The problem of ecosystem damage is international, and probably no country in the world is unaffected. Every continent has suffered; in western Europe it is estimated that several millions of hectares of land require attention, while in eastern Europe the degree of devastation is awesome. A recent estimate suggests that 43% of the earth's terrestrial surface has a reduced capacity to supply benefits to humanity because of recent direct impacts of land use.

The discipline of restoration ecology aims to provide a scientifically sound basis for the reconstruction of degraded or destroyed ecosystems and to produce self-supporting systems which are, to some degree, resilient to subsequent damage. The problems are international, and this book looks at the main issues with a broad perspective, using case studies where appropriate and considering the economic and social context in which restoration is carried out.

The main message of the book is that, if we are to achieve sustainable development, it is essential to reverse current trends of environmental degradation by developing and using our knowledge of how to restore ecosystems.

RESTORATION ECOLOGY AND
SUSTAINABLE DEVELOPMENT

RESTORATION ECOLOGY AND SUSTAINABLE DEVELOPMENT

Edited by
KRYSTYNA M. URBANSKA, NIGEL R. WEBB,
AND PETER J. EDWARDS

CAMBRIDGE
UNIVERSITY PRESS

PUBLISHED BY THE PRESS SYNDICATE OF THE UNIVERSITY OF CAMBRIDGE
The Pitt Building, Trumpington Street, Cambridge CB2 1RP, United Kingdom

CAMBRIDGE UNIVERSITY PRESS
The Edinburgh Building, Cambridge CB2 2RU, United Kingdom
40 West 20th Street, New York, NY 10011-4211, USA
10 Stamford Road, Oakleigh, Melbourne 3166, Australia

First published 1997

Printed in the United Kingdom at the University Press, Cambridge

Typeset in Times 10/13 pt [VN]

A catalogue record for this book is available from the British Library

Library of Congress Cataloguing in Publication data

Restoration ecology and sustainable development/edited by Krystyna M. Urbanska,
Nigel R. Webb, and Peter J. Edwards.
    p. cm.
    Papers from a conference sponsored by the Swiss Federal Institute of Technology
Zurich, and others.
    Includes indexes.
    ISBN 0-521-58160-5 (hardback).
    1. Restoration ecology – Congresses.   2. Restoration ecology – Economic
aspects – Congresses.   3. Sustainable development – Congresses.   I. Urbanska, K. M.
(Krystyna M.)   II. Webb, N. R. (Nigel R.)   III. Edwards, Peter J.
QH541.15.R45R5 1997
333.7'153 – dc21   96-52176   CIP

Contents

Contributors

Cyrus Abivardi
Swiss Federal Institute of Technology, Geobotany, Zurichbergstrasse 38
CH-8044 Zurich, Switzerland
FAX: +41 1 632 12 15   e-mail. abivardi@umnw.ethz.ch

Jan P. Bakker
Department of Plant Biology, University of Groningen, Kerklaan 30, PO
Box 14 9750, AA Haren, Groningen, The Netherlands.
FAX: +31 50 63 22 73   e-mail: J.P.Bakker@biol.RUG.NL

Anthony D. Bradshaw
Department of Environmental and Evolutionary Biology, University of
Liverpool, Liverpool L69 3BX, UK
FAX: +44 151 494 3120

Reinhard Bornkamm
Oekologisches Institut, TU Berlin, Rothenburgstrasse 12, D-12165 Berlin,
Germany
FAX: +49 4930 314 71355

Jeanne C. Chambers
USDA Forest Service, Intermountain Research Station, 920 Valley Rd,
Reno, Nevada 89512, USA
FAX: +1 702 784 4583   e-mail: chambers@ers.unr.edu

Michael J. Clark
Geodata Institute and Department of Geography, University of
Southampton, Southampton SO17 1BJ, UK
FAX: +44 1703 592 849   e-mail:mjc@soton.ac.uk

Kees S. Dijkema
Institute for Forest and Nature Research, PO Box 167, 1790 Den Burg

(Texel) The Netherlands
FAX: +31 222 319 235

Peter J. Edwards
Swiss Federal Institute of Technology, Geobotany, Zurichbergstrasse 38,
CH-8044 Zurich, Switzerland
FAX: +41 1 632 12 15   e-mail: edwards@umnw.ethz.ch

Peter Esselink
Laboratory of Plant Ecology, University of Groningen, PO Box 14, 9750
AA Haren, The Netherlands
and Stichting Het Groninger Lanschap, Ossenmarkt 9, 9712 NZ
Groningen, The Netherlands
FAX: 31 50 363 22 73

Steven N. Handel
Department of Ecology, Evolution & Natural Resources, Rutgers
University, New Brunswick, New Jersey 08903-0231, USA
FAX: +1 908 445 5870   e-mail: handel@biology.rutgers.edu

Kurt Haselwandter
Institut für Mikrobiologie, Universität Innsbruck, Technikerstrasse 25,
A-6020 Innsbruck, Austria
FAX: +43 512 507 2928   e-mail: Kurt.Haselwandter@uibk.ac.at

Sigurður H. Magnússon
Agricultural Research Institute, Keldnaholt, 112 Reikjavik, Iceland
FAX: +354 58 73 230   e-mail: sigurdur@rala.is

Jonathan D. Majer
School of Environmental Biology, Curtin University of Technology PO
Box U1987, Perth WA 6001, Australia
FAX: +61 9 351 2495   e-mail: imajerj@info.curtin.edu.au

William A. Niering
Department of Botany, Connecticut College, 270 Mohegan Avenue, New
London, Connecticut 06320, USA
FAX: +1 860 439 2519   e-mail: wanie@conncoll.edu.

V. Thomas Parker
Department of Biology, San Francisco State University, 1600 Holloway
Avenue, San Francisco, California 94132, USA
FAX: +1 415 338 2295   e-mail: parker@mercury.sfsu.edu

Steward T. A. Pickett
Institute of Ecosystem Studies, Box AB (Route 44A), Millbrook, New York 12545-0129, USA
FAX: +1 914 677 5976   e-mail: STAPickett@aol.com.

Krystyna M. Urbanska
Swiss Federal Institute of Technology, Geobotany, Zurichbergstrasse 38, CH-8044 Zurich, Switzerland
FAX: +41 1 632 12 15   e-mail: urbanska@umnw.ethz.ch

René van der Wal
Zoological Laboratory, University of Groningen, PO Box 14, 9750 AA Haren, The Netherlands
FAX: +31 50 363 22 05

Nigel R. Webb
Furzebrook Research Station, NERC Institute of Terrestrial Ecology, Wareham, Dorset BH20 5AS, UK
FAX: +44 1929 551 087   e-mail: NRW@wpo.nerc.ac.uk

Kathy S. Williams
Department of Biology, San Diego State University of California, San Diego, California 92182-5700, USA
FAX: +1 619 594 5676   e-mail: kwilliam@sunstroke.sdsu.edu

Foreword

The steady growth of restoration ecology may be recognized not only in the increased number of individuals and organizations involved, but also in a shift from the single-species focus to deductions at all levels of biological organization. The understanding of these various processes will ultimately help us to assess damage and to develop restoration approaches based on sound ecological science. The organization of the first international conference on restoration ecology in Zurich provides a clear measure of the vitality of the field. The Zurich conference was held under the patronage of European Ecological Federation (EEF) which is a co-operative body formed by national ecological societies in Europe. At present about 20 societies are EEF Members, but the total number of the involved countries approaches 30, since some societies (e.g., British Ecological Society, Gesellschaft für Oekologie, the Nordic Ecological Society OIKOS, and Société d'Ecologie) include members from more than one country. The EEF encourages broad international co-operation, but at the same time maintains a European focus, needed for more effective consideration of specifically European environmental problems. The EEF promotes the formation of specialist groups: three such groups active at present are Restoration Ecology, High Mountain Ecology, and River-Estuary Continuum.

The considerable interest in restoration ecology on a truly international scale was clearly documented by the great success of the Zurich conference; the European Ecological Federation has an important role to play in promoting further development. The Second International Conference on restoration ecology is already planned for spring 1998 in The Netherlands. A special symposium on restoration ecology is planned for the next EEF Congress in Thessaloniki in early autumn 1998. We hope that further development of restoration in Europe and co-operation with restoration-ists from all over the world will prove helpful in repairing at least a part of the considerable environmental damage resulting from human activities. The present book undoubtedly provides valuable references for many years to come.

Pehr H. Enckell
Vice President EEF

Acknowledgements

The First International Conference on 'Restoration Ecology and Sustainable Development' was sponsored financially by four Swiss institutions. The generous support of the Swiss Federal Institute of Technology Zurich, the Federal Office for Environment, Forest, and Landscape BUWAL, the Swiss National Science Foundation, and the Swiss Academy of Sciences is gratefully acknowledged.

Various staff members of the Geobotanical Institute SFIT provided cheerful assistance throughout the conference and also during the preparation of this volume. We are particularly grateful to Karin Lee, Marzio Fattorini, Johannes Killmann, Roger Stupf, and Thomas Wilhalm who answered many e-mail or fax messages, faithfully staffed the registration desk, and solved dozens of minor problems prior to the conference, during the meeting, and also afterwards. Anita Hegi, Rene Graf, and Stefan Locher helped with all technical aspects.

Many reviewers, too numerous to name, generously helped reading the submitted papers and providing reviews in record time. We would like to thank these colleagues for their freely given time.

Last but not least, we thank Dr Alan Crowden and the staff of Cambridge University Press for their encouragement and help.

Part I
Introduction

1

Why restoration?

KRYSTYNA M. URBANSKA, NIGEL R. WEBB,
AND PETER J. EDWARDS

One of the undesirable legacies of technical progress has been the creation of huge areas in which ecosystem processes and structures have been so damaged that the land cannot be used productively without major improvement. The catalogue of devastation is a long one: it includes mine and quarry sites, derelict industrial land (often contaminated with toxic materials), agricultural land damaged either by excessive salinity from irrigation or from lowered water tables, fragile alpine ecosystems which have been destroyed – for example through the creation of machine-graded ski slopes, arctic ecosystems damaged through on- and off-shore resource exploitation, arid and semi-arid regions which have been overgrazed, and large areas of the wet tropics in which rainforest has been indiscriminately felled to leave bare, infertile soil which is soon washed away.

The problem of ecosystem damage is international, and probably no country in the world is unaffected. In western Europe it is conservatively estimated that several million hectares of land require major attention. In Eastern Europe and Russia the degree of devastation is awesome, and in many regions causes serious problems of public health and hinders economic development. In many parts of the Third World, the situation is even more serious. The felling of tropical rainforest, for example, has proceeded at unprecedented rates in the last 25 years, and produced growing problems of soil loss. Recently Daily (1995) estimated that 43% of the earth's terrestrial surface has a reduced capacity to supply benefits to humanity because of recent, direct impacts of land use. Very clearly, our present situation, in which the earth's capacity to produce renewable natural resources is increasingly damaged while the demand for those resources increases as the world population grows, is not sustainable. One of the challenges we face in achieving sustainability is to reverse the trend of ecosystem damage through restoration and rehabilitation of ecosystems.

3

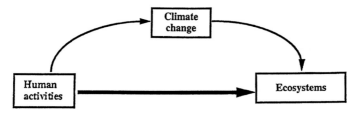

Figure 1.1. Human-induced disturbance of ecosystems: indirect disturbance due to the global climate change and direct disturbance or destruction of habitat (modified after Urbanska 1997).

Fortunately, there is a great potential for recovery inherent in most land types, and ecological research has greatly increased our ability to restore damaged ecosystems. More importantly, ecology has also contributed to a way of thinking about natural resources and natural processes, in which we recognize that ecosystems, including natural systems which are not directly exploited, have a value to humans; it is the restoration of that value which provides the motivation for restoration ecology. The discipline of restoration ecology aims to provide a scientifically sound basis for the reconstruction and function of damaged or destroyed ecosystems, and produce self-supporting systems which are, at least to some degree, resilient to subsequent damage. As will become clear in this book, exactly what is meant by restoration is far from simple. In its strict sense it means the restoring of something which was already there; and, indeed, the objective of ecological restoration is often to create an ecosystem with the same species composition and functional characteristics as a system which existed previously. However, sometimes restoration in the strict sense is not a practical option. Possible reasons are that we do not always know how to recreate a particular assemblage of species, or that the time needed to achieve the desired result is far too long. Another reason is that ecosystems are not precisely defined and invariable entities. Human activities affect ecosystems both directly, through the types of damage already described, and also indirectly through such processes as climatic change and regional pollution (Figure 1.1). Because of long-term environmental change, it may simply be impossible to restore an ecosystem to a particular reference condition which existed in the past. Thus, restoration often has a broader meaning of creating an ecosystem with desirable functional characteristics, though not one which matches precisely a particular reference system.

In the last few years, restoration ecology has developed rapidly as a scientific discipline and, more importantly, as a profession. At present, most of the practitioners in this new profession are to be found in the developed world, and in particular in Europe and the United States of America. Most conferences on the topic are held at the national level, particularly in the USA where the Society for Ecological Restoration (SER) is very active, and, as yet, there is no global forum for the exchange of ideas and experiences in restoration ecology. However, as the importance of ecological restoration grows, the need for such a forum becomes increasingly important. All too often restoration is carried out on an *ad hoc* trial-and-error basis, with little regard to well-established theoretical principles or to technical advances which have been made in other countries. The result is that projects fail unnecessarily, or take too long, or cost too much.

No truly international meeting on restoration ecology had been organized before the First International Conference on Restoration Ecology and Sustainable Development, held in March 1996 at the Swiss Federal Institute of Technology in Zurich, Switzerland. The need for an international forum was clearly demonstrated by the multinational audience (21 countries were represented from throughout the world) and by the decision that a second international conference should be held in the near future.

The organizer's objectives for the conference were the following:

1. to consolidate the scientific framework of restoration ecology;
2. to improve experimental methodology and establish standards for the design of field trials and their assessment;
3. to improve the use of technology for ecological restoration;
4. to improve transfer of ecological understanding and restoration technology to countries most afflicted by problems of ecosystem damage, particularly in eastern Europe and in the Third World.

This book is based on the invited papers presented at the Zurich conference. Apart from this short introduction defining the rationale for the restoration ecology, the first part includes a contribution dealing with the current problems and discrepancies in terminology used in restoration science and applied work (chapter 2 by A. D. Bradshaw). This short chapter is an important contribution to clarifying the differences between various types of ecological amelioration.

Part II with the overall theme 'Ecological basis of restoration' consists of six chapters which bring important aspects of structure and function of ecosystems in relation to restoration science. Chapter 3 by Parker and Pickett partly deals with ecosystem science and specifically with the modern ecological paradigm as a reference point for restoration. The two following chapters deal with the soil problems; they respectively include soil ecology (chapter 4 by Bradshaw) and soil micro-organisms (chapter 5 by Hasel-wandter). Relationships between various ecosystem inhabitants are dealt with in two further chapters which relate to important aspects of plant population ecology (chapter 6 by Urbanska) and plant–animal interactions (chapter 7 by Handel). The last chapter in this part of the book offers a landscape-based approach to restoration, and stresses the need to be aware of spatial relationships at all scales (chapter 8 by Webb).

Part III 'The Implementation and Assessment of restoration schemes' deals with ecosystem-specific approaches to restoration in various situations. Insights from particularly fragile ecosystems were selected to illustrate the problem. This part of the book consists accordingly of chapters dealing with alpine and Nordic areas, on the one hand (chapters 9 by Chambers and 10 by Magnússon), and wetlands, on the other hand (chapter 13 by Niering and chapter 14 by Bakker *et al.*). Two chapters in this section focus on the important role of invertebrates (chapter 11 by Majer and chapter 12 by Williams). Authors of those chapters demonstrate study cases from very different geographical areas; they offer different approaches and assessment criteria.

Part IV 'Ecological restoration, economics, and sustainability' focuses on the way that ecological restoration is inextricably linked to social, political, and economic issues, a topic which has been until now rather neglected. In chapter 15, Edwards and Abivardi emphasize that an essential step in applying restoration techniques is to develop a proper economic case for such work, which takes account of the full value of ecosystem services provided by natural and semi-natural systems. Chapter 16 by Clark reviews the social context of ecological restoration, and the responsibilities that it places upon practitioners to recognize the needs and expectations of the society in which they work.

In the short concluding chapter, Edwards *et al.* draw together some of the main themes of the preceding chapters. They argue that progress in ecological restoration must be based not only on improved understanding of the scientific issues and more effective use of technology, though both of these are crucial, but also upon a proper regard for the social and economic context in which restoration work is carried out. As a way to achieve these three objectives, they emphasize the need for better education of professionals, and also for improved public awareness of the urgency for ecological restoration.

References

Daily, C. G. (1995). Restoring value to the world's degraded lands. *Science*, 269, 350–4.

Urbanska, K. M. (1997). Reproductive behaviour of arctic/alpine plants and ecological restoration. In *Disturbance and Recovery of Arctic Terrestrial Ecosystems – an Ecological Perspective*, ed. R. M. M. Crawford, pp. 481–501. Dordrecht: Kluwer Academic Publishers.

2
What do we mean by restoration?
ANTHONY D. BRADSHAW

Words both define and guide our thinking, as much in restoration as in all other matters. A number of different words are commonly used. Although words can change their meaning, it is important to appreciate what they have been taken to mean up to the present, because this is the way most people will understand them. In ecological restoration four words are in common use – *restoration, rehabilitation, remediation, reclamation* – although there are others. Perhaps the most complete guidance to what these usually mean is the complete *Oxford English Dictionary* (1971).

The relevant definition of *restoration* is: 'the act of restoring to a former state or position ... or to an unimpaired or perfect condition'. To *restore* is: 'to bring back to the original state ... or to a healthy or vigorous state'. There is both the implication of returning to an original state, and to state that is perfect and healthy. This seems to be the way in which we continue to use the word on both sides of the Atlantic (Box 1978), even although it does have perfectionist implications (Francis *et al.* 1979).

Rehabilitation is defined as: 'the action of restoring a thing to a previous condition or status'. This appears rather similar to restoration, but there is little or no implication of perfection. Indeed, in common usage, something that is rehabilitated is not expected to be in as original or healthy a state as if it had been restored (Francis *et al.* 1979). For this reason the word can conveniently be used to indicate any act of improvement from a degraded state (Box 1978; Wali 1992).

Remediation is: 'the act of remedying'. To *remedy* is: 'to rectify, to make good'. Here the emphasis is on the process rather than on the endpoint reached.

Reclamation is a term used by many practitioners, especially in Britain but also in North America. It is defined as: 'the making of land fit for cultivation'. But to *reclaim* is given as: 'to bring back to a proper state'.

8

There is no implication of returning to an original state but rather to a useful one. *Replacement* may therefore be involved. To *replace* is: 'to provide or procure a substitute or equivalent in place of' (although an alternative meaning is to restore).

Enhancement is sometimes used in the USA to indicate the establishment of an alternative ecosystem (Pratt & Stevens 1992). This seems an unsatisfactory use of the word which is defined in the *OED* as: 'to raise in degree, heighten, intensify; or to increase in value, importance, attractiveness'. This is, in fact, the use suggested by Francis *et al.* 1979. There is no implication of making something bad better, but of making something already good better.

Mitigation is another word often used when restoration is considered. It is important to note that it is nothing directly to do with restoration. To *mitigate* is to 'appease . . . or to moderate the heinousness of something'. So, although mitigation can be an outcome of restoration (or rehabilitation or reclamation), it is a separate consideration (Clark this volume). It may well involve the improvement of quite another ecosystem.

To what characteristics are these words applied?

The great problem at present is that the word restoration is now widely used to cover all sorts of activities including those that are better called rehabilitation. This is obvious, for instance, in the activities of the Society for Ecological Restoration and in the coverage of its journal.

This problem must be addressed, because here is where perhaps the greatest confusion lies about what we are doing. From our ecological point of view we can apply it to ecosystems, habitats, communities, species, water or soil quality, or to some other ecological characteristic of the degraded or damaged area. All these are different and therefore their use has specific implications.

The word *ecosystem* covers the biological and non-biological elements occurring together in a particular area. So it is all inclusive. However, because 'system' is included, there is an emphasis on the overarching functions and interactions of these elements. So, when the restoration of *ecosystems* is being referred to, the suggestion is that we are particularly interested in the restoration of the fundamental processes by which ecosystems work. This has been well argued by Cairns (1988).

It is common now to talk about *habitat* restoration. Because habitat refers just to the place where organisms live, it tends to imply less than ecosystem. Its use therefore puts more emphasis on the restoration of place than of important ecological functions. We can also talk about restoration of *communities* or of *species*. In this case the emphasis is on just the plants and animals occurring in a particular place, or on a single species.

We also talk about restoration of *quality*. This is particularly true in discussions of soil or water restoration, perhaps because the species in these habitats are multifarious and their individual occurrences difficult to predict. The implication is therefore different. It is the perceived attributes of what is in an area, or of a component of the environment, that are considered to be important. To what is referred depends on the particular situation; it could be either an important factor such as BOD or level of contaminants, or a derivative of well-being such as species diversity. In some of these options complete restoration is not achieved. It can therefore be proper to refer to them as examples of *partial restoration* (Jordan *et al.* 1987).

Whatever we may think deserves attention, our intention should always be to focus on the restoration of functions, of processes, of biological potential, because without this the communities of organisms in which we are interested cannot persist (Bradshaw & Chadwick, 1980). Our ultimate aim should be the restoration of the whole ecosystem, even if we sometimes emphasise some particular component or attribute (National Research Council 1992, chapter 1).

The options in more detail

There are many attributes to an ecosystem. These can usefully be simplified into two main components, structure and function. What has happened in a damaged ecosystem can then be represented graphically with these components as the two axes (Magnuson *et al.* 1980; Bradshaw 1987) (Figure 2.1). Both components will have suffered, and will have to be restored. Rehabilitation, in which progress has been made but the original state not achieved, and reclamation, to something different, can be represented on the same figure.

This clarifies our options. In particular it points to the fact that restoration may not be easy. It may be possible, perhaps, to restore the functions fairly completely, but to achieve the original structure may be more difficult. This may not be so true in aquatic ecosystems where the rate of re-establishment of populations can be rapid, but it will certainly be true in a forest ecosystem where the full age structure may be impossible to achieve in less than 500 years. It may not be possible to achieve an original soil profile in less than 5000 years, although the biological functions of a soil can perhaps be restored in less than 10 years (Bradshaw this volume). It must be remembered that ecosystems are not static, but in a state of dynamic equilibrium. So what we aim for in restoration may well be a moving target (Parker & Pickett this volume). This suggests again that it is restoration of function(s) that is more important than restoration of precise structure. If a reference ecosystem is used, this must particularly be borne in mind.

There is also the problem that the perfectionist definition of restoration has sometimes been taken to involve re-establishing indigenous ecosystems rather than just the ecosystem that existed before degradation occurred. This immediately leads to confusion because of the difficulty of deciding what was the indigenous ecosystem. In areas where the ecosystem before degradation has essentially been determined by human activity, the original indigenous ecosystem may be irrelevant. This means that the ecosystem which restoration is intended to achieve must be defined and decided.

In many situations restoration in the narrow sense may be unrealistic. It may also be impossibly expensive. So we should realize that rehabilitation can be a proper option, as can be replacement. Both these alternatives, by offering something different, may provide an endpoint that is more valuable than what was there in the first place. Replacement is a particularly interesting option since it may allow restoration of a component, such as productivity, to a higher level than existed previously. In the heavily developed agricultural land of Britain, sand and gravel workings left to fill with water have contributed enormously to the diversity of wildlife and landscape in many areas. This is valuable reclamation; it is not, however, true restoration, although there may be restoration of particular attributes such as biodiversity.

Aftercare

In a recent note on the definition of ecological restoration, the Society for Ecological Restoration (1995) has included both renewal and maintenance in its suggested definition – 'Ecological restoration is the process of renewing and maintaining ecosystem health.' In the preceding arguments only the process of renewal has been considered. This is because it would seem confusing to extend this process to include maintenance. When any construction or reconstruction is undertaken in other areas of human endeavour, the processes are considered as separate actions.

This does not however mean that maintenance is not very important.

A. D. Bradshaw

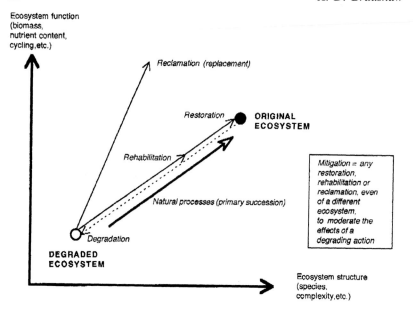

Figure 2.1. The different options for the improvement of a degraded ecosystem expressed in terms of the two major characteristics of structure and function. Used in its proper sense, *restoration* implies bringing back the ecosystem to its original or previous state in terms of both structure and function; there are then a number of other alternatives, including *rehabilitation* in which this is not totally achieved, and *replacement* of the original by something different – usually termed *reclamation* . . . *Mitigation* is a different consideration.

When it comes after an action of restoration and is directed to ensuring that the restored ecosystem finishes its development, it can very properly be termed *aftercare*. This word and the activities associated with it are an essential part of all restoration policy, but they are recognized to be separate considerations, as in, for instance, the UK 1990 Town and Country Planning Act.

What is difficult with all ecological restoration is that what is produced is something living and still capable of development, indeed something which will inevitably continue to develop as a result of further growth and successional processes. This can be allowed, or even encouraged. But, if the desired ecosystem is not climax vegetation, then it will be crucial to ensure that the appropriate factors arresting succession are allowed, or made, to occur (Bradshaw, 1989). This is where *maintenance* rather than aftercare becomes a specific consideration.

Conclusions

It is therefore very important that, when any work is undertaken, the different options and what they each might involve are clearly worked out and understood. Figure 2.1 can provide useful guidelines. Then it must be made clear what is to be the aim – whether full restoration, restoration of only certain attributes, or only rehabilitation or reclamation – and what is to be the actual endpoint. Full restoration, although it may seem ethically the most justifiable, and therefore the most obvious to adopt, may in fact not always be the most sensible in practical or biological terms.

Acknowledgement

This is developed from part of a paper (Bradshaw 1996) entitled 'Underlying principles of restoration', given at a workshop on Habitat Conservation and Restoration Strategies in the Great Lakes Basin held in Ontario in November 1994.

References

Box, T. W. (1978). The significance and responsibility of rehabilitating drastically disturbed land. In *Reclamation of Drastically Disturbed Lands*, eds. F. W. Schaller & P. Sutton, pp. 1–10. Madison: American Society of Agronomy.

Bradshaw, A. D. (1987). The reclamation of derelict land and the ecology of ecosystems. In *Restoration Ecology*, eds. W. R. Jordan, M. E. Gilpin, & J. D. Aber, pp. 53–74. Cambridge University Press.

Bradshaw, A. D. (1989). Management problems arising from successional processes. In *Biological Habitat Reconstruction*, ed. G. P. Buckley, pp. 68–78. London: Belhaven Press.

Bradshaw, A. D. (1996). Underlying principles of restoration. *Canadian Journal of Fisheries and Aquatic Sciences*, 53, suppl. 1, 3–9.

Bradshaw, A. D. & Chadwick, M. J. (1980). *The Restoration of Land*. Oxford: Blackwell Scientific Publications.

Cairns, J. (1988). Increasing diversity by restoring damaged ecosystems. In *Biodiversity*, ed. E. O. Wilson, pp. 333–43. Washington: National Academy Press.

Francis, G. R., Magnuson, J. J., Regier, H. A., & Talhelm, D. R. (1979). *Rehabilitating Great Lakes Ecosystems*. Ann Arbor, Michigan: Great Lakes Fishery Commission.

Jordan, W. R., Gilpin, M. E., & Aber, J. D. (1987). Restoration ecology: ecological restoration as a technique for basic research. In *Restoration Ecology*, eds. W. R. Jordan, M. E. Gilpin, & J. D. Aber, pp. 3–21. Cambridge University Press.

Magnuson, J. J., Regier, H. A., Christien, W. J., & Sonzogi, W. C. (1980). To rehabilitate and restore Great Lakes ecosystems. In *The Recovery Process in Damaged Ecosystems*, ed. J. Cairns, pp. 95–112. Michigan: Ann Arbor Science.

National Research Council (1992). *Restoration of Aquatic Ecosystems: Science, Technology and Public Policy.* Washington: National Academy Press.

Oxford English Dictionary (1971). *The Oxford English Dictionary.* Oxford University Press.

Pratt, J. R. & Stevens, J. (1992). Restoration ecology: repaying the national debt. In *Proceedings of the High Altitude Revegetation Workshop No.10,* eds. W. G. Hassell, S. K. Nordstrom, W. R. Keammerer, & W. J. Todd, pp. 40–9. Fort Collins: Colorado State University.

Society for Ecological Restoration (1995). *Definition of Ecological Restoration.* Madison: Society for Ecological Restoration.

Wali, M. (1992). Ecology of the rehabilitation process. In *Ecosystem Rehabilitation,* ed. M. Wali, vol. I, pp. 3–26. The Hague: SPB Academic Publishing.

Part II
Ecological basis of restoration

3
Restoration as an ecosystem process: implications of the modern ecological paradigm

V. THOMAS PARKER AND
STEWARD T. A. PICKETT

The problem: what do modern ecological principles have to say to restoration?

The goal of ecological restoration ostensibly is to return ecosystems to a state or condition from which they can be self-sustaining thereafter. Consequently, the fundamental problem we will address in this chapter is the question, how can ecological principles inform restoration? Such principles include the concepts used to analyse ecological systems, the role that history plays in ecological systems, the nature of the processes that are included in our view of nature, and the models we use to understand it. Unfortunately, ecology has more than one perspective that influences our thinking. We will argue that one set of principles, what we shall refer to as the contemporary paradigm, is the only valid approach for restoration. To set the stage, let us consider some alternatives. For instance, how we think of ecosystems affects restoration, and to illustrate this consider the question: are ecosystems strictly biogeochemical processing or productivity factories, or do they include a site or collection of species? A second set of important questions concerns the nature and impact of history: what role does history play in the current state of the system of interest? Is the past trajectory of a system a regular course of stages, or is it an idiosyncratic series of events? Finally, how we see ecological processes can affect restoration. To what extent are the processes within ecosystems congruent with the system boundaries and do such processes direct systems to well-defined endpoints?

Because answers to such questions form the basis for restoration, it is important to have an account of the current understanding of the issues they raise. How these questions might be answered has changed and evolved over the last few decades (Simberloff 1980; Botkin 1990; Pickett, Parker, & Fiedler 1992). Restoration can benefit from changes in ecological thinking (Pickett & Parker 1994) and we see features of modern ecology that are significant for restoration ecology.

The first aspect of modern ecology of value to restoration ecology is the return to a broader perspective of the ecosystem. The ecosystem has been viewed, by many ecologists and people engaged in using ecological principles to manage, conserve, and restore nature, as a narrow concept suitable only for understanding energy or nutrient flux and mineral cycling. We will show below how the more inclusive concept of the ecosystem can help improve restoration practice.

The second feature of modern ecology of relevance to restoration is the paradigm of the discipline. A new paradigm suggests general principles that can be useful in the application of the science. A paradigm is nothing more than the viewpoint and set of background assumptions of the discipline (Margolis 1993). The world view includes those most general principles that structure the science, as well as the judgements about what areas and questions are of interest, how to approach those questions, and what constitutes a valid answer. Here, we will be concerned with the general principles that the paradigm summarizes.

A problem in applying ecological principles is how to relate the general principles, which must suit a wide variety of ecological conditions and environments, to the idiosyncrasies of specific sites. Recognizing the important role of history and the specific conditions that influence a site, some practitioners have despaired of effectively applying ecological principles in 'real world' situations (Shrader-Frechette & McCoy 1993). However, ecology is beginning to deal effectively with the historical nature of its subject-matter (e.g., Davis 1986). 'Contingency' is the label we will use that highlights the historical and local specificity that has to be accounted for in complete understanding and effective manipulation of ecological systems.

Problems in restoration

Modern ecological principles show the shortcomings of some cases of restoration practice. Restoration practice is often based on the assumption that nature is fixed and unchanging (Jordan 1993). In the United States, several national parks have been treated that way. Examples include Yellowstone, the Grand Tetons, Yosemite and Everglades National Parks (Cronon 1995). These are places we wish to preserve forever, and which in general are perceived by most people as climax communities that are ever persistent. What happens when these systems experience a relatively infrequent but rather dramatic event from the public perspective? Extensive fires in Yellowstone National Park in 1988 resulted in a public outcry and review of management policies. This public response indicates how poorly people understand the dynamics of natural systems and instead tend to objectify and idealize nature. An idealized view of nature, however, makes it more difficult to understand that natural communities are constantly changing and that a number of internal and external processes maintain these systems. If natural and dynamic systems are viewed as in some ideal state, systems are presumed to have a single range of characteristics that can be preserved. This assumption might be applied to various system attributes, like biogeochemical dynamics, productivity, or composition. But such an assumption of objectification and idealization may thwart successful restoration.

An additional problem with the assumption that nature is fixed or in balance is the adoption of simplistic goals for restoration. What should be our goals when we begin the restoration of a natural system? Our experience is that many projects begin with vague goals such as returning the system to some primeval state in which it can take care of itself. This common view of ecological systems de-emphasizes the role of dynamic and multidimensional processes that have created these systems, and lacks the understanding of the human and landscape contexts in which processes and ecosystems occur. Modern ecology offers an alternative approach.

We begin an overview of these ideas by noting that an inclusive ecosystem concept should be used, and that it has implications that can help avoid taking static and ideal views of nature as the motivation of restoration practice. We then summarize the contemporary paradigm, detail the nature of ecological contingency as a feature of the natural world that influences restoration, and move to examples of the application of these principles in the natural world. More crucial in restoration is the problem of balancing the need to work with idiosyncratic sites, and, in the absence of detailed information on all sites, the need to use the general principles of ecology. This last theme appears throughout much of the chapter in specific principles and examples.

The ecosystem concept

The inclusive ecosystem concept is an excellent starting place for relating modern ecology to restoration practice. It can serve as a cornerstone for a theory of ecological restoration that is realistic, clear, and complete. Tansley (1935) articulated the first clear definition of the ecosystem that continues to be used and reinforced (Likens 1992). Although there have been interpretations that see the ecosystem as only a series of black boxes connected by the flow of energy and matter (reviewed by Golley 1993), the ecosystem is considered to be a collection of interacting organisms along with the physical environment, including matter and energy that they may assimilate, in some specified location. This definition of the ecosystem invites ecologists to understand the fluxes of energy, matter, and information, but it also invites understanding of the evolution of system components, the historical trajectory of the system, the interaction of assemblages of organisms, the behaviour and persistence of populations, and the fluxes of information embodied in the genetic and other structures of the ecosystem.

The inclusiveness of the definition of the ecosystem suggests an inclusive perspective on the discipline of ecology as a whole. Classical definitions of ecology emphasized the organism (e.g., Haeckel 1866), and early restoration, conservation, and management approaches similarly focused on one or several species. However, taking the inclusive nature of the ecosystem seriously, and accounting for the rich variety of phenomena ecologists routinely examine, suggests the need for a broader definition of the field: 'Ecology is the scientific study of the processes influencing the distribution and abundance of organisms, the interactions among organisms, and the interactions between organisms and the transformation and flux of energy and matter' (Likens 1992). Each of the subdisciplines of ecology emphasizes different aspects of this broad suite of interactions and influences. For restoration, the broad definition suggests that the goals and tools of restoration must also be broad indeed. And, given whatever the target chosen, it surely is embedded in the network of interactions. The implications can be emphasized by considering three aspects of the term 'ecosystem'. These aspects are the basic meaning, the models used to put the meaning into practice, and the metaphorical breadth of the term. We explain these aspects below.

The basic definition of the ecosystem is the fundamental meaning that ecologists and practitioners must use. We have already provided the essence of the definition. Here we recall two aspects of the definition. First, common to all instances of ecosystem is the need to specify a spatial location and extent. Secondly, the ecosystem involves biotic structure, physical environment and setting, and the exchanges within and among these two. But in order to use such an abstract definition, the meaning must be operationalized in an explicit model. Models can show the components of a system, the interactions among them, and the controls on the interactions.

In the case of ecosystems, the interactions can include transfers of energy, matter, and information, impact on biotic structure and composition through competitive, feeding, and mutualistic interactions among organisms, and other sorts of interactions. Because of the number of interactions and structures that can be found within a single ecosystem, ecologists and those who work with real ecosystems must specify the model they base their studies, conclusions, and applications upon. Failing to specify a model that can be communicated to the various parties involved in restoration may lead to confusion and disappointment.

The final way to use the ecosystem concept is as a metaphor. The image is much less exact than a model, but it is likely to be broader than any particular model. Such breadth may allow people to detect key features of real ecosystems that have been left out of the model used to motivate, plan, and assess a restoration. Because ecosystems have a necessary spatial extent, the metaphor, in combination with the insights of the modern paradigm, alerts ecologists to look beyond the boundary they have had to set, to determine whether important influences appear from outside the boundaries, or outside the spatial extent assumed by the model. Thus the metaphor invites consideration of the context of the focal ecosystem to be understood or restored, issues which are generally the focus of landscape ecology. The metaphor also reminds us of the temporal dimension of ecosystems. Because transformation, interactions, and fluxes are part of the basic definition of the ecosystem, and because each of these phenomena must be expressed as a rate, a time dimension is a necessary part of an ecosystem.

The consideration of the ecosystem as meaning and metaphor brings us to an understanding of one of the key elements in the title of this chapter: ecosystem process. We detail that understanding below.

Ecosystem processes and the contemporary ecological paradigm

Ecosystem theories emphasize the flux of energy and materials and are inclusive of processes as disparate as nitrogen flow and community dynamics. Recently, ecosystem definitions more inclusive of interactions among ecological entities have been proposed (Likens 1992; Jones & Lawton 1995). Ecosystem theories, however, have developed from two distinct sets of assumptions. Classically, ecosystems are thought to reach stable successional endpoints, after which processes are in dynamic equilibrium. This model of ecosystems suggests that systems are closed and self-regulating, that, during succession, ecosystems will increasingly control the flow of minerals and energy. Consequently, such models of ecosystems are seen as deterministic, and processes or events that move the ecosystem away from this equilibrium are considered disturbances. Disturbances are thought, under the classical view, to be exceptional.

In contrast, the contemporary paradigm assumes that ecosystems are open, can be regulated by external processes, and are subject to natural disturbances. They may have multiple and probabilistic successions, which at some scales may lead to multiple equilibria, while at other scales may fail to reach an equilibrium. Because systems are open to external regulation, humans and their effects must be incorporated in ecological models for restoration ecology to be effective. Thus, rather than viewing ecosystems as being 'in balance', systems are seen as in flux from some scale or perspective (Pickett *et al.* 1992). Ecological theory has shifted to this contemporary view because of both empirical explorations of natural systems (e.g., Wiens 1986) as well as the prominent failure of management based on older equilibrial assumptions (Botkin 1990).

Implicit in the contemporary approach to ecosystem dynamics is a requirement to understand process and context. Processes refer to system dynamics and the mechanisms underlying them, while context refers to the spatial influences on a system. First we consider processes. Because stable endpoints only play a small role, if any, in system structure, attention must move to ongoing processes. Processes contribute to variation. Events like disturbances can affect systems because systems are open. Dynamics of ecosystems can be seen at a variety of scales as exemplified by the movement of, and interactions among, individual organisms, the transformation of energy and materials, successional trajectories, patch dynamics, and responses to 'large' (regional–global) scale environmental change. If restoration is focused on re-establishing functioning and self-sustaining systems, then recapturing the dynamics of systems may be dependent on ensuring that appropriate processes are returned (e.g., Niering & Warren 1980; Niering 1987; Race 1985; D'Avenzo 1990). This requires understanding of the degree to which external processes or events in the past were important in the dynamics of the system, and whether they can continue in the restored site.

Processes refer to biotic or abiotic interactions that influence dynamics. Any process may influence a number of ecosystem characteristics simultaneously. A clear example of this is the differential effect of a fire, killing some individuals or species while stimulating the germination of others. Fires also transform nutrient dynamics by mineralizing nutrients previously bound up in organic matter. Furthermore, fires alter substantially local microclimates by the loss of cover and the presence of dark ash over the soil surface. All these changes together increase the rate and nature of vegetation dynamics, triggering succession. The fact that processes affect the dynamics of a variety of ecosystem aspects simultaneously illustrates the need to approach restoration from a variety of perspectives rather than relying on composition or some other characteristic alone to evaluate restoration success. The example of fire expands our attention from process to include spatial context.

Context specifically refers to the spatial connections of the site of interest with landscape around it. For example, differences in continuity of vegetation strongly influence the movement and propagation of a number of processes such as fire or pathogens. Fire is also a good example of a process which often starts outside a particular site and depends upon the relative continuity of vegetation to permit its flow from site to site. The context of the site is critical to whether historical fire regimes continue. Similarly, the rain of propagules into a site depends greatly on the types of vegetation nearby and how disturbed they are. The heterogeneity of adjacent landscapes impacts the flux of water and nutrients of sites downslope. All these examples emphasize the importance of the interactions of a site with its surroundings. Ecosystems are open to processes that arise externally to them at any scale considered, whether global atmospheric changes or the immigration of fungal spores. The spatial extent that needs to be included in the context depends on a number of considerations, such as the scale of the process of interest and how other features of the landscape may influence processes (Naveh & Lieberman 1984; Forman & Godron 1986; Turner 1989).

Humans have a significant influence on a number of processes and have modified much of the landscape. Human impacts can be an overwhelming influence on site restoration through disturbances and through processes arising in adjacent habitats modifying historical patterns. When houses dominate areas next to wildland reserves, humans tend to increase the frequency or magnitude of some processes while reducing others. For example, in central California, urban – wildland boundaries force managers to suppress wildfire in vegetation dependent on fire for its maintenance. At the same time, urban areas become sources of invasive species, of trails and roads into the managed site, and of other impacts. Restoring or managing vegetation in such a human-modified context requires active and ongoing intervention to maintain natural vegetation influenced by the frequency and composition of processes arising outside of the site. Systems cannot be 'self-sustaining' from the idealized perspective because contextual processes have been modified.

These concepts of contemporary ecology lead to a simple model of ecosystem dynamics. In this model, ecosystem characteristics and dynamics are dependent on two general sets of processes, those that are contained within the site and those external processes that influence the system. Both kinds of processes maintain the structure and the functioning of the ecosystem. While we have referred to the external set of processes as context, we emphasize that processes represent continua of extent, of origin, of magnitude, and of other characteristics; therefore, for any subset of processes, whether nitrogen cycling or species recruitment, reference to both internal and contextual influences is necessary. Ecosystems are in continuous flux for all characteristics at some scale. We emphasize that such a dynamic model is critical for successful restoration ecology, because it is the restoration or maintenance of the responsible processes underlying structure and function that will meet long-term restoration objectives.

The remainder of this chapter explores the nature of the spatial and temporal dynamics of ecosystems as a foundation for restoration. The nature of these dynamics and spatial contexts suggest that restoration ecology must use models that treat ecological systems as constantly dynamic and open to outside processes. Recognizing process and context indicates the inherent contingency of natural systems. Such contingency requires that two concepts must underlie that development of restoration models and approaches. One is that restoration must be seen as part of an ongoing process, not as a discrete event. A second concept is that historical uniqueness means no ideal reference states exist for systems, instead, more than one reference state must be considered to develop criteria for restoration projects; the diversity of potential reference conditions should be analysed from the context of the site being managed.

Examples of process and context in light of the contemporary paradigm

When we consider process and context together, as well as their temporal patterns, we are forced to conclude that any particular site results from the historically unique combination of processes for that location, which we refer to as contingency. In extensive landscapes of natural vegetation, unique features may not seem significant due to the influence of larger-scale processes that unify the structure and dynamics of the landscape. Fragmentation of areas by human management and the growth of human populations, however, has significantly shifted the importance of processes. Remaining historical natural processes are restricted to either smaller scales that are contained within sites, or to larger-scale processes like atmospheric or meteorological characteristics not directly influenced by fragmentation. Although the interactions among species or the interaction of species with their physical environment can be generalized, the specific dynamics of any system and the trajectories it may take after initiating restoration practices all depend on its prior history, accidental arrival or extinction of species, current processes acting on the site, and the site's place in the landscape.

Different plant communities may exhibit stable points in composition. Ecosystems that are species poor or that are strongly governed by a limited array of processes may well result in repeatable stable states in a variety of locations. Other systems, however, even relatively species poor systems, may offer a range of ecologically valid reference states. Ecologists who have reconstructed the history or palaeohistory of particular vegetation types are often struck by the differences between current and past composition. But to provide objectives for restoration projects, it is critical to decide on reference conditions. We can use the history as well as the current diversity of conditions to determine a set of possible reference states. What is important is that there is no one ideal reference state for any type of community or ecosystem. Instead, the context and history of the site being restored should be used to determine valid reference states.

Restoration of a site is driven by a number of societal as well as ecological goals; explicit identification of those objectives, as we have emphasized before (Pickett *et al.* 1992, Parker 1993; Pickett & Parker 1994; Pickett & Ostfeld 1994), is fundamental for the establishment of restoration ecology as a science. For an array of different sites to be restored, restricting restoration objectives to a single ideal reference state can create fundamental problems because the environmental context may differ among the sites (Pickett & Parker 1994). While no single ideal reference state exists, some argue that reference states can be chosen arbitrarily under certain circumstances (e.g., Aronson, Dhillion, & Le Floc'h 1994). We strongly disagree with the use of 'arbitrary' reference states (Aronson *et al.* 1994); instead, a reference system should be based upon the range of what is possible, illustrated by spatial and temporal variation in natural systems, and on contextual issues of how influential processes have been modified. Without focusing on the condition of a site and the external processes acting on the site, restoration can only pretend to create self-sustainability in most circumstances. Because any 'ecosystem of reference' is simply a manifestation of the goals and objectives of the restoration, we find it important to re-emphasize that it is by managing processes that the structure and function of an ecosystem is restored.

We can illustrate our concerns about process and context with an example of variation within vegetation types provided by coastal scrub vegetation in California. This is a shrub-dominated system restricted to near-coastal locations from northern California into Baja California. The vegetation is found on a diversity of soil types, exposures, and climatic conditions, and contains a large number of species. As a consequence, there is great variation in the compositional expression of this ecosystem type and there have been a number of attempts to classify sites within the broad vegetation types (e.g., Westman 1983). Clearly, such broad regional shifts in composition would restrict reference states to something relatively local, but local variation can also be great. High species diversity is expressed among sites and this diversity is sensitive to shifts in topography, distance from the ocean, and soil type. Sites within a few kilometres of each other can share less than half the total species in common when comparing north-facing communities on clay with south-facing communities on granite or any exposure on sand-dunes. Sites may express a range of topography, soil, or contextual processes that make each location distinct in consideration from the others. Each of these conditions alone requires a variety of reference states. Yet the vegetation reflects all of those conditions. Hence, the variety of possible reference states is huge.

A number of highly disturbed sites in the region of San Francisco, California, are currently receiving restoration efforts or are to be restored in the near future. Two specific restoration sites within this area illustrate our meaning of context. One example lies along a ridgeline surrounded by high-density urban development, and contains a large proportion of invasive species. Even with restoration, propagules of the invasives will continue to rain onto the site and represent an ongoing contextual process. People from the surrounding neighbourhoods will visit the site providing continuous fine disturbances. The second example is located only a few kilometres away on a large point of land surrounded by the Pacific Ocean on three sides. At this second location, coastal scrub had been disturbed by the presence of an off-road vehicle club for the last several decades before the purchase of the site for preservation. This ocean site is relatively isolated, and for most of the perimeter is in contact with natural coastal vegetation.

Two aspects of these examples are relevant to the choice of reference states. One is that, even though close in proximity to one another, the plant communities of the two sites are substantially different. The reasons for this difference lies in environmental differences between ridgeline and ocean edge sites, like soil type, exposure to wind and summer fog, historical isolation, and a number of other factors. Within the two restoration sites, substantial variation in composition and structure results from the same processes influenced by topography, soils, and exposures. There is no ideal reference state for this vegetation throughout the region or for these two sites. Adding other restoration sites within coastal scrub to this example only increases the emphasis on how, with variation in soil, slope, exposure, and other conditions, all sites and areas within sites should have different reference conditions for composition and processes.

These two sites also illustrate how context can influence our understanding of what restoration actually is. For the ocean site, restoration might be a relatively easy process in which soils are reconstructed and new plants established. Because a matrix of natural vegetation exists, and because the surrounding areas are mostly natural, a functioning, self-sustaining natural system may result from this restoration 'event'. Unfortunately, this may be an exception to more typical restoration sites. The ridgeline site surrounded by urban housing may seem more appropriate as a restoration example. Here contextual processes have been modified completely by humans, and restoration should be viewed as an ongoing intervention. As a general approach, we feel restoration is more appropriately considered a process, with the degree of active intervention being determined by contextual circumstances (Figure 3.1). In this sense, distinctions between restoration ecology and management of natural vegetation begin to break down.

Conclusions: enhancing restoration ecology

Contemporary approaches in ecology have established that, at most scales of investigation or levels of organization, ecological systems are not deterministic in characteristics like composition, successional pathways, mineral flow, energy flow, or productivity. As a consequence, the variation in ecosystems is simply the reflection of a history of species invasions responding to biotic interactions and the continuous influence of a number of abiotic processes. Crucially, our view of ecosystems recognizes that processes arising outside the system can regulate the system as much as can internal processes (Turner 1989). Together, these concepts lead to an inclusive model of ecosystems as open and variable in successional pathways and stable points, fluctuating in energy and mineral flow, and, especially from a restoration or conservation perspective, to a model that must include the role and impact of humans.

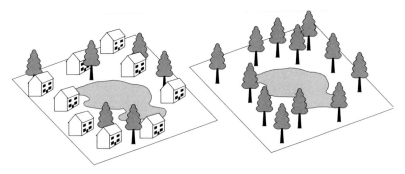

Figure 3.1. The context of restoration sites can strongly influence the processes that influence site dynamics. The two sites illustrated above show a site in a context of high-density housing, in the first case, while, in the second, the site is surrounded by natural vegetation. In the first case, many natural processes will have been suppressed, while other processes, like the dispersal of invasive species, are enhanced. Restoration of this first site will require continuous intervention. Restoration of the second site places it into continuity with ongoing natural processes that enhance restoration rates. The scale at which processes can impact sites suggests that the landscape context can be overwhelmingly important in assessing restoration.

Human impact varies in its rate and magnitude, but in almost all cases has increased the rate of change within ecosystems. Understanding the role of both internal and external processes is critical for developing restoration models. The natural world has hard-and-fast limits in its ability to respond to human-generated pressures. The basic physiological limits, historical availability of suitable species, and the rates of evolution all constrain the ability of nature to adapt successfully or to accommodate change (Pickett & Ostfeld 1994). The new paradigm suggests that the more we understand about these limits, the better we can predict or evaluate the effect of a human-caused change, and successfully intervene in our management.

Historically many cultures have tended to either idealize or anthropo-morphize 'nature'. The use of the word 'nature' in the United States tends to evoke an image of an entity 'out there', separate and distinct from human communities (Cronon 1995). This objectification of natural ecosys-tems has contributed to the metaphor of ecological systems as balanced in processes and capable of maintaining themselves in a climax condition. Too often conservation of a system means saving it 'as it is', imposing a concept of stability onto dynamic systems. For restoration ecology, this metaphor would suggest that such deterministic systems would only require a single restoration event to initiate a self-regulating process returning to an ideal reference state or climax. These perspectives deny the complex dimensionality and dynamic condition of ecological systems.

Ecologists tend to celebrate the distinction of new approaches to the science by the erection of disciplines. New societies and journals soon follow and these are often useful for specialists working out concepts and principles unique to, or focused on, that discipline. In the context of separating themselves from the objectives of traditional applied ecology, scientists concerned with the restoration, conservation, and management of natural systems have laid claim to their place as new disciplines. We agree with this process for the development and maturation of models and applications based on these practical goals and new perspectives. Even now, in the early states of the history of these disciplines, it seems appropriate to point out some of the ways in which they are beginning to converge. The underlying basis for this convergence is based on two points, that basic ecological models unify these disciplines on the one hand, and that contingency limits the usefulness of applying general models indiscriminately.

Previously, differences in the scale of the ecosystem or the level of interest distinguished the disciplines of conservation, management, and restoration. For example, a focus on rare animals and plants dominated conservation biology early on, while restoration was focused on the initial states of assembling ecosystems in highly disturbed locations such as former mine sites or newly created sites for wetlands. However, it has become clear that species cannot be preserved without their genetic and ecological contexts, and that sites cannot be restored without considering their historical and current ecological contexts.

We feel the contemporary paradigm emphasizes this convergence among ecological applications. Systems are dynamic and are maintained by a continuous environmental regime of processes. Furthermore, because ecosystems are open to regulation from external processes as well as from internal processes, the environmental regime of any site receiving restoration efforts includes the context of that site. When contextual processes begin to dominate a local restored site and shift the trajectory of site dynamics away from restoration objectives, more or modified intervention is required. At this stage, restoration objectives, conservation objectives, and management objectives begin to converge completely.

If this congruence of disciplines and approaches is true, then what are the unique aspects of restoration ecology that provide it with the status of a distinct discipline? Our conclusion is that, because restoration is concerned with tangible locations, restoration ecology must balance the use of general models of ecological systems with the unique problems provided by the context of each particular location. If we use the analogy of restoration as managing succession, then the problem for restoration is that most ecological models are articulated at higher, more general levels of hierarchical frameworks of processes (Pickett, Collins, & Armesto 1987), while restoration ecologists must somehow determine the differential impacts of local circumstances, processes found at the lowest level of the conceptual hierarchical framework (Luken 1990).

We conclude by emphasizing the need for restoration ecology to develop models that combine general principles with unique site conditions. The detailed points of the contemporary paradigm point out the ways ecologists have come to understand the linkages, processes, opportunities, and constraints that shape the various components of biodiversity. Systems are open to important controlling factors, often externally regulated, frequently probabilistic in their dynamics, subject to natural disturbances and episodic events, not necessarily in short-term or fine-scale equilibrium, and contain humans. In this context, an ecosystem's structure and dynamics are maintained by a particular and historical environmental regime of biotic and abiotic processes. This model, based on contemporary views of ecosystem dynamics (e.g., Pickett *et al.* 1987; Pickett & McDonnell 1989; Wu & Loucks 1995; Brand & Parker 1995; Parker & Pickett 1997), incorporates the essential aspects we have argued for in this chapter. The challenge for restoration ecology is to abandon the 'balance of nature' for a balance of approaches incorporating the general with the specific.

References

Aronson, J., Dhillion, S. & Le Floc'h, E. (1994). On the need to select an ecosystem of reference, however imperfect: a reply to Pickett and Parker. *Restoration Ecology*, 3, 1–3.
Botkin, D. B. (1990). *Discordant Harmonies: A New Ecology for the Twenty-First Century*. New York: Oxford University Press.
Brand, T. & Parker, V. T. (1995). Scale and laws of vegetation dynamics. *Oikos*, 73, 375–80.
Cronon, W. (1995). The trouble with wilderness; or, getting back to the wrong nature. In *Uncommon Ground: Toward Reinventing Nature*, ed. W. Cronon, pp. 69–90. New York: Norton.
D'Avanzo, C. (1990). Long-term evaluation of wetland creation projects. In *Wetland Creation and Restoration*, eds. J. A. Kusler & M. E. Kentula, pp. 487–97. Washington, DC: Island Press.
Davis, M. B. (1986). Climatic instability, time lags, and community disequilibrium. In *Community Ecology*, eds. J. Diamond, & T. J. Case, pp. 269–84. New York: Harper & Row.

Forman, R. T. T. & Godron, M. (1986). *Landscape Ecology*. New York: Wiley.

Golley, F. B. (1993). *A History of the Ecosystem Concept in Ecology*. New Haven: Yale University Press.

Haeckel, E. (1866). Generalle Morphologie der Organismen: Allgemeine Grundzuege der organischen Formen-wissenschaft, mechanisch begruendet durch die von Charles Darwin reformirte Descendenz-Theorie, vols. 1–2. Berlin: Reimer.

Jones, C. G. & Lawton, J. H. (1995). *Linking Species and Ecosystems*. New York: Chapman & Hall.

Jordan, W. R., III. (1993). Restoration as a technique for identifying and characterizing human influences on ecosystems. In *Humans as Components of Ecosystems: The Ecology of Subtle Human Effects and Populated Areas*, eds. M. J. McDonnell & S. T. A. Pickett, pp. 271–9. New York: Springer-Verlag.

Likens, G. E. (1992). *Excellence in Ecology, 3: The Ecosystem Approach: Its Use and Abuse*. Ecology Institute, Oldendorf/Luhe, Germany.

Luken, J. O. (1990). *Directing Ecological Succession*. London: Chapman and Hall.

Margolis, H. (1993). *Paradigms and Barriers: How Habits of Mind Govern Scientific Beliefs*. University of Chicago Press.

Naveh, Z. & Lieberman, A. S. (1984). *Landscape Ecology: Theory and Application*. New York: Springer-Verlag.

Niering, W. A. (1987). Vegetation dynamics ('Succession' and 'Climax') in relation to plant-community management. *Conservation Biology*, 1, 287–95.

Niering, W. A. & Warren, R. S. (1980). Vegetation patterns and processes in New England Salt Marshes. *BioScience*, 30, 301–7.

Parker, V. T. (1993). Conservation issues in land management. In *Interface Between Ecology and Land Development in California*, ed. J. E. Keeley, pp. 53–60. Los Angeles, CA: Southern California Academy of Sciences.

Parker, V. T. & Pickett, S. T. A. (1997). Historical contingency and multiple scales of dynamics within plant communities. In *Scale Issues in Ecology*, eds. D. Peterson & V. T. Parker. New York: Columbia University Press.

Pickett, S. T. A. & McDonnell, M. J. (1989). Changing perspectives in community dynamics: a theory of successional forces. *Trends in Ecology and Evolution*, 4, 241–5.

Pickett, S. T. A. & Ostfeld, R. S. (1994). The shifting paradigm in ecology. *Ecology and Environment*, 3, 151–9.

Pickett, S. T. A. & Parker, V. T. (1994). Avoiding the old pitfalls: opportunities in a new discipline. *Restoration Ecology*, 2, 75–9.

Pickett, S. T. A., Collins, S. L. & Armesto, J. J. (1987). A hierarchical consideration of causes and mechanisms of succession. *Vegetatio*, 69, 109–14.

Pickett, S. T. A., Parker, V. T. & Fiedler, P. L. (1992). The new paradigm in ecology: Implications for conservation biology above the species level. In *Conservation Biology: The Theory and Practice of Nature Conservation, Preservation, and Management*, eds. P. Fiedler & S. Jain, pp. 65–88. New York: Chapman & Hall.

Race, M. S. (1985). Critique of present wetlands mitigation policies in the United States based on an analysis of past restoration projects in San Francisco. *Environmental Management*, 9, 71–82.

Shrader-Frechette, K. S. & McCoy, E. D. (1993). *Method in Ecology: Strategies for Conservation.* New York: Cambridge University Press.

Simberloff, D. (1980). A succession of paradigms in ecology: essentialism to materialism and probabilism. *Synthèse*, 43, 3–39.

Tansley, A. G. (1935). The use and abuse of vegetational concepts and terms. *Ecology*, 16, 284–307.

Turner, M. G. (1989). Landscape ecology: the effect of pattern on process. *Annual Review of Ecology and Systematics*, 20, 171–97.

Westman, W. E. (1983). Xeric mediterranean-type shrubland association of Alta and Baja California and the community/continuum debate. *Vegetatio*, 52, 3–19.

Wiens, J. A. (1986). Spatial scale and temporal variation in studies of shrubsteppe birds. In *Community Ecology*, eds. J. Diamond & T. J. Case, pp. 154–72. New York: Harper & Row.

Wu, J. & Loucks, O. L. (1995). From balance of nature to hierarchical patch dynamics: a paradigm shift in ecology. *Quarterly Review of Biology*, 70, 439–66.

4

The importance of soil ecology in restoration science

ANTHONY D. BRADSHAW

Introduction

Successional processes

When ecosystems are degraded for whatever reason, either the vegetation or both the vegetation and the soil suffer; the animals, of course, suffer also because their primary resource is lost. It is the loss of vegetation which is the most significant event, besides being the most obvious. We can all hold in our minds visions of the results of overgrazing or a hurricane to remind ourselves of the catastrophic degradations of vegetation that can occur.

But if all that has happened is that the vegetation has been destroyed, recovery can occur very quickly. Once the damaging factor has been withdrawn, the fragments of original plants remaining can quickly shoot again, often making use of existing root systems. New plants can also arise quickly from dormant seeds. Although the available space may, for a time, be occupied by opportunistic ruderal species, there is a subsequent process of readjustment as the species of the original community reassert their presence and finally their original dominance.

All this is termed secondary succession. What can happen is particularly well documented for arable fields after farming has been abandoned (Bazzaz 1979). This is an extreme case, because the previous tillage will have removed all the previous original vegetation, normally woodland, including most of its propagules. The first colonists are fugitive species with a high growth rate; subsequent recolonization comes from small areas where the species of the original vegetation exist, from the small woodlands and field headlands which are a part of most farmland.

A study of this sort of succession suggests that natural regeneration is easy and that, as a result, artificial restoration of degraded land will also be easy. But in the situations described only part of the previous ecosystem has been destroyed – the soil has been left in place. In some cases some

Table 4.1. *The range of factors hostile to plant growth likely to occur in different types of degraded land (from Bradshaw & Chadwick 1980): the most common and serious problems are soil structure and nitrogen content*

Materials	Physical problems				Chemical problems				
	Texture & structure	Stability	Water supply	Surface temperature	Nitrogen	Other nutrients	pH*	Toxic materials	Salinity
colliery spoil	– –	– – –/o	–/o	o/+++	– –	– – –	– – –/o	o	o/++
strip mining	– –/o	– – –/o	–/o	o/+++	– –	– – –/o	– – –/o	o	o/++
fly ash	– –/o	–/o	o	o	– –	– –	+/+++	++	o/++
oil shale	– –	– – –/o	– –	o/++	– –	– –	–/o	o	o/+
iron ore	– –/o	– –/o	–/o	o	– –	–/o		o	o
bauxite	o	o	o	o	–/o	–/o	o	o	o
heavy metals	– –	– – –/o	–/o	o	– –	– –	– –/+	+++/+	o/+++
gold wastes	– –	– –	– –	o	– –	– –	– –/–	o/++	o
kaolin wastes	– – –/–	– –	– –	o	– –	– –	–	o	o
acid rocks	– –	o	– –	o	– –	–	–	o	o
calcareous rk	– –	o	– –	o	– –	–	+	o	o
sand/gravel	–/o	o	– –/++	o	– –	–/o		o	o
coastal sand	– –/o	– – –/o	–/o	–/o	– –/o	– –/o	–/o	o	o/+
urban land	– – –/o	o	o	o	– – –/o	o	o	o/++	o
roadsides	– – –/o	– –	– –/o	– –/o	– – –/o	–/o	o	o	o
ski runs	– –	o	– –	o/+	– –	–/o	o	o	o

Note: Deficiency: – – – severe, – – slight   adequate: o   excess: + slight, +++ severe   (*for pH: – low, + high)
actual score can vary between limits shown owing to site conditions and history of disturbance

concomitant soil damage may have occurred as a result of loss of the vegetation cover, but this is not usually serious.

From the point of view of a functioning ecosystem, what is important is that the soil holds some of the most important non-renewable resources of the ecosystem, particularly the mineral nutrients and the soil organic matter and mineral particles that hold them. Some mineral nutrients will be lost when the vegetation is destroyed, but the amount is usually small in comparison with what is stored in the soil. If, therefore, the soil part of the ecosystem remains, the original species can quickly make a new start and the vegetation can regrow without delay. This is the essence of secondary succession.

Unfortunately, human beings undertake many types of development in which not only the vegetation, but also the soil, is destroyed or degraded. This can arise when the soil itself is being exploited, as in agriculture, or when the soil is overlaid with buildings, as in urban or industrial developments, or where the soil suffers major disturbance such as mining in order to exploit another, usually mineral, resource underneath (Bradshaw & Chadwick 1980). In nature, similar conditions occur on glacial moraines left by retreating ice, on alluvial deposits in rivers and coasts, and after startling events such as landslips and volcanic eruptions (Miles & Walton 1993).

In such situations, what is produced will vary, depending on the situation. But essentially all that remains will be a skeletal material, composed of raw mineral fragments and particles, in the form of pieces of undecomposed rock, or of material of a single size such as sand. The minerals will be undecomposed, so that the normal breakdown products such as clay minerals, as well as finer rock particles, are not present. There will be no secondary minerals, such as hydroxy-apatites and carbonates. There will be no organic matter with its store of available nutrients, especially nitrogen. At the same time the lack of a range of fine particles may offer an environment physically hostile to plant roots. The range of possible hostile soil factors is considerable (Table 4.1).

In these circumstances the scope for plant growth and ecosystem regeneration is much more bleak. The natural successions which occur are known as primary successions. Since there will be an almost complete absence of propagules, the first limitation will be problems of immigration of species. The second limitation will be the physical hostility and the third the deficiency in essential resources. Only few species will be able to tolerate these, and as a result the process of ecosystem development may take a long time. The primary colonists may persist for several decades.

Ultimately the natural processes of soil and ecosystem development will create improved conditions and a properly functioning and structured ecosystem will result. But this can take up to 100 years, as shown, for instance, by the primary succession taking place on the moraines left by retreating glaciers at Glacier Bay, Alaska (Crocker & Major 1955).

Soil as a critical factor

Soil is therefore a critical controlling component of ecosystems at the early stages of their development. Without the natural processes of soil development, ecosystems would remain in a very depauperate condition.

Soil is, however, also a critical factor controlling the final ecosystems that develop in any situation. Any description of the ecosystems of the world indicates the interrelationships between vegetation and soil. But it is often difficult to understand which is cause and which is effect. It is easier to understand the dominating effect that soil can have on the distribution of species and ecosystems from studies on a more local scale, within a single climate, such as those of the Sheffield region of England (Grime & Lloyd 1973).

The most critical evidence, perhaps, comes from experiments where an initially uniform area has been subject to different manurial treatments. The outstanding example of this is the Park Grass Experiment at Rothamsted, begun by Lawes and Gilbert in 1856 and continued up to the present day (Brenchley & Warrington 1969; Thurston 1969). This shows not only progressive divergence of the plant communities on the different plots, but also startling effects on the presence or absence of different species (Figure 4.1). Underlying this is our increasing awareness of the subtle differences between species in their response to ordinary mineral nutrients, for example nitrogen (Figure 4.2).

Principles of repair

In situations where the soil has been destroyed or lost, an engineering solution is possible. Good soil can be purchased from another site, brought in and spread to a suitable depth. But this is expensive and is only possible if the area to be treated is small. Since the process requires another area from which soil can be taken, it will also only be possible if such a supply area exists. Soil brought in from elsewhere may also not have any of the characteristics of the original soil, although it may have some useful components.

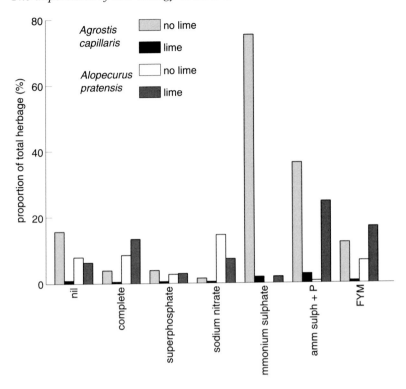

Figure 4.1. The percentage contributions of the grasses *Agrostis capillaris* and *Alopecurus pratensis* to the total yield of herbage from seven of the different manurial treatment plots of the 100 year Park Grass Experiment at Rothamsted (from Brenchley & Warrington 1969). The effects of the nutrient treatments on the balance of species in an originally uniform grassland ecosystem are considerable.

It is therefore more likely that the degraded site materials will need to be treated directly. In view of what occurs in primary succession, this should not be impossible, particularly if the natural processes occurring in such successions can be harnessed. The processes leading to the development of biological soil fertility will be important, rather than the processes involved in long-term pedogenesis, especially since (i) the timescales of these two processes are very different and (ii) it is the former that determines productivity and ecosystem structure and function (Table 4.2).

Excellent plant growth can, of course, be achieved by a rooting medium that provides nothing but water and soluble plant nutrients. Biological soil

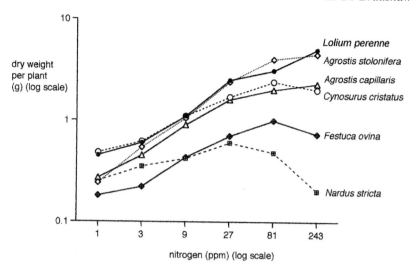

Figure 4.2. The growth responses of different grass species to variation in nitrogen level in sand culture (from Bradshaw *et al.* 1964). Such results provide evidence for the contrasting adaptations of different species to soil conditions.

fertility is essentially related to the capacity of the soil to provide adequate supplies of these, because if plant growth can be supported, so can the development of a whole ecosystem, providing the long-term supplies of water and nutrients are adequate for the complete development. It might be thought that this fertility could take a long time to develop. Observations on primary successions as well as on experimental restoration of derelict land suggest, however, that development can be a rapid process, particularly if assistance, by suitable intervention treatments, can be given in those aspects where natural processes might be slow or inhibited.

Natural primary successions usually take 50–100 years to reach some sort of maturity and equilibrium, for example forest development on glacial moraines at Glacier Bay (Figure 4.3) or on ironstone spoil banks in Minnesota (Leisman 1957). It is impossible to get a mature woodland in much shorter time, but it is not unreasonable to plan to achieve a satisfactorily biologically active soil, supporting an adequate plant cover and forming a simple but self-sustaining ecosystem, within 5–10 years. This may seem optimistic, but in many areas where there is dereliction we need to think about the environment that affects the lives not of ourselves but of our children. Ten years represents the length of a childhood, and we should

Table 4.2 *Processes involved in ecosystem development on degraded land (with approximate periods of time over which process is likely to be important): the biological processes are those most important in enabling plant growth to occur*

Biological processes		Pedological processes	
Time (yrs)	Process	Time (yrs)	Process
1–50	1 Immigration of appropriate plant species	1–1000	1 Accumulation of fine material by rock weathering
1–50	2 Establishment of appropriate plant species		
1–10	3 Accumulation of fine mineral materials captured by plants	1–1000	2 Decomposition of soil minerals by weathering
1–100	4 Accumulation of nutrients by plants from soil minerals	1–100	3 Improvements of soil available water capacity
1–100	5 Accumulation of nitrogen by biological fixation and from atmospheric inputs	1–1000	4 Release of mineral nutrients from soil minerals
1–20	6 Immigration of soil flora and fauna supported by accumulating organic matter		
1–20	7 Changes in soil structure and organic matter turnover due to plant, soil micro-organism and animal activities		
1–20	8 Improvements in soil water holding capacity due to changes in soil structure		
10–1000	9 Reduction in toxicities due accumulation of organic matter	10–10 000	5 Leaching of mobile materials from surface to lower layers
		100–10 000	6 Formation of distinctive horizons in the soil profile

A. D. Bradshaw

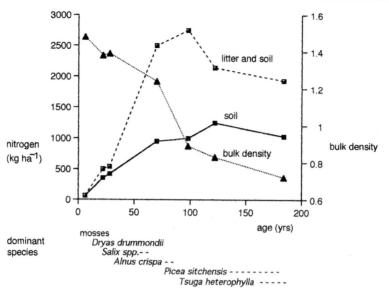

Figure 4.3. The soil bulk density and nitrogen changes occurring naturally as the dominant species, indicated below the graph, replace one another in the plant succession occurring on moraines at Glacier Bay, Alaska (from Crocker & Major 1955). The increase in soil nitrogen is due particularly to *Dryas drummondii* and *Alnus crispa*, fixing about 15 kg and 65 kg N ha^{-1} yr^{-1} respectively.

not inflict dereliction on the next generation for any longer than this. Indeed, in view of what dereliction can mean, the aim should be not more than half a childhood (Burt & Bradshaw 1986).

The individual processes

To achieve an effective and rapid restoration of the soil we need to review the different processes involved in soil development and how much they need to be, and can be, assisted. To do this we can choose a number of illustrative, but certainly not exhaustive, examples.

To enable natural successional processes to occur, the first essential is for plants to be established (Table 4.2). It is these plants that then bring about a whole series of important changes in the soil material. This means that the first requirement is for at least some plant species to arrive, and for conditions to be adequate for them to become established. These will immediately begin the process of accumulation of nutrients and organic matter in the surface layers of the developing soil. So, although we are considering soil processes, we must start by considering plants.

Immigration
Processes

It is often assumed that plants can always reach a new site. This may be true of lower plants, which are distributed by spores. But it is certainly not true of seed plants unless, as for example in orchids, their seeds are very small. Areas derelict for 100 years have been shown to be still missing species ecologically suited to them, although these species have well-established populations not more than 50 km away (Ash *et al.* 1994). For many plants even a distance of 1 km is an insuperable obstacle.

So natural immigration processes cannot be relied on, and it can be important to carry out simple introductions of appropriate species. Some local species may arrive and be entirely suitable, but other species, from further away, need to be introduced. This is particularly true of leguminous and other nitrogen-fixing species which play an important role in suc-cession and tend to have large seeds.

Assistance

There are many different methods of introduction, ranging from normal agricultural methods to hand seeding and planting (Williamson *et al.* 1982; Coppin & Bradshaw 1982). Even trees can be established by direct seeding, although normal forestry techniques usually may be more suitable. Sometimes complete pieces of the original ecosystem, rooted in blocks of original soil, can be moved, to act as island sources of propagules. This is very clear in many reclamation experiments, where losses of nitrogen due to leaching become considerably reduced by the second year, even when readily soluble nutrients are added by fertilization (Robinson, Handel, & Schmalhofer 1992; Handel this volume).

Establishment
Processes

Once propagules arrive the problem for them is not over, because they have to establish. This means that they have to overcome the physical difficulties of the raw environment. Seeds can have very specific adaptations to extreme substrates; both size and shape play an important role. Soil physical conditions occurring at the outset can play an important part in determining what individuals establish. Good evidence comes from studies of what happens following volcanic eruptions, such as at Mount St Helens in 1980 (del Moral 1993). The eruption produced a wide variety of materials differing markedly in their physical characteristics. Although colonization has been slowest on the coarse pumice materials, the best colonization has not taken place on smooth fine material; micro-sites produced by pebbles and small rocks provide the best sites for all species. This preference is supported by experimental interventions showing the great value of spreading an inert mulch. The evidence suggests that it is the water relations of the seed and seedling which are important, which fits in with previous experimental work (Harper 1977).

Essentially this implies that the seedling germinating on a raw substrate is very much exposed to the vicissitudes of weather conditions. There will be little trouble if conditions remain permanently wet, but fluctuating wetness can cause great difficulties. These may have to be overcome by interventions applied directly to the raw substrate.

Assistance

The first essential is to relieve any serious compaction (a common problem) by ripping or scarification to allow root penetration. There is now a variety of machinery available. Then the seed has to be put in conditions favourable to germination and establishment. The simplest method is to place the seed below the surface by mechanical means, drilling or cultivation, simulating the effects of the disturbance and burying processes that would occur in mature soils. But if the seed is going to arrive or be placed artificially on the surface, almost the same effect is obtained if the surface has been broken up, since this offers a range of microsites in which microclimatic and physical conditions are suitable for germination (Cotts & Redente 1995). But protection of the seed on an inhospitable substrate can also be provided by a layer of mulch covering the seed, often chopped straw spread over the surface by blower (Kay 1978).

The most elaborate intervention is hydroseeding, in which the seed is applied to the surface suspended in a liquid mixture containing an organic mulch, a stabilizer, and nutrients. This, although expensive, can be very effective. But, since the seed is effectively being laid on the surface, germination and establishment remains at the mercy of the weather, the surface conditions and the possible toxic effects of the nutrients, so that the process must be carried out with care (Figure 4.4).

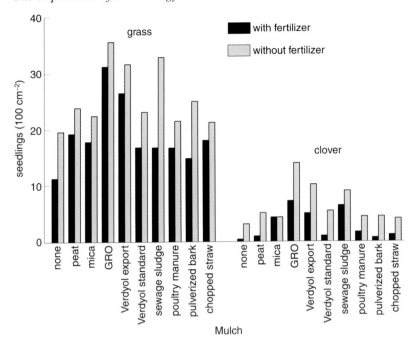

Figure 4.4. The effect of different mulches (at 20 m^3 ha^{-1}) and complete fertilizer (at 500 kg ha^{-1}) on the establishment of grass and clover in a grass/clover seed mixture applied hydraulically in the autumn onto kaolin sand waste in Cornwall (from Roberts & Bradshaw 1985). The most effective mulches are those made from organic fibres and alginates; fertilizer has a considerable adverse effect, especially on clover.

Accumulation and retention of fine materials

Processes

Physical weathering processes will cause the gradual breakdown of rocks and the production of fine particles. In most situations these are then liable to be washed or blown away unless vegetation is present. The importance of vegetation in this respect is made very clear in situations where vegetation has been killed by pollution or other factors. In the area round the nickel smelters at Sudbury, Ontario, the destruction of the vegetation by SO$_2$ has led to the complete loss of the accumulated fine soil material down as far as the underlying rock (Gunn 1995). Vegetation not only ensures accumulation and retention of fine particles by its obvious above-ground effects, but also by its root growth. Roots not only stabilize the soil by simple mechanical effects, but the finer roots and root hairs cause the aggregation of the finer soil particles into soil crumbs. Where slopes are steep, vegetation has a particularly critical role.

Assistance

Little can be done to hasten the weathering process. The accumulation process, however, will be enormously hastened by the presence and growth of plants, encouraged in the many different ways already mentioned. They can actually capture loose material coming from elsewhere, forming miniature dunes. In situations where the degradation has left behind predominantly fine material, in waste heaps and tailings ponds, the presence of plants has a very important role in preventing its erosion. As a result, plants may be introduced specifically to achieve early erosion control in advance of the desired vegetation. Such so-called 'nurse' species are commonly cereals, such as rye or wheat, or even sorghum. They grow rapidly and die, leaving a matrix of protective material, through which the permanent vegetation can grow. On steep slopes vegetation can be used in many ways to great advantage (Schiechtl 1980; Coppin & Richards 1990).

A more radical solution, possible in certain situations, is to amend the site with fine materials. These are often available as a by-product of the original degrading operation, such as the fines from rock-tunnelling operations or the mica from kaolin extraction. The material can either be placed specifically, in planting pits, or spread and mixed into the surface. The effect can be to improve both water-holding capacity and nutrient retention (Figure 4.5 but see also Figure 4.8). It must not be forgotten that if some original topsoil is available it can be used; even in small quantities (about 15 cm) it can have significant effects on moisture retention and plant growth (Brown *et al.* 1992).

Accumulation of mineral nutrients
Processes

An established ecosystem can only persist and grow if it can obtain supplies of nutrients. The approximate amounts required by different ecosystems, on an annual basis, are given in Table 4.3. In any mineral soil there is a slow release of all these nutrients, except nitrogen, from the minerals in the soil. In an initial skeletal soil composed of unweathered fragments, these will have to be released directly from the component minerals by the complex process of weathering; they will then pass into secondary minerals. There

Table 4.3 *The total amounts of nutrients required annually by different ecosystems (Bradshaw 1983): nitrogen is the nutrient required in the greatest amount*

		Productivity level (kg ha^{-1} year^{-1})			
	Nutrient content assumed (%)	1000	5000	10 000	20 000
Nitrogen	2.0	20	100	200	400
Potassium	1.1	11	55	110	220
Magnesium	0.51	5.1	26	51	102
Calcium	0.26	2.6	13	26	52
Phosphorus	0.18	1.8	9	18	36
Type of ecosystem		Tundra and desert	Poorly productive temperate	Productive temperate and poorly productive tropical	Tropical

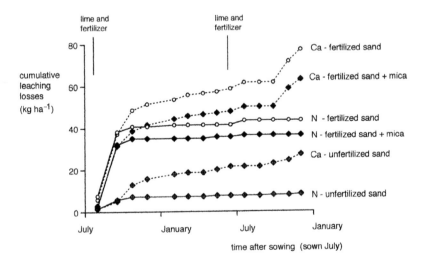

Figure 4.5. Leaching losses, from lysimeters, of nitrogen and calcium from kaolin sand waste with and without amendment with mica, given complete fertilizer and limestone on sowing and after one year (from Smith 1985). The presence of the fine particle mica reduces leaching losses considerably; but the presence of the well-developed grass sward in the second year reduces any further loss of nitrogen to a very low level.

Table 4.4 *The average chemical composition (%) of different rock types (Clarke 1924): there are differences in important plant nutrients such as phosphorus and calcium which can have major effects on the type of ecosystem which can develop*

Component	Rhyolites	Granites	Diorites	Basalts	Dolerites	Shales	Sandstones	Limestones
SiO_2	72.8	70.2	58.9	49.1	50.5	58.1	78.3	5.2
TiO_2	0.3	0.4	0.8	1.4	1.5	0.7	0.3	0.06
Al_2O_3	13.5	14.5	16.5	15.7	15.3	15.4	4.8	0.8
Fe_2O_3	1.5	1.6	2.9	5.4	3.8	4.0	1.1	0.5
FeO	0.9	1.8	4.0	6.4	7.8	2.5	0.3	
MnO	0.08	0.1	0.1	0.3	0.2			
MgO	0.4	0.9	3.6	6.2	5.8	2.4	1.2	7.9
CaO	1.2	2.0	6.1	9.0	8.9	3.1	5.5	42.6
Na_2O	3.4	3.5	3.5	3.1	3.1	1.3	0.5	0.05
K_2O	4.5	4.1	2.1	1.5	1.0	3.2	1.3	0.3
H_2O	1.5	0.08	1.3	1.6	1.9	5.0	1.6	0.8
P_2O_3	0.08	0.2	0.3	0.5	0.3	0.2	-0.08	0.04
CO_2						2.6	5.0	41.5
SO_3						0.6	0.07	0.05
BaO						0.05	0.05	
C						0.8		

will usually be more than adequate supplies of micronutrients, but the nutrients required in larger amounts may not all be available initially in sufficient amounts. Which elements are freely available, and which are not, depends ultimately on the particular soil minerals present (Table 4.4). Interactions are possible; phosphorus for instance can be rendered unavailable by the presence of high levels of iron or calcium with which it forms insoluble phosphates.

To understand fully what mineral nutrients will be available in a material and which will be in short supply requires a chemical and, if possible, a mineralogical analysis. But it must be remembered that when plants grow they acquire nutrients by active uptake processes taking place in a diffuse root system. Some species, especially woody species, have very diffuse systems and associated mycorrhiza, which allows them to act as scavengers and collect small amounts of nutrients occurring over a wide area and large soil volume. Because of this scavenging, losses by leaching are substantially reduced once vegetation becomes established. These nutrients become concentrated in the plant, are shed in dying plant parts, and so ultimately accumulate in the surface layers of the soil. In this way plant growth leads to an improvement of available nutrient levels in the soil immediately beneath them (Figure 4.6). Since these accumulated nutrients are initially in organic matter they are made readily available by the decomposition of the organic matter.

Assistance

Plant growth has therefore an important positive contribution to make to soil nutrient status. But basic deficiencies of nutrients in the starting material cannot be overcome by this. Plant growth can be completely restricted, for instance, by a deficiency of phosphorus, particularly if at the same time there are other elements present which will complex it. In such situations intervention is necessary, by addition of the deficient element. This will usually be by an artificial fertilizer, such as superphosphate or ground rock phosphate for phosphorus. But organic materials may be available; sewage sludge for instance contains high levels of phosphorus.

The amount to be added will depend on the particular situation, and will need to be determined by soil analysis. For some nutrients such as phosphorus, which are not very soluble and not required in large amounts, a single application may be all that is required, although if the phosphorus becomes bound then a second application will be needed after a few years. Potassium is needed in larger amounts and is easily leached, but because it

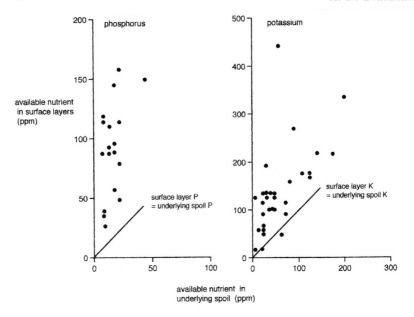

Figure 4.6. The levels of available potassium and phosphorus in the surface layers of different afforested colliery spoil heaps in W. Germany compared with the levels in the underlying spoil (from Knabe 1973). The elevated amounts in the surface layers are due to the power of nutrient accumulation of the tree species.

is a common component of many soil minerals extra amounts are usually not needed.

The amount to be added, however depends also on the endpoint required, the two extremes being represented by productive agriculture and diverse low growing species-rich vegetation. Since all species have individual requirements, the nutrient levels achieved will determine whether or not a particular species will be prominently represented or not in the final ecosystem. This is illustrated for white clover by Figure 4.7, growing on a very deficient sand waste, where its presence or absence is obviously completely dependent on phosphorus and calcium levels.

Since plants have a scavenging effect, particularly for nutrients in short supply, plant establishment leads to a considerable reduction in leaching. This is very clear in many reclamation experiments, where losses of nitrogen due to leaching become considerably reduced by the second year, even when readily soluble nutrients are added by fertilization (Marrs & Bradshaw 1980 see also Figure 4.5).

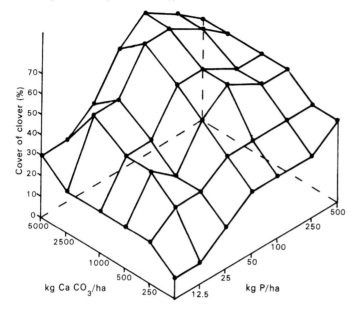

Figure 4.7. The effects of lime and phosphorus aftercare treatments on the growth of 2-year-old white clover (*Trifolium repens*) on reclaimed kaolin sand waste (from Bradshaw *et al.* 1978). A sensitive species such as clover will not persist on poor soils without further addition of both lime and phosphorus.

Accumulation of nitrogen
Processes

Unlike other plant nutrients, almost no nitrogen occurs in soil minerals. It is present in soils in the soil organic fraction, in which it has accumulated by biological processes. A large amount is stored in the organic matter, from which a small amount is released annually by mineralization. A greater amount of nitrogen is required for plant growth than of any other soil nutrient (Table 4.3). There is a simple relationship between nitrogen supply and required soil nitrogen capital depending on the rate of organic matter breakdown (Table 4.5). This suggests that, in normal temperate conditions, the soil nitrogen capital required is about $1000 \, \mathrm{kg\,N\,ha^{-1}}$. Yet a skeletal soil starts effectively with none. The breakdown process is dependent on the presence of decomposer organisms, mainly bacteria and fungi. But these readily colonize new soils. The rate of breakdown can, however, be affected by the carbon/nitrogen ratio of the material as well as soil pH.

In temperate regions between 10 and $25 \, \mathrm{kg\,N\,ha^{-1}\,yr^{-1}}$ is contributed by

Table 4.5 *The organic soil nitrogen capital (kg N ha⁻¹) needed to provide for different ecosystem requirements (kg N ha⁻¹ yr⁻¹) assuming various annual rates of organic matter decomposition (k) (Bradshaw, 1983): because nitrogen is stored in soil in organic matter and is released only slowly by decomposition, a large amount of nitrogen has to be stored in order to provide sufficient for ecosystem growth*

	Decomposition rate			
Annual requirement	0.02	0.1	0.2	1.0
200	10 000	2 000	1 000	200
100	5 000	1 000	500	100
50	2 500	500	250	50
Type of ecosystem	Montane	Cool temperate	Warm temperate	Tropical

precipitation, although it may be more in industrial areas. 25 kg N ha⁻¹ yr⁻¹ is neither enough to provide for the annual requirement nor will it do very much to build up the overall soil capital. The critical source is by biological fixation. A small amount, about 5 kg N ha⁻¹ yr⁻¹, is fixed by free living micro-organisms; the greatest amount is provided by symbiotic micro-organisms, notably rhizobia occurring on members of the Leguminosae, and actinomycetes such as *Frankia* occurring on other species such as *Alnus* and *Casuarina*. These fix between 50 and 150 kg N ha⁻¹ yr⁻¹, providing a major source of nitrogen, enough for immediate ecosystem needs and forming a major contribution to the soil capital (Marrs *et al.* 1983).

Scavenging species can have an important role early in primary successions, collecting the nitrogen from precipitation, but vegetation and soil development are essentially driven by the arrival of species capable of symbiotic nitrogen fixation. In the Glacier Bay chronosequence, the major development is due to the arrival and establishment firstly of *Dryas drummondii* and then of *Alnus crispa*. Even so, this succession, like many others, has taken about 100 years to reach maturity.

Assistance

Although natural processes will work in the end, intervention is usually more important with regard to nitrogen supply than for any other soil attribute. Following agronomic principles, it is easy to provide nitrogen by mineral fertilizer. But the total amount required, 1000 kg N ha⁻¹, is large

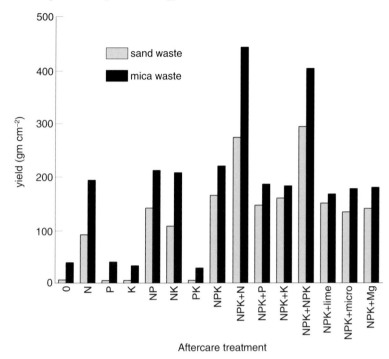

Figure 4.8. The growth responses to the addition of different nutrients to moribund swards established on kaolin sand and mica wastes (from Bradshaw *et al.* 1975 and unpublished). The poor growth must have been almost entirely due to shortage of nitrogen; the recovery in growth with the addition of nitrogen is consistently better on the mica waste, probably due to the better retention of nitrogen by the finer particles of the mica.

and expensive. In order for it to be taken up by plants, it would have to be given at a rate commensurate with plant uptake, about $100\,\text{kg}\,\text{ha}^{-1}\,\text{yr}^{-1}$, and, unless provided in an expensive slow-release form, it will be liable to leaching. On skeletal soils, leaching can account for half the nitrogen applied (Dancer 1975). So, where nitrogen has been applied in restoration by fertilizer, regression at the end of the first year, that can be shown to be due to nitrogen deficiency, is commonplace if not universal (Bloomfield, Handley, & Bradshaw 1982). On the wastes produced by kaolin mining in Cornwall, the nitrogen deficiencies that can arise are considerable, and can be the only factor holding back ecosystem development (Figure 4.8). It is interesting that, on the finer-grained, mica wastes, the deficiencies are not so great as on sand, and the retention and release of higher applications of nitrogen more effective.

Table 4.6 *The amount of nitrogen and phosphorus contributed by a single heavy application of two different types of sludge (200 t ha^{-1} in each case; Byrom & Bradshaw 1991): a single application of sewage sludge can provide all the nutrients needed in a soil however much degraded*

Sludge type	Dry solids %	Total nitrogen t ha^{-1}	Total phosphorus		Total phosphorus	
			N% ds	kg N ha^{-1}	P % ds	kg P ha^{-1}
Liquid digested	4	8	5	400	1.7	140
Digested cake	25	50	3	1500	1.5	750

In suitable circumstances it is possible to use heavy applications of nitrogen-rich organic matter. A single application of digested sewage sludge, for instance, can provide all the capital of soil nitrogen required as well as substantial amounts of phosphorus (Table 4.6). It is in a form readily available to plants and yet resistant to leaching (Byrom & Bradshaw 1991). Sludge is only available in some situations, but there may be other organic materials instead. Topsoil, even if available only in small amounts, is, of course, a possible source.

Normally the major way in which nitrogen accumulation can be assisted is by the use of legumes. These can be used either for their contribution to the growth of other species or in their own right. In temperate grassland, herbaceous legumes such as *Trifolium repens* and *Trifolium pratense* can contribute well over 100 kg N ha^{-1} yr^{-1} (Dancer, Handley, & Bradshaw 1977). The permanence of their contribution in comparison to fertilizer nitrogen is easily demonstrated in field experiments. There are a large number of species to choose from, adapted to different soils and climates (Bradshaw & Chadwick, 1980). The nitrogen accumulated is soon released as mineral nitrogen for other plants to take up; decomposition of the organic matter is greatly assisted by the low C/N ratio of the plant material. As a result, in herbaceous legumes, the release of nitrogen into associated vegetation can be detected after one year. In woody species such as tree lupin (*Lupinus arboreus*), however, release may not occur for 4 years (Figure 4.9). Nevertheless tree lupin is used very successfully in forestry on poor soils (Gadgil 1971). Spectacular long-term improvement in growth can be induced in non-N-fixing woody species on degraded soils when they are planted in mixtures with N-fixing woody species (Figure 4.10).

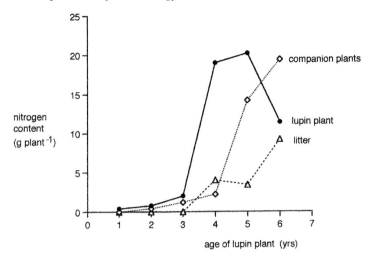

Figure 4.9. The accumulation of nitrogen in single colonizing plants of *Lupinus arboreus*, the companion vegetation, and the associated litter, growing on kaolin wastes over a period of 6 years until the lupin plants die (from Palaniappan *et al.* 1979). Nitrogen is accumulated first in the N-fixing lupin, but after 3 years it becomes available to the companion vegetation which suddenly grows very vigorously.

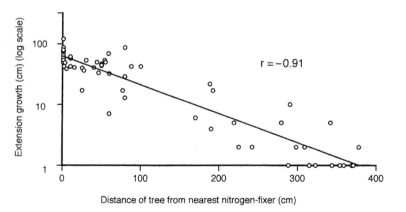

Figure 4.10. The annual extension growth after 10 years of various non-N-fixing tree species planted on kaolin mining waste at different distances from N-fixing *Alnus* species (Kendle & Bradshaw 1992). The effect of proximity to the *Alnus* is to increase growth by a factor of 50.

Again, as with other nutrients, the use of any assistance must be planned in relation to the desired endpoint. All plant communities require some nitrogen, and on skeletal materials some nitrogen must always be given if establishment is to be successful. But if a low-productivity high-diversity ecosystem is required, it may be better to contribute the nitrogen by fertilizer, giving two or three applications, rather than by a legume, since there is the possibility, if other conditions such as phosphorus and calcium levels are adequate, the legume may flourish excessively and by its continuous contribution of nitrogen encourage unwanted strongly competitive species. It is the absence of adequate levels of phosphorus that renders untreated limestone quarries, for instance, such a favourable habitat for uncommon and rare species intolerant of competition (Davis 1976).

Immigration of soil organisms

There have been too few studies of the soil organisms in degraded soil materials. However it is clear that the accumulating organic matter, both live and dead, will immediately support a variety of soil organisms, most of which have little difficulty in immigration. The fungi and bacteria will have an immediate effect in bringing about the decomposition of the organic matter, permitting nutrient turnover. Populations of 3×10^9 bacteria gm^{-1} of soil are rapidly achieved. It is not possible to estimate the fungal component in the same way, but linear estimates suggest that about 3×10^3 m of hyphae gm^{-1} of soil is common (Swift, Heal, & Anderson 1979). Such population densities can have a crucial influence on soil structure. The growth forms of the fungi are particularly effective in causing the aggregation of soil particles into crumbs; but the colloidal and other similar sticky materials, such as polysaccharides and waxes, produced by both bacteria and fungi, can also be important in causing the formation of soil crumb structure. Mycorrhizal fungi, also, have an important role in assisting nutrient uptake, so important in skeletal soils.

Very large populations of soil fauna also develop, feeding on the fungi, bacteria, plant organic matter, and each other, helping in the decomposition processes (Majer 1989 and this volume). Their passage through the soil also creates small voids which contribute to the total pore space of the soil. As a result of these and other agents, progressive reductions in bulk density occur over time in primary successions, on both natural and artificial materials. This reduction in bulk density allows the more free passage of plant roots. But it has a major effect on increasing the available water-holding capacity of the materials, which depends to a large extent on pore space as well as on organic matter content.

There is one soil organism that deserves special attention – the earthworm. In a mature soil there can be as many as 1 million ha^{-1} ($100\,m^{-2}$). Their burrowing activity has three major effects: (i) forming drainage channels – up to 10 times the number of earthworms, (ii) bringing fine soil to the surface in wormcasts – approximately $5\,mm\,yr^{-1}$, (iii) pulling litter down from the soil surface into the soil profile. The physical effects were first pointed out by Darwin (1881). In calcareous materials such as urban brick waste, favourable to earthworms, colonization can readily occur, and the effects of the worms on soil development is quickly noticed (Bradshaw 1983).

Assistance

When legumes are introduced into a skeletal soil, it is unlikely that their appropriate rhizobia will be present, so it is normal to ensure that the seed is inoculated. Otherwise assistance is rarely, if ever, given to soil organisms. Bacteria and fungi are so mobile and so prolific that there is no need. This is usually true with soil microfauna. But there is a growing realization that this may be an over-optimistic approach (Haselwandter this volume). Appropriate mycorrhizal fungi, in particular, may not be present and it can be sensible to remedy this. Planted material can be inoculated before planting by being grown in a suitable soil. But seed material is more difficult and too little work has been done. Perhaps the only sensible solution is to bring in and scatter some appropriate soil as an inoculum.

Certain soil conditions can reduce microbial growth and activity. This is very obvious on soils which are either very acid or contaminated with heavy metals, and can be recognized by the accumulation of undecayed organic matter and reduced nutrient cycling. Any treatment that reduces the effects of these two toxicities will improve the situation.

Among soil fauna, some arthropods can have problems of dispersal and need to be introduced (Williams this volume). Earthworms certainly have little mobility. Their introduction in soil or turf can have startling effects on drainage and litter accumulation, for instance, on newly reclaimed polder soils (Hoogerkamp, Rogaar, & Eijsackers 1983) and coal-mine sites (Figure 4.11). But, as with the micro-organisms, soil chemical conditions must be suitable for introductions to be successful.

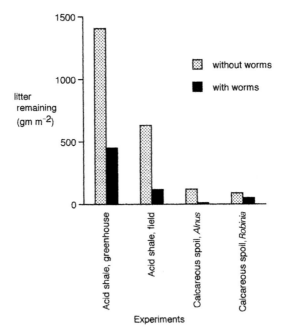

Figure 4.11. The effects of presence or absence of introduced populations of earthworms (*Lumbricus terrestris*) on the amount of litter remaining on different areas of afforested colliery spoil, after approximately 6 months (from Vimmerstedt 1983). In all cases the amount of litter is reduced by at least half.

Improvement in water holding capacity

Processes

All the processes which improve soil structure, and particularly bulk density, will improve the available water capacity, because this depends so much on pore space. Organic matter itself will be particularly important because its own available water capacity can be three of four times that of a mineral soil. At the same time, because the hydraulic conductivity of soils is poor, the more that roots can penetrate into the soil, the greater is the soil volume and therefore amount of water from which plants can draw. Developed soils are therefore more likely to offer plants equable water conditions, with less fluctuations in supply.

Assistance

The value of small applications of a developed soil or an organic mulch has already been mentioned. But an organic material applied to the surface will

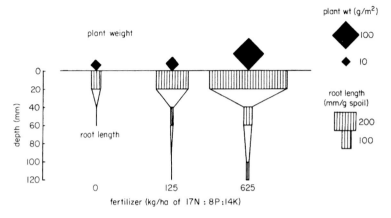

Figure 4.12. The amount and depth of root growth of ryegrass (*Lolium perenne*) in colliery shale given different fertilizer treatments (Bradshaw & Chadwick 1980). The added nutrients have a major effect in increasing the amount and depth of rooting; this reduces the susceptibility of the plants to drought.

have little effect on the soil as a whole. It is very difficult to apply and mix into a skeletal material enough organic matter to affect it to a substantial depth, although sewage sludge is a possibility. But organic matter can be used in a localized manner in tree-planting pits (Sheldon & Bradshaw 1976). Recently, the possibility of using hydrophilic polymers, which can absorb and hold up to 200 times their own weight of water, has been demonstrated (Woolhouse & Johnson 1991), but these are expensive to use on a large scale.

Deep cultivation will always be valuable in allowing deeper rooting. But what is not always realized is that plant rooting is very dependent on plant nutrition (Figure 4.12). Plants that are suffering from an inadequate supply of nutrients may well actually die of drought. At the same time, since plants have a highly significant role in improving soil structure by their root growth and their contribution of organic matter to the soil, a complex set of positive interactions exist in which anything that helps to assist one aspect of soil development is likely to assist other aspects.

Toxicity
Processes

Toxicity is, in general, a localized problem usually related to particular types of mining disturbance. Acidity, at the sort of extremes that can inhibit growth, is mainly associated with the presence of pyrite, FeS, which oxidizes on exposure to air to give sulphuric acid. Pyrite is mostly commonly found in the wastes produced by mining for coal, and metals. When levels of pyrite in a soil material reach about 3–5%, the soil pH can be well below 3, totally preventing growth.

Heavy metal contamination can have equally traumatic effects. Much depends on the form in which the metal is present, but levels of total copper, lead, or zinc above 0.5% are likely to prevent growth completely, except of tolerant plant populations if these exist. Without any protective cover, metal contaminated sites are therefore very liable to erosion and to be a source of serious pollution to surrounding areas.

Under natural conditions the acidity from pyrite will slowly be leached away, so that the toxicity will disappear and allow the main soil-forming processes to operate. However, if there is great deal of pyrite present, this will not all oxidize at once, and a pH as low as 2.5 may be maintained for 30–50 years.

Heavy metals are relatively immobile and will not leach away. As a result, metal toxicity is an almost permanent feature. This is not only reflected in the almost complete lack of plant growth on metal wastes over hundreds of years, but even on natural metal anomalies. However, if metal-tolerant plants can gain a foothold, they may accumulate slowly sufficient organic matter at the surface to ameliorate conditions sufficiently for other plants to colonize.

Assistance

With regard to acidity, except for finding acid-tolerant plant species, the only soil treatment is to neutralize the acidity by the application of lime. The amount to be added is not just that sufficient to neutralize the available acidity, which would be the agricultural approach, but that sufficient to neutralize also the potential acidity. This is related to the amount of unweathered pyrite, which can readily be determined (Costigan, Bradshaw, & Gemmell 1981). If this is done, the amount of lime that may need to be added can rise from 20 tonnes ha^{-1} to 150 tonnes ha^{-1}. This can be expensive, but is the only solution if restoration of the site material itself is to be achieved.

The situation with metal contamination is even more difficult, because there is no effective and reliable way of getting rid of metals or their effects. At one stage it was considered possible to alleviate metal toxicity by the addition of organic matter. Although this does work on a temporary basis,

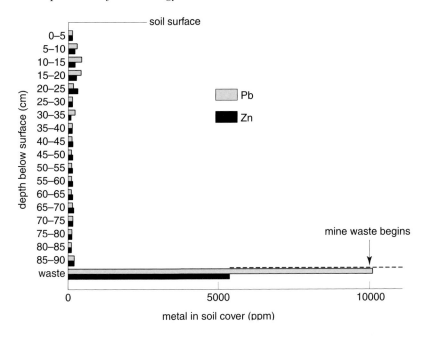

Figure 4.13. Metal concentrations in the inert cover placed over highly contaminated lead/zinc mine wastes at Y Van, N. Wales, 5 years previously (from Shu & Bradshaw 1995). The inert cover prevents the upward movement of toxic elements almost completely and allows the establishment of a normal vegetation.

its effects disappear within about 5 years as the organic matter breaks down. In some situations, metal-tolerant plant populations can be found. These can provide an effective cover, but will need to be given additions of nutrients, particularly nitrogen, from time to time to maintain growth. There do not seem to be any useful metal-tolerant legumes.

This means that the only permanent solution is to cover the contaminated material with some other, uncontaminated, material. This can be a waste material, not containing metals, from the mine itself, or it can be subsoil or waste from elsewhere. The fertility of this covering can then be restored, by the ways already discussed. Even on very toxic wastes, such a layer need not be more than 30–50 cms deep to ensure that the surface is well isolated from metal contamination, because upward movement of contaminants is minimal (Figure 4.13). On some wastes it can be even less (Trlica *et al.* 1995).

Table 4.7 *A simple table of the physical and chemical problems that can be found in the soils of degraded terrestrial ecosystems and their short- and long-term treatments (from Bradshaw 1983): the long-term treatments are closest to the natural ecological processes and are most likely to be self-sustaining*

Category	Problem	Immediate treatment	Long-term treatment
Physical			
Texture	coarse	organic matter or fines	vegetation
	fine	organic matter	vegetation
Structure	compact	rip or scarify	vegetation
	loose	compact	vegetation
Stability	unstable	stabilizer or nurse	regrade or vegetation
Moisture	wet	drain	drain
	dry	irrigate or mulch	tolerant vegetation
Nutrition			
Macronutrients	nitrogen	fertilizer	N-fixing species
	others	fertilizer and lime	fertilizer and lime
Micronutrients	deficient	fertilizer	-
Toxicity			
pH	low	lime	lime or tolerant species
	high	pyritic waste or organic matter	weathering
Heavy metals	high	organic matter or tolerant plants	inert covering
Salinity	high	weathering or irrigate	weathering or tolerant species

Conclusions

All this can be summarized in a very practical way as a series of problems with short- and long-term solutions (Table 4.7). Further details are given in the various handbooks that are now available for individual types of degraded land and ecosystems.

It is important to realize that, without soil, ecosystem processes cannot be supported, and that the proper functioning of these processes is critical for ecosystem development. In restoration this principle is particularly critical, since ecosystem degradation nearly always involves soil degradation, and often the soil degradation is total. So the first problem to be addressed in restoration is the way in which the restoration of the soil is to be tackled.

Although there are short-term solutions, long-term solutions are what are important. They have their basis in natural ecological processes by which biologically satisfactory soils are originally formed. Such processes take place without human intervention and without cost. To employ them is therefore to save costs and to ensure self-sustaining endpoints. The problem is that some of them act rather slowly. It is therefore tempting to disregard them and to apply more artificial solutions. But these can either have only short-term effects or, as in the use of imported topsoil, be expensive.

Any improvement of soil characteristics, however, has to be balanced against the endpoint required. Within limits, soil conditions are adjustable, and initially restrictive factors can be retained if required. Maximum productivity will only be achieved by maximum soil fertility, but the ecosystem is then likely to be dominated by only a few species. If an ecosystem of lower productivity, containing species less adapted to competition, is sought then less intervention should be undertaken, appropriate to the species required. But two ecological points must be remembered: (i) because of the original site conditions, the species to be favoured can only be those adapted to those basic conditions; (ii) eventually natural successional processes, even with minimum intervention, are likely to lead to changes in soil conditions which may ultimately cause the replacement of the desired species by others. In choosing a particular level of adjustment, analysis and experimentation stretching over several years will be important.

Good ecological restoration involves a full understanding of natural soil processes if they are to be harnessed to the practical end of restoration, and if a particular desired endpoint is to be achieved.

Acknowledgements

I am very grateful for the invitation and support of RTH and the Geobotanisches Institut enabling me to attend the First International Conference on Restoration Ecology and Sustainable Development held at Zurich, and for the work of many former graduate students and research associates who have contributed so much to understanding the role of soil in restoration ecology.

References

Ash, H. J., Gemmell, R. P., & Bradshaw, A. D. (1994). The introduction of native plant species on industrial waste heaps: a test of immigration and other factors affecting primary succession. *Journal of Applied Ecology*, 31, 74–84.

Bazzaz, F. A. (1979). The physiological ecology of plant succession. *Annual Review of Ecology and Systematics*, 10, 351–71.

Bloomfield, H. E., Handley, J. F., & Bradshaw, A. D. (1982). Nutrient deficiencies and the aftercare of reclaimed derelict land. *Journal of Applied Ecology*, 19, 151–8.

Bradshaw, A. D. (1983). The reconstruction of ecosystems. *Journal of Applied Ecology*, 20, 1–17.

Bradshaw, A. D. & Chadwick, M. J. (1980). *The Restoration of Land*. Berkeley: University of California Press.

Bradshaw, A. D., Chadwick, M. J., Jowett, D., & Snaydon, R. W. (1964). Experimental studies into the mineral nutrition of several grass species. IV Nitrogen level. *Journal of Ecology*, 52, 665–76.

Bradshaw, A. D., Dancer, W. S., Handley, J. F., & Sheldon, J. C. (1975). The biology of land revegetation and the reclamation of the china clay wastes of Cornwall. In *The Ecology of Resource Degradation and Renewal*, eds. M. J. Chadwick & G. T. Goodman, pp. 363–84. Oxford: Blackwell Scientific Publications.

Bradshaw, A. D., Humphries, R. N., Johnson, M. S., & Roberts, R. D. (1978). The restoration of vegetation on derelict land produced by industrial activity. In *The Breakdown and Restoration of Ecosystems*, eds. M. W. Holdgate & M. J. Woodman, pp. 249–74. New York: Plenum.

Brenchley, W. E. & Warrington, K. (1969). *The Park Grass Plots at Rothamsted 1856–1949*. Harpenden: Rothamsted Experimental Station.

Brown, R. W., Sidle, R. C., Amacher, M. C., & Kotuby-Amacher, J. (1992). Reclamation of gold mine soils in the pinyon-juniper zone of the Great Basin. In *Proceedings of the High Altitude Revegetation Workshop No. 10*, eds. W. G. Hassell, S. K. Nordstrom, W. R. Keammerer, & W. J. Todd, pp. 215–38. Fort Collins: Colorado State University.

Burt, A. & Bradshaw, A. D. (1986). *Transforming our Land: the Way Forward*. London: Her Majesty's Stationery Office.

Byrom, K. & Bradshaw, A. D. (1991). The potential value of sewage sludge in land reclamation. In *Alternative Uses of Sewage Sludge*, ed. J. E. Hall, pp. 1–20. Oxford: Pergamon.

Clarke, F. W. (1924). *The Data of Geochemistry (5th edn)*. Washington: United States Geological Survey.

Coppin, N. J. & Bradshaw, A. D. (1982). *Quarry Reclamation. The Establishment of Vegetation in Quarries and Open Pit Non-Metal Mines*. London: Mining Journal Books.

Coppin, N. J. & Richards, I. G. (1990) *The Use of Vegetation in Civil Engineering*. London: Butterworths.

Costigan, P., Bradshaw, A. D. & Gemmell, R. P. (1981). The reclamation of acidic colliery soil. I Acid production potential. *Journal of Applied Ecology*, 18, 865–78.

Cotts, N. R. & Redente, E. F. (1995). Restoration approaches in Grand Teton National Park: a case study. In *Proceedings of the High Altitude Revegetation Workshop No. 11*, eds. W. R. Keammerer & W. G. Hassell, pp. 41–69. Fort Collins: Colorado State University.

Crocker, R. L. & Major, J. (1955). Soil development in relation to vegetation and surface age at Glacier Bay, Alaska. *Journal of Ecology*, 43, 427–48.

Dancer, W. S. (1975). Leaching losses in the reclamation of sand spoils in Cornwall. *Journal of Environmental Quality*, 4, 499–504.

Dancer, W. S., Handley, J. F., & Bradshaw, A. D. (1977). Nitrogen accumulation in kaolin mining wastes in Cornwall. II Forage legumes. *Plant and Soil*, 48, 303–14.

Darwin, C. (1881). *The Formation of Vegetable Mould through the Action of Worms with Observations on their Habits.* London: Faber and Faber.

Davis, B. N. K. (1976). Wildlife, urbanisation and industry. *Biological Conservation*, 10, 249–91.

del Moral, R. (1993). Mechanisms of primary succession on volcanoes: a view from Mount St Helens. In *Primary Succession on Land*, eds. J. Miles & D. W. H. Walton, pp. 79–100. Oxford: Blackwell Scientific Publications.

Gadgil, R. L. (1971). The nutritional role of *Lupinus arboreus* in coastal sand dune forestry. I The potential influence of undamaged lupin plants on nitrogen uptake by *Pinus radiata*. *Plant and Soil*, 34, 357–67.

Grime, J. P. & Lloyd, P. S. (1973). *An Ecological Atlas of Grassland Plants.* London: Edward Arnold.

Gunn, J. M. (1995). *Restoration and Recovery of an Industrial Region.* New York: Springer-Verlag.

Harper, J. L. (1977). *Population Biology of Plants.* London: Academic Press.

Hoogerkamp, M., Rogaar, H., & Eijsackers, H. J. P. (1983). Effects of earthworms on recently reclaimed polder soils in the Netherlands. In *Earthworm Ecology*, ed. J. E. Satchell, 241–6. London: Chapman and Hall.

Kay, B. L. (1978)., Mulch and chemical stabilisers for land reclamation in dry regions. In *Reclamation of Drastically Disturbed Lands*, eds. F. W. Schaller & P. Sutton, pp. 467–83. Madison, Wisconsin: American Society of Agronomy.

Kendle, A. D. & Bradshaw, A. D. (1992). The role of soil nitrogen in the growth of trees on derelict land. *Arboricultural Journal*, 16, 103–22.

Knabe, W. (1973). Investigations of soils and tree growth on five deep-mine refuse piles in the hard-coil region of the Ruhr. In *Ecology and Reclamation of Devastated Land*, eds. R. L. Hutnik & G. Davis, pp. 307–24. New York: Gordon and Breach.

Leisman, G. A. (1957). A vegetation and soil chronosequence on the Mesabi Iron Range spoil banks, Minnesota. *Ecological Monograph*, 27, 221–45.

Majer, J. D. (1989). *Animals in Primary Succession: the Role of Fauna in Reclaimed Lands.* Cambridge University Press.

Marrs, R. H. & Bradshaw, A. D. (1980). Ecosystem development on reclaimed china clay wastes. II Leaching of nutrients. *Journal of Applied Ecology*, 17, 727–36.

Marrs, R. H., Roberts, R. D., Skeffington, R. A., & Bradshaw, A. D. (1983). Nitrogen and the development of ecosystems. In *Nitrogen as an Ecological Factor*, eds. J. A. Lee, S. McNeill, & I. H. Rorison, pp. 113–36. Oxford: Blackwell.

Miles, J. & Walton, D. W. H. (1993). *Primary Succession on Land.* Oxford: Blackwell.

Palaniappan, V. M., Marrs, R. H. & Bradshaw, A. D. (1979). The effect of *Lupinus arboreus* on the nitrogen status of china clay wastes. *Journal of Applied Ecology*, 16, 825–31.

Roberts, R. D. & Bradshaw, A. D. (1985). The development of a hydraulic seeding technique for unstable sand slopes. II Field evaluation. *Journal of Applied Ecology*, 22, 979–94.

A. D. Bradshaw

Robinson, G. R., Handel, S. N., & Schmalhofer, V. R. (1992). Survival, reproduction, and recruitment after 14 years on a reforested landfill. *Environmental Management*, 16, 265–71.

Schiechtl, H. (1980). *Bioengineering for Land Reclamation and Conservation.* Edmonton: University of Alberta Press.

Sheldon, J. C. & Bradshaw, A. D. (1976). The reclamation of slate waste tips by tree planting. *Landscape Design*, 113, 31–3.

Shu, J. & Bradshaw, A. D. (1995). The containment of toxic wastes: I Long term metal movement in soils over a covered metalliferous waste heap at Parc lead-zinc mine, North Wales. *Environmental Pollution*, 90, 371–7.

Smith, A. F. (1985). Amelioration of china clay mining wastes for vegetation Establishment. Ph.D. thesis: University of Liverpool.

Swift, M. J., Heal, O. W. & Anderson, J. M. (1979). *Decomposition in Terrestrial Ecosystems.* Oxford: Blackwell Scientific Publications.

Thurston, J. (1969). The effect of liming and fertilizers on the botanical composition of permanent grassland, and on the yield of hay. In *Ecological Aspects of the Mineral Nutrition of Plants*, ed. I. H. Rorison, pp. 3–9. Oxford: Blackwell Scientific Publications.

Trlica, M. J., Brown, L. F., Jackson, C. L., & Jones, J. (1995). Depth of soil over molybdenum tailings as it affects plant cover, production, and metal uptake. In *Proceedings of the High Altitude Revegetation Workshop No. 11*, eds. W. R. Keammerer & W. G. Hassell, pp. 119–44. Fort Collins: Colorado State University.

Vimmerstedt, J. P. (1983). Earthworm ecology in reclaimed opencast coal mining sites in Ohio. In *Earthworm Ecology*, ed. J. E. Satchell, pp. 229–40. London: Chapman and Hall.

Williamson, N. A., Johnson, M. S., & Bradshaw, A. D. (1982). *Mine Wastes Reclamation. The Establishment of Vegetation on Metal Mine Wastes.* London: Mining Journal Books.

Woolhouse, J. & Johnson, M. S. (1991). Water storing soil polymers and the growth of trees. *Arboricultural Journal*, 15, 27–35.

5

Soil micro-organisms, mycorrhiza, and restoration ecology

KURT HASELWANDTER

Introduction

A number of different factors can lead to the disturbance of the stability of natural or man-made ecosystems. It is well known that natural, i.e. climatic, geomorphic, or palaeotectonic, processes can affect the equilibrium of natural ecosystems (Herrera, Salamanca, & Barea 1993). Such natural agents are capable of damaging irreversibly the biological, chemical, and physical components of soil quality, accompanied by a degeneration of the vegetation (Francis & Thornes 1990). Especially in moisture-deficient areas the decline in soil and plant productivity leads to the, apparently irreversible, development of deserts (desertization, Figure 5.1).

Additionally, human impact, such as deforestation or overgrazing, can also cause ecosystem degeneration, and hence, particularly in arid areas, the development of desert-like conditions (desertification; Skujins & Allen 1986). Under more favourable climatic conditions, the man-mediated ecosystem degeneration may be reversible and accessible to restoration through attempts to establish the original environmental conditions. Desertified ecosystems can be subjected to reclamation strategies including the use of native plant species which eventually leads to the establishment of a natural ecosystem with functions identical with or similar to those of the original ecosystem (Figure 5.1). Under some circumstances, desertified land can be revegetated with species from different ecosystems, with the ultimate goal of developing new ecosystems for different land use or ecological functioning different from the original ecosystem.

Concomitant with ecosystem degradation is generalized damage of the soil microbiota. This inevitably leads to disturbances of the nutrient cycling and hence the functioning and sustainability of the ecosystem. Soil micro-organisms form a major component of the soil biomass, and their activities play a key role in the turnover of nutrients, affecting nutrient

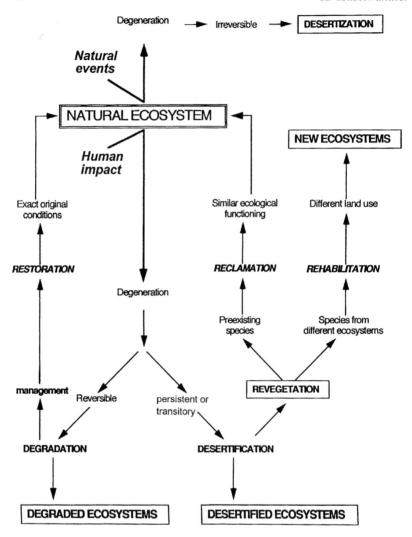

Figure 5.1. Factors leading to degeneration of natural ecosystems and management strategies for their recovery (modified from Herrera *et al.* 1993).

availability (Coleman, Reid, & Cole 1983; see also Figure 5.2). It must be emphasized that the turnover rate of a relatively small pool of labile nutrients is far more important than the pool size. The larger, but less dynamic, non-labile organic and inorganic pools may contribute only a small fraction to annual nutrient fluxes, compared with the small highly labile pool of nutrients (Coleman 1985).

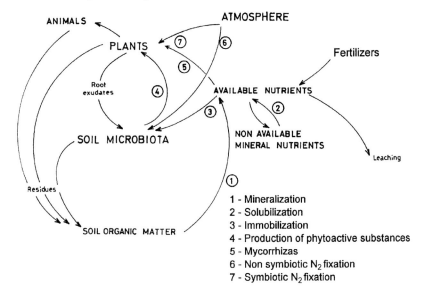

Figure 5.2. Relations of main microbially mediated processes to nutrient cycling (modified from Jeffries & Barea 1994).

Mycorrhizal fungi represent an integral part of the soil microbiota. Almost all families of vascular plants contain species which form at least one type of mycorrhiza (Newman & Reddell 1987; Harley & Harley 1987). The major kinds of mycorrhiza (Table 5.1) are the arbuscular mycorrhiza (AM), ectomycorrhiza (EM), mycorrhiza of the Ericales, and orchidaceous mycorrhiza (Harley & Smith 1983; Moser & Haselwandter 1983). There is a shift in the predominance of certain kinds of mycorrhiza concomitant with increasing latitude or altitude, prevailing climate, and soil types (Read 1984).

In addition to the mycorrhizal fungi listed in Table 5.1, dark-septate fungi are found to colonize a wide range of different plants, not only in alpine plant communities in Europe (Haselwandter & Read 1980; Read & Haselwandter 1981; Blaschke 1991) and North America (Currah & Van Dyk 1986; Trappe 1988), but also in the tropics (Thoen 1987). Under some circumstances, such fungi may lead to a statistically significant increase in the dry weight or/and shoot phosphorus content of host plants (Haselwandter & Read 1982).

Soil harbours a multidimensional, complicated web of interactions involving a large number of soil organisms and, mostly, micro-organisms dependent processes (Coleman 1994), all of which are subject to changes

Table 5.1. *Some characteristics of the different kinds of mycorrhiza*

	Fungi	Hosts	Fungi enter host cells	Sheath
Arbuscular mycorrhiza	Zygomycetes	Bryophyta Pteridophyta Gymnospermae Angiospermae	+	–
Mycorrhiza in Ericales				
ericoid type	Ascomycetes	Ericales	+	–
arbutoid type	Basidiomycetes	Ericales	+	+
monotropoid type	Basidiomycetes	Monotropa	+	+
Mycorrhiza in Orchids	Basidiomycetes	Orchidaceae	+	–
Ectomycorrhiza	Zygomycetes Ascomycetes Basidiomycetes	Gymnospermae Angiospermae	–	+

under stress conditions leading to soil degradation. Disturbance to the soil and vegetation adversely affects the microbial population including mycorrhizal fungi (Jha, Sharma, & Mishra 1992). Hence, for an assessment of the success of strategies to restore or reclaim degraded land, the effects of the strategies employed on the soil microbiota, including mycorrhizal fungi and their activities, has to be monitored. The following paragraphs do not intend to review inclusively all the literature; rather, the aim is to provide examples of the microbial impact required for successful soil rehabilitation. Special emphasis will be placed on the effects of restoration strategies on integrative soil microbial parameters such as soil respiration or microbial biomass, and on specific features, for example, nitrogen fixation or mycorrhization.

Soil microbiota with particular reference to non-mycorrhizal components

The primary objectives of restoration are to minimize environmental degradation and to facilitate re-establishment of a functional plant–soil system exhibiting long-term stability. This relies entirely on the development of a functioning soil microbial community (Tate 1985). Many of the functions of the microbial community can be induced through amendment of the soil with organic materials, but long-term stability of the system requires the development of an indigenous microbial community that can contribute to biogeochemical cycling processes, independently of further organic amendments. The microbial fraction forms a substantial part (8–15%) of the pool of N in revegetated and native woodland ecosystems, with the potential to contribute substantially to nutrient cycling (Sparling, Brandenburg, & Zhu 1994).

Both disturbance as well as restoration or rehabilitation of soils affect a huge number of different microbiological phenomena. As the number of such phenomena which can be analysed is limited, attempts have been made to select those which are manageable and indicate most reliably any positive or negative effects on soil biota. The success of restoration may be inferred from studies of the microbial community structure. But process studies may provide even better indicators for ecosystem recovery, such as the ratio of soil microbial respiration to total microbial biomass (metabolic quotient, qCO_2; Anderson & Domsch 1986). According to Odum (1969) the respiration/biomass ratio is expected to decrease in ecosystems under rehabilitation. This hypothesis was tested in two studies, both in connection with the development of the soil microflora in relation to plant succession.

The first study refers to the primary succession in plant colonization of a moraine in the Tyrolean Central Alps of Austria. The corresponding glacier has been retreating for more than 200 years, with the positions of the ice-front well documented, which allows precise dating of soil development. Samples of soils representing different age were analysed with regard to soil respiration and microbial biomass (determined by substrate-induced respiration, SIR). Plant succession was accompanied by a rise in soil microbial respiration and an even greater increase in microbial biomass, resulting in an exponential decrease in the metabolic quotient qCO_2 (Insam & Haselwandter 1989). Physical and chemical soil characteristics changed also with time; the percentage of sand in the 2 mm fraction decreased steadily, and the organic carbon and total nitrogen content increased considerably.

In the second study, the same methods as mentioned above were applied to determine the short-term development of the soil microflora at a high-elevation site above timberline where a reclamation trial was established in 1982. Immediately after initiation of ecosystem development through seeding and fertilizer application, the metabolic quotient was low, rising in the following 2 years, and decreasing in the subsequent years approaching the value determined for soil under natural climax vegetation (Insam & Haselwandter 1989).

It has been observed that the microbial biomass decreased with increasing soil moisture stress and increased strongly after remoistening of the soil

(Hassink, Lebbink, & van Veen 1991). This renders the metabolic quotient dependent on climatic conditions. Nevertheless, determination of the metabolic quotient appears to yield valuable information for soil monitoring because it integrates several key ecosystem functions (Zak, Fresquez, & Visser 1992).

In some cases, studies of specific functional groups of the microbial soil community may have more significance in assessing soil quality. For example, the community structure of species involved in nitrogen transformations, including nitrogen fixation, or of mycorrhizal fungi (see next section of this chapter) may provide useful and ecologically significant information on the general quality of soil.

With regard to nitrogen fixation, studies of nitrogenase activity may prove useful in high-altitude revegetation programmes. Legume species such as *Trifolium badium, T. pallescens*, and *Lotus alpinus* were carefully excavated from their natural habitat at 2000 m above sea-level and transferred to a Caricetum curvulae at 2600 m, where their nitrogenase activity was measured under field conditions. Even well above the natural area of distribution, nitrogenase activity of the leguminous plants was shown to reach a remarkably high level, thus potentially contributing substantial amounts of nitrogen to the vegetation system (Holzmann & Haselwandter 1988). This may be of particular relevance for revegetation at high elevation (Johnson & Rumbaugh 1986), in which seeds of Fabales might be included in the seed mixtures applied. Once established, a plant cover with nitrogen-fixing legumes may become less dependent on nitrogen fertilization than a community without plants with symbiotic nitrogen fixation. Asymbiotic nitrogen fixation was shown to yield only insignificant amounts of nitrogen fixed in the rhizosphere of plants growing in the alpine grass heath (Holzmann & Haselwandter 1988) or in the nival zone (Haselwandter *et al.* 1983; Table 5.2).

Similarly, woody legumes inoculated with selected strains of rhizobia (and mycorrhizal fungi) can be used in revegetation strategies for desertified land (Herrera *et al.* 1993). This is another example illustrating the importance of information on specific functions of micro-organisms within the microbial soil community for designing and evaluating the restoration strategy applied.

Soil microbiota with particular reference to mycorrhizal components

The aim of ecosystem restoration is to return degraded biological communities to their original state (Jordan, Peters, & Allen 1988). Of the myriad of

Table 5.2. *Maximum values for nitrogenase activity (nmol ethylene production per pot 24 h^{-1}) of intact systems measured by acetylene reduction assay* in situ *in the Tyrolean Central Alps of Austria (data from Holzmann & Haselwandter 1988, and Haselwandter et al. 1983)*

Plant species	Mode of N_2 fixation	nmol C_2H_4 pot^{-1} 24h^{-1}
Transplanted to alpine grass heath at 2550 m		
Trifolium badium	symbiotic	14×10^3
Trifolium pallescens	symbiotic	14×10^3
Lotus alpinus	symbiotic	12×10^3
Alpine grass heath plants growing at 2550 m		
Leucanthemopsis alpina	asymbiotic	150
Potentilla aurea	asymbiotic	75
Veronica bellidioides	asymbiotic	220
Nival zone plants growing at 3150 m		
Cerastium uniflorum	asymbiotic	trace
Poa laxa	asymbiotic	trace

organisms living in soil, it is the mycorrhizal fungi that provide a direct link between the plants as primary producers and the decomposers. The mycorrhizal fungal hyphae create a physical connection between the root surface and soil particles, and increase the water and nutrient absorbing surface area of the root system through establishing closer contact with the soil (Haselwandter & Bowen 1996). This connection between roots, fungal hyphae, and soil matrix is of paramount importance with regard to water relations (Sanchez-Díaz & Honrubia 1994) and plant uptake of nitrogen and phosphorus (George, Marschner, & Jakobsen 1995). It seems likely that the potential of mycorrhizal fungi to produce siderophores affects the iron nutrition of host plants (Haselwandter 1995). The extraradical hyphae of the mycorrhizal fungi also contribute substantially to soil structure development (Tisdall 1994). Overall, the mycorrhizal association affects significantly plant succession (Janos 1980a; Gange, Brown, & Foster 1990) and community structure (Francis & Read 1994). Numerous studies have revealed that the success of restoration directly depends on the establishment of mycorrhizas. Hence, it appears appropriate to evaluate the success of restoration strategies with regard to their effect on mycorrhizal associations.

Almost any ecosystem perturbation serves to reduce the mycorrhizal population in soil. Thus the restoration of disturbed land depends, at least in part, on the restoration of the mycorrhizal symbiosis (Allen 1989). In early stages of succession, many plants are either non-mycorrhizal or facultatively mycorrhizal. In later stages of recovery from disturbance, an increasing proportion of the plants, for example, in tropical ecosystems, becomes obligately mycorrhizal (Janos 1980b). The rate of restoration or plant succession may be hastened by manipulation of the mycorrhizal fungus population or inoculation programmes (Reeves *et al.*, 1979; Janos 1980a). Most importantly, mycorrhizal fungi may prevent stagnation of community development rather than facilitate skipping of successional stages (Miller & Jastrow 1992).

A comparison of native prairie grasses has shown that one species produced approximately five times longer mycorrhizal infected roots than the other two species tested, making this species suitable as an early succession species for increasing the propagule density of indigenous arbuscular mycorrhizal fungi (Noyd, Pfleger, & Russelle 1995). This is likely to enhance the successful reclamation of coarse tailing deposits by more persistent, mycorrhiza dependent plant species. Similarly, in the nursery inoculated trees may serve as inoculum source for neighbouring plants susceptible to mycorrhizal infection. Although at present very little is known of the spread of mycorrhizal mycelium along the roots of a tree under field conditions, and the rate of colonization of roots next to this tree, this principle may well prove to be important with regard to the use of trees for agroforestry and land rehabilitation (Haselwandter & Bowen 1996).

Restoration of surface-mined areas is essential for reducing erosion and dust problems and producing an aesthetically pleasing landscape. Restoration or revegetation of such areas is particularly difficult under harsh climate conditions and when the substrate to be revegetated is unweathered, blasted rock with low microbial activity. Introduction of essential soil micro-organisms such as mycorrhizal fungi or rhizobia may enhance the chances of success. This is facilitated when, for example, surface soil (topsoil) which is reapplied after mining, is stored under conditions allowing for maximum survival of beneficial soil micro-organisms.

A number of studies has shown that stockpiling reduces vital bacterial and fungal biomass in soil, including the propagule density of mycorrhizal fungi (e.g. Visser *et al.* 1984; Harris *et al.* 1987; Jasper, Abbott, & Robson 1989; Williamson & Johnson 1990). Miller, Carnes, & Moorman (1985) demonstrated that soil moisture content during stockpiling was critical for survival of AM fungal propagules, i.e. the drier the soil, the higher the remaining mycorrhizal infection potential. These results suggest that the design of stockpiles should be appropriate for regional climatic conditions in order to maximize survival of mycorrhizal fungi. When soils are stored

Table 5.3. *Arbuscular mycorrhizal infection intensity (percentage of root length infected) of dominant grass species determined 7 yr after establishment of a revegetation trial at 1620 m in the Glungezer area near Innsbruck*

Plots were fertilized annually with mineral fertilizer (NPK 15:15:15; 50 g m^{-2}) or organic fertilizer (200 g m^{-2}; 'Biosol' = fungal biomass, product of Biochemie Ges.m.b.H., A-6250 Kundl, Austria; composition: organic matter 80–90%, N$_{total}$ 5–8%, N$_{water\ soluble}$ <0.5%, P$_2$O$_5$ 0.5–2.5%, K$_2$O 3–4%, trace elements, vitamines and siderophores). Indicated mean values ± SD

Plant species	Fertilizer	% infected root length
Poa annua	organic	94 ± 9
	mineral	36 ± 30
	none	23 ± 18
Agrostis tenuis	organic	83 ± 14
	mineral	29 ± 21
	none	26 ± 17
Festuca rubra	organic	85 ± 19
	mineral	33 ± 23
	none	25 ± 29

under relatively dry conditions, the duration of storage appears to determine survival of AM propagules. In mesic environments the depth of the stockpiles should be restricted to the rooting depth of the covering vegetation through which accumulation of moisture in the soil can be minimized (Miller & Jastrow 1992).

Topsoil replacement is essential for re-establishment of mycorrhizas, as topsoil represents the primary source of mycorrhizal inoculum. Without topsoil, the development of mycorrhizae on spoil or tailings can be quite slow (Waaland & Allen, 1987). The addition of topsoil can promote both the establishment of mycorrhizas and vegetation (Lambert & Cole 1980). If topsoil is not available, adding of organic amendments may enhance the mycorrhiza formation (Johnson & McGraw 1988). This has also been observed in an alpine environment in which an organic fertilizer appeared to enhance arbuscular mycorrhiza development, whereas infection intensity on the mineral fertilized plot was in the range of the unfertilized control (Table 5.3). This observation is of preliminary nature, but such an effect, if confirmed, could have important implications for restoration strategies.

In cases where the indigenous populations of infective and effective mycorrhizal fungi are inadequate, inoculation with mycorrhizal fungi may prove to be a prerequisite for the success of any restoration attempts (Jasper 1994). Inoculation may be necessary even for rehabilitation of soils which are not severely disturbed, but in which the return of effective mycorrhizal fungi would be too slow to ensure establishment of a diverse range of plant species before canopy closure (Jasper, Abbott, & Robson 1992). In general, plant growth is limited when heavy metals are present either in trace concentrations or at high and hence toxic concentrations. In both cases, mycorrhizal infection may play a key role with regard to the potential of a given plant species to colonize a particular habitat (Hasel-wandter, Leyval, & Sanders 1994).

Inoculum production and inoculation techniques have been developed for AM and EM fungi (see e.g., Jeffries & Dodd 1991; Kuek 1994; Sylvia & Jarstfer 1994). In general, these techniques are feasible in the intensive plant production of horticulture and in nurseries. Ecosystem restoration or revegetation of disturbed soils is quite different from these situations in many respects, for example with regard to the dimension of the area to be inoculated. Therefore, except for very special cases which absolutely require the investment of inoculation, soil-management strategies appear to be currently the major practical option for enhancing mycorrhiza development in soils which are to be rehabilitated. In case of man-made ecosystem disturbance, such strategies should, for example, minimize loss of infectivity of mycorrhizal fungi and maximize their survival in the soil to be revegetated (Jasper, 1994).

In a 4-year trial, Herrera et al. (1993) have shown that inoculation of the seedlings to be used for revegetation with selected mycorrhizal fungi (and rhizobia) improved outplanting performance, plant survival, and biomass development. The approach included production of mycorrhizal and nodulated plantlets of woody legumes after screening for the appropriate plant species–microsymbiont combinations. Such a result is particularly promising with regard to recovery of desertified ecosystems.

An important mechanism by which AM fungi benefit restoration is based upon their contribution to nutrient cycling and improvement of soil structure (Allen et al. 1992). The development of a self-sustaining system requires the establishment of a nutrient reserve on basis of various, in particular organic, forms of inputs (Bradshaw et al. 1982). Without stabilization of the organic inputs, accumulation of organic matter and buildup of nutrient reserves are minimal. Aggregate formation is a prerequisite for stabilization of organic residues in soil (Elliott & Coleman 1988). Therefore, a major goal of restoration is enhancement of soil aggregate development thereby facilitating creation of a nutrient reserve.

Soil aggregates are relatively resistant to breakdown and known to prevent water and wind erosion.

Mycorrhizal fungi increase soil aggregation by means of physical action exerted by the hyphae, and the production of polysaccharides by the fungi or the associated microflora. Together with fine roots, especially individual mycorrhizal and saprophytic fungal hyphae bind soil particles into larger, aggregated units (Tisdall & Oades 1979; Miller & Jastrow 1990). Thus mycorrhizal fungi add to the stability of soil (Tisdall 1994) and improvement of soil structure (Forster 1990).

If the ultimate goal of restoration is to return a degraded ecosystem into its original state, that implies making it again stable and sustainable. In this respect, soil micro-organisms including mycorrhizal fungi play a key role. Especially in the later stages of succession, mycorrhizal fungi short-circuit nutrient cycles by acquiring nutrients from organic resources (Jeffries & Barea 1994). In addition, mycorrhizal fungi have been shown to re-allocate nutrients between individuals of the same or even different plant species, thus preventing loss of resources from the entire ecosystem (Read, Francis, & Finlay 1985; Pankow, Boller, & Wiemken 1991). Consequently, it is clear that mycorrhizal fungi are essential for the sustainability of natural and agricultural ecosystems (Bethlenfalvay & Linderman 1992; Barea & Jeffries 1995; Hooker & Black 1995), and of any restored ecosystem as well.

Conclusions

Nutrient cycling is essential for ecosystem functioning. Soil micro-organisms play a key role in the turnover of nutrients. Mycorrhizal fungi form an integral part of the soil microbiota. Hence, for an assessment of the success of strategies to restore or reclaim degraded land, their effects on the soil microbiota, including mycorrhizal fungi and their activities, should be monitored. Such criteria seem to represent valuable indicators for soil rehabilitation assessment. Useful soil microbial characteristics may include biomass, respiration, and the metabolic quotient. Analysis of specific functional groups of the soil microbiota, such as nitrogen fixing micro-organisms and mycorrhizal fungi, may have particular significance in assessing soil quality.

So far, the potential contribution of fungi with dark septate hyphae to ecosystem restoration has been neglected. In comparison to AM fungi, these fungi are relatively easy to isolate and propagate. However, the function of this type of infection under ecologically relevant conditions is still not well understood. Therefore justification to include such fungi in an inoculation programme would have to be examined on a case by case basis. Soil micro-organisms including mycorrhizal fungi are essential for the establishment and preservation of nutrient cycles, in particular within sustainable ecosystems. In general, contributions of different members of the soil microbiota are specific. Hence it is necessary to have information about individual microorganisms in order to be able to predict their role within the soil community. This may seem unrealistic considering that only a small percentage of the microbial populations in soil is identified or in culture, leaving a vast share of the soil microbiota unknown and unstudied (Kennedy & Smith 1995). On the other hand, the molecular tools which are now available enable soil microbiologists to track specific components of microbial communities, including non-culturable soil microorganisms (Amann et al. 1991; Hahn & Zeyer 1994). Future investigations will show to what extent these techniques can contribute to the solution of questions pertinent to restoration ecology.

References

Allen, M. F. (1989). Mycorrhizae and rehabilitation of disturbed arid soils: Processes and practices. *Arid Soil Research*, 3, 229–41.
Allen, M. F., Clouse, S. D., Weinbaum, B. S., Jeakins, S., Friese, C. F., & Allen, E. B. (1992). Mycorrhizae and the integration of scales: From molecules to ecosystems. In *Mycorrhizal Functioning: An Integrative Plant-Fungal Process.* ed. M. F. Allen, pp. 488–516. New York, London: Chapman & Hall.
Amann, R. I., Springer, N., Ludwig, W., Görtz, H.-D., & Schleifer, K.-H. (1991). Identification *in situ* and phylogeny of uncultured bacterial endosymbionts. *Nature*, 351, 161–4.
Anderson, T.-H. & Domsch, K. H. (1986). Carbon assimilation and microbial activity in soil. *Zeitschrift für Pflanzenernährung und Bodenkunde*, 149, 457–68.
Barea, J. M. & Jeffries, P. (1995). Arbuscular mycorrhizas in sustainable soil-plant systems. In *Mycorrhiza.* eds. A. Varma & B. Hock, p. 521–60. Berlin, Heidelberg: Springer.
Bethlenfalvay, G. J. & Linderman, R. G. (1992). *Mycorrhizae in Sustainable Agriculture.* ASA Special Publication No. 54. Madison, WI: American Society of Agronomy.
Blaschke, H. (1991). Multiple mycorrhizal associations of individual calcicole host plants in the alpine grass-heath zone. *Mycorrhiza*, 1, 31–4.
Bradshaw, A. D., Marrs, R. H., Roberts, R. D., & Skeffington, R. A. (1982). The creation of nitrogen cycles in derelict land. Philosophical Transactions of the Royal Society of London, Series B 296, 557–61.
Coleman, D. C. (1985). Through a ped darkly: An ecological assessment of root–soil–microbial–faunal interactions. In *Ecological Interactions in Soil: Plants, Microbes and Animals*, eds. A. H. Fitter, D. Atkinson, D. J. Read, & M. B. Usher, pp. 1–21. Oxford: Blackwell.

Coleman, D. C. (1994). The microbial loop concept as used in terrestrial soil ecology studies. *Microbial Ecology*, 28, 245–50.

Coleman, D. C., Reid, C. P. P., & Cole, C. V. (1983). Biological strategies of nutrient cycling in soil systems. *Advances in Ecological Research*, 13, 1–55.

Currah, R. S. & Van Dyk, M. (1986). A survey of some perennial vascular plant species native to Alberta for occurrence of mycorrhizal fungi. *Canadian Field-Naturalist*, 100, 330–42.

Elliott, E. T. & Coleman, D. C. (1988). Let the soil work for us. *Ecological Bulletins*, 39, 23–32.

Forster, S. M. (1990). The role of microorganisms in aggregate formation and soil stabilization: Types of aggregation. *Arid Soil Research and Rehabilitation*, 4, 85–98.

Francis, C. F. & Thornes, J. B. (1990). Matorral: Erosion and reclamation. In *Soil Degradation and Rehabilitation in Mediterranean Environmental Conditions*, eds. J. Albaladejo, M. A. Stocking, & E. Díaz, pp. 87–115. Murcia: Consejo Superior de Investigaciones Científicas.

Francis, R. & Read, D. J. (1994). The contributions of mycorrhizal fungi to the determination of plant community structure. In *Management of Mycorrhizas in Agriculture, Horticulture and Forestry*, eds. A. D. Robson, L. K. Abbott, & N. Malajczuk, pp. 11–25. Dordrecht: Kluwer.

Gange, A. C., Brown, V. K., & Foster, L. M. (1990). A test of mycorrhizal benefit in an early succession plant community. *New Phytologist*, 115, 85–91.

George, E., Marschner, H. & Jakobsen, I. (1995). Role of arbuscular mycorrhizal fungi in uptake of phosphorus and nitrogen from soil. *Critical Reviews in Biotechnology*, 15, 257–70.

Hahn, D. & Zeyer, J. (1994). *In situ* detection of bacteria in the environment. In *Beyond the Biomass*, eds. K. Ritz, J. Dighton, & K. E. Giller, pp. 137–48. Chichester: Wiley.

Harley, J. L. & Harley, E. L. (1987). A check-list of mycorrhiza in the British flora. *New Phytologist*, 105, 1–102.

Harley, J. L. & Smith, S. E. (1983). *Mycorrhizal Symbiosis*. London: Academic Press.

Harris, J. A., Hunter, D., Birch, P. & Short, K. C. (1987). Changes in the microbial community and physico-chemical characteristics of topsoils stockpiled during opencast mining. *Soil Use and Management*, 5, 161–7.

Haselwandter, K. (1995). Mycorrhizal fungi: Siderophore production. *Critical Reviews in Biotechnology*, 15, 287–91.

Haselwandter, K. & Bowen, G. D. (1996). Mycorrhizal relations in trees for agroforestry and land rehabilitation. *Forest Ecology and Management*, 81, 1–17.

Haselwandter, K., Hofmann, A., Holzmann, H.-P., & Read, D. J. (1983). Availability of nitrogen and phosphorus in the nival zone of the Alps. *Oecologia*, 57, 266–9.

Haselwandter, K., Leyval, C., & Sanders, F. E. (1994). Impact of arbuscular mycorrhizal fungi on plant uptake of heavy metals and radionuclides from soil. In *Impact of Arbuscular Mycorrhizas on Sustainable Agriculture and Natural Ecosystems*, eds. S. Gianinazzi & H. Schüepp, pp. 179–89. Basle: Birkhäuser.

Haselwandter, K. & Read, D. J. (1980) Fungal associations of roots of
dominant and sub-dominant plants in high-alpine vegetation systems with
special reference to mycorrhiza. *Oecologia*, 45, 57–62.

Haselwandter, K. & Read, D. J. (1982). The significance of a root–fungus
association in two *Carex* species of high-alpine plant communities.
Oecologia, 53, 352–54.

Hassink, J., Lebbink, G., & van Veen, J. A. (1991). Microbial biomass and
activity of a reclaimed-polder soil under a conventional or a reduced-input
farming system. *Soil Biology and Biochemistry*, 23, 507–13.

Herrera, M. A., Salamanca, C. P. & Barea, J. M. (1993). Inoculation of woody
legumes with selected arbuscular mycorrhizal fungi and rhizobia to recover
desertified mediterranean ecosystems. *Applied and Environmental
Microbiology*, 59, 129–33.

Holzmann, H.-P. & Haselwandter, K. (1988). Contribution of nitrogen fixation
to nitrogen nutrition in an alpine sedge community (*Caricetum curvulae*).
Oecologia, 76, 298–302.

Hooker, J. E. Black, K. E. (1995). Arbuscular mycorrhizal fungi as
components of sustainable soil-plant systems. *Critical Reviews in
Biotechnology*, 15, 201–12.

Insam, H. & Haselwandter, K. (1989). Metabolic quotient of the soil
microflora in relation to plant succession. *Oecologia*, 79, 174–8.

Janos, D. P. (1980a). Mycorrhizae influence tropical succession. *Biotropica*, 12,
56–64.

Janos, D. P. (1980b). Vesicular-arbuscular mycorrhizae affect lowland tropical
rain forest plant growth. *Ecology*, 61, 151–62.

Jasper, D. A. (1994). Management of mycorrhizas in revegetation. In
Management of Mycorrhizas in Agriculture, Horticulture and Forestry, eds.
A. D. Robson, L. K. Abbott, & N. Malajczuk, pp. 211–19. Dordrecht:
Kluwer.

Jasper, D. A., Abbott, L. K., & Robson, A. D. (1989). The loss of VA
mycorrhizal infectivity during bauxite mining may limit the growth of
Acacia pulchella R.Br. *Australian Journal of Botany*, 37, 33–42.

Jasper, D. A., Abbott, L. K., & Robson, A. D. (1992). Soil disturbance in
native ecosystems – the decline and recovery of infectivity of VA
mycorrhizal fungi. In *Mycorrhizas in Ecosystems*, eds. D. J. Read, D. H.
Lewis, A. H. Fitter, & I. J. Alexander, pp. 151–5. *Oxon: CAB
International*.

Jeffries, P. & Barea, J. M. (1994). Biogeochemical cycling and arbuscular
mycorrhizas in the sustainability of plant-soil systems. In *Impact of
Mycorrhizas on Sustainable Agriculture and Natural Ecosystems*, eds. S.
Gianinazzi & H. Schüepp, pp. 101–15. Basle: Birkhäuser.

Jeffries, P. & Dodd, J. C. (1991). The use of mycorrhizal inoculants in forestry
and agriculture. In *Handbook of Applied Mycology*, eds. D. K. Arora, B.
Rai, K. G. Mukerji, & G. R. Knudsen, vol. I, pp. 155–85. New York:
Dekker.

Jha, D. K., Sharma, G. D. & Mishra, R. R. (1992). Ecology of soil microflora
and mycorrhizal symbionts in degraded forests at two altitudes. *Biology
and Fertility of Soils*, 12, 272–8.

Johnson, D. A. & Rumbaugh, M. D. (1986). Field nodulation and acetylene
reduction activity of high-altitude legumes in the Western United States.
Arctic and Alpine Research, 18, 171–9.

Johnson, N. C. & McGraw, A. C. (1988). Vesicular-arbuscular mycorrhizae in taconite tailings. I. Incidence and spread of endogonaceous fungi following reclamation. *Agriculture, Ecosystems and Environment,* 21, 135–42.

Jordan, W. R., Peters, R. L., & Allen, E. B. (1988). Ecological restoration as a strategy for conserving biological diversity. *Environmental Management,* 12, 55–72.

Kennedy, A. C. & Smith, K. L. (1995). Soil microbial diversity and the sustainability of agricultural soils. *Plant and Soil,* 170, 75–86.

Kuek, C. (1994). Issues concerning the production and use of inocula of ectomycorrhizal fungi in increasing the economic productivity of plantations. In *Management of Mycorrhizas in Agriculture, Horticulture and Forestry,* eds. A. D. Robson, L. K. Abbott, & N. Malajczuk, pp. 221–30. Dordrecht: Kluwer.

Lambert, D. H. & Cole, H. (1980). Effects of mycorrhizae on establishment and performance of forage species in mine spoil. *Agronomy Journal,* 72, 257–60.

Miller, R. M., Carnes, B. A. & Moorman, T. B. (1985). Factors influencing the survival of vesicular-arbuscular mycorrhiza propagules during topsoil storage. *Journal of Applied Ecology,* 22, 259–66.

Miller, R. M. & Jastrow, J. D. (1990). Hierarchy of root and mycorrhizal fungal interactions with soil aggregation. *Soil Biology and Biochemistry,* 22, 579–84.

Miller, R. M. & Jastrow, J. D. (1992). The application of VA mycorrhizae to ecosystem restoration and reclamation. In *Mycorrhizal Functioning: An Integrative Plant-Fungal Process,* ed. M. F. Allen, pp. 438–67. New York: Chapman & Hall.

Moser, M. & Haselwandter, K. (1983). Ecophysiology of mycorrhizal symbioses. In *Encyclopedia of Plant Physiology,* New Series, vol. 12 C, eds. O. L. Lange, P. S. Nobel, C. B. Osmond, & H. Ziegler, pp. 391–421. Berlin: Springer.

Newman, E. I. & Redell, P. (1987). The distribution of mycorrhizas among families of vascular plants. *New Phytologist,* 106, 745–51.

Noyd, R. K., Pfleger, F. L., & Russelle, M. P. (1995). Interactions between native prairie grasses and indigenous arbuscular mycorrhizal fungi: implications for reclamation of taconite iron ore tailing. *New Phytologist,* 129, 651–60.

Odum, E. P. (1969). The strategy of ecosystem development. *Science,* 164, 262–70.

Pankow, W., Boller, T. & Wiemken, A. (1991). The significance of mycorrhizas in protective ecosystems. *Experientia,* 47, 391–4.

Read, D. J. (1984). The structure and function of the vegetative mycelium of mycorrhizal roots. In *The Ecology and Physiology of the Fungal Mycelium,* eds. D. H. Jennings & A. D. Rayner, pp. 215–40. Cambridge University Press.

Read, D. J., Francis, R., & Finlay, R. D. (1985). Mycorrhizal mycelia and nutrient cycling in plant communities. In *Ecological Interactions in Soil: Plants, Microbes and Animals,* eds. A. H. Fitter, D. Atkinson, D. J. Read, & M. B. Usher, pp. 193–217. Oxford: Blackwell.

Read, D. J. & Haselwandter, K. (1981). Observations on the mycorrhizal status of some alpine plant communities. *New Phytologist,* 88, 341–52.

Reeves, F. B., Wagner, D., Moorman, T., & Keil, J. (1979). The role of endomycorrhizae in revegetation practices in the semi-arid west. I. A comparison of incidence of mycorrhizae in severely disturbed vs. natural environments. *American Journal of Botany*, 66, 6–13.

Sanchez-Díaz, M. & Honrubia, M. (1994). Water relations and alleviation of drought stress in mycorrhizal plants. In *Impact of Arbuscular Mycorrhizas on Sustainable Agriculture and Natural Ecosystems*, eds. S. Gianinazzi & H. Schüepp, pp. 167–78. Basle: Birkhäuser.

Skujins, J. & Allen, M. F. (1986). Use of mycorrhizae for land rehabilitation. MIRCEN Journal 2, 161–76.

Sparling, G. P., Brandenburg, S. A. & Zhu, C. (1994). Microbial C and N in revegetated wheatbelt soils in Western Australia: Estimation in soil, humus and leaf-litter using the ninhydrin method. *Soil Biology and Biochemistry*, 26, 1179–84.

Sylvia, D. M. & Jarstfer, A. G. (1994). Production of inoculum and inoculation with arbuscular mycorrhizal fungi. In *Management of Mycorrhizas in Agriculture, Horticulture and Forestry*, eds. A. D. Robson, L. K. Abbott, & N. Malajczuk, pp. 231–8. Dordrecht: Kluwer.

Tate, R. L. III. (1985). Microorganisms, ecosystem disturbance and soil-formation processes. In *Soil Reclamation Processes*, eds. R. L. Tate III. & D. A. Klein, pp. 1–33. New York: Dekker.

Thoen, D. (1987). First observations on the occurrence of vesicular-arbuscular mycorrhizae (VAM) in hydrophytes, hygrophytes, halophytes and xerophytes in the region of Lake Retba (Cap-Vert, Senegal) during the dry season. *Mémoires de la Société Royal de Botanique de Belgique*, 9, 60–66.

Tisdall, J. M. (1994). Possible role of soil microorganisms in aggregation in soils. In *Management of Mycorrhizas in Agriculture, Horticulture and Forestry*, eds. A. D. Robson, L. K. Abbott, & N. Malajczuk, pp. 115–21. Dordrecht: Kluwer.

Tisdall, J. M. & Oades, J. M. (1979). Stabilization of soil aggregates by the root system of ryegrass. *Australian Journal of Soil Research*, 57, 429–41.

Trappe, J. M. (1988). Lessons from alpine fungi. *Mycologia*, 80, 1–10.

Visser, S., Fujikawa, J., Griffiths, C. L., & Parkinson, D. (1984). Effect of topsoil storage on microbial activity, primary production and decomposition potential. *Plant and Soil*, 82, 41–50.

Waaland, M. E. & Allen, E. B. (1987). Relationships between VA mycorrhizal fungi and plant cover following surface mining in Wyoming. *Journal of Range Management*, 40, 271–6.

Williamson, J. C. & Johnson, D. B. (1990). Determination of the activity of soil microbial populations in stored and restored soils at opencast coal sites. *Soil Biology and Biochemistry*, 22, 671–5.

Zak, J. C., Fresquez, P. R. & Visser, S. (1992). Soil microbial processes and dynamics: Their importance to effective reclamation. In *Evaluating Reclamation Success: The Ecological Consideration*. General Technical Report NE-1643, pp. 3–16. Radnor: N.E. Forest Experiment Station, Forest Service, US Department of Agriculture.

6

Safe sites – interface of plant population ecology and restoration ecology

KRYSTYNA M. URBANSKA

Introduction

The development of populations which together form the plant cover is influenced by reproductive processes, of which the establishment phase is of particular importance. Regeneration at a population level has been studied for a long time (Grime 1979; Grubb 1977) but some aspects remain to be fully clarified and certain opinions need reconsideration (Grubb, personal communication).

The importance of the establishment phase to plant population dynamics is clearly recognizable even in an undisturbed environment. It takes on new dimensions in recovery after disturbance, and becomes crucial in situations where landscape and ecosystems have been destroyed or so far damaged that unassisted recovery is not possible.

Much landscape reconstruction is still designed by engineers and landscape architects, and yet ecologists have a great deal to offer in this regard (Bradshaw 1983; Saunders, Hobbs, & Ehrlich 1993). Contributions from restoration ecologists are thus urgently needed to create a solid scientific basis for reconstruction work, and a population-oriented approach represents a very pertinent component (Figure 6.1).

This chapter deals with the safe-site problem which clearly represents an interface to plant population ecology and restoration ecology. I intend first to sum up the current state of knowledge on the subject, and then to show the value of the safe-site concept to planning, implementation, and assessment of restoration schemes. I will also indicate some future research needs. Data from our long-term research above the timberline, and also those from other cold-dominated areas, will be used to illustrate some aspects, but the proposed general concepts apply to many other ecosystems. Unless otherwise indicated, the data presented are my own unpublished results.

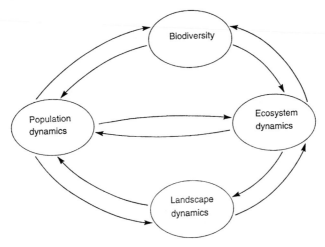

Figure 6.1. Population dynamics in relation to ecosystem, landscape, and biodiversity.

Safe-site concept in plant population ecology

The original concept of a safe site was introduced by Harper and his co-workers (Harper *et al.* 1961; Harper, Williams, & Sagar 1965) who defined a safe site as an environment immediately surrounding a seed which is favourable to germination and establishment. They argued that safe sites are species-specific and that the availability and diversity of safe sites represents a necessary condition for development of a species-rich vegetation. The scale of the safe site was emphasized by the 'microsite' or 'microhabitat' terminology used instead of 'safe site' by e.g., Chambers (1995a), Fowler (1986), Grime (1979), Pavlik 1995, and Ryser (1993).

More recent studies on the safe-site concept include work of our group in which the safe-site issue was addressed with reference to an extreme alpine environment (Flüeler 1992; Schütz 1988; Urbanska 1992, 1995a; Urbanska & Schütz 1986). We postulated that safe sites should be defined not only by attributes advantageous to recruitment, but also by a hierarchy of ecosystem-specific hazards from which safe sites should protect propagules and developing plants. The hierarchy depends on the local conditions. For instance, in our research area situated in the north-east Swiss Alps, the most frequent risk is clearly frost with associated phenomena, while overgrazing has a much lower place in the hierarchy of hazards. On the other hand, in some sites located in the south Tyrolean Alps, which are characterized by hot, dry summers, the number one risk is the instability of the geological substratum, and overgrazing comes up as a close second (Wilhalm, personal communication). We suggested furthermore the safe sites are not species-specific but may be available to propagules which belong to different species yet have similar morphological and physiological features. Finally, the safe-site concept applies, in our opinion, not only to seed, but also to specialized vegetative propagules (Urbanska 1990) and/or plant fragments arising from spontaneous or enforced cloning (see e.g., Chou, Vardy, & Jefferies 1992).

Safe sites and dispersal in plants

Dispersal is the first component in the sequence of events which ensures the viability of a species in the long run. I argued previously (Urbanska 1989, 1990, 1992) that reproduction is not completed by the propagule formation alone and dispersal should accordingly be regarded as an integral part of the process.

Considered in the context of dispersal, safe sites may be regarded as targets towards which propagules are directed and natural selection operates to increase the efficacy of the process. The success of dispersal, i.e. deposition of propagules in safe sites, is influenced by two principal factors, namely (i) distance from the diaspore source to possible safe sites and (ii) availability and density of safe sites.

In a model proposed by Green (1983), the dispersal curve is convex, unimodal, and monotonically decreasing; on the other hand, abundance of safe sites is presented as a monotonically increasing function of the distance from the mother plant, though Green remarks that it does not need to be linear (Figure 6.2). Green recognized that spatial distribution of safe sites may not always be uniform, random, or moderately clumped but argued that his model does hold also in cases where safe sites are strongly clumped within the dispersal distance, on the condition that variations in number of safe sites in each clump are considered.

Although Green's model may indeed apply to many species, it can hardly be considered representative of plants with complex dispersal modes, because the relationship between area and distance then becomes obscured. As a result, both the safe-site abundance curve and partly also the dispersal curve will have to be modified. Amphicarpic species (e.g., *Amphicarpum purshii*) which combine subterranean diaspore production and virtual achory with above-ground dispersal represent an extreme example (see e.g., Cheplick & Quinn 1982). Given the fact that a large part of the diaspores are produced underground and develop within an immediate area of the

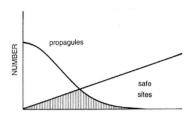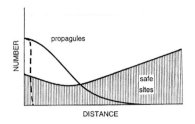

Figure 6.2. Relationships between dispersal and safe-site abundance. Left: the original model of Green (1983): the curve labelled 'propagules' represents a typical dispersal curve. The graph shows the number of propagules and the number of safe sites available at all distances from the parent (located at the origin). Near the parent, there exists an overabundance of propagules but too few safe sites to accommodate them, while, at greater distances, safe sites are abundant but there are too few propagules to occupy them all. The shaded area is equal to the number of propagules or safe sites, whichever is less, integrated over all distances from the parent, and is therefore equal to the maximum number of propagules that can occupy safe sites under these conditions. For purposes of illustration, the scale for the graph of safe-site abundance has been exaggerated. Reproduced by permission of the publisher. Right: the model of Green modified for amphicarpic plants. Dashed line shows the 'dispersal' of subterranean diaspores.

mother plant, the safe-site abundance curve in Green's model would have to be altered; the dispersal curve might generally be considered convex and unimodal, but it includes in fact two distinct components (Figure 6.2).

Amphicarpic plants are admittedly rather rare, but more recent studies increasingly indicate that combined dispersal strategies occur more often than formerly thought. Discrete dispersal patterns occurring in a single plant are often accompanied by differences in temporal pattern of germination (e.g., *Heterotheca latifolia*, Venable & Levin 1985). An interesting example is that of *Lotus alpinus* previously regarded as autochorous (Müller-Schneider 1986). My recent studies (Urbanska 1994a) revealed that *L. alpinus* produces both dehiscent and non-dehiscent pods. While the dehiscent pods spring open (pod shattering) and then seeds become dispersed over some distance, the ripe indehiscent pods are deposited on the ground and remain unopened at least until the following summer when the pericarp becomes damaged by fungi. The exposed seeds then remain mostly in groups and small juvenile cohorts may often be observed in a close vicinity to the mother plants or within the mother canopy (Urbanska, unpublished).

The safe-site curve in *L. alpinus* clearly does not correspond to Green's model. Our studies in the alpine vegetation belt strongly suggest that this

Table 6.1. *Differences in seed input between islands of secondary vegetation and adjacent degraded pastures in the Poco das Antas Biological Reserve, Brazil*

The total number of seeds is given for all seed traps pooled over the 11-month sampling period. (After Kolb unpublished Ph.D. thesis).

Sample origin	Total number of seeds
Pasture	13 702
Vegetation island	37 190

may also be the case for numerous other species (see further parts of this chapter). Detailed studies on seed rain, diaspore deposition patterns, and safe-site status in species with complex dispersal modes would be most helpful to clarify the general usefulness of the traditional bell-shaped dispersal curve, especially in predictions concerning the short-distance distribution of diaspores and their subsequent fate.

Structure of safe sites

The first step towards the possible establishment of a seedling is the deposition of diaspores (Ash, Gemmell, & Bradshaw 1994) and diaspore entrapment may be the primary factor determining the fate of propagules (Chambers, MacMahon, & Haefner 1991). Soil-surface characteristics especially micro- and possibly also nano-relief are thus exceedingly important (see e.g., Chambers & MacMahon 1994). Extant plants or vegetation patches considerably enhance diaspore entrapment in windy arid environments (Nelson & Chew 1977), high-alpine sites (Chambers *et al.* 1991, Chambers 1995a,b, and also chapter 9 in this volume; Urbanska 1994a,b, 1995a,b) and/or subarctic and arctic tundra (Urbanska 1997a,b). They also play an essential role in vertebrate-mediated seed slow and particularly in ornithochorous species (Robinson & Handel 1993). The elegant study of Kolb (unpublished) demonstrates that differences in seed input between vegetation 'islands' and adjacent open pastures may be indeed dramatic (Table 6.1).

Even if the diaspores succeed in travelling over shorter or longer distances and become trapped, the destiny of seedlings is ultimately determined by safe-site availability. Not all places which diaspores reach are favourable to a successful germination (Chambers 1995a). Also, not all places in which germination takes place are suitable for recruitment; for that reason, I proposed to distinguish between germination sites and safe sites (Urbanska 1992).

Safe sites promoting actual recruitment are characterized by diverse combinations of attributes which ensure a favourable microclimate (Flüeler 1992), adequate soil structure/texture (Bradshaw & Chadwick 1980; Fowler 1986, 1988), nutrient and water content (Kellman 1979; Uhl *et al.* 1981), and also protection e.g., from herbivores (McAuliffe 1986). At least some of those features are influenced by plants occurring in a close vicinity to the developing seedlings.

Neighbouring plants often compete for resources with newcomers, but there is an increasing body of evidence that they may also enhance establishment. I propose to focus on the latter aspect, which is particularly interesting to plant population and community ecology, but not fully appreciated so far. It is, perhaps, not very surprising that most available data originate from extreme ecosystems, but recent studies from more mesic areas (see e.g., Ryser 1993) suggest that the phenomenon is rather general.

Neighbour plants as components of safe site

A plant occurring in the immediate surroundings of a seedling/juvenile may be (a) its mother, (b) an individual representing the same species, or (c) a non-conspecific juvenile/adult. Depending on the status, the function of a neighbour plant as safe-site component may thus be either regarded as a form of maternal care or considered in terms of commensalism. Differences in chronological age or age-state between the neighbour and the newcomer are clearly recognizable in most cases.

Post-dispersal maternal care

Close proximity of the mother plant to its established offspring seems to be favourable in some situations. Our experimental studies in strongly disturbed high-alpine sites demonstrate that small juvenile cohorts occurring within the mother canopy or close to it are a fairly common feature in patchy vegetation, and seem to be the norm, not the exception, in some species. Population mapping in experimental plots indicated that this trend was apparently not restricted to a single plant species or a particular life form, for its was observed in legumes (*Lotus alpinus, Trifolium thalii*), grasses (*Trisetum spicatum, Poa laxa*), and also in herbs (*Potentilla dubia, Alchemilla nitida, A. dumosa, Senecio carniolicus*). Reproduction by seed mostly resulted in locally increased patch density, although in some species

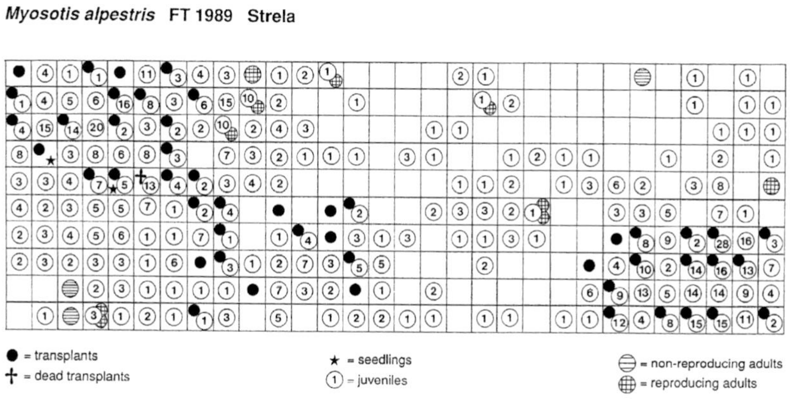

Myosotis alpestris FT 1989 Strela

● = transplants
✝ = dead transplants
★ = seedlings
① = juveniles
⊖ = non-reproducing adults
⊕ = reproducing adults

Figure 6.3. *Myosotis alpestris* in a restoration plot at Strela Mountain, NE Swiss Alps (dolomite, *ca.* 2500 m.a.s.l.): age-state oriented population mapping Strela 6 years after restoration. Slow-release organic fertilizer supplement. Initial number of introduced clonal transplants was 60 (3 × 20), the current population size N = 1525. *M. alpestris* shared the safety island with 21 other species.

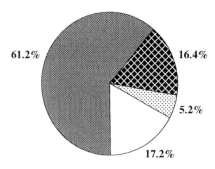

Figure 6.4. *Trisetum spicatum* in restoration site at Jakobshorn Mountain, NE Swiss Alps (silicate, *ca.* 2500 m.a.s.l.): age-state structure (%) of the plants spread outside the safety islands. Sectors correspond respectively to seedlings (dotted), established juveniles (grey), non-reproducing adults (checked), and reproducing individuals (white). (After Urbanska 1995b).

(e.g., *Myosotis alpestris*, Figure 6.3) the boundaries among sectors were obscured. The whole population area extending beyond the trial plots was observed so far only in *Trisetum spicatum* (Urbanska 1995a); it is interesting to note that the plants growing outside the plots mostly represented established individuals belonging to various age-state classes (Figure 6.4). The positive effect of mother plants on the establishment of their offspring in lowland sites were also clearly observed by Tischew (personal communication) in her recent experimental studies on population development of *Corynephorus canescens* in a former area of coal exploitation in Eastern Germany characterized by exceedingly hostile edaphic conditions.

Maternal care operating as a component of the safe site may be recognized, on the one hand, in shelter provided for developing offspring by the mother canopy, and, on the other hand, in both protection and local litter supply offered by decaying remains of pericarp and inflorescence to germinating seeds, seedlings, and juveniles. Both these aspects often occur together; the former is related to achory, the latter often occurs in plants which produce fruits as dispersal units and is particularly distinct in synaptospermous species. Various forms of group dispersal combined with achory were recently observed in many high-alpine plants (Hasler 1992; Urbanska 1992, 1997b). One of them is *Biscutella levigata* regarded as uniformly anemochorous until Gasser (1986) revealed its population patchiness to be at least partially influenced by autodeposition of diaspore groups. Synaptospermy is apparently advantageous in environments susceptible to disturbance, and may be particularly important to founding new populations, especially those of dioecious species (see e.g., Quinn 1987; Cox 1985). It would be most desirable to assess the frequency of the phenomenon both within species and at the community level. Highly stressed sites with open vegetation would be of particular interest.

The apparent role of the mother plant as a component of the safe site observed in some plants raises the evolutionary question of selective advantages of the 'post-dispersal maternal care'. The problem was previously discussed in amphicarpic species; early hypotheses proposed pre-sampling safe site by the mother plant, and also active choice of safe sites (for some references see van der Pijl 1982), but additional empirical tests are needed. As to partly autochorous high-alpine species which include synaptospermy in their dispersal strategies, it may be hypothesized that deposition of diaspores in clumps accompanied by maternal care is adaptive and contributes to the spreading of risks in hazardous, cold-dominated environments; in this way, fitness would be improved via diversified safe sites. More detailed studies in alpine tundra are urgently needed to test this hypothesis, and genetic patch analyses would be indispensable.

Conspecific neighbours

Competition among siblings belonging to the same cohort is probably frequent, but there are some indications that juveniles situated on the outside of a dense cluster may sometimes protect the inner ones from, for example, desiccation or frost. Such a situation has been reported, for instance, in dense seedling cohorts of *Floerkea proserpinacoides* (Smith 1983), and has often been observed in viviparous *Poa alpina*. In our research area, whole clumps of developing propagules were often deposited on the ground; the surviving juveniles apparently profited both from shelter and local litter/nutrient supply provided by the dead siblings; this issue should be clarified in further studies.

Relationships between conspecific individuals representing various age classes which do not correspond to mother/offspring associations seem to be rather complex. Asymmetric competition was regarded as the most frequent explanation for size hierarchies in populations (Weiner & Thomas 1986), but symmetric competition was also observed (Bonan 1988; Weiner 1990; Wilson & Gurevitch 1995). It is conceivable that other relationships may also occur, especially in some extreme environments, but to the best of my knowledge no experimental data are available so far. Cold- or drought-dominated ecosystems, where need for protection is obvious but distribution of nutrients patchy (better vs. poorer sites), would be a natural choice for such studies.

Nurse phenomenon

Non-conspecific adults often provide protection and favourable edaphic conditions to the newcomers. This 'nurse' phenomenon is particularly well known in slowly growing cacti occurring in various arid ecosystems (Figure 6.5, Table 6.2, see also e.g., Turner *et al.* 1966; Franco & Nobel 1989; Valiente-Banuet, Vite, & Zacada-Hurtado 1991, Suzan, Nabhan, & Patten 1994). However, it was also reported in other plant groups (McAuliffe 1986).

The nurse-like relationships are not restricted to hot and dry areas, but occur equally frequent though perhaps less spectacularly in other ecosystems. In high-alpine and arctic sites, for instance, healthy clonal structures (e.g., well-developed cushions) of established species are frequently colonized by later arrivals (Figure 6.6A).

In more productive environments competition is frequently regarded as the most important community-shaping interaction among species, and gaps received much attention as places which particularly promote

Figure 6.5. Ajo Mountains, S Arizona: Young saguaro (*Carnegiea gigantea*) and its nurse plant *Larrea tridentata*. Photo taken by the author.

establishment on account of reduced inference (e.g., Grubb 1976; Pickett 1980). More recent studies show, however, that not only gaps but also nurse-like phenomena are important in, for example, grassland ecosystems (see e.g., Fenner 1987; Ryser 1993).

Table 6.2. *Organ Pipe Cactus National Monument, Arizona*

Total soil nitrogen content beneath nurse plants of *Carnegiea gigantea* and in exposed regions outside influence of their roots. Means ± 1 S.E. followed by the same letter are not significantly different (student's *t*-test, P < 0.001; *n* = 6; after Franco and Nobel 1989).

Soil	Nurse species	N (% by dry mass)
exposed	none	0.014 ± 0.001^a
under canopy	*Ambrosia deltoidea*	0.035 ± 0.005^b
under canopy	*Cercidium microphyllum*	0.037 ± 0.004^b

The Arctic presents an interesting aspect of nurse-like relationships. Contrary to most other environments where these associations are characterized by interactions among angiosperms, the beneficial influence of cryptogams on establishment of vascular plants in permafrost areas is often very conspicuous (Figure 6.6B). Cryptogram mats provide both root isolation from the permafrost layer, and shelter on the soil surface (Bell & Bliss 1977; Sohlberg & Bliss 1984; Bliss & Peterson 1992). Poikilohydric mosses, especially *Sphagnum* species, often play an essential role (Walker *et al.* 1989), but fruticose lichens may also largely control soil processes (Kershaw & Field 1975; Tenhunen *et al.* 1992). Nurse cryptograms were widely observed in arctic sites but, to the best of my knowledge, no experimental data are available so far except for an interesting report of Barrett (1975) on a small-scale restoration project in the High Arctic.

The nurse phenomenon may sometimes be characterized by the more or less exclusive relationship between a single nurse species and a single protected species; it seems, however, that multiple species combinations are more frequent, although this aspect remains largely unexplored. More detailed studies and statistical evaluations are necessary to assess possible preferential species combinations. It would be most desirable to have data from various areas.

Dynamics of safe sites

Safe sites are obviously changing in time and space and the patterns of change may be varied. Unoccupied safe sites may be either directly influenced by abiotic factors and/or, for example, burrowing animals, or there may be indirect changes related to the development of nearby vegetation. Occupied safe sites on the other hand change mostly as a result

(A)

(C)

Figure 6.6. Nurse plants in primary and secondary safe sites. (A) (top left)
Jatzhorn Mountain, NE Swiss Alps (silicate, *ca.* 2630 m.a.s.l.): *Myosotis
alpestris* well established within the healthy cushion of its nurse *Minuartia
sedoides*. Photo taken by the author. (B) (top right) NE Greenland (*ca.*
72°14′N, *ca.* 5 m.a.s.l.): *Saxifraga oppositifolia* established within cryptogam
mats. Photo courtesy of Dr S. Sivertsen.

(C) (bottom left) NW Svalbard (78°56.12' N, *ca.* 20 m. a. s. l.): *Cerastium arcticum* within partly self-reduced cushion of *Silene acaulis.* Photo courtesy of Dr P. A. Wookey. (D) (bottom right) Tällihorn Mountain, NE Swiss Alps (*ca.* 2600 m. a. s. l.): Juveniles of *Phyteuma hemisphericum* established within self-thinned tusock of *Carex curvula.* Photo taken by the author.

of growth and development of the established plants. This development may bring about changed relationships, for example, the initial commensalism may in time turn into competition (see e.g., Yeaton 1978; McAuliffe 1984; Vandermeer 1980; Yeaton & Romero-Manzanares 1986). I have previously suggested (Urbanska 1992) that changes in safe-site status represent an underlying process of succession. The intriguing question of how long a safe site remains a safe site would be most interesting to study experimentally in contrasting environments.

The development of established perennial plants often leads to the appearance of secondary safe sites resulting from self-thinning. Many secondary safe sites may accordingly be interpreted as a facet of the nurse phenomenon. The secondary colonization of that type may be routinely observed in extreme ecosystems. In the arctic tundra of Svalbard for instance, self-thinned mats of *Dryas octopetala* or cushions of *Silene acaulis* influenced by partial dieback are often colonized by other species (Figure 6.6C). No detailed microclimatic data are available to date, but it may be safely assumed that the temperature within the clonal structures is higher than in the adjacent bare soil on account of the dark surface and consequent lower albedo; also, the moisture regime with a mat or a cushion is probably more mesic than in the vegetation-free area nearby (Wookey, personal communication). This explanation is possibly also valid for secondary safe sites resulting from natural dieback of some tiller groups in the high-alpine sedge *Carex curvula* (Figure 6.6D). The small openings in the self-thinned tussocks apparently promote establishment by screening dicot juveniles from the rough climate, and also provide favourable edaphic conditions. My recent studies revealed that difference in mean number of seedlings per cm^2 between the tussock openings and the adjacent bare ground was negligible, but the corresponding difference in number of established juveniles was highly significant (Table 6.3).

The dynamics of safe sites are particularly complex in disturbed ecosystems, and obviously depend on the extent and pattern of disturbance. Minor local disturbances may be beneficial, but strong recurrent disturbances which occur at a large scale may dramatically alter abundance and diversity of safe sites in a given area (Urbanska 1992).

Plants living in extreme environments have apparently evolved risk-distribution strategies to cope with changes in temporal and spatial availability of safe sites. One of these strategies is distribution of dispersal and germination in space achieved via diversified behaviour. The patterns of diaspore deposition and pod dehiscence in *Lotus alpinus* are accom-

Table 6.3. *Jatzhorn Mountain, NE Swiss Alps, ca. 2600 m.a.s.l.*

Seedlings and juveniles within partly decayed tussocks of *Carex curvula* and in bare surfaces nearby. Area measured using a formula for an ellipse $A = \pi 1/4\ ab$ with *a* being the longer axis perpendicular to *b*. Means ± SD in a column followed by different letters are not significantly different (Mann-Whitney, $p < 0.0001$); unpublished data of the author.

Surface	n	Area (cm^2)	Seedlings/cm^2	Juveniles/cm^2
Tussock	23	1.8 ± 0.1	3.8 ± 0.2^a	2.3 ± 0.1^a
Bare	21	1.8 ± 0.1	3.6 ± 0.1^a	0.2 ± 0.1^b

panied by germination distributed over at least two growth periods (see the comments on p. 84). A sequential seed germination influenced by a successive decay of pods distributed throughout one growth period was observed in achorous *Trifolium thalii* (Urbanska, unpublished). Seed dormancy represents a further important feature relating to safe-site availability.

Safe-site concept in restoration

Conceptual models in assisted recovery and/or restoration must be based on adequate ecological information. In the following part of this chapter I propose to consider the safe-site concept in relation to various phases of restoration.

Evaluation of disturbance

Each restoration project should have a pre-operational evaluation to select the best of an array of alternatives (Cairns 1993). The safe-sites concept may be used in the evaluation following a two-step procedure: (1) safe sites have to be identified; (2) based on this identification, disturbance thresholds may be defined by safe-site availability and density in relation to some landscape features.

Identification of safe sites includes evaluation of (i) ecosystem-specific risks, and (ii) safe-site attributes. The hierarchy of risks, and possible safe-site attributes should be based on information including both more general factors, for example, climate or hydrology, and the actual data gathered in the area to be restored. Data on soil, especially the topsoil/seed bank status, is exceedingly important (for soil, see e.g., Bradshaw 1983; Ash *et al.* 1994, and, in particular, Bradshaw, chapter 4 in this volume; for seed bank see e.g., van der Valk & Pederson 1989; Parker, Simpson, & Leck 1989; Urbanska 1997a).

Selection of reference ecosystems from the range of undisturbed ecosystems in the ecoregion may be crucial to the safe-site oriented approach because information on pre-disturbance conditions may be vague or insufficient. It is important that several reference ecosystems are selected instead of only one (see Pickett & Parker 1994; Pickett, Parker, & Fiedler 1992; and also Parker & Pickett, chapter 3 in this volume). To assess abundance and diversity of safe sites, spatial structure of plant communities will have to be studied; however, the traditional phytosociological releves are not helpful in this respect, since conditions advantageous to successful establishment are recognizable in the performance of juveniles. The mapping should accordingly focus on age-state classes (Fattorini, in press; Urbanska 1994a,b, 1995a,b).

Assessment of the disturbance threshold should include the disturbance scale, since it permits the areas to be restored to be placed in the context of the landscape with which they are expected to interact ecologically. Evaluation of the scale of disturbance also permits a more realistic assessment of the environmental hazards operating within the area, and thus a better evaluation of the safe-site status. Distance to remnant natural habitats or earlier restored areas which represent diaspore sources is of primary importance (see e.g., Crowe 1979; Davis 1986; Handel, Robinson, & Beattie 1994; Urbanska 1994a,b, 1995a,b).

Based on the above information, three disturbance thresholds may be distinguished and incorporated into an evaluation chart (Table 6.4).

As far as our restoration research in the alpine area is concerned, the disturbance threshold may be generally estimated as being at level three because the topsoil in machine-graded ski runs was removed and discarded. Spontaneous colonization of the exposed mineral soil is exceedingly slow and most frequently very limited in spite of the fact that the construction work took place about 27 years ago and diaspore sources are often nearby. Commercial revegetation efforts using lowland grass seed accompanied by massive fertilizer dosage failed to bring about any lasting success at high altitude. An extensive restoration programme would accordingly be required.

Planning and implementation

Safe-site planning is obviously based on the evaluation of disturbance in the site to be restored, but specific aspects to be considered in the actual

Table 6.4. *Evaluation chart: disturbance threshold rating and planning decisions*

Scale	Topsoil/seed bank	Safe sites	Diaspore source	Threshold	Decision
1	1	1	1	ONE	X
2	2	2	1–2	TWO	XX
2–3	3	3	1–3	THREE	XXX

Note: Scale: 1 = disturbance local; 2 = disturbed area medium-sized; 3 = disturbed area extensive
Topsoil/seed bank: 1 = present; 2 = damaged; 3 = absent.
Safe sites: 1 = numerous and diverse; 2 = few; 3 = none or virtually none.
Diaspore source: 1 = nearby; 2 = distant; 3 = none.
Threshold: 1 = disturbance local and/or not intensive; 2 = deterioration considerable and/or extensive; 3 = site destroyed.
Decisions: X = unassisted recovery probable, no intervention necessary, perhaps only diaspore entrapment might be improved. XX = recovery should be assisted by some site manipulations, e.g., diversification of microrelief, site protection, diaspore entrapment. XXX = a full restoration programme with extensive soil and plant manipulations required.

work are addressed as well. They include suitable mixture of plant species to be initially installed, abundance and diversity of safe sites per unit of area, and also adequate procedures to provide the required attributes and protection measures.

Native plants are the obvious choice for restoration (Bradshaw 1983; Handel *et al.* 1994; Urbanska & Hasler 1992). The use of native plants in restoration schemes may have an additional benefit in reintroducing plants which have become rare in the area (Urbanska 1995a, see also Pavlik 1995 for comments on historical species range). However, the market supply of native plant material is insufficient in most countries and restorationists must often rely on wild populations. I discussed recently the need for a reasonable compromise between a sufficient amount of material and a minimum damage to native populations (Urbanska 1995b). A non-destructive sampling of wild populations followed by single-ramet cloning most frequently provides satisfactory results (Hasler 1992; Keigley 1988; Urbanska & Hasler 1992) but not all native plants are suited to the procedure (Tschurr 1992).

Native plant material includes seeds and pre-grown transplants. The latter are nowadays widely used, not only for shrubs and trees, but also for herbs (e.g., Francis & Morton 1995; McEachern, Bowles, & Pavlovic 1994). Both the genetic transplants grown from seed and clonal transplants

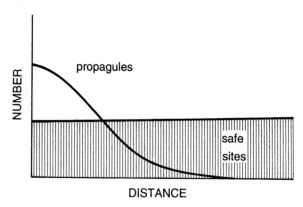

DISTANCE

Figure 6.7. Safety island: relationships between dispersal and abundance
presented in a modified model of Green (see Figure 6.2).

obtained by vegetative multiplication were extensively used in our restoration trials above the timberline (see e.g., Hasler 1992; Tschurr 1990;
Urbanska 1994a,b, 1995a,b; 1997a,b); graminoids were particularly well-
suited to cloning (e.g., Urbanska, Hefti-Holenstein, & Elmer 1987; Fattorini 1996), but excellent results were also obtained with many legumes
and/or forbs (Gasser 1989; Hasler 1992; Tschurr 1992).

An important feature in restoration planning is a local abundance of safe
sites. I propose therefore to outline here the concept of safety islands.

Safety islands are understood as patches characterized by a high
abundance and availability of various safe sites. Compared to Green's
model, the abundance of safe sites is thus represented by a flat line
regardless of distance (Figure 6.7). Safety islands include pre-grown
transplants representing an appropriate mixture of various species and life
forms (e.g., saplings, young shrubs, transplants of grasses, legumes and
herbs). Seeds might also be included. The structural complexity of safety
islands would represent *per se* a factor promoting seed deposition rate
(McDonnell & Stiles 1983; McClanahan & Wolfe 1987) but establishment
of the initial plant community should be followed by measures ensuring
protection and enhancing diaspore entrapment. Introduction of grown
plants and their possible symbiotic partners plays an important role in
accelerated development of vegetation in safety islands.

It may be expected that the favourable microclimate provided in the
safety islands would enhance both survival and reproduction of the
installed pre-grown plants as well as recruitment from seeds brought as
restoration materials, produced *in situ*, or representing immigrant diaspores (Figure 6.8).

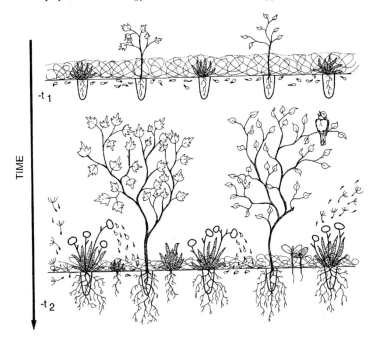

Figure 6.8. Plant cover development in safety islands: t_1–initial phase; t_2–later phase.

Determining an adequate size of safety islands is a very important problem. A cluster of smaller islands may represent a reasonable alternative to a single larger island, but the choice largely depends both on the conditions in the restoration site and on the surrounding landscape.

Safety islands should serve as diaspore sources for future colonization of the area (Figure 6.8). To promote this development, it may be necessary to provide 'migration corridors' (e.g., with geotextile mats) without further site manipulations.

The concept of safety islands has been tested in our alpine restoration trials since 1985. The stripe-shaped plots of varied length (1×3–10 m) included transplants of various high-alpine species grown in containers prior to their installation above the timberline. Extensive soil amendment was not included in most earlier trials, but a small amount of nutrient-rich garden soil was consistently brought with each transplant into the site. Transplants were mostly non-reproducing at the time of planting. Plots were mostly installed in clusters (Figure 6.9); the 'migration corridors' were established in a recent trial, but it is too early yet to assess their efficacy.

Figure 6.9. Freshly installed clusters of safety islands on a black diamond* ski run, N slope of Jakobshorn Mountain (*ca.* 2400 m.a.s.l.). Note the considerable environmental damage due to machine-grading. Photo courtesy of M. Fattorini. * = the highest difficulty grade.

Table 6.5. *Transplant survival in plots MG at Jakobshorn Mountain (siliceous substratum, ca. 2500 m.a.s.l.)*

Code	Restoration year	ITN	NLT 1992	S%
MG1	1986	602	334	55.5
MG2	1986	440	322	73.4
MG3	1987	400	314	78.5
MG4	1987	471	297	63.0

Note: ITN = number of transplants used initially; NLT 1992 = number of live transplants recorded during the 1992 census. S% = survival 5 and 6 years after restoration, respectively (after Urbanska 1994b).

Table 6.6. *Plots MG at Jakobshorn Mountain 5 to 6 years after restoration: age-state classes distribution.*

Code	s	j	nr	r	NR	R	T	EN	DD
MG1	1122	1443	156	174	149	144	3188	1773	6
MG2	639	443	51	41	188	164	1526	535	6
MG3	79	109	30	32	135	163	548	171	6
MG4	19	192	99	30	160	108	608	321	6

Note: s = seedlings, j = juveniles, nr = non-reproducing newcomers, r = reproducing newcomers, NR = non-reproducing transplants: R = reproducing transplants. T = total community size; EN = total number of established newcomers; DD = delta-diversity index, i.e., number of age-state classes. Status as of summer 1994.

Assessment

The safe-site status in post-restoration assessment may be well documented with age-state-oriented mapping of populations and/or whole communities. In this way, both the survival and further development of initially introduced plant populations, and spontaneous colonization, may also be assessed (Tables 6.5–6.6). The indices gathered in these inventories may be listed as follows:

- safe sites are expected to ensure survival of introduced plants. Total survival rate of the transplants is thus an index of initial safe-site efficacy (Table 6.5).
- safe sites are indispensable for successful recruitment; the minimum number of established newcomers indicates thus the minimum number of safe sites (Table 6.6). There may still be some unoccupied safe sites at the time of the inventory.

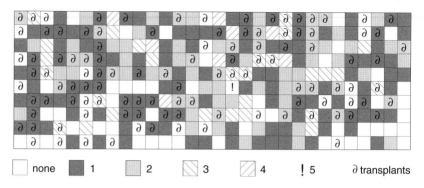

none ▢   1 ■   2 ▨   3 ◤   4 ◩   ! 5   ∂ transplants

Figure 6.10. A restoration plot at Strela Mountain: alpha diversity 8 years after restoration. Distribution of species number in 10×10 cm quadrats. Total number of registered species $N_{1992} = 27$, the initial species number (transplants) $N_{1987} = 6$.

– safe sites promote both establishment and further development of population and community; the delta diversity, i.e. range of age-state classes, is thus another useful index of safe site efficacy (Table 6.6; see also Urbanska 1994a,b, 1995a,b; Fattorini 1996) whereas age–state-oriented mapping gives clues as to spatial distribution of safe sites.
– safe sites should enhance immigration of further species and thus increase alpha diversity. The number of immigrant species (Figure 6.10) and their contribution to the whole community size (Figure 6.11) may thus serve as an index of safe-site abundance (Urbanska 1994a,b, 1995a,b; 1997a,b; Fattorini 1996; Etter unpublished).

Colonization of safety islands by further species might also be assessed in terms of the equilibrium theory of island biogeography (MacArthur & Wilson 1963, 1967, see also e.g., Crowe 1979 or Gray 1982). The theory represents an interesting proposition for assessment of restoration because it clearly may be interpreted as extension of the safe site concept; however, some details should be modified because the departure point is not bare ground but an island 'community' which includes a finite number of transplants.

Assessment based on the data gathered soon after restoration is not very reliable, especially as far as extreme ecosystems are concerned, because most losses may occur within the first 3–4 years; demographic studies should thus be carried out in the mid-term. On the other hand, it seems that the immigration in safety islands may begin as early as one year after

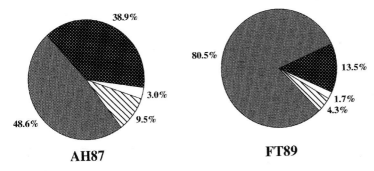

Figure 6.11. Group contribution (%) to the whole community size in two restoration plots at Strela Mountain. Initial community size in the plot AH87 was 188 vs. 1181 8 years later; that of the plot FT89–200 vs. 1929 6 years later. The sectors correspond respectively to surviving transplants (striped), transplant offspring (grey), identified immigrants (dotted), and non-identified new-comers (white).

restoration, and a considerable increase in species diversity may be registered after only three years (Hasler 1992; Tschurr 1992; see also Schütz 1988 for data on seeding trials). Evaluation three years after restoration might accordingly bring about first indications of the restoration success, but our studies demonstrate that a second inventory carried out 3 years later is very informative indeed.

Aftercare

Restoration success may be defined by three main ecosystem attributes, namely identity, resilience, and correspondence; the target ecosystem should thus be self-sustaining (Cairns 1993). Considered in the context of safe-site concept, it means that there should be a dynamic development resulting in changes in number and diversity of safe sites. However, in some situations safe sites may have to be occasionally provided anew as a part of mid- or long-term aftercare.

Measures which may be clearly recognized as improvement of safe-site status are often recommended in biological conservation of plants inhabiting more productive ecosystems. For instance, small-scale sod cutting around adult plants was indicated as a good strategy for the rare *Gentiana pneumonanthe* (Oostermeier *et al.*, in press). A local enhancing the substratum dynamics seems to be suitable for conservation of some valuable species in the Swiss Plateau (Holdenegger 1994, and unpublished).

Our studies in the alpine area revealed that biodegradable wood-fibre mats used in restoration trails were largely decomposed after three years and did not offer much further protection. However, the dynamic development of populations and communities registered in older plots suggests that a further improvement may in fact not be necessary (Urbanska 1994a,b, 1995a,b; Fattorini 1996). The question of safe sites as a part of aftercare remains open to further verifications, and experimental studies would be very valuable.

Conclusions

An approach focusing on safe sites is clearly useful in planning, implementation, and assessment of restoration schemes. It may also be helpful in aftercare. It would be most desirable for the safety island concept to be tested in various restoration schemes.

Safe sites are clearly related to selection in restored habitats, and the suitability of the plants used as restoration material is thus decisive. Indigenous plants are the obvious choice because (i) they are adapted to life conditions in the area to be restored and (ii) their safe sites may be defined more easily than those of exotic plants.

A major problem in ecological restoration is the availability of suitable indigenous material on the market. The nursery industry should be encouraged to supply an ecologically wider selection of material for restoration originating from local biological reserves and natural habitats (Handel, Robinson, & Beattie 1994). There is no reason at all why, with appropriate ecological understanding, wild species cannot be treated with the same simplicity as cultivated plants. But investigations are required if the most effective treatments are to be found (Bradshaw 1983).

The above suggestions do not imply that the commercial enterprises should give up the basic economic principle of profit. On the contrary; they indicate that profit-gaining and environment-friendly work are not mutually exclusive. A successful reconstruction of ecosystems is the ultimate proof of our ecological understanding but it also tests the ability of very different specialists to work together (Bradshaw 1983; see also Edwards & Abivardi, chapter 15 in this volume).

Acknowledgements

Various colleagues and friends offered valuable comments on the early drafts; I particularly thank Drs P. A. Wookey (University of London) and

S. Sivertsen (University of Trondheim). Dr T. Wilhalm helped with some statistics, Ms Anita Hegi made drawings. Permission from Springer Verlag, Heidelberg, to reproduce Figure 6.1 from a paper by D. S. Green (1983) in *Oecologia* (Berlin) 56: 357, is gratefully acknowledged. An anonymous reviewer provided constructive criticism to improve the manuscript.

References

Ash, H. J., Gemmel, R. P., & Bradshaw, A. D. (1994). The introduction of native plant species on industrial waste heaps: a test of immigration and other factors affecting primary succession. *Journal of Applied Ecology*, 31, 74–84.

Barrett, P. E. (1975). Preliminary observations of off-road vehicle disturbance to sedge-meadow tundra at a coastal lowland location, Devon Island, N.W.T. *ALUR Report* 73-74-71, Department of Indian & Northern Affairs, Ottawa, Ontario, Canada.

Bell, K. L. & Bliss, L. C., 1977. Overwintering phenology of plants in a polar semidesert. *Arctic*, 30, 118–21.

Bliss, L. C. & Peterson, K. M. (1992). Plant succession, competition, and the physiological constrains of species in the Arctic. in *Arctic Ecosystems in a Changing Climate – an Ecophysiological Perspective*, eds. F. S. Chapin, R. L. Jefferies, J. F. Reynolds, G. R. Shaver, & J. Svoboda, pp. 111–36. San Diego: Academic Press.

Bonan, G. B. (1988). The size structure of theoretical plant populations: spatial patterns and neighbourhood effects. *Ecology*, 69, 1721–30.

Bradshaw, A. D. (1983). The reconstruction of ecosystems. *Journal of Applied Ecology*, 20, 1–17.

Bradshaw, A. D. & Chadwick, M. J. (1980). *The Restoration of Land.* Oxford: Blackwell Scientific Publications.

Cairns, J. Jr. (1993). Ecological restoration: replenishing our national and global ecological capital. In *Reconstruction of Fragmented Ecosystems*, eds. D. A. Saunders, R. J. Hobbs, & P. R. Ehrlich, pp. 193–208. Norton: Surrey Beatty & Sons.

Chambers, J. C. (1995a). Relationships between seed fates and seedling establishment in an alpine ecosystem. *Ecology*, 76, 2124–33.

Chambers, J. C. (1995b). Disturbance, life history strategies, and seed fates in alpine herbfield communities. *American Journal of Botany*, 82, 421–33.

Chambers, J. C. & MacMahon, J. A. (1994). A day in the life of a seed: movements and fates of seeds and their implications for natural and managed systems. *Annual Review of Ecology and Systematics*, 25, 263–92.

Chambers, J. C., MacMahon, J. A., & Haefner, J. H. (1991). Seed entrapment in alpine ecosystems: effects of soil particle size and diaspore morphology. *Ecology*, 72, 1668–77.

Cheplick, G. P. & Quinn, J. A. (1982). *Amphicarpum purshii* and the 'pesimistic strategy' in amphicarpic annuals with subterranean fruits. *Oecologia* (Berlin) 52, 327–32.

Chou, R., Vardy, C., & Jefferies, R. L. (1992). Establishment from leaves and other plant fragments produced by the foraging activities of geese. *Functional Ecology*, 6, 297–301.

Cox, P. A. (1985). Islands and dioecism: insights from reproductive ecology of *Pandanus tectorius* in Polynesia. In *Studies on Plant Demography: a Festschrift for John Harper*, ed. J. White, pp. 359–72. London: Academic Press.

Crowe, T. M. (1979). Lots of weeds: insular phytogeography of vacant urban lots. *Journal of Biogeography*, 6, 169–81.

Davis, B. N. K. (1986). Colonization of newly created habitats by plants and animals. *Journal of Environmental Management*, 22, 361–71.

Fattorini, M. (1996) Post-restoration development of plant cover in a machine-graded alpine ski run. In *Proceedings of 12th High Altitude Revegetation Workshop*, ed. W. R. Keammerer, pp. 306–16. Fort Collins: Colorado Water Resources Research Institute Information Series.

Fenner, M. (1987). Seedlings. *New Phytologist*, 106 (Supplement), 35–47.

Flüeler, R. P. (1992). Experimentelle Untersuchungen über Keimung und Etablierung von alpinen Leguminosen. *Veröffentlichungen des Geobotanischen Institutes ETH Zürich, Stiftung Rübel*, no. 110.

Fowler, N. L. (1986). Microsite requirements for germination and establishment of three grass species. *American Midland Naturalist*, 115, 131–45.

Fowler, N. L. (1988). What is safe site? Neighbour, litter, germination date and patch effects. *Ecology*, 69, 947–61.

Francis, J. L. & Morton, A. J. (1995). Restoring the woodland layer in young plantations and new woodlands. In *Restoration Ecology in Europe*, eds. K. M. Urbanska, & K. Grodzinska, pp. 1–13. Zurich: Geobotanical Institute SFIT.

Franco, A. C. & Nobel, P. S. (1989). Effect of nurse plants on the microhabitat and growth of cacti. *Journal of Ecology*, 77, 870–86.

Gasser, M. (1986). Genetic-ecological investigations in *Biscutella levigata* L. *Veröffentlichungen des Geobotanischen Institutes ETH Zürich, Stiftung Rübel*, 85.

Gasser, M. (1989). Bedeutung der vegetativen Phase bei alpinen Pflanzen für die biologische Erosionsbekämpfung in der alpinen Stufe. *Berichte Geobotanisches Institutes ETH Zürich, Stiftung Rübel*, 55, 151–76.

Gray, H. J. (1982). Plant dispersal and colonization. In *Ecology of Quarries*, ed. B. N. K. Davies, pp. 27–31. Cambridge: NERC/ITE.

Green, D. S. (1983). The efficacy of dispersal in relation to safe site density. *Oecologia* (Berlin), 65, 356–8.

Grime, J. P. (1979). *Plant Strategies and Vegetation Processes*. New York: J. Wiley & Sons.

Grubb, P. J. (1976). A theoretical background to the conservation of ecologically distinct groups of annuals and biennials in the chalk grassland ecosystem. *Biological Conservation*, 10, 53–76.

Grubb, P. J. (1977). The maintenance of species richness in plant communities: the regeneration niche. *Biological Review*, 52, 107–45.

Handel, S. N., Robinson, G. R., & Beattie, A. J. (1994). Biodiversity resources for restoration ecology. *Restoration Ecology*, 2, 230–41.

Harper, J. L., Clatworthy, J. N., McNaughton, I. H., & Sagar, G. R. (1961). The evolution and ecology of closely related species living in the same area. *Evolution*, 15, 209–27.

Harper, J. L., Williams, J. T., & Sagar, G. R. (1965). The behaviour of seeds in soil. Part I. The heterogeneity of soil surface and its role in determining the establishment of plants from seed. *Journal of Ecology*, 53, 273–86.

Hasler, A. R. (1992). Experimentelle Untersuchungen über klonal wachsende alpine Leguminosen. *Veröffentlichungen des Geobotanischen Institutes ETH Zurich Stiftung Rübel*, no. 111.

Holdenegger, R. (1994). Zur Flora und Vegetation der Küstnachtertobels: Veränderungen innerhalb der letzten fünfzig Jahre. *Botanica Helvetica*, 104, 55–68.

Keigley, R. B. (1988). Developing methods of restoring vegetation communities while preserving genetic integrity. In *Proceedings of 8th High Altitude Revegetation Workshop*, eds. W. R. Keammerer & L. F. Brown, pp. 129–38. Fort Collins: Colorado Water Resources Research Institute.

Kellmann, M. (1979). Soil enrichment by neotropica savanna trees. *Journal of Ecology*, 67, 565–77.

Kershaw, K. A. & Field, G. F. (1975). Studies on lichen-dominated systems. XV. The temperature and humidity profiles in a *Cladina alpestris* mat. *Canadian Journal of Botany*, 53, 2614–20.

MacArthur, R. H. & Wilson, E. O. (1963). An equilibrium theory of insular biogeography. *Evolution*, 17, 373–87.

MacArthur, R. H. & Wilson, E. O. (1967). *The Theory of Island Biogeography*. Princeton University Press.

McAuliffe, J. R. (1984). Sahuaro-nurse tree associations in the Sonoran desert: competitive effects of sahuaro. *Oecologia* (Berlin) 64, 319–21.

McAuliffe, J. R. (1986). Herbivore-limited establishment of a Sonoran Desert tree, *Cercidium microphyllum*. *Ecology*, 67, 276–80.

McClanahan, T. R. & Wolfe, R. W. (1987). Dispersal of ornithochorous seeds from forest edges in central Florida. *Vegetatio*, 71, 107–12.

McDonnell, M. J. & Stiles, E. W. (1983). The structural complexity of old field vegetation and the recruitment of bird-dispersed plant species. *Oecologia*, 56, 109–16.

McEachern, K. A., Bowles, M. L., & Pavlovic, N. B. (1994). A metapopulation approach to Pitscher's thistle (*Cirsium pitcheri*) recovery in southern Lake Michigan dunes. In *Restoration of Endangered Species*, eds. M. L. Bowles & C. J. Whelan, pp. 194–218. Cambridge University Press.

Miller, T. E. & Weiner, J. (1989). Local density variation may mimic effects of asymmetric competition on plant size variability. *Ecology*, 70, 1188–91.

Müller-Schneider, P. (1986). Verbreitungsbiologie der Blütenpflanzen Graubündens. *Veröffentlichungen des Geobotanischen Institutes ETH Zürich, Stiftung Rübel*, no. 85.

Nelson, J. F. & Chew, R. M. (1977). Factors affecting seed reserves in the Mojave Desert ecosystem, Rock Valley, Nye County, Nevada. *American Midland Naturalist*, 97, 300–20.

Oostermeier, J. G. B., Luijten, S. H., Krenova, Z. V., & den Nijs, H. C. M. Changes in population and habitat characteristics limit reproductive success of the rare *Gentiana pneumonanthe*. *Conservation Biology* (in press).

Parker, V. T., Simpson, R. L., & Leck, M. A. (1989). Pattern and process in the dynamics of seed banks. In *Ecology of Seed Banks*, eds. M. A. Leck, V. T. Parker, & R. L. Simpson, pp. 367–84. San Diego: Academic Press.

Pavlik, B. M. (1995). The recovery of an endangered plant. II. A three-phased approach to restoring populations. In *Restoration Ecology in Europe*, eds. K. M. Urbanska, & K. Grodzinska, pp. 49–69. Zurich: Geobotanical Institute SFIT.

Pickett, S. T. A. (1980). Non-equilibrium coexistence of plants. *Bulletin of Torrey Botanical Club*, 107, 238–48.

Pickett, S. T. A. & Parker, V. T. (1994). Avoiding the old pitfalls: opportunities in a new discipline. *Restoration Ecology*, 2, 75–9.

Pickett, S. T. A., Parker, V. T., & Fiedler, P. (1992). The new paradigm in ecology: implications for conservation biology above the species level. In *Conservation Biology; the Theory and Practice of Nature Conservation*, eds. P. Fiedler, & S. Jain, pp. 56–88. New York: Chapman & Hall.

Quinn, J. A. (1987). Relationship between synaptospermy and dioecy in the life history strategies of *Buchloe dactyloides* (Gramineae). *American Journal of Botany*, 74, 1167–72.

Robinson, G. R. & Handel, S. N. (1993). Forest restoration on a closed landfill: rapid addition of new species by bird dispersal. *Conservation Biology*, 7, 271–8.

Ryser, P. (1993). Influences of neighbouring plants on seedling establishment in limestone grassland. *Journal of Vegetation Science*, 4, 195–202.

Saunders, D. A., Hobbs, R. J., & Ehrlich, P. R. (1993). Reconstruction of fragmented ecosystems – problems and possibilities. In *Reconstruction of Fragmented Ecosystems*, eds. D. A. Saunders, R. J. Hobbs, & P. R. Ehrlich, pp. 305–13. Norton: Surrey, Beatty & Sons.

Schütz, M. (1988). Genetisch-ökologische Untersuchungen an alpinen Pflanzen auf verschiedenen Gesteinunterlagen: Keimungs- und Aussastversuche. *Veröffentlichungen des Geobotanischen Institutes ETH Zürich, Stiftung Rübel*, no. 99.

Smith, B. H. (1983). Demography of *Floerkea proserpinacoides*, a forest-floor annual. III. Dynamics of seed and seedling populations. *Journal of Ecology*, 71, 413–25.

Sohlberg, E. & Bliss, L. C. (1984). Microscale pattern of vascular plant distribution in two high-arctic communities. *Canadian Journal of Botany*, 62, 2033–42.

Suzan, H., Nabhan, G. P., & Patten, D. T. (1994). Nurse plant and floral biology of a rare night-blooming cereus, *Peniocereus striatus* (Brandeggee) F. Buxbaum. *Conservation Biology*, 2, 461–70.

Tenhunen, J. D., Lange, O. L., Hahn, S., Siegwolf, R., & Oberbauer, S. F. (1992). The ecosystem role of poikilohydric tundra plants. In *Arctic Ecosystems in a Changing Climate – an Ecophysiological Perspective*, eds. S. F. Chapin, R. L. Jefferies, J. F. Reynolds, G. R. Shaver, & J. Svoboda, pp. 213–37. San Diego: Academic Press.

Tschurr, F. R. (1990). Single-ramet-cloning (SRC) and multi-ramet-cloning (MRC): an example of basic and applied revegetation research. In *Proceedings of 9th High Altitude Revegetation Workshop*, eds. W. R. Keammerer, & J. Todd, pp. 234–7. Fort Collins: Colorado Water Resources Research Institute.

Tschurr, F. R. (1992). Experimentelle Untersuchungen über das Regenerationsverhalten bei alpinen Pflanzen. *Veröffentlichungen des Geobotanischen Institutes ETH Zürich, Stiftung Rübel*, no. 108.

Turner, R. M., Alcron, S. M., Olin, G., & Booth, J. A. (1966). The influence of shade, soil and water on saguaro seedling establishment. *Botanical Gazette*, 127, 95–102.

Uhl, C., Clark, K., Clark, H., & Murphy, P. (1981). Early plant succession after cutting and burning in the Upper Rio Negro region of the Amazon Basin. *Journal of Ecology*, 69, 631–49.

Urbanska, K. M. (1989). Reproductive effort or reproductive offer? – A revised approach to reproductive strategies in flowering plants. *Botanica Helvetica*, 99, 49–63.

Urbanska, K. M. (1990). Biology of asexually reproducing plants. In *Biological Approaches and Evolutionary Trends in Plants*, ed. S. Kawano, pp. 273–92. London: Academic Press.

Urbanska, K. M. (1992). *Populationsbiologie der Pflanzen*. Stuttgart: G. Fischer.

Urbanska, K. M. (1994a). Use of *Lotus alpinus* in alpine ecosystem restoration. In *The First International Lotus Symposium*, eds. P. R. Beuselinck, & C. A. Roberts, pp. 172–6. St. Louis: University of Missouri–Columbia.

Urbanska, K. M. (1994b). Ecological restoration above the timberline: demographic monitoring of whole trial plots in the Swiss Alps. *Botanica Helvetica*, 104, 141–56.

Urbanska, K. M. (1995a). Ecological restoration above the timberline and its demographic assessment. In *Restoration Ecology in Europe*, eds. K. M. Urbanska & K. Grodzinska, pp. 15–36. Zurich: Geobotanical Institute SFIT.

Urbanska, K. M. (1995b). Biodiversity assessment in ecological restoration above the timberline. *Biodiversity and Conservation*, 4, 679–95.

Urbanska, K M. (1997a). Reproductive behaviour of arctic/alpine plants and ecological restoration. In *Disturbance and Recovery of Arctic Terrestrial Ecosystems – an Ecological Perspective*, ed. R. M. M. Crawford, pp. 481–501. Dordrecht: Kluwer Academic Publishers.

Urbanska, K. M. (1997b). Restoration ecology of the alpine and the arctic areas: are the classical concepts of niche and succession directly applicable? In *Variation and Evolution in Arctic and Alpine Plants*, eds. B. E. Jonsell & L. Borgen, *Opera Botanica*.

Urbanska, K. M. & Hasler, A. R. (1992). Ecologically compatible revegetation above the timberline: a model and its application in the field. In *Proceedings of 10th High Altitude Revegetation Workshop*, eds. W. G. Hassell, S. K. Nordstrom, W. R. Keammerer, & J. Todd, pp. 247–53. Fort Collins: Colorado Water Resources Research Institute.

Urbanska, K. M., Hefti-Holenstein, B., & Elmer, G. (1987). Performance of some alpine grasses in single-tiller cloning experiments and in the subsequent revegetation trials above the timberline. *Berichte des Geobotanischen Institutes ETH Zürich Stiftung Rübel*, 53, 64–90.

Urbanska, K. M. & Schütz, M. (1986). Reproduction by seed in alpine plants and revegetation research above timberline. *Botanica Helvetica*, 96, 43–60.

Valiente-Banuet, A., Vite, A. F., & Zavada-Hurtado, J. A. (1991). Interaction between the cactus *Neobuxbaumia tetezo* and the nurse shrub *Mimosa Luisana*. *Journal of Vegetation Science*, 2, 11–14.

Van der Pijl, L. (1982). *Principles of Dispersal in Higher Plants*. Berlin: Springer-Verlag.

Van der Valk, A. G. & Pederson, R. L. (1989) Seed banks and the management and restoration of natural vegetation. In *Ecology of Soil Seed Banks*, eds. M. A. Leck, V. T. Parker, & R. L. Simpson, pp. 329–46. San Diego: Academic Press.

Vandermeet, J. (1980). Saguaros and nurse trees: a new hypothesis to account for population fluctuations. *The Southwestern Naturalist*, 25, 357–60.

Venable, D. L. & Levin, D. A. (1985). Ecology of achene dimorphism in *Heterotheca latifolia*. I. Achene structure, germination and dispersal. *Journal of Ecology*, 73, 133–45.

Walker, D. A., Binnian, E., Evans, B. E., Lederer, N. D., Nordstrand, E., & Webber, P. J. (1989). Terrain, vegetation, and landscape evolution of the R4D research site, Brooks Range Foothills, Alaska. *Holarctic Ecology*, 12, 238–61.

Weiner, J. (1990). Assymmetric competition in plant populations. *Trends in Ecology and Evolution*, 5, 360–4.

Weiner, J. & Thomas, S. C. (1986). Size variability and competition in plant monocultures. *Oikos*, 47, 211–22.

Wilson, C. & Gurevitch, J. (1995). Plant size and spatial patterns in a natural population of *Myosotis micrantha*. *Journal of Vegetation Science*, 6, 847–52.

Yeaton, R. I. (1978). A cyclical relationship between *Larrea tridentata* and *Opuntia leptocaulis* in the northern Chihuahuan desert. *Journal of Ecology*, 66, 651–6.

Yeaton, R. I. & Romero-Manzanares, A. (1986). Organization of vegetation mosaics in the *Acacia schaffneri – Opuntia streptocantha* association, Southern Chihuahuan Desert, Mexico. *Journal of Ecology*, 74, 211–17.

7

The role of plant–animal mutualisms in the design and restoration of natural communities

STEVEN N. HANDEL

Introduction

The restoration of native plant communities can be approached from the perspective of many different disciplines. Scientists are interested in testing ideas about community organization and structure, and patterns of succession in manipulated systems. Landscape architects are interested in adding ecological principles into design, to extend their options and 'palette' of plants for different sites. Land managers need to develop methods to more easily sustain natural communities for many public uses. Public officials want more area for recreation and amenity. Developers are interested in buffers between construction projects and neighbouring areas.

Although the focus and interest of each group differs, the need for effective and efficient protocols for planting remains the same. Effective protocols will give us communities that will be sustainable, with minimal human intervention and management. Efficient protocols will minimize the expenditure of funds, so often from hard-pressed government sources, while maximizing the number of plants, and the area covered. In these ways the *economics* of restoration ecology cannot be separated from the other, ecological design limitations that a restorationist always must consider.

What can the restoration ecologist offer to maximize extent and complexity in a project, while keeping costs down to satisfy economic concerns? I would like to explore how a focus on the principles of plant–animal mutualisms can improve both the demographic functioning of an ecological restoration, and also the economic balance sheet that is integral to projects aimed at improving our natural areas. Can research into these mutualisms facilitate improvement in both these areas of concern?

111

Mutualisms in ecological theory

In many natural communities the co-occurrence of certain species is not associated with a competition for resources, or a battle for an ecological advantage, but with a benefit to both parties. Living together improves the performance of both, yielding, for example, a higher rate of population growth and the ability to spread more quickly into the habitat. Sometimes the association is an *obligate* mutualism; each species requires the other at a critical stage of the life history for survival. Sometimes the association is *facultative*, causing an enhanced performance when both are present, but persistence is still possible when one partner deserts or never finds the other. Theoretical consequences and predictions deriving from these simple concepts are under active investigation (Boucher, James, & Keeler 1982; Boucher 1985; Price 1991). Both types of mutualisms can occur in a restored community, and will affect the fate of many species.

The demographic principle that operates when two species are mutualists is a simple modification of the logistic growth equation, where the presence of one species increases the numbers of the other. In this way the two populations increase their respective sizes when co-occurring, although there are obvious constraints to ever-increasing populations (May 1981).

Attention to the requirements of mutualisms and their protocols would increase the probability of them becoming established. These positive interactions must receive comparable attention to negative plant–animal interactions, particularly herbivory, that are a regular concern of restoration biologists.

Pollination mutualisms and restoration

Ecological symmetry at the project site

The addition of a plant species to a restoration plan does not guarantee that pollinators will be attracted in numbers or types adequate to ensure abundant seed set. Seed set can be low or absent if the pollinators are not present and spread of the plants in numbers and in space may fail. Even if the precise pollinator guild is not known for all the plant species in a restoration, important groups of pollinators can usually be determined by the floral syndrome, or suite of characters, that is associated with major classes of floral visitors (Barth, 1985; Howe & Westley, 1988; Proctor, Yeo, & Lack 1996). For example, some plant species have generalized, open, radially symmetrical flower shapes, and can be successfully pollinated by many different insects. Other plants have an intricate zygomorphic floral shape, restricting the spectrum of pollinators that is attracted to the plant and can deliver pollen.

A successful restoration must ensure that there is a match between the installed plant species and the habitat's pollination guild. The guild will develop through time, of course, and the project must focus on two problems: do the existing pollinators visiting the plants in the first few years produce seed; and what is the probability that the developing guild will be similar to the pollinators typical of the target plant community on undisturbed sites? For example, many early spring flowering herbs in temperate North America require queen bumble-bees (*Bombus* spp.), often the only large insect flying on the chilly days, for pollination. Other spring plants require visits by solitary bees (Andrenidae) for pollination. Later in the warming spring other plants have floral traits that attract migrating hummingbirds. Consequently, characteristics of the physical habitat of the restoration must be appropriate for these required mutualists, as well as for the plants. If the plants need these unusual mutualists, but they are unavailable, the species is unlikely to survive.

Several ecological factors can be identified as acting on the expression of this mutualism. For example, although bumble-bees are relatively wide-ranging and will visit many species of flowers, they have a series of behavioural requirements. Queens make new nests in existing holes in the ground, such as those made by rodents or rotting wood (Wilson 1971). Early in the spring only these nest-founding queens are flying and pollinating. New workers are produced later, and will take over the pollination role as their numbers increase. Consequently, a restoration of spring woodland plants might be pollinator-limited if isolated from land where bumble-bee colonies are not quickly founded.

Scientific attention to foraging insects searching for flowers has been concentrated on species of *Apis*, honey-bees (e.g., Waddington 1983; Seeley 1985; Gould & Gould 1988), and of *Bombus*, bumble-bees (Heinrich 1979), the most conspicuous but certainly not most typical temperate pollinators. Data on smaller bees are available, but they are much less studied (Richards 1978; Buchmann & Nabhan 1996; Proctor, Yeo, & Lack 1996). The large social bees, wide-ranging and active over most of the growing season, are not useful mutualists for all members of an installed plant community. These bees choose among available plants, and are sensitive to the requirement for a positive energy balance during their foraging flights. They will disregard smaller, less rewarding flowers with which no mutualism can be established.

The larger bees do, however, forage over quite long distances for nectar. Honey-bees have been shown to forage over 8 km from the hive (Visscher & Seeley 1982), suggesting that a restored plant community could be visited by distant workers, if these plants compete favourably as energetic rewards with other stands nearer to the nest.

Similarly, bumble-bees can travel long distances (Heinrich 1979; Thomson, Maddison, & Plowright 1982). Some bumble-bees, for example, have been tracked foraging many kilometres from their nest, sequentially visiting ('traplining') nectar producers. However, these bees do not communicate nectar locations to their sisters so that plant populations close to the nest are likely to be visited by many workers. Restoration projects using spring flowers (such as *Dicentra* species), that require visits by queen bumble-bees, must be near nests for any chance of pollination. The numbers of overwintering queens is fewer than the number of new workers that are produced and forage later in the growing season. Consequently, the relative efficiency of pollination by bumble-bees will vary over a season, with more workers being present for late flowering species.

Smaller bee species from families such as Andrenidae and Halictidae are virtually unavailable from commercial sources, and natural invasion of these pollinators to the restoration site might take many years, and be difficult to guarantee. Only a few, apparently hymenopteran vagabonds or fugitive species such as *Halictus ligatus*, regularly enter newly restored areas at an early stage (Reed 1995). Since these bees probably forage over very restricted areas (Buchmann & Nabhan 1996), adding small patches of artificial habitats for some important bee pollinators may be possible, to induce these species to come into the area (Figure 7.1).

Most solitary bee species apparently have a patchy distribution across the landscape, and cannot be relied upon to appear on a restoration site until several years have passed, as a result of chance invasion from the scattered bee populations. The element of chance is high, and study of restored prairies in North America (Reed 1995) shows very different bee faunas in nearby patches (Table 7.1).

Adding a plant population to a restoration site can be considered in a similar way to recovery after a disturbance. The chance that a pollinator will reinvade a disturbance area unassisted is a function of the favourableness of the new habitat and the pollinator's dispersal behaviour, again poorly known for many species. For one highly specialized, obligate pollinator, the agaonid wasp pollinating the fig, *Ficus aurea*, population levels reached near equilibrium levels only months after a major hurricane disturbance (Bronstein & Hossaert-McKey 1995). However, too few

Table 7.1. *Distribution of bee species on eight native and restored prairies in the northern United States (from Reed 1995)*

On each site there were bee species found at no other site.

Distribution	Number of bee species
Total bee species found in study	298
Only found on prairie remnants	83
Only found on restored prairies	73
Found on both remnants and restored prairies	129
Found only on one site	121
Found on all eight sites	6

Figure 7.1. Creation of open, sandy soil plots can be used to speed the introduction of ground-nesting pollinators to newly restored sites, especially to areas which have highly engineered soils (Yurlina & Handel in preparation).

studies with insect pollinators and disturbance patterns have been reported to make generalizations. Some bees, such as the well-studied tropical euglossines (Dressler 1968; Janzen 1971; Williams 1982) can travel over many kilometres, but the dispersal behaviour of most small bees remains to be uncovered.

The introduction of plants known to require pollinators of low occurrence is undesirable during early stages of restoration. There will even be cases where local extinction of the original pollinator guild precludes the mutualisms from ever being re-established. Plants without access to essential mutualists have been called the 'living dead', meaning that their future reproduction is impossible. It is pointless to insist on keeping such species in a restoration scheme, when ecological function is the goal!

The foraging behaviour of these solitary bee species is also poorly known (Eickwort & Ginsberg, 1980), though we do know that they behave quite differently from the larger, social genera. For example, *Ceratina calcarata* flies at the edges of wildflower stands, and visits fewer blossoms than a typical honey-bee which has just left its hive (Ginsberg 1984). Study of a new *Brassica campestris* population planted in different densities and arrays showed that flowers were only visited by solitary bee species, even when in dense (plants at 20 cm spacing) arrays. Indeed, it was notable that no honey bees visited these new populations of plants, even though several large hives were within 50 metres of the planting; the nectar reward of the plants was too low to be used by the honey-bees (Handel 1985).

Plant populations, community structure, and pollination

The interplay between number of available pollinators and number of nectar-rewarding plants must be addressed in determining the scale of a local restoration. When number of pollinators is relatively low compared with the number of flowers, many flowers fail to set seed. When there are too many pollinators compared with flower number, the insects cannot receive adequate rewards, and they move to other resources or their numbers decline.

For the restorationist, a large population of flowers may yield few seeds when pollinators are sparse, or if the local pollinator guild is inappropriate for the plant species that have been introduced. A small population of a plant may be ignored if the pollinators have the floral equivalent of 'greener pastures' elsewhere. For example, studies of *Viscaria vulgaris* and *Dianthus deltoides* in Europe have shown that larger populations receive significantly more visits and seed set than smaller or fragmented stands (Jennersten 1988; Jennersten & Nilsson 1993). Similarly, in Argentina, fragmented forest stands suffered decreases in pollination success (Aizen & Feinsinger 1994). Very small plant populations may have different breeding systems and genetic structures than is typical of larger populations (Falk & Holsinger 1991; Washitani 1996). In this way, lower seed set is only the most overt effect of pollinator loss. The higher seed set in large stands may be due to more visits or to more pollen being deposited at each visit; these two components of plant reproductive success are related in a complex way.

The nature of the balance between insect and plant numbers that optimizes reproduction is poorly known, but a cautious restoration should avoid extremely large or small stands of single plant species. Certainly the members and proportions of taxa in the pollination guild will change as the number of rewarding plants increases and as the insects colonize the area (e.g., Conner & Neumier 1995). Clusters that resemble local natural population sizes and distribution patterns seem likely to be the most effective initial restoration plan. However, if a longer time period can be tolerated before the target of seed reproduction is reached, this design criterion can be relaxed, since, given time, pollinators should colonize all but the most isolated patches. This is an area where careful monitoring of reproductive success (such as proportion of flowers that set seed, or number of plants which produce any seed) at comparable restorations would provide valuable information. If time is available, preliminary plantings before the main installation may be useful to indicate whether appropriate pollinators are in the area.

To sustain any plant population, reproduction is necessary to replace the inevitable deaths. Any steps that increase natural regeneration and make a long-term replanting programme unnecessary are obviously desirable.

The microsite placement of a plant may also affect its attractiveness to pollinators. Many insects are restricted to narrow portions of larger landscapes. For example, geometrid moths prefer the cover of woods, and only forage at the edge of fields, while noctuid moths range more broadly into the open (Morse & Fritz 1983). Milkweeds (*Asclepias* spp.) in the field have different lepidopteran pollinator guilds because of this microsite preference (Morse & Fritz 1983).

In shady forests growing on formerly disturbed land, there is interest in restoring wildflowers (Kubikova 1993–4; Francis & Morton 1995). There is a sharp difference in the temperature regimes experienced by plants in sunflecks, and plants under continual shade. Although woodland herbs are able to photosynthesize and persist in shady sites, seed production is often confined to sunnier microsites. One reason is that flowers in the sunny microsites have several-fold more visits by pollinators (Figure 7.2). Installation of wildflowers in a woodland restoration must concentrate on these microsites, not follow a regular grid on the land, as in most ornamental plantings, if seed set and population spread is an immediate goal of the restoration.

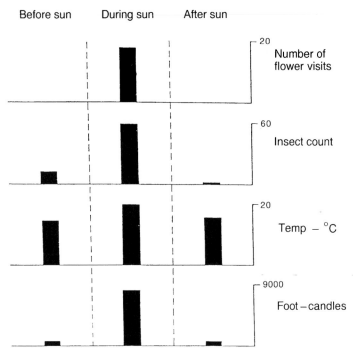

Figure 7.2. Woodland pollinators often prefer to forage in sun flecks. Beattie (1971) showed that the number of flower visits and illumination from ephemeral flecks were highly correlated. Microhabitat will strongly influence pollination success for woodland herbs.

Finally, there is a community interplay in pollination ecology that will effect the reproductive performance of the stand. Many more pollinators sample the components of the plant community than visit the most energetically rewarding species (Dafni 1992). This process may have helped drive the temporal distribution of flowering that we see in many communities (Kochmer & Handel 1986; Rathcke 1988). Potential competition for pollinators can be relieved in a restoration plan by constructing communities, as far as is possible, of sequentially flowering species. Bronstein (1995) has developed a framework for thinking about the temporal match between pollinators and their food plants, and how this relationship affects successful reproduction (Table 7.2). Flowering times can be obtained from many local floras, or be recorded in model communities that the restorationist wishes to imitate.

Table 7.2. *Pollinator/plant 'landscapes' that influence the effectiveness of the mutualism, and their consequences* (from Bronstein 1995)

1. Highly specialized pollinators and synchronously flowering plants. Rare, a mismatch in timing is very costly. 2. Highly specialized pollinators and asynchronously flowering plants. More common, less of a chance for failure. 3. Relatively generalist pollinators and synchronously flowering plants. Most common, especially in temperate interactions. 4. Relatively generalist pollinators and asynchronously flowering plants. Mobility of the visitors can persist, allowing continuation of the mutualism. 5. Generalist pollinators that may migrate. Visitors may be able to use geographic gradients in flowering time, allowing persistence of mutualisms across this range.

Sequential flowering may maximize seed set among plant species, and also enhance populations of generalist pollinators in the area. In situations where the local pollinator guild is poorly known, planning for sequential flowering will be a prudent course, increasing the probability that some fraction of the plant community can be visited by the local pollinators. This has a positive feedback on the next year's probability of pollination success, in a similar way that the flower species themselves can act as 'sequential mutualists', increasing the overall success to each component (Waser & Real 1979). In this way a longer-term season of flowering in the plant community, appealing to many on aesthetic grounds, can also be ecologically important.

Seed dispersal mutualisms and restoration

Seed dispersers as facilitators in restoration

Seed production has many important functions in plant communities, for example expanding existing populations, starting new ones, usually introducing new genotypes into the population, allowing perennation during stressful periods (Fenner 1992), and many of these functions are necessary components of a successful restoration. Although it would be possible to continue to add seeds to aid in the maturation of a project, taking advantage of natural dispersers to spread seed is like having a free assistant whose work schedule can span many years (Harmer & Kerr 1995). The seed-dispersers' activity and behaviour may eventually make them the primary 'landscape architects' of the site, in the sense that their actions determine which species of plants predominate on the site, and how they are distributed. How can one facilitate this activity, and what will be its impact?

Seed dispersal by animals is generally a diffuse mutualism, and there are few known examples where only one animal species is the sole agent for a plant species. In contrast, there are many cases of pollination mutualism where an animal specializes on one or several closely related plant species (Proctor, Yeo, & Lack 1996). This functional difference has been explained in several ways, focusing on the necessity of pollen to reach a very specific and small-scale location (a conspecific stigma) in the habitat, while a deposited seed has potentially much broader favourable destinations, usually away from another individual of the same species (Wheelwright and Orians 1982).

The kinds of animals that act as seed dispersers have long been studied, and offer wonderful stores of natural history, as well as windows into ecological function (e.g., Sernander 1927; Ridley 1930; Howe & Smallwood 1982; van der Pijl 1982; Fenner 1992). Some animal dispersal syndromes such as passive dispersal by adhesion to fur and feathers (Sorensen 1986) are not true mutualisms. Many others can be classified as mutualism as the diaspore includes a reward for the disperser. This often takes the form of energy-rich tissue surrounding the seed or seed cluster. Birds, bats, and other mammals, reptiles, and even fish participate in these mutualisms in various habitats, but invertebrates, especially ants, also play a major role in dispersal in some areas, including temperate woodland forests and the sterile soil shrublands of Australia and South Africa (Beattie 1985; Huxley & Cutler 1991).

Each animal involved in a mutualism has its own foraging and dispersal behaviour which, combined with its social structure, moulds the quality of its role as a mutualist (e.g. Pratt & Stiles 1983; Herrera 1984; Levey 1986). Distance of seed dispersal, microhabitats where seeds are most often deposited, clustering of seeds, and proportion of seeds that survive the dispersal event are all parameters that the ecologist can measure (Murray 1986; Jordano 1992). Long-distance dispersal has received much attention for its dramatic and important role in initiation of plant communities on distant islands (Carlquist 1974), but it is the mundane, more local dispersal that is of relevance to those who restore sites embedded in a matrix of terrestrial habitats.

Shape of the seed shadow

In restoring degraded landscapes, two aspects of seed dispersal will contribute to future plant community patterns. The first aspect is the removal and deposition of seeds from the plants that we introduce. This activity increases population size and local range, and begins the slow development of an age-distribution and genetic structure in the restored population that is typical for the species. We may want to accelerate this process by installing plants that will produce seeds quickly during the restoration process. Rapid spread of progeny from installed plants can take advantage of a relatively open substrate, before ground cover clogs microsites needed for seedling emergence.

The second aspect is the transport of seeds onto the site from surrounding vegetation. This process has the potential to add new species to the community, and thus commence the demographic changes mentioned for installed plants. This process is a two-edged sword. On the one hand, species and genotypes that are typical of native communities of the area are added including those which may not be available from the nurseries used to supply the restoration. In this way the local biodiversity can increase incrementally, and ecological 'communication' between the project and its landscape matrix can begin (Handel, Robinson, & Beattie 1994). On the other hand, unwanted species may invade. Often plants of alien origin sweep through restorations, using the sites which one has reserved for native species (Drake, *et al.* 1989; di Castro, Hansen, & Debussche 1988). If the goal is to mimic native stands, these plants must be removed by management of the restoration until the threat of invasion is curbed. A constant, low-level management may be needed if the surroundings have large populations of the unwanted plants.

Some installed plants will not require mutualists for dispersal (most gymnosperms, wind-dispersed angiosperms) because they spread in response to the vagaries of wind speed and direction. Others have passively dispersed seeds (by adhesion, for example) and need sympatric animal populations for seed movement. Lack of true mutualisms does not negate the importance of plant–animal interplay for these species. The shape of seed shadows for these species has been explored in many systems, using techniques ranging from mathematical simulations to ingenious field manipulations (e.g., Bullock & Primack 1977; Greene & Johnson 1989; Okubo & Levin 1989).

For plants requiring mutualisms for dispersal, animal behaviour becomes critical in understanding the pace of the population spread. Different birds, for example, have idiosyncratic foraging and flight behaviours (Wegner & Merriam 1979; Howe and Westley 1988; Abrahamson 1989). Deposition of seed will not necessarily decline with increasing distance from the source plant, but may peak at particular locations where the birds nest or perch (Stiles 1989; Izhaki Walton, & Safriel 1991) (Figure 7.3).

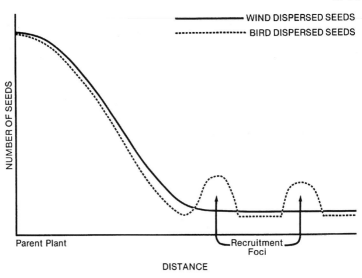

Figure 7.3. Animal dispersal behaviour influences the pattern of seed deposition from a plant source. Recruitment foci, often tree perches in open areas, can be quite different from wind-dispersed systems (from Stiles 1989).

Much seed deposition, by regurgitation or defecation, is remarkably close to the parent plant (Willson 1993). Chemicals encouraging the fast passage of seed through the gut are common in the fruits of bird-dispersed species and are of obvious advantage to the plant (Levey 1986). For example, Hoppes (1988) surveyed a variety of native temperate species, and produced data showing that most deposition was within 10–15 m of the source plant (Figure 7.4). Whether seeds travel from the edge of a site or from plants installed on the body of a site, knowledge of the seed shadow patterns allow the designer to estimate the possible location of seedlings in the next plant generation.

Once deposited on the ground, new seed becomes the object of many additional ecological forces. Seeds are often dispersed again, for example by small rodents who tear through animal droppings for seeds or find wind-dispersed seeds, and cache them elsewhere (Janzen 1983; Vander Wall 1992). This interaction may lengthen the tail of the seed shadow and cause clustering of seedlings. Many factors can then limit the number of seedlings, such as herbivory at the young stages, competition from other established plants, and attack by pathogens (Silvertown & Lovett-Doust 1993). Although the dispersal phase is critical and may be a limiting factor on a newly restored site, dispersal is only the first ecological hurdle in the contest for a mature plant community. Other mutualists may play their part during these later stages, such as ants protecting plants against herbivores in return for the rewards of extra-floral nectaries (Abrahamson 1989; Koptur 1992). These numerous ecological strands make the whole cloth of restoration, but it is my purpose to emphasize only the interactions in the earliest stages, as this is where the most planning is required.

Factors effecting the pattern of dispersal

Given an empty site availability for restoration, what can be done to increase the probability of many seed dispersers visiting the site, and thus increase seed deposition? Again, as more is learned about the behavioural requirements of the animals, we can modify the planting regime to exploit certain preferences. One successful approach has been to increase the amount of perching space for visiting birds. Birds do not move across and rest on random locations in a habitat, but search out areas most favourable for food, shelter, and protection from their enemies (Smith 1975).

Addition of perches in an open field has been shown to highly increase the number of seeds deposited on that site (McDonnell & Stiles 1983; McClanahan & Wolfe 1993). When perches are present, apparently they act as lures to focus bird movement onto the site. Where no tall structures are present, few seeds are deposited since those sections of the field are avoided by birds. The threshold height of an attracting structure may be relatively short, only 2 m (McDonnell 1986), similar to the height of many woody plants which are introduced during restorations. Similarly, in natural settings Kollmann & Pirl (1995) found that most seed rain was in mature shrub, not into adjacent grasslands. McDonnell's studies showed that simple structures – they need not even be living plants – could act as efficient attractors. The seeds found in these studies were mostly brought in from surrounding areas. Use of early successional woody plants that have large displays of fruit might maximize the quality of the plant lure for birds, and subsequently increase the number of seed introduced to the site. But even modest fruit displays can lure birds into open areas to feed (Davidar & Morton 1986).

Actual plants have been used in experimental work to show the speed with which new plantings can attract birds carrying seeds of new species into a restoration area (McClanahan & Wolfe 1993; Robinson & Handel 1993). In the latter study, 20 new species were added to a woodland restoration. After only 1 year following their introduction, over 1000

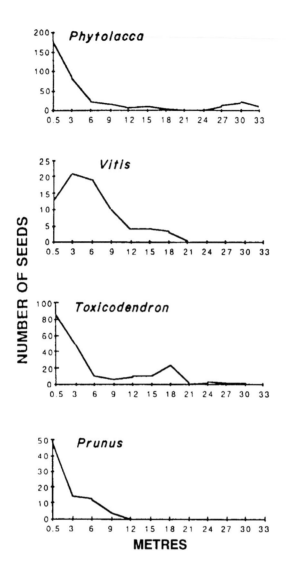

Figure 7.4. Although birds can carry seeds long distances (e.g. Ridley 1930), many seed shadows by frugivores foraging on fleshy-fruited species are quite close to the source plant (from Hoppes 1988).

Figure 7.5. Traps placed beneath perching sites (patches of hackberry, *Celtis occidentalis*, in a woodland restoration on an urban hillside), can be used to estimate the speed, quantity, and diversity of seeds brought into a site by frugivores (Mattei & Handel in preparation).

seedlings were found, of which 95% came from surrounding areas. In this particular restoration, only 20% of the installed plants were reproductive. One could predict that, if the fruit display were greater, the number of attracted birds would have been significantly greater.

Spatial pattern of plants across the landscape may also affect bird activity. This is being tested in a large experiment where seven woody species have been installed in four size patches: 7, 21, 42, and 70 plants, representing 1, 3, 6, and 10 individuals of each species. Patch diameter range from 3 to 12 m. Seeds can be transported into the patches from birds living in surrounding forest remnants, mostly on one side of the experimental area. During the first growing season, seed deposition was recorded from traps placed in each patch (Figure 7.5). The amount of seed deposited

Table 7.3. *Deposition of seeds beneath clusters of woody plants planted in an open field*

Data are averages of 5 replicates of each patch size, from seeds collected August–November, 1994 (Mattei & Handel in preparation).

Patch size (number of plants)	Seeds/patch	Seeds/trap
7	3203	641
21	1996	200
42	4921	328
70	4137	165

was very high, and many new species were found. Although the largest patches received more seed in total the average seed number per trap was highest in the smallest patch (Table 7.3). Apparently small patches still attract many frugivores, and flocks of birds will congregate even on patches of only 7 plants. These data suggest that initial plant dispersion can be high (many small patches), and still facilitate this mutualism. The resultant seed shadows may then fill the whole area more quickly, though more data are needed before detailed recommendations can be made.

These field studies illustrate a concept of using nucleating centres to initiate the successional process on barren restoration sites. Yarranton & Morrison (1974) discussed a similar concept termed 'nucleation', as a model for plant migration into open sites. The general pattern seen is that the initial plantings can attract mutualist dispersers quite rapidly, adding biodiversity and numbers to the site.

Secondary phases of restoration may be necessary, as not all mutualists will visit a sunny, open site. Ant foragers, important for many woodland species, would come into the habitat only later, when soil conditions had developed a structure more amenable for the ant nests. Planting herbs that need ants as dispersers (myrmecochores) must be considered as something which comes later in an effective restoration. When shady conditions have developed, the initial mutualist links will themselves be modified. Many of the frugivorous birds prefer openings and disturbed microhabitats at the edges of woodlands to hunt for fruit (Thompson and Willson 1978; Moore & Willson 1982). The tempo and pattern of mutualist service will change through time, and create the mosaic and complexity that is typical of mature, self-sustaining stands.

A new mutualism

The enticing of mutualists to a site, their activity in developing the stand, and the interplay between the restoration site and the surrounding landscape conditions, all complement each other. This process, once initiated, becomes a low-cost economic engine of ecological change, allowing the land managers to concentrate more of their efforts on routine maintenance and protective measures, instead of on endless, additional plantings. The mutualists, when present, take over much of the fundamental job of species introduction and population expansion.

Ecologists have a valuable role to play working with land development and management experts in identifying areas where ecological impacts of development can be minimized, delineating areas of habitat that must be protected, and determining how much buffer zone is needed between human activities and natural resources that must be sustained. An understanding of the advantages of mutualists in the development of new natural areas, can be important in making restoration economically viable. The ecologists can identify the processes that facilitate community structure and change, and ecological economists, applying these findings, can exploit ecological processes into cost-effective management.

Conclusions

Population growth and community development in a restored habitat requires a variety of plant mutualists. For plant reproduction, pollinator guild composition and pollinator numbers must be adequate for the number and types of flowers introduced during the first stages of the project. Successful pollination will depend on the rates of invasion of the pollinators to the site. Protocols for restoration must include provisions for attracting pollinators, as well as for the habitat requirements of the plant community itself. Plant species that require specialized pollinator species may suffer the greatest limitation of seed set during early stages of the restoration process.

Similarly, increase in local biodiversity and population spread will depend on attracting seed dispersers to the site. Frugivores must have adequate food and resting microsites in the restoration area, which can be manipulated by structural components of the design. Experiments on plant restorations show that bird frugivore movements can be shaped by perches placed in the new habitat, and that birds have non-random movements across the site. Many new plant species can be introduced, over a short period of time, by attracting seed dispersers. The number of seeds introduced to the site can be orders of magnitude more than seeds produced on site by the new plants themselves. In these ways, attention to the critical role of mutualists can increase the speed and success of a restoration, at no additional cost to the land manager.

Acknowledgements

I thank many collaborators for their efforts, especially George R. Robinson, Jennifer H. Mattei, Mary E. Yurlina, and Joan G. Ehrenfeld. I have had wonderful field assistance notably from Susan E. Fede, Paul Dudas, William F. Parsons, and Georgeanne Keer. Support for this work is from the US National Science Foundation (Conservation and Restoration Biology), the City of New York Department of Sanitation, the Schumann Fund for New Jersey, and the Rutgers University Bureau for Biological Research. I thank these organizations, and also Krystyna M. Urbanska for her constant encouragement.

References

Abrahamson, W. G., ed. (1989). *Plant–Animal Interactions*. New York: McGraw-Hill.
Aizen, M. A., & Feinsinger, P. (1994). Forest fragmentation, pollination, and plant reproduction in a Chaco dry forest, Argentina. *Ecology*, 75, 330–51.
Barth, F. G. (1985). *Insects and Plants: the Biology of a Partnership*. Princeton University Press.
Beattie, A. J. (1971). Itinerant pollinators in a forest. *Madroño*, 21, 120–4.
Beattie, A. J. (1985). *The Evolutionary Ecology of Ant–plant Mutualisms*. Cambridge University Press.
Boucher, D. H., ed. (1985). *The Biology of Mutualism: Ecology and Evolution*. New York: Oxford University Press.
Boucher, D. H., James, S. & Keeler, K. H. (1982). The ecology of mutualism. *Annual Review of Ecology and Systematics*, 13, 15–47.
Bronstein, J. L. (1995). The plant-pollinator landscape. In *Mosaic Landscapes and Ecological Processes*, eds. L. Hansson, L. Fahrig, & G. Merriam, pp. 256–88. London: Chapman & Hall.
Bronstein, J. L. & Hossaert-McKey, M. (1995). Hurricane Andrew and a Florida fig pollination mutualism, resilience of an obligate interaction. *Biotropica*, 27, 373–81.
Buchmann, S. L. & Nabhan, G. P. (1996). *The Forgotten Pollinators*. Washington, DC: Island Press.
Bullock, S. H. & Primack, R. B. (1977). Comparative experimental study of seed dispersal on animals. *Ecology*, 58, 681–6.
Carlquist, S. (1974). *Island Biology*. New York: Columbia University Press.
Conner, J. K. & Neumier, R. (1995). Effects of black mustard population size on the taxonomic composition of pollinators. *Oecologia*, 104, 218–25.

Dafni, A. (1992). *Pollination Ecology: A Practical Approach.* Oxford University Press.

Davidar, P. & Morton, E. S. (1986). The relationship between fruit crop sizes and fruit removal rates by birds. *Ecology*, 67, 262–5.

di Castro, F., Hansen, A. J. & Debussche, M., eds. (1988). *Biological Invasions in Europe and the Mediterranean Basin.* Dordrecht: Kluwer Academic Publishers.

Drake, J. A., Mooney, H. A., di Castro, F., Groves, R. H., Kruger, F. J., Rejmanek, M. & Williamson, M., eds. (1989). *Biological Invasions: A Global Perspective.* Chichester: John Wiley & Sons.

Dressler, R. L. (1968). Pollination by euglossine bees. *Evolution*, 22, 202–10.

Eickwort, G. C. & Ginsberg, H. S. (1980). Foraging and mating behavior of Apoidea. *Annual Review of Entomology*, 25, 421–6.

Falk, D. A. & Holsinger, K. E., eds. (1991). *Genetics and Conservation of Rare Plants.* New York: Oxford University Press.

Fenner, M., ed. (1992). *Seeds: The Ecology of Regeneration in Plant Communities.* Wallingford: C-A-B International.

Francis, J. L. & Morton, A. J. (1995). Restoring the woodland field layer in young plantations and new woodlands. In *Restoration Ecology in Europe*, eds. K. M. Urbanska & K. Grodzinska, pp. 1–13. Zurich: Geobotanical Institute, SFIT.

Ginsberg, H. S. (1984). Foraging behavior of the bees *Halictus ligatus* (Hymenoptera: Halictidae) and *Ceratina calcarata* (Hymenoptera: Anthophoridae): foraging speed on early-summer composite flowers. *Journal of the New York Entomology Society*, 92, 162–8.

Gould, J. L. & Gould, C. G. (1988). *The Honey Bee.* New York: Scientific American Library.

Greene, D. F. & Johnson, E. A. (1989). A model of wind dispersal of winged or plumed seeds. *Ecology*, 70, 339–47.

Greene, D. F. & Johnson, E. A. (1996). Wind dispersal of seeds from a forest into a clearing. *Ecology*, 77, 595–609.

Handel, S. N. (1985). Pollen flow and the creation of local genotypic variation. In *Structure and Functioning of Plant Populations. 2. Phenotypic and Genotypic Variation in Plant Populations*, eds. J. Haeck & J. W. Woldendorp, pp. 251–66. Amsterdam: North-Holland Publishing.

Handel, S. N., Robinson, G. R. & Beattie, A. J. (1994). Biodiversity resources for restoration ecology. *Restoration Ecology*, 2, 230–41.

Harmer, R. & Kerr, G. (1995). Creating woodlands: to plant trees or not? In *The Ecology of Woodland Creation*, ed. R. Ferris-Kaan, pp. 113–28. Chichester: John Wiley and Sons.

Heinrich, B. (1979). *Bumblebee Economics.* Cambridge, Massachusetts: Harvard University Press.

Herrera, C. M. (1984). A study of avian frugivores, bird-dispersed plants, and their interaction in Mediterranean scrublands. *Ecological Monographs*, 54, 1–23.

Hoppes, W. G. (1988). Seedfall pattern of several species of bird-dispersed plants in an Illinois woodland. *Ecology*, 69, 320–9.

Howe, H. F. & Westley, L. C. (1988). *Ecological Relationships of Plants and Animals.* New York: Oxford University Press.

Howe, H. F. & Smallwood, J. (1982). Ecology of seed dispersal. *Annual Review of Ecology and Systematics*, 13, 201–28.

Huxley, C. R. & Cutler, D. F., eds. (1991). *Ant–plant Interactions*. Oxford University Press.

Izhaki, I., Walton, P. B. & Safreil, U. F. (1991). Seed shadows generated by frugivorous birds in an eastern Mediterranean scrub. *Journal of Ecology*, 79, 575–90.

Janzen, D. H. (1971). Euglossine bees as long-distance pollinators of tropical plants. *Science*, 171, 203–5.

Janzen, D. H. (1983). Dispersal of seeds by vertebrate guts. In *Coevolution*, eds. D. J. Futuyma & M. Slatkin, pp. 232–62. Sunderland, Massachusetts: Sinauer Associates.

Jennersten, O. (1988). Pollination in *Dianthus deltoides* (Caryophyllaceae), effects of habitat fragmentation on visitation and seed set. *Conservation Biology*, 2, 359–66.

Jennersten, O. & Nilsson, S. G. (1993). Insect flower visitation frequency and seed production in relation to patch size of *Viscaria vulgaris* (Caryophyllaceae). *Oikos*, 68, 283–92.

Jordano, P. (1992). Fruits and frugivory. In *Seeds: The Ecology of Regeneration in Plant Communities*, ed. M. Fenner, pp. 105–56. Wallingford: C-A-B International.

Kochmer, J. P. & Handel, S. N. (1986). Constraints and competition in the evolution of flowering phenology. *Ecological Monographs*, 56, 303–25.

Kollmann, J. & Pirl, M. (1995). Spatial patterns of seed rain of fleshy-fruited plants in a scrubland-grassland transition. *Acta Oecologia*, 16, 313–29.

Koptur, S. (1992). Extrafloral nectary-mediated interactions between insects and plants. In *Insect–Plant Interactions*, ed. E. Bernays, vol. IV, pp. 81–129. Boca Raton: CRC Press.

Kubikova, J. (1993–1994). Oak–pine afforestation of agricultural land: an attempt to enrich its understory diversity. *Novitates Botany Charles University, Prague*, 8, 63–73.

Levey, D. J. (1986). Methods of seed processing by birds and seed deposition patterns. In *Frugivores and seed dispersal*, eds. A. Estrada & T. H. Fleming, pp. 147–58. Dordrecht: Dr W. Junk.

May, R. M., ed. (1981). *Theoretical Ecology, Principles and Applications*. 2nd edn. Oxford: Blackwell Scientific Publications.

McClanahan, T. R. & Wolfe, R. W. (1993). Accelerating forest succession in a fragmented landscape: the role of birds and perches. *Conservation Biology*, 7, 279–88.

McDonnell, M. J. (1986). Old field vegetation height and the dispersal pattern of bird-disseminated woody plants. *Bulletin of the Torrey Botanical Club*, 113, 6–11.

McDonnell, M. J. & Stiles, E. W. (1983). The structural complexity of old field vegetation and the recruitment of bird-dispersed plant species. *Oecologia*, 56, 109–16.

Moore, L. A. & Willson, M. F. (1982). The effect of microhabitat, spatial distribution, and display size on dispersal of *Lindera benzoin* by avian frugivores. *Canadian Journal of Botany*, 60, 557–60.

Morse, D. H. & Fritz, R. S. (1983). Contributions of diurnal and nocturnal insects to the pollination of common milkweed (*Asclepias syriaca* L.) in a pollen limited system. *Oecologia*, 60, 190–7.

Murray, D. R., ed. (1986). *Seed dispersal*. Sydney: Academic Press.

Okubo, A. & Levin, S. A. (1989). A theoretical framework for data analysis of wind dispersal of seeds and pollen. *Ecology*, 70, 329–38.

Pratt, T. K. & Stiles, E. W. (1983). How long fruit-eating birds stay in the plants where they feed, implications for seed dispersal. *American Naturalist*, 122, 789–805.

Price, P. W., ed. (1991). *Plant–animal Interactions: Evolutionary Ecology in Tropical and Temperate Regions.* New York: John Wiley.

Proctor, M., Yeo, P., & Lack, A. (1996). *The Natural History of Pollination.* Portland, Oregon: Timber Press.

Rathcke, B. (1988). Flowering phenologies in a shrub community: competition and constraints. *Journal of Ecology*, 76, 975–94.

Reed, C. C. (1995). Insects surveyed on flowers in native and reconstructed prairies (Minnesota). *Restoration and Management Notes*, 13, 210–13.

Richards, A. J., ed. (1978). *The Pollination of Flowers by Insects.* London: Academic Press.

Ridley, H. N. (1930). *The Dispersal of Plants Throughout the World.* Ashford, Kent: Reeve.

Robinson, G. R. & Handel, S. N. (1993). Forest restoration on a closed landfill: rapid addition of new species by bird dispersal. *Conservation Biology*, 7, 271–8.

Seeley, T. (1985). *Honey Bee Ecology.* Princeton University Press.

Sernander, R. (1927). Zur Morphologie und Biologie der Diasporen. Nova Acta Regiae Societatis scientiarum Upsaliensis, vol. extraordinary edition, 1927, pp. 1–104.

Silvertown, J. & Lovett-Doust, J. (1993). *Introduction to Plant Population Biology*, 3rd edn. London: Blackwell Scientific Publications.

Smith, A. J. (1975). Invasion and ecesis of bird-disseminated woody plants in a temperate forest sere. *Ecology*, 56, 19–34.

Sorensen, A. E. (1986). Seed dispersal by adhesion. *Annual Review of Ecology and Systematics*, 17, 443–64.

Stiles, E. W. (1989). Fruits, seeds, and dispersal agents. In *Plant–animal Interactions*, ed. W. G. Abrahamson, pp. 87–122. New York: McGraw-Hill.

Thompson, J. N. & M. F. Willson, (1978). Disturbance and the dispersal of fleshy fruits. *Science*, 200, 1161–3.

Thomson, J. D., Maddison, W. P., & Plowright, R. C. (1982). Behavior of bumble bee pollinators of *Aralia hispida* Vent. (Araliaceae). *Oecologia*, 54, 326–36.

van der Pijl, L. (1982). *Principles of Dispersal in Higher Plants.* 3rd edn. New York: Springer-Verlag.

Van der Wall, S. B. (1992). The role of animals in dispersing a "wind-dispersed" pine. *Ecology*, 73, 614–21.

Visscher, P. K. & Seeley, T. D. (1982). Foraging strategy of honeybee colonies in a temperate deciduous forest. *Ecology*, 63, 1790–801.

Waddington, K. D. (1983). Foraging behavior of pollinators. In *Pollination Biology*, ed. L. Real, pp. 213–39. Orlando: Academic Press.

Waser, N. M. & Real, L. A. (1979). Effective mutualism between sequentially flowering plant species. *Nature*, 281, 670–2.

Washitani, I. (1996). Predicted genetic consequences of strong fertility selection due to pollinator loss in an isolated population of *Primula sieboldii*. *Conservation Biology*, 10, 59–64.

Wegner, J. F. & Merriam, G. (1979). Movement by birds and small mammals between a wood and adjoining farmland habitats. *Journal of Applied Ecology*, 16, 349–58.

Wheelwright, N. T. & Orians, G. H. (1982). Seed dispersal by animals, contrasts with pollen dispersal, problems of terminology, and constraints on coevolution. *American Naturalist*, 119, 402–13.

Williams, N. H. (1982). The biology of orchids and euglossine bees. In *Orchid Biology: Reviews and Perspectives, II*, ed. J. Arditti, pp. 120–71. Ithaca, New York: Cornell University Press.

Willson, M. F. (1993). Dispersal mode, seed shadows, and colonization patterns. *Vegetatio*, 107/108, 261–80.

Wilson, E. O. (1971). *The Insect Societies*. Cambridge, MA: Harvard University Press.

Yarranton, G. A. & Morrison, R. G. (1974). Spatial dynamics of a primary succession: nucleation. *Journal of Ecology*, 62, 417–28.

8

The development of criteria for ecological restoration

NIGEL R. WEBB

Introduction

It is more than 30 years since attempts were first made to repair the damaged landscapes left as the heavy industry, which had dominated the economies of Europe, began its long decline. Much of this restoration was in the hands of civil engineers and landscape architects, and relied to a considerable extent on agricultural techniques. However, a few pioneering ecologists seized the opportunities which the restoration of this land offered to apply their science to a pressing and challenging problem. Previously, the attention of ecologists had been focused on describing the composition, structure, and functioning of what we call natural or semi-natural communities. Communities in which there has been a strong human influence have largely been ignored by ecologists; yet, as Bradshaw (1987) has pointed out, ecological processes still operate in such communities, and the restoration or reconstruction of vegetation to a state comparable with that occurring naturally presents almost the ultimate challenge to ecologists in the application of their science.

The restoration of derelict or degraded land has depended largely upon one area of ecology – that concerned with the identification, description, and provision of the habitat for species. By understanding the requirements for nutrition, growth, and reproduction (the autecology) of particular species, considerable success has been achieved in restoration schemes. This approach continues the traditions of plant ecology which, unlike animal ecology, where the emphasis had been on the dynamics of populations and communities, saw the occurrence of species very much in terms of their habitat and, in particular, of their physical and chemical requirements. The success of this approach depended on a sufficient understanding of the habitat requirements of the various species of plant. The damaged or degraded land was altered using agricultural techniques to

133

create the right habitat conditions. An alternative approach was to make use of varieties or forms of the species which, through natural selection, had slightly modified habitat requirements which conferred tolerance in these species to many of the pollutants and toxins to be found in the degraded land. It is from these beginnings that modern restoration ecology has developed.

Over recent decades, the traditional approach to plant ecology has been replaced by one which emphasizes the dynamics between individuals in populations and of species within communities: plant ecology has drawn closer to the approaches used by animal ecologists. In parallel, restoration ecology has widened its perspectives, particularly in relation to the construction or assembly of communities of conservation value. The concept of constructing communities has offered ecologists unique opportunities for the experimental manipulation of species assemblages in order to gain insights into community composition, structure, and assembly, and generates opportunities to test the resilience and response of communities to change, particularly those arising from management or climate. There is a lack of general theory to link the activities of individual organisms, population dynamics, and community assemblages to ecosystem structure and function (Jones & Lawton 1995). The sustainability of biodiversity is only possible through the satisfactory functioning of natural and semi-natural ecosystems.

Autecology, population dynamics, and community assembly are three areas of ecological science which have contributed considerably to restoration ecology. Furthermore, there are reciprocal benefits to ecological science from the practice of restoration ecology. However, there remain other areas of ecological science which are now opening up and which will contribute substantially to restoration ecology. Prominent among these is that concerned with scale, both temporal and spatial, and, in particular, with large scales (Edwards, May, & Webb 1994). A great deal of dynamic ecology has been concerned with the changes which take place over time. There has been considerable interest in all aspects of succession for many decades; however, there have been few studies in which spatial relationships have been examined. This imbalance stems largely from the ease with which data forming time-series can be analysed in comparison with data referenced spatially. The last decade has seen the rapid development of computer-based procedures which enable spatially referenced data to be analysed easily – the developments in geographic information systems (GIS) are an example. As a result of these developments, it is now possible to consider not only 'when' things happen but 'where' they happen. We have seen the same course being followed in restoration ecology: much of restoration ecology has been concerned with 'how' and 'when', but now we are in a position to consider 'where', and it is the ecological aspects of 'where' which I want to develop in this chapter, taking what Bullock & Webb 1995a called a landscape approach to ecological restoration.

There is not only a sound ecological basis for this approach, but also a practical one. Formerly, the challenge to restoration ecology was to create vegetation, if not communities of both plants and animals, on damaged or degraded areas, and this approach depended on the nature of the site to be restored. Little consideration was given to assessing the surrounding biotopes and habitats to see how the restored area fitted in. Recent years have seen even this change. What was not foreseen was the extent to which agricultural land would become surplus to the needs of farming. Government policies in many countries in the years since World War II have been directed towards increasing food production and eliminating dependency on external sources. As a result, a complex system of subsidies and price support was developed; however, by the mid 1980s it was evident that excessive food surpluses had accumulated which were proving expensive to maintain and disperse, and that there were adverse effects on the diversity of wildlife (Firbank *et al.* 1993).

By the late 1980s, the concepts of extensification and set-aside had gained ground. A number of environmental concerns can be addressed in set-aside programmes (Firbank *et al.* 1993). These include conservation of wildlife, biocontrol of pests on adjacent arable land, increase of game and fish stocks, reduction of groundwater pollution, management of run-off of nutrients and pollutants, provision of public access and amenity, improvement of the rural landscape, reduction of carbon dioxide emissions, and production of biomass fuels. The loss of diversity through the decline of both species and habitats can be offset by set-aside programmes. There is no single biotope which should be given top priority, but Firbank *et al.* (1993) made the point that set-aside should be used locally to restore habitat diversity, to promote the expansion of existing biotopes, to provide buffer zones and corridors, and to provide new sites.

The availability of previously farmed land to meet the objectives of wildlife conservation has provided a new focus, and Biodiversity Action Plans have now gone as far as setting targets for the creation of new areas of biotope. For instance, in Britain the Biodiversity Action Plan has set a national target of increasing the area of lowland heathland by 10% (6000 ha)–an additional area approximately equivalent to the present extent of the Dorset heathlands.

The foregoing sets the scene for this chapter. Previously, restoration projects were site-based. Land was restored with little reference to its surroundings, other than, perhaps, to consider what was appropriate. However, two developments have changed this perception: first, within ecological science an interest has developed in spatial relationships at all scales; secondly, and perhaps more importantly, the availability of land caused by the decline in agriculture has increased. For the first time, this latter factor provides us with a choice of where to restore, and forces us to consider how ecological restoration can increase the diversity of habitats and ensure the survival of species. In saying this, I am assuming that the technology for creating habitats is now largely available. The principal question is 'where' should we create new habitats and biotopes?

Where a landscape approach is adopted, ecological restoration can be seen as a three-stage process. First, ecological principles (such as island biogeography and metapopulation theories) and features of organisms – what Southwood (1977) calls their habitat templet (such as their dispersal and persistence) – should be used in combination to develop criteria which can be used to determine where restored areas should be located in relation to existing biotope patches and to promote the dynamics of the species. Secondly, once a location has been selected, the conditions require assessment. Thirdly, the practical problems of undertaking the restoration must be considered.

The focus of this chapter will be on the first stage – the development of ecological criteria for choosing sites. It will draw on the extensive research into the ecology of patches of dwarf shrub heathland in southern England. As a result of current land use changes, it is now possible to consider increasing the areas of patches, infilling and linking patches, and creating new patches to offset the loss of some 85% of the area of these heathlands over the last two centuries, and to meet current policies to increase biodiversity.

The Dorset heathlands

The Dorset heathlands provide us with an excellent case history typical of many areas of semi-natural vegetation throughout Europe and in other parts of the world. Losses or agricultural improvement and urban expansion have affected most open biotopes, particularly grasslands and wetlands. Many semi-natural woodlands, small woodlots, and hedgerows (Watt & Buckley 1994) have also been destroyed or converted into plantation woodlands, broad-leaved species often being replaced by conifers.

On the global scale, major vegetation types are determined primarily by climatic patterns. Within regions dominated by a particular type of climate, further modification occurs depending on the patterns of topography, soils, and water. Dwarf shrub heathland, dominated by members of the Ericaceae, is characteristic of the Atlantic zone of western Europe – the Cfb zone of Köppen – where this formation occurs on soils with suitable characteristics as a result of past land uses (Gimingham 1972; Webb 1986).

The heathlands of Dorset developed following forest clearances which began at least 4500 years ago (Webb & Haskins 1980) and which led to most of the area of suitable soils in south-east Dorset being covered with heath vegetation. Today no more than 15% of the original area of heathland remains, and remnant patches of this biotope exist in a matrix of farmland, forest, and urban and industrial land. They have long provided us with one of the best-documented examples of the effects of fragmentation and isolation of a semi-natural biotope (Moore 1962; Webb 1990).

We can view the original heathland landscape as a patchwork of different vegetation types, the pattern of which was largely determined by variations in topography and soils. These patches can be considered as environmental resource patches (*sensu* Forman & Godron 1986). Disturbance, in this case the removal of trees by humans, led to the spread of dwarf shrub vegetation. This process created a series of disturbance patches overlying the pattern of topography and soils. This position existed roughly at the late Iron Age and Roman times (*c.* 2000 BP), when the extent of these heathlands was greatest and amounted to at least 300 km² (Webb & Haskins 1980). Subsequently, as a result of disturbance to land surrounding these large heathland patches or continents, a series of remnant patches of heathland was created which today occupies slightly less than 60 km² (Webb 1990). For most purposes, we recognize 141 patches, their shape and distribution largely reflecting the pattern of land ownership rather than natural or biotic boundaries. In a sense, these remnant patches are secondary in that they are remnants of the disturbance patches and not remnants of the mosaic of primary vegetation. Yet underlying them are the patterns of topography, soils, and water which determined the original patchwork. The management and use of these heathlands have followed well-established practices over many centuries (Webb 1986). Today there is little management of the remaining fragments except for those which are nature reserves. Where management occurs it is often constrained by the size and shape of the patches.

The pattern outlined above is characteristic not only of heathland but of most other remnants of semi-natural vegetation, such as woodlands and grasslands, throughout western Europe, as well as many other parts of the world. Such systems have attracted ecologists, particularly those interested in the problems of survival for those species characteristic of this community. To this and similar systems, various models have been applied to express the dynamics of such systems. From the point of view of the restoration ecologist, the principal question is 'where' should we create new patches of heathland? One type of 'where' has already been determined. First, it is evident that the heathland must be created within the climatic zone within which it is possible for heathland to occur. Secondly, there are restrictions within this zone, determined by the occurrence of suitable soils and hydrological regimes. In the case of Dorset, heathland can potentially occur over an area 100 000 ha (Figure 8.1) where the geological formations are suitable. It is difficult for us to know whether heathland extended over almost all of this potential area, but we know that in the mid eighteenth century the extent of the heathlands was about 40 000 ha (Webb & Haskins 1980) and that today 6–7000 ha remain (Webb 1990). The picture is more or less the same throughout the range of Atlantic heathlands in western Europe, with 10–15% of the former area remaining.

Creating new biotope patches

Taking heathlands as our example, we have seen how their former extent has been greatly reduced and that there is now, as a result of changing priorities in agricultural production, potential to create new areas. There has been considerable research into restoration techniques (reviewed by Putwain & Rae 1988) and this aspect will not be discussed here. Many techniques have been developed to repair damage to heathland, such as where oil and gas pipelines have been laid or to create heathland on the bare soils and mineral substrates which remain after the extraction of minerals

Figure 8.1. Maps showing the distribution of heathland in Dorset, southern England, in the mid-eighteenth century and at the present time. The solid line is the coast and the dashed line indicates the area of soils which surround Poole Harbour and which are suitable for heathland formation. The distribution of heathland in the eighteenth century has been reconstructed from old maps which show that the heathland was in a few large continuous areas between the river valleys with a total area of about 40 000 ha. By 1978, the field survey of Webb & Haskins (1980) showed that the heathlands had been reduced in area to less than 6000 ha and had been split up in to 141 fragments. The loss and fragmentation of these heathlands had been caused by conversion to agricultural land, afforestation, and urban and industrial development.

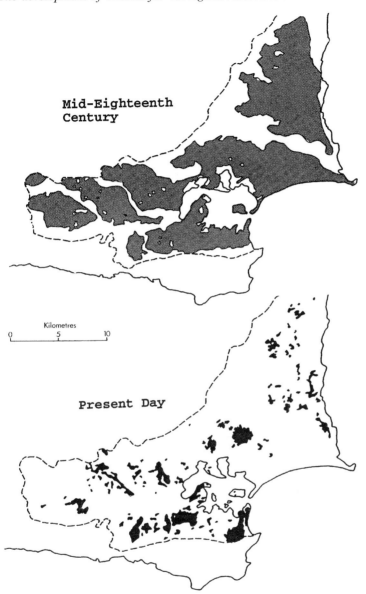

(Putwain & Rae 1988). In both instances the damage or disturbance fixes the location to be restored and therefore little consideration has been given to the relationship with existing patches of the biotope. The restoration of heathland from grassland, scrubland, and woodland is a less well-developed subject, and grades into conservation management. However, the conversion to heathland of grasslands and afforested areas is now being attempted (Smith, Webb, & Clarke 1991; Webb, Veitch, & Pywell 1995; Pywell, Webb, & Putwain, 1995). In these instances, the areas to be restored are not so precisely defined and there is considerable flexibility to restore areas within the boundaries of given ownerships. In these cases it is possible to ask where new biotope patches are best located.

The question of 'where' to create new areas of a particular biotope can be answered in several ways, and there are several types of 'where'. The simplest approach is to create new patches within the former extent of the biotope without relating the positioning of the new patches to the positions of the existing patches. Clearly, the climate and soil conditions are likely to be suitable, but the soils may have been altered through cultivation, and the manipulation of soil fertility may be required before restoration can be effected. A more refined approach to the positioning of new patches is likely to address a variety of factors, some of which meet ecological requirements and others which address purely practical ones.

Ecological requirements

First, we might consider linking unconnected patches. Large patches might be linked, but more often the linkage of a cluster of small patches, in which edge effects are likely to be great, will have a greater priority. In this type of exercise it is useful to know how large the patches of a particular biotope need to be, and we would seek to link those that fell below this threshold.

Secondly, we might consider infilling patches and altering their shape in an attempt to minimize the length of edge. As in the previous case, the aim would be to establish patches which exceeded the minimum size-threshold.

On a more ambitious scale, we might consider the re-creation of an entire hydrological unit. In the case of lowland heath in southern England, such a unit would comprise a catchment of high, drier ground surrounding a valley mire system. As a result of this topography, a series of related heathland vegetation types could be created as well as re-establishing the hydrological conditions for the maintenance of this system. In this case, where the topography was suitable or could be restored, the selection of sites to be restored would be focused. This exercise would involve a wide range of ecological engineering techniques.

A fourth approach would be to provide the conditions that will enhance and sustain populations of particular threatened or endangered species. Such species might be confined to a few of the existing patches and, by increasing the area of habitat for these species, their status might be maintained or enhanced. In some cases, enlargement of the biotope might be needed to create home-ranges of an adequate size to support the species.

Another approach might be to create corridors or stepping-stones. Although this seems a good idea, our knowledge of their use by species as an aid to dispersal is poor and the extent to which these features are used is equivocal (Dawson 1994).

Practical requirements

First amongst these is the past use of the land. In some cases this will make restoration of the biotope difficult, if not impossible. Many of the biotopes of conservation interest that we wish to create are dependent on soils of low fertility. On many agricultural soils there will have been modification and improvement through the addition of fertilizers. This can be difficult to reverse (Marrs & Gough 1989; Gough & Marrs 1990; Marrs 1993; Evans, Marrs, & Welch 1993).

Next we need to consider the pattern of land ownership. This will have changed from the historical pattern, which was more closely related to the patterning of the vegetation, to a modern pattern which can be independent of natural variation in soils and vegetation. Not only will the land to be restored need to be acquired, but it will require management once restored. If, for instance, heathland is restored, future management might involve grazing. Livestock may not be on the heathland for all of the time and adjacent holding pastures will be required – again, a constraint on where restoration can take place.

Finally, in restoring ancient vegetation types or biotopes, we need to address aesthetic consideration of landscape and amenity as well as conservation needs. The general public may well value appearance of the landscape more highly than the detailed requirements of the conservationist.

The potential for creating a biotope within its former area

Where patches of a biotope of high conservation value are embedded in a matrix of farmland, forests, and urban land, as a first step one might like to know what overall potential exists within this area to create additional areas of the biotope. In principle, this is a straightforward task. First, we establish where the biotope formerly occurred, and secondly we identify the current land use. Some forms of land use will enable the land to be converted to the biotope again while other forms will not. A variety of approaches can be used. We can use a geological or soil map and work within the boundary which provides the right conditions for the biotope. We can refine this by using topographic maps from which the historical extent of the biotope can be plotted. We can then overlay this on a map of the current land use and identify areas which are suitable for the creation of new patches. The interpretation of old maps sometimes poses problems, and likewise new field surveys to establish current land use may be difficult and costly. Frequently, as in the case of the Dorset heathlands, we know the extent of the biotope of high conservation value, but almost nothing about the matrix in which the patches are embedded.

An approach using a geographic information system to combine historical maps and remotely sensed images has been described for the Dorset heathlands by Veitch, Webb, & Wyatt (1995). In this case, good quality historical topographic maps covering the last two centuries exist. First, the extent of the Dorset heaths was defined from first (1811) and second (1896) editions of the Ordnance Survey maps to create a map of heathland in the mid nineteenth century. A map of the distribution of heathland in 1960 (Moore 1962) was also available. These historical maps were digitized and rasterized at a resolution of 25×25 m to generate a dataset which depicted the changes in the distribution of the Dorset heathlands from the early nineteenth century to the recent past.

The next step was to prepare a map of the current extent of the heathlands and the land use of the areas surrounding them. This is possible in a variety of ways, using either field survey, aerial photography, or remote-sensing. Veitch et al. (1995) made use of a national land cover map prepared by the Institute of Terrestrial Ecology from the Landsat Thematic Mapper (Fuller, Groome, & Jones 1994). This map expressed the land cover of Britain in 25 classes at a spatial resolution of 25×25 m. For this exercise, a 33×44 km pixel covering the required section of the Dorset heathlands was selected. These data were processed using the IDRISI raster geographical information system mounted on an IBM PS/2 Model 70 personal computer. First, an image was extracted showing the current distribution of dwarf shrub heath in Dorset. Secondly, the composite boundary of heathland in the nineteenth century was overlaid

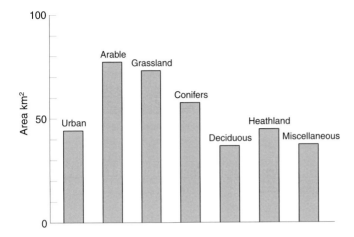

Figure 8.2. The area of the principal land cover types derived from remote sensed images of the land which was heathland at the beginning of the nineteenth century. In this exercise the total area of former heathland was estimated as 36 500 ha. The present area of heathland was estimated to be 4430 ha and the remaining area made up of grasslands, arable land, coniferous woodland and plantations, deciduous woodland, and urban land. The land which is not heathland varies in its potential to be converted to heathland again (after Veitch, Webb, & Wyatt 1995).

on the land cover map for the heathland area. This enabled the current land cover types of the former heathland to be determined and classified. Finally, these land cover types were reclassified into five classes which represented the ease with which the land could be converted to heathland again. It proved possible to classify all of the land lying between the present and the eighteenth-century heathland boundaries in terms of its suitability for the reconstruction as heathland, and to calculate the areas of the various types of land with potential for reconstruction as heathland (Figure 8.2).

In this exercise, only two datasets have been combined; however, with additional datasets, such as the distribution of soil fertility, the distribution of past land use patterns, surface water hydrology, and so on, it would be possible to refine its use. By using such data, it is possible to identify areas where heathland might most easily be restored. This approach can be extended to other biotopes. In the highly managed landscapes of western Europe, maps are often available from which the extent of these biotopes at various times in the past can be reconstructed. Hence, it is possible to make overall assessments of the potential to increase the extent of various biotopes.

Making new patches

The creation of new patches of a biotope within the area of its former extent needs to address three factors: the size of the patches, their shape, and their degree of isolation. To some extent these three factors are interrelated. Size cannot be altered without altering the shape and the relationship between the area of a patch and its circumference. Likewise, altering the size of the patches affects the degree to which they are isolated. Frequently, small patches tend to be isolated. They exist as satellites of large patches or at the fringes of the former extent of the biotope.

Patch area

If we enlarge existing patches of a particular biotope, we can examine the benefits in terms of species–area relationships. Likewise, if we create new patches within the former boundary of the biotope, how big should they be? For both type of patch, we can seek answers in the theories of species–area relationships.

Much time has been devoted in ecological science to discussion of the nature of the relationships between species and area. This discussion has mainly focused on the problems created by reducing the area of remaining patches and the consequences of increasing their isolation. This process has resulted in a decline in biodiversity in protected areas and nature reserves. In our case, we are considering the reverse: what will be the consequences of increasing the area of patches?

In general, the larger an area the more species it contains (Preston 1962; Connor & McCoy 1979; Williamson 1981). This has been expressed in the general form of $S = cA^z$ where S in the number of species, A the area, and c and z are constants. The constant z measures the slope of the line relating numbers of species to area and generally has a value of 0.3. Species area curves have been presented for a variety of taxa, most often for higher plants and particularly for birds. In almost all cases, positive correlations have been obtained, although the significance of the correlation has varied. In some instances, such as beetles (Coleoptera) on heathland fragments (Webb & Hopkins 1984), negative correlations have been obtained (Hopkins & Webb 1984). The greater richness of species on large areas has been attributed to the greater number of habitats present when larger areas are considered.

There are two factors affecting the richness of species on a given area of biotope. First, the correct set of species should be considered. If one considers heathland spiders on fragments of heathland then a positive relationship is obtained; however, if one considers all spiders on the same heathland patches, a negative relationship is found because of the presence of transient species from the surrounding biotopes (Webb 1989). For heathland patches, a similar effect has been found for plant diversity (Webb & Vermaat 1990). Secondly, the question of defining the area must be considered. If one considers topographic areas of different sizes, these areas may or may not coincide with the so-called 'natural boundaries' of biotopes or habitats; in such cases a misleading result can be obtained Webb (1994).

The relationship between species and area was developed more formally by MacArthur & Wilson (1967) in their theory of island biogeography. They proposed that on islands where species are colonizing, a dynamic equilibrium is attained in which immigration and extinction rates balance one another. The species number at which the equilibrium is reached depends on the area of the island and its proximity to a source of colonists. In suggesting that species richness was the result of a dynamic equilibrium, MacArthur & Wilson (1967) provided a biological explanation for the observed richness.

The theories of island biogeography were developed for oceanic islands, and it was suggested that an analogy could be drawn between such islands and biotope of habitat islands which might form nature reserves or protected areas. In a region such as Europe where, at best, areas of semi-natural communities, which could form nature reserves, exist within the matrix of other land uses, this concept was limited in its application. A more satisfactory analogy can be drawn between remnants of primary vegetation and islands than between remnants of secondary vegetation. Furthermore, the nature of the intervening areas modified the isolation effects. At one stage, there was considerable interest in using these theories as a basis for selecting reserves and protected areas (Simberloff & Abele 1976; Diamond 1975; May 1975).

There has been considerable criticism of the theory of island biogeography (Gilbert 1980; Boecklen & Gotelli 1984). On the one hand it simply deals with species-richness, and is less concerned with species composition and community structure. From the point of view of assembling communities, the composition of the flora and fauna is equally important, as conclusions drawn from species-richness alone may be ambiguous (Simberloff & Abele 1976; Higgs & Usher 1980; Higgs 1981). Small and isolated heathlands tend to be invaded by vagrant or ephemeral species from the surrounding biotopes. Therefore, Webb, & Hopkins (1984) considered that species-richness alone was inappropriate to assess patches of heathland of different sizes. Despite this, species-richness in isolation has been given considerable weight in conservation assessments (Ratcliffe 1977; Margules, Higgs, & Raffe (1982). What is more appropriate is some measure of representativeness or typicalness: thus, a patch of heathland containing more heathland species would be preferred to one containing fewer species.

Quite clearly, if we create patches of a particular biotope within the range over which that biotope formerly occurred, we might expect that biodiversity of the patches would respond in the classical fashion with the final species-richness depending on the size of the patch. Isolation is likely to be of little importance, because in creating the patch we have manipulated this. However, this factor comes into play once the patch is established, and the medium- to long-term persistence of the patch will depend on the proximity of sources of further colonists unless we continue to manipulate the process of immigration to the patches: this latter approach might not be acceptable in conservation practice.

A related problem is the question of whether a cluster of small patches will result in greater species-richness. This topic has been reviewed recently by Spellerberg (1991). The answer is equivocal, as much depends on the range of habitats provided by the cluster of patches, which by chance could be greater than that of a single large patch of the same area. The confusion results from the use of the terms 'biotope' and 'habitat'. The biotope is the habitat of the community (Whittaker, Levin, & Root 1973; Webb 1994) whereas the habitat is the location which provides the conditions required by an individual species. We can expect a species to be present only when its habitat is present. Boundaries of patches may coincide with those of either an area of biotope or an area of habitat. If we simply define topographic areas then the boundaries may include several biotopes. Even where the boundary coincides with that of the biotope, a varying number of habitats may be included. It is also possible that some habitats will be absent, despite an area of biotope being delimited. The extent to which patch boundaries correspond with habitat and biotope boundaries will determine richness; hence, it is possible to achieve a greater richness on a cluster of small patches, although it might be difficult to maintain.

Enlarging existing patches is a related problem. A patch might be enlarged to infill an irregular boundary, to make the overall shape of the patch more regular, and to reduce the length of perimeter in relation to the area. A patch might simply be enlarged and this might absorb smaller satellite patches. Once again, similar conditions apply and a greater area of biotope is likely to contain more species. Increasing patch size will help support species with large home-ranges, which would not persist on smaller patches. In some instances it has been suggested that the minimum area requirements for species can be met by using a cluster of small patches (Hinsley, Bellamy, & Newton 1995).

Patch shape

Much of the species area discussion has concentrated on area or isolation. The relative importance of these factors depends on whether or not one believes that the control of extinction rates on a patch is more or less important than the rates of immigration to the patch. Clearly, in order to minimize extinction rates, patch size should be as large as possible, and where remnant patches are being protected this is likely to be the most valuable approach. In this case, where immigration is seen as of little importance, it does not matter how close the patches are to each other.

In creating new patches, immigration is likely to be an important factor. In the initial stages this is manipulated, but once the elements of the biotope are established it is widely expected that additional species will reach the patch by themselves. Game (1980) suggests that, to an immigrating individual, the apparent size of a patch is determined by the linear dimension of the patch perpendicular to the direction of travel of the dispersing species; hence, immigration rate will depend on shape and not simply on area.

In many cases, created patches represent the early successional stages of particular biotopes. In the landscapes of much of western Europe, the biotopes most highly valued for conservation are representatives of early stages in succession. It has been clearly demonstrated (Thomas & Morris 1994) that most of the species with a high conservation status are dependent for their habitats on early successional communities. In the absence of management to maintain their condition, these patches will change, and where later successional stages surround them they will be prone to invasions. The size and shape of the restored patch will be of importance in controlling this process.

For patches of heathland, the invasion by species from the surroundings was demonstrated for invertebrates (Webb & Hopkins 1984; Webb, Clarke, & Nicholas 1984) and vegetation (Webb & Vermaat 1990). In general, it was found that overall species-richness declined with increasing area (Figure 8.3) and only when small patches exceeded about 12 ha was their species-richness comparable with that of large patches. Similar effects and similar calculations can be made for other biotopes; however, heathland patches are particularly interesting because the species-richness of heathland is characteristically low and evidence of invasion by non-heathland species easy to detect.

The described changes in species-richness reflect the geometry of the patches. Petersen (1997) has noted that if area/circumference is plotted against patch size, a curve of similar shape to that of Webb & Vermaat (1990) is obtained (Figure 8.3). The more regular the shape of the patch, the steeper the angle of the curve. This accords with the change in shape of the curves observed by Webb & Vermaat (1990), which became flatter over a period of 9 years as species-richness on heathland patches increased as a result of invasion from the edges.

This simple geometric approach could be used to decide how to alter the shapes of the existing patches and to decide the shapes of new patches. The necessary information could be mounted on a GIS and an optimal solution calculated for particular landscapes, the aim being to steepen the curve. In this way, a priority could be established by which the shapes of the patches are modified using restoration techniques. Monitoring the shape of the curve provides an alternative use in conservation management. It would highlight where management effort should be directed to maintain the highest conservation value throughout the landscape. Of course, this assumes that species-richness is the sole conservation criterion.

Isolation

In terms of recreated patches of a biotope, the degree of isolation is difficult to interpret. Those species which are the essential elements in the biotope will be placed there during the restoration activity. In addition, certain other species, such as rarities or specialist indicators of the biotope, might be introduced. The extent to which species introductions of this type are carried out is a controversial topic which currently lacks clear principles. Many conservationists would hesitate to encourage a wide range of introductions of this type. They would, however, expect critical species to establish on the new patches of biotope under their own powers of dispersal. The extent to which species move within the landscape, while not persisting at any given location, is difficult to assess. Nevertheless, over the longer term we might expect our patch to persist, to acquire characteristic species, and to interact with other patches of the same biotope, especially where long-term persistence is an aim of the restoration. It is the maintenance of the interaction between other patches which is important

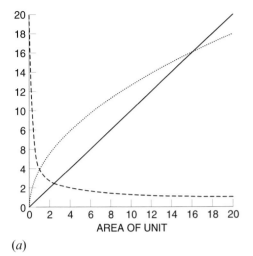

(a)

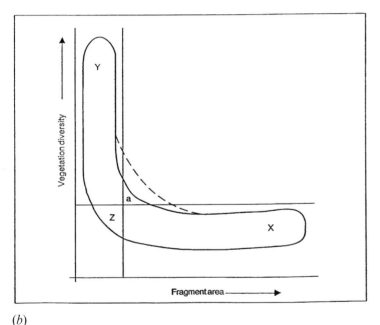

(b)

Figure 8.3. The geometric relationship obtained by Petersen (1997) by plotting the ratio of circumference to the area of a patch against the area of a patch (a). This is compared (b) with the relationship between vegetational diversity and patch area for patches of heathland in Dorset (Webb & Vermaat 1990). The more regular the shape of the patch the steeper the curve. In Figure 8.3b the invasion of heathland patches by vegetation from the surroundings results in a more irregular boundary and a more shallow curve.

when we consider where to locate new patches. In selecting the location of our new patch, we require information on how this will affect the overall degree of isolation of the existing patches.

There are two related points to be considered. The creation of the remnant patches often results in large patches surrounded by satellite patches. Frequently, there is a pattern of a few large core patches, but as one moves outwards towards the periphery of the potential distribution of the biotope, the patches not only become smaller but are more isolated. This characteristic pattern is well illustrated by the distribution of heathland patches in Dorset (Figure 8.1), where the smallest and most isolated patches tend to occur towards the periphery of the area of soils on which heathland can form. As a consequence of this distribution of patches, the movement of dispersing individuals will have a direction. Individuals dispersing from heathland patches, both large and small, within the central area of the heathlands are likely to encounter heathland in whatever direction they move, but individuals dispersing from the patches at the edges of the heathland will encounter more heathland only by moving in certain directions. What is needed is a statistic which encapsulates the effects of both area and isolation.

To this end, Bullock & Webb (1995a) derived a measure of landscape isolation by taking each of the 4 ha-survey squares used in the Dorset heathland surveys (Webb & Haskins 1980; Webb 1990) and calculating the harmonic mean distance of each square from every other square containing heathland in Dorset using Ranges IV software (Kenward 1990). They plotted a contour map showing the relative isolation of heathland in every part of Dorset heathland landscape. In further analyses, they showed that, for 6 species out of a set of 11 heathland indicator species, the squares occupied by them has a significantly lower harmonic mean distance than those squares from which the species were absent. This analysis has been made simply on the presence of the biotope, but the approach could be refined by using the presence or absence in the survey squares of the habitats of various species. Employing approaches which account for differences of scale at which different species perceive the landscape will be discussed later.

The ease with which spatial analyses of the type outlined can now be carried out, using the software available in geographic information systems, offers considerable opportunities to organize the landscape on ecological principles. We could take the contour map and calculate an optimum solution by adding new patches of heathland at locations which would reduce the isolation of each square as much as possibl. We could predict where to place new patches of heathland either on the basis of the biotope in general or for patches of habitat of particular species. Once we have identified the locations of the new patches, these locations can then be examined to see whether they are suitable for the re-creation of heathland.

Species area vs. landscape approach

In much of the previous discussion we have concentrated on the properties of the patches. Nevertheless, we have recognized that any new patches we make will form part of a population of patches of our reconstructed biotope and there is an implicit recognition of an interaction between the patches. At this point, therefore, it is worth comparing a patch-based approach with a landscape approach in which we see a population of patches distributed within the landscape in a way which supports the interactions between them.

The species-area concept leads us to a static view of the patches in the landscape and focuses our attention on the within-patch dynamics and not on the between-patch dynamics. It emphasizes species-richness, rather than which species, and there is little recognition of the dynamics that exist between the patch and its surroundings. It is perhaps interesting to note that in conservation biology the dominant position of the within-patch approach contrasts with that adopted for the matrix, whereas in agriculture and pest control dynamic interactions are emphasized. The studies on heathland patches and on a wide range of other biotope patches have raised a number of interesting questions of how we should view such a patchwork, and this is particularly relevant if we wish to add new patches.

The way in which we define and identify patches is of particular importance. For the most part, patches have been defined at what is effectively a human scale. Conservation science has interested itself considerably with this approach since it has provided a means by which areas could be chosen to receive protection (May 1975; Margules, Higgs, & Rafe 1982; Reed 1983). It is understandable that we should wish to relate the distribution and abundance of species to the pattern of fragments which exist. This pattern of fragments not only matches the scale at which we see the patches, but is the scale at which they are owned, managed, and conserved. Although this scale may be appropriate for vertebrates and some higher plants, it is not so for invertebrates and many other taxa. It is essential to view the landscape and to delimit patches at a scale relevant to the organisms under consideration. Likewise, while ownership may continue at the scale of the patch, conservation management will need to be on an appropriate scale within the boundaries of the patches.

Landscape ecology considers the operation of ecological processes over larger spatial scales than either those occupied by species populations, communities, or even biotope patches. It considers how these processes operate over an entire landscape or geographical region. Although species populations will occur on the patches, they do not exist in isolation within the respective patches. There is interaction with other, sometimes distant, populations through the movement of individuals in what has become recognized as metapopulation dynamics (Gilpin & Hanski 1991).

Individual species approach

Up to now we have considered creating new patches of heathland at the human scale, and we have a clear description of the size, shape, and distribution of these patches within the landscape. We have also been concerned with the species-richness of these biotope patches. However, it is now widely recognized that even in fragmented landscapes there are important dynamics to be considered in the ecology of individual species. First, we need to develop a picture of the landscape at a scale appropriate to the species under consideration. For an insect, the concept of patch which we have used up to now is not appropriate. The insect will be seeking patches of its habitat and not examples of the biotope as a whole. If our restoration is to be successful from the point of view of this group, we need to ensure that not only are biotope patches created in the right places, but patches of habitat are created at locations which match the dynamics of the individual insect species.

Another example from the Dorset heathlands illustrates the species approach. As a result of the accumulation of long-term datasets (Webb & Haskins (1980; Chapman, Clarke, & Webb 1989: Webb 1990), it is possible to define precisely the habitats of a number of species which are characteristic of these heaths and to estimate how well the heathland biotope provides these habitats. This approach draws a clear distinction between the terms 'habitat' and 'biotope'. The patches of heathland represent the biotope within which are to be found the habitats of heathland species. Without detailed study it is difficult to form a general view of a patch of heathland to gain an impression of the quantity of habitat available for an insect or any other particular species. What we are observing is the biotope – the heathland on a broad scale – the heathland as humans see it. To the conservationist it may be assumed that the presence of heathland is alone sufficient to provide habitat to all species of interest, but this may not be the case.

Webb & Thomas (1994) defined the habitats of heathland species using existing information, and expressed the habitat in terms of the vegetation composition and structure and the topography of the 4 ha recording squares used in the Dorset heathland surveys. They were able to prepare a map for their selected species showing the distribution of the habitat of each one over the entire heathland landscape, and to relate the distribution of the habitat patches to the distribution of the biotope patches.

In this analysis it was shown that the current management of the heathlands failed to provide patches of the habitat at the right time and in the right location to ensure the survival of the selected species. For other species, the frequency of occurrence in both time and space of new patches of habitat was satisfactory. A good example is provided by the Silver-studded blue butterfly (*Plebejus argus*), where on average new habitat occurred within 80 m of existing patches of habitat. This distance was well within the dispersal powers of the butterfly, enabling it to track the occurrence of its habitat. It has to be remembered that heathland is a successional community, and that patches of habitat for the Silver-studded blue persist for no more than 8 years at any one location. After this time, successional changes make the patch uninhabitable. In this instance, the intensity of management of the heathland vegetation to control succession is of importance. It would be perfectly possible to extend the suitability of a patch beyond 8 years by managing it.

Furthermore, we can ask whether a better arrangement of habitat patches is possible within the existing configuration of biotope patches. This aspect is of interest to the conservationist who could, by managing heathland appropriately, create as much of the habitat for the butterfly as possible. Ultimately, the amount of habitat that could be created by suitable management would be restricted by topography, soils, and hydrology. Again, we could construct a map illustrating the maximum amount of habitat possible.

In the case we have been discussing, the total amount of habitat which could be created is constrained by the configuration of the patches of heathland. However, we could create new patches of habitat at locations which were within the likely range of dispersal of the butterfly, or whatever species we chose, and which could be colonized. Again, taking the Silver-studded blue as our example, it has been shown that this butterfly is capable of colonizing patches of its habitat within 1 km of existing patches over the time period for which they remain suitable (<8

years) (Thomas & Harrison 1992). Therefore, if we make new patches of heathland containing the habitat of the Silver-studded blue within 1 km of existing patches of habitat, there will be a strong likelihood that these patches will be colonized. We can combine data on the habitat requirements of a species, on the current distribution of its habitat, and on its dispersal ability to suggest where new patches of habitat are best located – a relatively straightforward procedure using the analytical facilities of geographic information systems. To do this exercise for every species would be difficult. Two approaches are possible: either we could confine the approach to a small number of critical species characteristic of the biotope, or we could select a few species which were representative of a group of species with similar dispersal characteristics and habitat requirements. The most difficult part of this exercise is obtaining detailed knowledge of the dispersal patterns of the target species within the landscape.

By creating new patches of habitat within the dispersal range of a species, I am assuming that the species will establish on the new patches and persist there so long as the patch remains suitable. We can expect that small populations on such patches will become extinct from time to time. In this respect we are expecting the classical dynamics of the metapopulation to operate. That is, there will be a population of populations of a species spread throughout the landscape but not existing permanently at any one location. Recolonization of an area will be from other populations; thus, we need to ensure that the habitat is provided at a suitable frequency and at the correct locations for this metapopulation dynamic to be maintained. Looking at the landscape as a whole, the picture will remain stable and sustainable. An example of this was demonstrated for the Dorset heathlands when Bullock & Webb (1995b) examined the changes to the composition of the heathland vegetation following severe heathland fires in 1976. At this time, 11% of the total area of heathland was burnt and the vegetation on some of the largest patches was completely destroyed. However, when they examined the picture 9 years later and considered the entire landscape of heathland patches, no overall change was found; the pattern of vegetation, although changed from site to site, had remained stable when examined over a large temporal and spatial scale. The establishment of populations on new areas of habitat is distinct from the concept of stepping-stones or corridors, which species may use in a transient way as they move through the landscape. The extent to which this occurs has been difficult to demonstrate (Dawson 1994).

Conclusions

One of the major divisions in ecological science is that separating population and community ecology from ecosystem ecology (Jones & Lawton 1995). The former is concerned primarily with organisms, their various assemblages, and their distribution and abundances. The latter takes a functional view and is concerned with the processes operating in ecosystems. Even within restoration ecology, this divergence of approach is evident.

More recently, ecologists have been interested in scale (Edwards, May, & Webb 1994), and particularly with large spatial and temporal scales. In this they have been assisted by the availability of powerful analytical tools, and in particular the ability to analyse spatially referenced datasets. Whether coincidentally or not, ecological science has broadened from a concern confined to the within-population, the within-community, or the within-patch view of species assemblages to a view which recognizes interactions between these units; the most widely influential model of these is the metapopulation.

From a practical point of view, we are now in a position where, instead of taking more and more land for development and agricultural production, agricultural land is now in surplus. The availability of this land presents us with the opportunity to reconstruct landscapes as functioning units, and to do this according to ecological principles. First, ecological principles and attributes of organisms such as their dispersal abilities and persistence should be used in combination to develop criteria for use in determining where restored areas should be located in relation to existing biotope patches. Secondly, once a location has been selected, the conditions require assessment. Thirdly, there are the practical problems of undertaking the restoration.

This coming together of themes presents an exciting challenge to restoration ecology. We can, as I have outlined, consider where it is best to create new patches of biotopes and new areas of habitat for certain species. We can contemplate this exercise at any scale. We might consider how to reinstate the small-scale pattern required for the functioning of the microarthropod community in tundra soils (Hertzberg, Leinaas, & Ims 1994), or we might consider, as I have done, what is the best distribution of biotope patches within a landscape. In all cases the emphasis is on function, on maintaining an operating system. Restoration ecologists need to employ their considerable technological skills, which are now well established, according to ecological principles. If we succeed in creating functional systems, we shall have gone a long way towards our goal of sustainability.

References

Boecklen, W. J. & Gotelli, N. J (1984). Island biogeographic theory and conservation practice: species-area or specious-area relationships? *Biological Conservation*, 29, 63–80.

Bradshaw, A. D. (1987). Restoration: an acid test for Ecology. In *Restoration Ecology: a Synthetic Approach to Ecological Research*, eds. W. R. Jordan III, M. E. Gilpin, & J. D. Aber. Cambridge University Press.

Bullock, J. M. & Webb, N. R. (1995a). A landscape approach to heathland restoration. In *Restoration Ecology in Europe*, eds. K. M. Urbanska & K. Grodzinska. Zurich: Geobotanical Institute SFIT.

Bullock, J. M. & Webb, N. R. (1995b). Responses to severe fires in heathland mosaics in southern England. *Biological Conservation*, 73, 207–14.

Chapman S. B., Clarke, R. T., & Webb, N. R. (1989). The survey and assessment of heathland in Dorset, England for conservation. *Biological Conservation*, 47, 137–52.

Connor, E. F. & McCoy, E. D. (1979). The statistics and biology of the species-area relationship. *American Naturalist*, 113, 791–833.

Dawson, D. G. (1994). Narrow is the way. In *Fragmentation in Agricultural Landscapes*, ed. J. W. Dover. Preston: International Association for Landscape Ecology (UK).

Diamond, J. M. (1975). Assembly of species communities. In *Ecology and the Evolution of Communities*, eds. M. L. Cody & J. M. Diamond. Harvard, Cambridge, MA: Belknap Press.

Edwards, P. J., May, R. M., & Webb, N. R. eds. (1994). *Large Scale Ecology and Conservation Biology*. Oxford: Blackwell Scientific Publications.

Evans, C., Marrs, R. S., & Welch, G. (1993). The restoration of heathland on arable farmland at Minsmere RSPB Reserve. *RSPB Conservation Review*, 7, 80–4.

Firbank, L. G., Arnold, H. R., Eversham, B. C., Mountford, J. O., Radford, G. L., Telfer, M. G., Treweek, J. R., Webb, N. R., & Wells, T. C. E. (1993). *Managing Set-Aside Land for Wildlife*. ITE Research Publication No. 7. London: HMSO.

Forman, R. T. T. & Godron, M. (1986). *Landscape Ecology*. New York: Wiley.

Fuller, R. M., Groom, G. B., & Jones, A. R. (1994). The land cover map of Great Britain: an automated classification of Landsat Thematic Mapper data. *Photogrammetric Engineering & Remote Sensing*, 60, 533–62.

Game, M. (1980). Best shape for nature reserves. *Nature (London)*, 287, 630–2.

Gilbert, F. S. (1980). The equilibrium theory of island biogeography: Fact or fiction. *Journal of Biogeography*, 7, 209–35.

Gilpin, M. E. & Hanski, I. (1991). *Metapopulation Dynamics: Empirical and Theoretical Investigations*. London: Academic Press.

Gimingham, C. H. (1972). *Ecology of Heathlands*. London: Chapman & Hall.

Gough, M. W. & Marrs, R. H. (1990). A comparison of soil fertility between semi-natural and agricultural plant communities: implications for the creation of species rich grassland on abandoned agricultural land. *Biological Conservation*, 51, 83–96.

Hertzberg, K., Leinaas, H. P., & Ims, R. A. (1994). Patterns of abundance and demography: Collembola in a habitat patch gradient. *Ecography*, 17, 349–59.

Higgs, A. J. (1981). Island biogeography and nature reserve design. *Journal of Biogeography*, 8, 117–24.

Higgs, A. J. & Usher, M. B. (1980). Should nature reserves be large or small? *Nature (London)*, 285, 568–9.

Hinsley, S. A., Bellamy, P. E., & Newton, I. (1995). Habitat fragmentation and the occurrence of breeding birds in small woodlands. *Institute of Terrestrial Ecology Annual Report 1994–95*, pp 33–5.

Hopkins, P. J. & Webb, N. R. (1984). The composition of the beetle and spider faunas on fragmented heathlands. *Journal of Applied Ecology*, 21, 935–46.

Jones, C. G. & Lawton, J. H., eds. (1995). *Linking Species and Ecosystems*. London: Chapman & Hall.

Kenward, R. E (1990). *RANGES IV. Software for Analysing Animal Location Data*. Wareham: Institute of Terrestrial Ecology.

MacArthur, R. H. & Wilson, E. O. (1967). *The Theory of Island Biogeography*. Princeton University Press.

Margules, C. R., Higgs, A. J., & Rafe, R. W. (1982). Modern biogeographic theory: are there lessons for nature reserve design? *Biological Conservation*, 24, 115–28.

Marrs, R. H. (1993). Soil fertility and nature conservation in Europe: Theoretical considerations and practical management solutions. *Advances in Ecological Research*, 24, 242–300.

Marrs, R. H. & Gough, M. W. (1989). Soil fertility: a potential problem for habitat restoration. In *Biological Habitat Restoration*, ed. G. P. Buckley. London: Belhaven Press.

May, R. M. (1975). Patterns of species abundance and diversity. In *Ecology and Evolution of Communities*, eds. M. Cody & J. M. Diamond. Harvard, Cambridge, MA: Belknap Press.

Moore, N. W. (1962). The heaths of Dorset and their conservation. *Journal of Ecology*, 50, 369–91.

Petersen, J. (1977). The effects of cultivation on adjacent heathland vegetation studied in up- and down-wind gradients between a cultivated field and heathland in SW Jutland, Denmark. Unpublished thesis: University of Århus, Denmark (in Danish).

Preston, F. W. (1962). The canonical distribution of commonness and rarity. *Ecology*, 43, 185–215, 410–32.

Putwain, P. D. & Rae, P. A. S. (1988). *Heathland Restoration: A Handbook of Techniques*. Southampton: British Gas (Southern).

Pywell, R. F., Webb, N. R., & Putwain, P. D. (1995). A comparison of techniques for restoring heathland on abandoned farmland. *Journal of Applied Ecology*, 32, 400–11.

Ratcliffe, D. A. (1977). *A Nature Conservation Review*. Cambridge University Press.

Reed, T. M. (1983). The role of species–area relationships in reserve choice: a British Example. *Biological Conservation*, 25, 263–71.

Simberloff, D. S. & Abele, L. G. (1976). Island biogeography theory and conservation practice. *Science*, 191, 285–6.

Smith, R. E. N., Webb, N. R., & Clarke, R. T. (1991). The establishment of heathland on old fields in Dorset, England. *Biological Conservation*, 57, 221–34.

Southwood, T. R. E. (1977). Habitat, the templet for ecological strategies. *Journal of Animal Ecology*, 46, 337–65.

Spellerberg, I. F. (1991). Biogeographical basis for conservation. In *The Scientific Management of Temperate Communities for Conservation*, eds. I. F. Spellerberg, F. B. Goldsmith, & M. G. Morris. Oxford: Blackwell Scientific Publications.

Thomas, C. D. & Harrison, S. (1992). The spatial dynamics of a patchily distributed butterfly species. *Journal of Animal Ecology*, 61, 437–46.

Thomas, J. A. & Morris, M. G. (1994). Patterns, mechanisms and rates of extinction among invertebrates in the United Kingdom. *Philosophical Transactions of the Royal Society London. Series B*. 344, 47–54.

Veitch, N., Webb, N. R., & Wyatt, B. K. (1995). The application of geographic information systems and remotely sensed data to the conservation of heathland fragments. *Biological Conservation*, 72, 91–7.

Watt, T. A. & Buckley, G. P. (1994). *Hedgerow Management and Nature Conservation*. Wye: Wye College Press.

Webb, N. R. (1986). *Heathlands*. London: Collins.

Webb, N. R. (1989). Studies on the invertebrate fauna of fragmented heathland in Dorset, UK, and the implications for conservation. *Biological Conservation*, 47, 153–65.

Webb, N. R. (1990). Changes on the heathlands of Dorset, England, between 1978 and 1987. *Biological Conservation*, 51, 273–86.

Webb, N. R. (1994). The habitat, the biotope and the landscape. In *Fragmentation in Agricultural Landscapes*, ed. J. W. Dover. Preston: International Association for Landscape Ecology (UK).

Webb, N. R., Clarke, R. T., & Nicholas J. T. (1984). Invertebrate diversity on fragmented *Calluna*-heathland: effects of surrounding vegetation. *Journal of Biogeography*, 11, 41–6.

Webb, N. R. & Haskins, L. E. (1980). An ecological survey of heathlands in the Poole Basin, Dorset, England in 1978. *Biological Conservation*, 17, 281–96.

Webb, N. R. & Hopkins, P. J. (1984). Invertebrate diversity on fragmented *Calluna*-heathlands. *Journal of Applied Ecology*, 21, 921–33.

Webb, N. R. & Thomas, J. A. (1994). Conserving insect habitats in heathland biotopes: a question of scale. In *Large Scale Ecology and Conservation biology*, eds. P. J. Edwards, R. M. May, & N. R. Webb. Oxford: Blackwell Scientific Publications.

Webb, N. R., Veitch, N., & Pywell, R. F. (1995). Increasing the extent of heathland in southern England. In *Restoration Ecology in Europe*, eds. K. M. Urbanska & K. Grodzinska. Zurich: Geobotanical Institute sfit.

Webb, N. R. & Vermaat, A. H. (1990). Changes in vegetational diversity on remnant heathland fragments. *Biological Conservation*, 53, 253–64.

Whittaker, R. H., Levin, S. A., & Root, R. B. (1973). Niche, habitat and ecotope. *American Naturalist*, 107, 321–38.

Williamson, M. (1981). *Island Populations*. Oxford University Press.

Part III

The implementation and assessment of restoration schemes

9

Restoring alpine ecosystems in the western United States: environmental constraints, disturbance characteristics, and restoration success

JEANNE C. CHAMBERS

Introduction

In the United States, alpine ecosystems constitute vital resources. Although they comprise only about 8% of the total US land area, they serve as critical watersheds for urban and agricultural centres and provide important wildlife habitat. In addition, they are valued for their abundant and diverse mineral resources, for livestock forage, and as recreational areas. With expanding human populations, the many diverse resources that these ecosystems support are being increasingly exploited. Disturbance is common and varied, ranging from recreational trails to mine sites characterized by acid soils with high concentrations of heavy metals. As early as 1978 it was estimated that 11.8% of the tundra ecosystems in the western US had received some type of human-mediated disturbance (Brown, Johnston, & Van Cleve 1978). The limited extent and importance of these ecosystems dictate that resource use or extraction be consistent with maintaining or restoring ecosystem integrity.

Alpine ecosystems have been described as being among the most difficult to restore following disturbance (Macyk in press). They are characterized by extreme and variable temperature and precipitation (MacMahon 1981) and the unpredictable nature of the environment increases the severity of disturbances. Only a limited suite of species are adapted to survive and reproduce in alpine ecosystems, and both naturally colonizing species and species selected for restoration must be members of that small pool. Seed production is highly variable between years, making it difficult to acquire adequate seeds for even a limited number of adapted species (Chambers 1989). Seedling establishment depends on obtaining the proper set of environmental conditions and is often episodic (Roach & Marchand 1984; Chambers, MacMahon, & Brown 1990). Rates of ecosystem development

161

are related to disturbance severity and are often low following severe disturbance.

Because of the climatic and biotic limitations, alpine areas are seldom capable of supporting urban populations or agronomic activities other than livestock grazing, and most non-extractive land uses depend on the maintenance of stable native ecosystems. In these ecosystems, the only restoration goal that makes ecological sense is the re-establishment of self-sustaining ecosystems with structure and function similar to predisturbance ecosystems or undisturbed native ecosystems with like environmental constraints. An important assumption is that, if ecosystem structure and function can be restored, other restoration goals such as environmental protection from erosion and pollution and hydrologic balance will also have been obtained. In the United States, alpine restoration methods have been developed over about the past 25 years in response to increased public concern about maintaining or restoring ecosystem integrity and stricter environmental laws. Early approaches to achieving functioning ecosystems were often based on the assumption that, once the soil surface had been stabilized and a protective vegetation cover had been established, natural successional processes would result in structure and function similar to undisturbed native ecosystems. It has become increasingly clear that the extreme environment, the disturbance characteristics, and restoration techniques have lasting effects on ecosystem structure and function and, thus, on restoration success (e.g., Brown, Johnston, & Chambers, 1984; Cargill & Chapin, 1987; Chambers, Brown, & Johnston 1987b; Densmore 1994).

This chapter reviews available information on the effects of the extreme environment and disturbance on alpine ecosystems and examines the implications for restoration. It also summarizes information on ecosystem development following restoration. Many of the examples provided stem from research conducted by my colleagues and myself in the Beartooth Mountains of Montana over the past 15 years. Details of the Beartooth study sites are in Chambers *et al.* 1987b and Chambers *et al.* 1990. Other reviews of alpine restoration include specific restoration techniques and are found in Brown *et al.* (1978), Brown & Johnston (1979); Ferchau (1988); Brown & Chambers (1989); and Macyk (in press).

The alpine environment

In alpine ecosystems, the physical environment compounds the effects of disturbance and increases the difficulty of restoration. The alpine climate imposes low heat budgets and temperatures may fall below 0 °C at any point during growing seasons that last only 60–90 days. Conversely, high-intensity solar radiation is common in alpine areas. Values recorded in July range from $21.2\,MJ\,m^{-2}\,d^{-1}$ in the Olympic Mountains, Washington (1960 m), to $28.3\,MJ\,m^{-2}\,d^{-1}$ in the Sierra Nevada Range (3540 m) (Bliss 1985). High and persistent winds are common in alpine environments, although wind speeds are spatially and temporally variable with summer wind speeds at 40 to 60 cm ranging from $1–2\,m\,s^{-1}$ in meadows but from $3–5\,m\,s^{-1}$ on ridges (Bliss 1985). On exposed sites, winds can be high enough to induce a 3–6 °C cooling on plant surfaces (Bell & Bliss 1979). Precipitation during the growing season is highly variable, increasing from western to eastern mountain ranges. July and August values range from 5.5 cm (1972 m) in the Olympic Mountains to 10.6 cm (3350 m) in the Medicine Bow Mountains, Wyoming (Bliss 1985).

Sharp topographic gradients in mid-latitude alpine areas interact with insolation, wind, and precipitation to produce abrupt environmental changes that influence soil development and plant species distributions (Billings 1988; Grabherr *et al.* 1995). Insolation increases with altitude under clear skies, but is highly dependent on aspect in mountainous terrain. In the Colorado alpine, south- and east-facing slopes on fellfield sites received respectively 18 and 14% more net radiation than a north-facing slope during clear summer days (Isard 1986). Also, evapotranspiration during dry periods was 40% lower on north-facing slopes than on south-facing slopes. Strong winter winds typically redistribute freshly fallen snow, resulting in deep, long-lasting snowfields on leeward slopes while leaving adjacent windward slopes snow free. These patterns significantly influence plant–soil water relations. Differences in soil moisture between dry, windswept knolls and topographic depressions on a single ridge are often larger than the variation among level alpine areas along the latitudinal gradient from the equator to the poles (Billings 1974). Snowbanks protect plants from desiccation and winter temperatures, but they shorten the effective growing season. Meltwater from snowbanks increases available soil water directly downslope. Differences in snow cover depth between windward and leeward slopes determine species distributions, influencing the locations of dry fellfield, dry meadow, moist meadow, and snowbed vegetation (May & Webber, 1982; Stanton, Rejmanek, & Galen 1994).

Alpine soils are generally young, heterogeneous and weakly developed. Cold soil temperatures reduce chemical reactions and biotic activity that result in soil genesis, and soil depths to fractured rock or bedrock range from a few centimeters to 1 m. Plant roots are concentrated in the top 5 to 25 cm (Ratcliffe & Turkington 1987), but can extend into the fractured rock zone (Eddleman & Ward 1984). Exposed ridges and slopes that are snow-free in winter typically have thin soils and surface horizons that are formed by the physical mixing of mineral and organic material (Eddleman & Ward 1984; Macyk, in press). They are often coarse-textured and well-drained, and low in organic matter, nutrients, and cation exchange capacities. In contrast, fellfields and dry meadows on well-drained slopes accumulate large amounts of organic matter in surface soils and have correspondingly high cation exchange capacities (Ratcliffe & Turkington 1987). Areas with maximum snow accumulation and the longest duration of snowbanks have saturated soils during the period of snow melt. Soils exhibit considerable mixing due to soil movement and are coarse-textured and low in organic matter (Eddleman & Ward 1984). Soils in areas of ponded run-off or groundwater discharge are frequently highly organic and peaty with mottled subsoils and dense silty layers deeper in the profile (Retzer 1974).

Nutrient availability in alpine soils is spatially and temporally variable and both nitrogen (NH_4 and NO_3) and phosphorus (PO_4) tend to be low (Chambers *et al.* 1987b; Ratcliffe & Turkington 1987). Cold soil temperatures and low rates of decomposition result in accumulation of organic matter. In fellfields and meadow surface soils, organic carbon ranges from 5 to 15% in surface soils, while total nitrogen on the same soils ranges from 0.23 to 1.1% (Nimlos & McConnell 1965; Eddleman & Ward 1984; Chambers *et al.* 1987b; Ratcliffe & Turkington 1987). Resulting C:N ratios range from 14 to 22. Incomplete oxidation of organic matter and accumulation of acidic end-products of microbial metabolism result in increased soil acidity. Because nitrification is low in alpine ecosystems, ammonium is the dominant form of inorganic nitrogen. Changes in nitrogen concentrations are influenced by soil moisture, temperature, microbial activity, and plant physiological responses (Everett *et al.* 1981). Litter decomposition is related to soil moisture and organic matter gradients with higher decomposition and nitrogen release occurring on sites with intermediate levels of snowpack than on sites with higher or lower levels (O'Lear & Seastedt 1994).

Environmental effects on species life histories and successional processes

The extreme environmental conditions have had a strong evolutionary influence on species life histories and physiological responses (Billings 1988; Körner 1995) and, consequently, on alpine successional processes. Growth rates of tundra species can be as high as those of temperate plants during the summer (Chapin 1987), but the short growing seasons restrict total production. Thus, leaf and flower development are often prolonged over several growing seasons (Körner & Larcher 1988). The result is that few species are adapted to both survive and reproduce in the extreme alpine environment. Floras are small with only 200 to 600 species occurring within the alpine zone on entire mountain ranges (Bliss 1962). Dominant life forms include low-growing, perennial cushion and rosette plants, forbs, graminoids, and deciduous and evergreen shrubs. Species-richness and the number of viable life forms decrease with increasing elevation (Grabherr *et al.* 1995). Annuals are rare, as few species are capable of completing the whole life cycle in one year. Species introduced from lower elevations are seldom capable of surviving more than a few years (Cargill & Chapin 1987). Alpine restoration species must necessarily be members of the small suite of species adapted to survive and reproduce in the extreme environment.

Because of the small floras and low stature of the plants, succession is less apparent in alpine ecosystems than in more temperate areas (Chambers, MacMahon, & Wade 1992). In alpine areas with moderate environmental regimes, distinct changes in species composition occur during succession. Depending on site characteristics and propagule availability, early seral dominants are often members of the Poaceae or Asteraceae, although species belonging to several plant families appear in early seral stages (Webber & Ives 1978; Chambers, Brown, & Johnston 1984). Small-scale disturbances where surface soils are left in place are often colonized by short-lived forbs (Freedman *et al.* 1982; Chambers 1993). On mineral soils low in nitrogen, such as those exposed by retreating snowbanks or eroded by wind, species with nitrogen-fixing symbionts are frequent colonizers (e.g., Walker 1989; Chapin *et al.* 1995). On environmentally extreme sites in general, early colonizers can facilitate establishment of other species by providing favourable micro-environments (Urbanska this volume). Under the most extreme conditions, few species can either colonize or persist. In most cases, early establishing species are members of the late seral community. Restoration implications are that, if species from a particular environmental regime can be established following disturbance, the site has the potential to rather quickly resemble the late seral community (Chambers *et al.* 1992).

Characteristics of alpine disturbances

The characteristics of a disturbance determine species establishment processes, affect the rate and trajectory of succession, and influence the

Table 9.1. *Generalized properties of alpine disturbances with topsoils in place, topsoils removed, or soils altered that influence the selection of restoration methods*

Property	Topsoils		Topsoils removed	Soils altered
	Organic	Mineral		
Topography	Slight-Mod	Mod-Ext	Mod-EWxt	Slight-Ext
Soil nutrient retention and cycling capacity	High	Int-Low	Low	Low
Propagule pool	High	High-Low	Absent	Absent
Vegetation production potential	High	Int-Low	Low	Low
Recovery rate	Rapid	Int-Slow	Slow	Slow

choice of restoration methods (MacMahon & Jordan 1994). One of the most important aspects of a disturbance is severity in relationship to the soil and physical environment (Körner 1995; Bradshaw this volume). Although disturbance characteristics represent a continuum, different types of disturbances with increasing severity can be recognized (Chapin 1983). In alpine ecosystems, these include topsoils developed and in place, topsoils poorly-developed but in place, topsoils removed, and soils altered. Generalized properties of disturbance characteristics that influence restoration approaches are in Table 9.1. The least severe are those in which topsoils are not removed even though vegetation has been removed or otherwise affected. These include areas affected by livestock grazing, camping, or trails that exhibit changes in species composition, decreased vegetation cover, or increased soil erosion (Willard & Marr 1970; Bell & Bliss 1973; Lent & Klein 1988). Organic topsoils usually have relatively high soil-water and nutrient retention capacities and contain propagules from the native community. Less-intensive restoration inputs are required and recovery processes often resemble secondary succession (Cargill & Chapin 1987). More severe are disturbances that occur on areas without well-developed topsoils, such as ridges or scree slopes, or that remove topsoils. These soils often have lower water and nutrient retention capacities and variable propagule pools. Amelioration of the extreme physical environment and plant establishment are primary restoration concerns. Disturbances in which topsoils are removed often result from roads and mining activities and are characterized by soils or subsoils that are poorly developed, low in nutrients, and devoid of propagules. Without topsoils, successful restoration often requires improvement of soil physical or chemical properties, and recovery can be a slow process. The most severely disturbed areas are those with altered soils or spoils resulting from mining activities that expose pyritic materials and initiate a cycle of sulphide oxidation that results in low soil pH and increased availability of heavy metals. Restoration of these areas focuses on environmental protection and surface stabilization (Brown & Johnston 1979).

Restoration of alpine disturbances

Restoration goals

Restoration goals influence both restoration approaches and outcomes. While the longer-term goal of alpine restoration is re-establishment of ecosystems with structure and function similar to predisturbed or undisturbed systems, other more immediate objectives influence restoration approaches. On severely disturbed sites with erosive or altered soils or spoils with high potentials for soil loss or acid generation, rapid surface stabilization is often an important restoration goal (Macyk in press). An implied goal, especially when surface stabilization is important, is often high vegetation production. Sites with poorly developed topsoils are not capable of supporting high vegetation production without repeated nutrient inputs and lower productivity is an acceptable outcome.

Soil considerations

Following removal of vegetation, soil characteristics as influenced by geology and topography are among the most important indicators of recovery potential. Sites with well-developed topsoils, such as meadows, often have highly organic, dark-coloured soils. Sites that lack topsoils, such as ridges, or that have had the topsoils removed are characterized by mineral soils or subsoils. Dark coloured organic soils have lower thermal conductivities, heat capacities, thermal diffusivities, and thermal contact coefficients than lighter-coloured mineral soils (Cochran 1969). On a 3200 m elevation site on the Beartooth Plateau, Montana, exposed organic soils in the alpine zone exhibited temperatures in excess of 40 °C and had higher surface and near-surface soil temperatures than adjacent sites with intact vegetation or exposed mineral soils. Air temperature plus soil temperature is highly related to shoot and root production of alpine species

(Chambers *et al.* 1990). Disturbance affects the plant environment on organic soils through large diurnal fluctuations in soil surface temperatures and generally higher soil temperatures at shallow depths during periods of moderate-to-high solar radiation. Exposed mineral soils have smaller daily temperature fluctuations and cooler temperatures during periods of high insolation.

The effects of disturbance on available soil water depend on topography and soil characteristics. Soil water potentials low enough to induce plant water deficits occur during August and September on exposed alpine areas, such as fellfields and ridges (Johnson & Caldwell 1975), but wet meadow sites are often saturated throughout the growing season (Taylor & Seastedt 1994). In general, organic soils and soils with higher percentages of soil fines have higher water-holding capacities than mineral soils. Vegetation removal greatly reduces transpiration while evaporation from the soil surface is increased to a lesser degree (e.g., Vitousek & Walker 1987). This results in drier surface soils but greater water availability below the soil surface on disturbed sites. Vegetated alpine communities can have significantly lower soil water potentials than adjacent disturbed areas during periods of low precipitation (Chambers *et al.* 1990). Further, differences between vegetated and disturbed communities on organic soils can exceed those between mineral and organic soils.

Well-developed organic soils typically have higher cation exchange capacities and greater nutrient pools and cycling capacities than mineral soils or subsoils. In contrast, mineral soils are characterized by high porosities, low soil organic matter and cation exchange capacities, and, thus, low nutrient retention. Following disturbance of organic soils, higher rates of mineralization and decomposition can further increase nutrient availability (Vitousek & Walker 1987). On the Beartooth Plateau, disturbed organic soils had levels of available nitrogen that were significantly higher than on adjacent undisturbed areas or on nearby fertilized or not fertilized mineral soils (Table 9.2). Phosphorus was also higher on disturbed organic soils than on adjacent undisturbed sites or mineral soils (Table 9.2). On organic soils, however, nutrient losses can occur before biomass uptake increases to where nutrients are utilized at the rate supplied by mineralization.

The soil amendments used depend on the effects of disturbance on soil characteristics and on restoration goals. Well-developed organic topsoils usually have the necessary properties to support soil surface stabilization through the rapid development of a vegetation cover and long-term vegetative productivity. Although fertilizers can increase plant biomass,

Table 9.2. *Soil properties of disturbed areas with organic or mineral soils on the Beartooth Plateau, Montana*

On the mineral soils the effects of N and P fertilization were evaluated, while on organic soils the effects of vegetation clearing were measured. Soils were sampled in August, 2 years after clearing of organic soils and fertilization of mineral soils. Values are mean ± S.E. (Chambers *et al.* 1990).

	Mineral Soils		Organic Soils	
Property	Fertilized	Not fertilized	Cleared	Not cleared
Organic matter (%)	0.61 ± 0.08	0.65 ± 0.13	10.2 ± 0.25	10.4 ± 0.58
Total nitrogen (%)	0.02 ± 0.08	0.02 ± 0.003	0.56 ± 0.04	0.50 ± 0.06
NO_3 (mg/kg)	4.30 ± 0.42	2.50 ± 0.34	30.33 ± 4.67	6.17 ± 0.43
NH_4 (mg/kg)	2.67 ± 0.48	1.50 ± 0.32	5.07 ± 0.32	4.73 ± 0.35
P (mg/kg)	37.50 ± 3.99	7.00 ± 0.45	17.3 ± 1.67	10.6 ± 0.47
K (mg/kg)	62.17 ± 0.70	66.67 ± 4.87	133.83 ± 6.94	164.0 ± 13.8
pH	6.18 ± 0.09	6.35 ± 0.08	5.38 ± 0.04	5.60 ± 0.13
CEC (umol/kg)	7.48 ± 0.20	7.21 ± 0.14	14.83 ± 0.40	14.28 ± 0.69

they are seldom necessary. On the Beartooth Plateau, higher seedling growth occurred on organic topsoils than on mineral soils (Chambers *et al.* 1990). In addition, organic topsoils had significantly higher long-term seedling survival (Figure 9.1).

In most cases, replacement of topsoils, even poorly developed topsoils or topsoils mixed with subsurface soils provide the best plant growing medium (Densmore 1994). On those sites with topsoils removed, the restoration goals influence the choice of soil amendments. If the goal of restoration is an ecosystem with vegetation production similar to native ecosystems with organic topsoils, amendments such as organic matter that improve soil nutrient and water retention are necessary. Soil organic matter is one of the slowest components to recover following disturbance (Chambers, Brown, & Williams 1994; Burke, Lavenroth, & Coffin 1995). Organic matter in the form of straw, peat, or manure improves soil structure by decreasing bulk densities, and increases nutrient retention through higher cation exchange capacities. Organic matter can provide a continuous, though limited, supply of plant nutrients, but if organic matter with high C:N ratios are used, application of nitrogen fertilizer is necessary to facilitate microbial decomposition and increase nitrogen availability to plants.

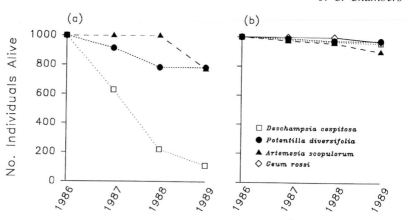

Figure 9.1. Four-year seedling survival of species with varying life histories that emerged in 1986 on disturbed mineral (a) or organic (b) soils on the Beartooth Plateau, Montana (Chambers 1995a and Chambers unpublished data).

If the goal of restoring mineral soils is rapid stabilization of surface soils, fertilizers can be used to increase plant establishment and growth. In the Beartooth Plateau study, fertilization of mineral soils with low levels of N and P resulted in significantly higher seedling weights, and increased long-term (5 yr) seedling survival (Figure 9.2). Fertilization also resulted in earlier and higher reproduction (Chambers, unpublished data). However, survival was still higher on disturbed areas with organic topsoils (Figure 9.1). In the absence of topsoil or organic matter additions higher nutrient levels, especially nitrogen, can be maintained only by repeated fertilization. On the Beartooth Plateau, mineral soils were fertilized with 8.2 and 15.6 g m^{-2} (80 and 150 lbs ac^{-1}) of N and P, respectively, and compared to plots that were not fertilized. Two years after fertilization, levels of available N and P were higher in fertilized than control plots, but only half the amount of P and less than a tenth the amount of N originally applied remained in the soil (Table 9.2). Nitrogen is highly mobile in mineral soils and fertilization results in a short-term nitrogen pulse (Marschner 1986). Phosphate is less mobile in soils and exhibits higher levels of retention. Long-term fertilization can be used to maintain higher levels of soil nitrogen (Macyk in press), but this approach is seldom economically feasible and can result in leaching and nutrification of ponds or streams. Slow-release nitrogen fertilizer applied at the time of restoration may be a viable option for increasing plant establishment. When the soil surface is relatively stable and lower vegetation productivity is an acceptable restora-

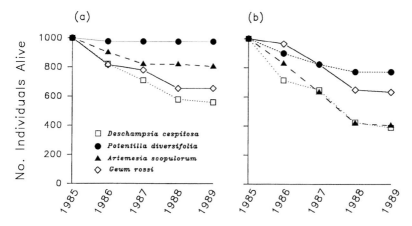

Figure 9.2. Five-year seedling survival of species with varying life histories that emerged in 1985 on mineral soils and that were either fertilized (a) or not fertilized (b) on the Beartooth Plateau, Montana (Chambers 1995a and Chambers unpublished data).

tion goal, minimal soil amendments are necessary. Lower vegetation productivity is a logical goal on sites with poorly developed and coarse-textured soils that exhibit little erosion, and for alpine communities that have inherently low vegetation production.

Selection of restoration species

Selection of species for restoration depends on the environmental characteristics of the disturbed site, species life-history characteristics, and restoration goals. Examining the species composition of old disturbances with similar environmental characteristics provides a direct indication of species adaptability (Chambers *et al.* 1984; Brown & Chambers 1989). Several alpine species have broad ecological amplitudes and colonize various types of disturbances. Some of these species, primarily graminoids, have been widely used in alpine restoration. They produce high numbers of easily harvested seeds during favourable years (Chambers 1989) and readily establish over a range of disturbance characteristics. These species respond favourably to high levels of nutrients and, given favourable nutrient regimes, exhibit high relative growth rates (Chambers *et al.* 1990). They are capable of rapidly producing a dense, vegetation cover that stabilizes the soil surface (Brown & Chambers 1989). The disadvantages are that dense stands can preclude establishment of later seral species, decrease species diversity, and retard succession (Brown *et al.* 1984). Further, if nutrient levels drop, as occurs when fertilization is discontinued, plant densities and productivity decline dramatically. Selecting species for restoration that exhibit a variety of life histories and physiological traits can increase species diversity and accelerate succession. Further, restoration with a variety of species can help to insure community stability (*sensu* Nilsson & Grelsson 1995) in response to disturbances such as changes in climate or nutrient regimes, herbivory, or small-scale soil disturbance.

   Species with low nutrient requirements or that have nitrogen-fixing symbionts provide a viable option for revegetating sites that lack well-developed topsoils. In temperate areas, species with low nutrient requirements have been used to successfully revegetate infertile soils, including areas lacking topsoil and mine spoils (Chapin 1983). Also, plants with symbiotic nitrogen-fixing organisms have been used to increase nitrogen capital on disturbed sites (Jeffries, Wilson, & Bradshaw 1981). In alpine areas, species exhibiting different life histories have been successfully established on disturbed sites from seed (Brown & Chambers 1989; Chambers *et al.* 1990). Legumes with nitrogen-fixing symbionts exist, such as species of *Lupinus, Astragalus*, and *Trifolium* (Johnson & Rumbaugh 1986), but little is known about their establishment ecology.

Plant materials considerations

Following disturbance, initial species establishment depends on seeds and other plant propagules that persist in topsoils or that can disperse to the site. Alpine restorationists can take advantage of residual propagule pools and natural dispersal, but can also add additional propagules to the site in the form of seeds, plants, or sod.

   On disturbed sites where topsoils are either left in place or returned, seed banks and vegetative propagules such as roots, rhizomes, and corms have the potential to serve as important sources of plant materials. Alpine seed bank densities and species composition vary according to topographic location, moisture regime, and composition of the above-ground vegetation (McGraw & Vavrek 1989; Chambers 1995a). Densities range from 0 to 3957 seeds m^{-2} and species composition tends to resemble the above-ground vegetation. Seed banks occur in a wide variety of community types and can be well developed within 30 years after a severe disturbance. Following disturbance, regeneration from vegetative propagules can equal or exceed that from seeds (Chambers *et al.* 1992). However, the ability of vegetative propagules to survive repeated disturbance or lengthy storage is less than that of many seeds.

Seed production varies among both years and sites, influencing plant establishment processes and restoration activities. Floral development may be initiated one or even two seasons prior to flowering, and seed production depends on the current and previous growing seasons (Billings 1974). Because of its dependence on environmental conditions, seed production is temporally and spatially variable. Differences in seed viability exist among years for individual species and among species within a given year (Chambers 1989). Seed rain at the community level also varies among years. Mean seed rain densities for a late seral *Geum*-turf area dominated by a clonal rosette species with low seed production (*Geum rossii*) ranged from 3375 to 6179 filled seeds m^{-2} over a 3-year period (Chambers 1993).

Variable seed production and the dependence on native species has resulted in limited commercial availability of alpine seed. Seed collection of native species is often limited to good seed production years. More than one year may be required to collect sufficient seed of the species required for a given restoration project. Seed-increase programmes at the Environmental Plant Center (EPC) at Meeker, Colorado and the Vegetation Branch of the Alberta Environmental Centre (AEC) are increasing the number of species available, but the focus has been primarily on grasses. In recent years, independent seed collectors have increased native seed availability of graminoids and forbs.

Valuable sources of plant materials other than seeds include sod and individual plants. Salvaging and replacing sod or transplanting sod from donor areas allows plants to quickly establish in the short alpine growing season and has been used for reclaiming pipelines, mined sites, and hiking trails (Marr, Buckner, & Johnson 1974; Brown *et al.* 1978; Walker, Sadasivaiah, & Weijer 1977). Successful establishment of sod requires handling techniques designed to maintain a favourable moisture status. Transplanting of individual species is an effective technique on sites with physical conditions or environmental conditions that limit establishment from seed (May, Webber, & May 1982; Urbanska 1986). Survival is usually high, although species with fibrous roots exhibit higher establishment than species with rhizomes or corms.

Plant establishment processes and revegetation

Disturbance characteristics and restoration methodologies influence all aspects of species establishment from seed entrapment and retention, to seed viability and germination, and, finally, to seedling emergence, growth, and survival (see Urbanska this volume). In the severe alpine environment, physical processes significantly influence seed and seedling fates. Following disturbance, seeds that are sown or naturally deposited on wind-exposed sites are moved over the soil surface until some type of surface depression or barrier traps them in that location. Seed entrapment and retention are determined by physical relationships between soil surface characteristics and seed morphological attributes (Chambers, MacMahon, & Haefner 1991; Chambers 1995b). Seed attributes, including size and the presence or absence of specialized appendages or seed coats affect both rates of seed movement and the distances moved (Chambers 1995b). Small seeds and seeds with adhesive seed coats are more likely to be trapped in place than large seeds, and show greater vertical movement through the soil column (Figure 9.3). In contrast, movement of large seeds is more highly dependent on soil surface properties. Thus, soil surface characteristics are important determinants of species establishment patterns during both natural colonization and restoration. Increasing soil surface roughness or using a protective organic mulch can result in higher seed retention and seedling establishment.

Seed germination and seedling emergence requirements vary among species and influence seeding approaches. Small seeds have lower nutrient reserves that restrict the depth from which emergence can occur and should be planted close to the soil surface. In contrast, larger seeds may desiccate during germination or seedling emergence if planted too close to the soil surface. Germination of many tundra species, but especially forbs and some *Carex* species, is enhanced by exposure to light (Amen 1966; Chambers, MacMahon, & Brown 1987a; Haggas, Brown, & Johnston 1987). This indicates that sowing species with a light requirement for germination close to the soil surface can maximize germination. In laboratory experiments, seeds of tundra species tend to exhibit high temperature optima for germination (Amen 1966). In the field, however, cold, wet stratification results in lower temperature optima for germination (Reynolds 1984). Stratification can increase the rate of germination of alpine species (Chambers *et al.* 1987a) and can result in germination at temperatures from 0 to 10 °C for Rocky Mountain alpine annuals (Reynolds 1984) and perennials (Chambers *et al.* 1987a). Seeding in the autumn ensures that seeds will receive a wet, cold stratification period and allows seedlings to take advantage of higher moisture during the spring and early summer in areas with limited growing season precipitation.

Several factors influence the seedling environment and affect seedling

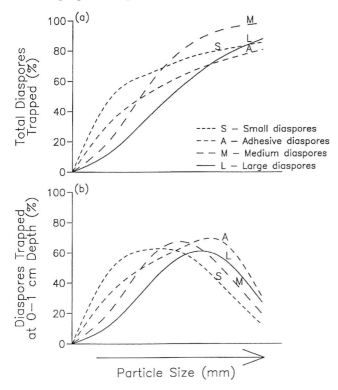

Figure 9.3. Generalized models of how small (S), medium-sized (M), large (L), and adhesive (A) seeds are trapped in soils over a range of increasing particle sizes in the entire soil column (a) and at the depth at which germination and emergence are likely to occur (0–1 cm) (b). Seeds shown in (a) do not leave the soil surface by horizontal processes nor the 0–1 cm depth by vertical processes. Curves were derived from Weibull probability distributions (Chambers *et al.* 1991).

emergence, growth, and survival. In alpine ecosystems, slow seedling growth (Bell & Bliss 1980), needle ice formation (Brink *et al.* 1967; Roach & Marchand 1984), and soil drought (Bonde 1968; Bell & Bliss 1980) contribute to low seedling survival. Because of the importance of air and soil temperatures on seedling growth and survival, disturbance characteristics have a significant effect on plant establishment. Although natural seedling establishment is often described as episodic, with the proper restoration techniques and species selection plants can be routinely established from seed (Brown & Chambers 1989; Chambers *et al.* 1990). The effects of disturbance characteristics on soil temperatures and nutrient and water retention capacities and, thus, seedling establishment were

discussed earlier. Regardless of disturbance characteristics, soil temperatures and water potentials can be ameliorated during the restoration
process by using an organic mulch. Similar to naturally occurring plant
litter, organic mulches have lower thermal conductivities, heat capacities,
and thermal diffusivities than underlying soils resulting in greater diurnal
fluctuations in surface temperatures (Cochran 1969). Mulches can decrease
soil water loss by decreasing surface evaporation and reduce the occurrence
of needle ice. On the Beartooth Plateau, seedling emergence was higher on
mulched plots than on plots that were not mulched. In these windy
environments surface mulches both ameliorate the surface environment
and hold surface-sown seeds in place. Mulches themselves must be held in
place by tackifiers or netting.

Ecosystem development and restoration success

Restoration success can be evaluated by examining the longer-term effects
of disturbance characteristics and restoration treatments on ecosystem
development. Because the ultimate goal of restoration is re-establishment
of self-sustaining ecosystems with structure and function similar to native
ecosystems with similar environments, comparisons of undisturbed native
ecosystems and restored ecosystems can be used to evaluate restoration
success. The available data on restoration success reported here is from
subalpine to low alpine sites and may not be representative of the more
extreme alpine sites.

As expected, the initial characteristics of the disturbance, the types of soil
amendments, and the species that are established have lasting effects on
rates and trajectories of succession, and, thus, restoration success. Properties of soils that are conducive to nutrient retention and the development of
active nutrient cycles, such as fine soil textures, total nitrogen, organic
matter, and water retention capacity, were good predictors of the rate and
pattern of succession on treeline sites following placer mining in Alaska
(Densmore 1994). Given favourable environmental conditions and organic
soils in tussock tundra, vegetation cover and biomass can quickly (within
10 yr) equal or exceed that of adjacent undisturbed areas (Chapin & Chapin
1980). Further, native early seral species will dominate the site in the
absence of seeding if the propagule pool is still intact or if these species can
disperse to the site (Chapin & Chapin 1980; Cargill & Chapin 1987;
Densmore 1994). Ecosystem response appears to be proportionate to the
amount of topsoil that is replaced following disturbance. On the placer
mined site in Alaska, sites where the topsoils were respread over regraded

soils recovered more rapidly than sites amended with a small amount of topsoil. The slowest to recover were sites with mineral spoils that lacked topsoils (Densmore 1994). On the Beartooth Plateau site, vegetation cover was only 25% on the mineral soils of a gravel borrow area 35 years after disturbance (Chambers 1993).

An early assumption in the restoration of mineral soils or soils lacking topsoils was that high densities of graminoids would increase the rate of organic matter accumulation and accelerate natural successional processes. Graminoids have substantial rates of tissue turnover and high litter quality that can enhance nutrient cycling (Hobbie 1995). Although dense stands of graminoids can be established with heavy or repeated applications of inorganic nutrients, this approach has little effect on soil organic matter or total nitrogen and, thus, nitrogen capital. In the Beartooth Mountains, vegetation and soil properties of severely disturbed alpine mine sites at treeline that had been revegetated 8 years earlier and fertilized for 4 consecutive years following revegetation were compared to naturally revegetated and undisturbed fellfield sites (Chambers *et al.* 1987b). Biomass of revegetated areas exceeded that of reference areas, but vegetation cover was similar to that of the reference areas. The revegetated and fertilized site had significantly higher levels of P and K than either the naturally revegetated or reference fellfield sites, but levels of organic matter and total nitrogen were two times higher on reference sites than on revegetated or naturally revegetated sites (Figure 9.4). Both NO_3 and NH_4 were higher on reference than on revegetated areas or naturally revegetated areas during the growing season. Low levels of organic matter or total nitrogen were also found in comparisons of native reference areas with 0–6-yr-old revegetated coal mine spoil on subalpine sites in the Canadian Rockies (Fyles, Fyles, & Bell 1985) and with the 5-yr-old placer mine spoil in Alaska (Densmore 1994).

Few data are available on the development of the soil microbial community or nutrient cycles on restored alpine areas. On the revegetated coal mine spoil in the Canadian Rockies, detritus biomass, soil CO_2 evolution in both field and laboratory and rate of cellulose decomposition increased with site age, indicating recovering systems (Fyles *et al.* 1985). In the Beartooth Mountains, total mycorrhizal spore densities and percentage infection for key plant species was as high on 3-yr-old revegetated sites as on native reference areas (Allen *et al.* 1987). However, only one mycorrhizal species occurred on the revegetated areas, while 11 different mycorrhizal species were found on the reference areas. It was uncertain whether the low species diversity on the revegetated area was due to limited

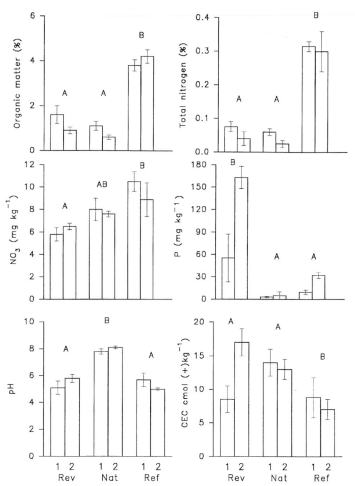

Figure 9.4. Major chemical properties of soils collected from seeded revegetated (Rev) and natural revegetated (Nat) sites on mine spoil and from adjacent reference (Ref) sites on the Glengary and McLaren mines in southern Montana. Values are means ± SE. Different letters indicate significant differences among site types (Fisher's Protected LSD; P < 0.05; Chambers *et al.* 1987b).

dispersal, soil conditions, or the dominance of a single life form – grasses.

Following severe disturbance, use of densely seeded grasses and heavy fertilization can promote site stability and vegetation productivity on both organic and mineral soils. However, these methods have either had no effect or, more frequently, retarded natural successional processes. On severely disturbed alpine mine sites that had been revegetated with high densities of native grasses and repeatedly fertilized, stand productivity remained high, but 8 years after seeding there was no increase in species diversity (Figure 9.5; Brown *et al.* 1984; Brown, personal communication). Only after fertilization was stopped and plant biomass and density decreased did significant colonization of native species occur. This is consistent with evidence that competitive interactions determining resource use can explain patterns of diversity in these ecosystems (Pastor 1995).

The available data indicate that successional trajectories are related to both the characteristics of the disturbance and the restoration methods, and differ depending on the ecosystem attribute measured (Figure 9.6). Recovery of restored sites on organic soils with favourable environmental regimes resembles secondary succession, and the restored site can quickly equal or exceed the undisturbed community in terms of vegetation productivity if the requirements for plant establishment are met. If graminoids are the primary early seral and restoration species, vegetation cover seldom exceeds that of adjacent native communities with more diverse life forms. Species composition and diversity (richness) depend on initial species establishment. If graminoids or a limited number of early seral species establish, change in species composition may occur slowly. Establishing both early and late seral species may accelerate this process, but no large-scale attempts to using this approach were found in the literature. Unfortunately, little is known about the development of soil microbial communities or nutrient cycles on either organic or mineral soils.

On sites with mineral soils that have had the topsoils removed, it is necessary to replace the topsoils or to increase the nutrient and water-holding capacities of the soils by incorporating organic matter for 'rapid' ecosystem development to occur. In the absence of such amendments, recovery processes occur slowly and resemble primary succession. High seeding densities of grasses and heavy fertilizer applications can temporarily increase vegetation cover and productivity and result in surface soil stability. As illustrated above, these treatments have little or no affect on organic matter pools and nitrogen retention, and can delay colonization by native species. Because of lower competition, plant species diversity on mineral soils may exceed that on organic soils during natural succession and following restoration. Treatments that effectively establish both early and late seral species, especially low nutrient adapted species and legumes, may result in lower initial plant productivity, but provide adequate surface stability and accelerate successional processes. Sites characterized by

1978

1983

1987

Figure 9.5. Restoration study plots on severely disturbed mineral soils on the McLaren mine above Cooke City, MT. Plots were seeded with high densities of native graminoids and received repeated fertilization for 4 years after seeding. Initial establishment was high (1978) (top left) and seeded plant density and biomass remained high while the plots were fertilized (1983) (bottom left). Four years after fertilization was stopped, plant density and biomass had declined significantly and species diversity was still low (1987) (above).

extreme environments due to elevation or topography appear to exhibit the lowest recovery potential. The best option for these sites may be developing land use plans that are designed to prevent severe disturbance.

Areas for future research

Alpine ecosystems will undoubtedly receive increased pressure as human populations and activities expand into the twenty-first century. Many of the general techniques that have been developed for restoring alpine ecosystems appear to have been successful, but methods for restoring ecosystem structure and functioning similar to predisturbance or adjacent native ecosystems are poorly developed for areas that lack well-developed topsoils. Methods still need to be devised for restoring successfully areas that exhibit the most extreme environments because of topographic location or elevation. Although our understanding of the combined effects

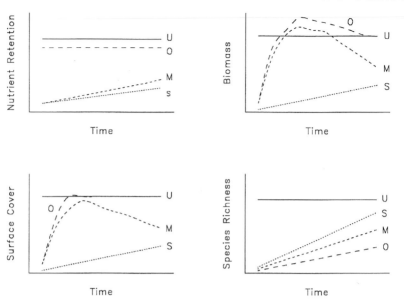

Figure 9.6. Possible successional trajectories of soil and vegetation attributes following disturbance in alpine ecosystems. Restored organic topsoils and organic topsoils with rapid natural establishment are indicated by O, intensive restoration of mineral soils with topsoils removed by M, natural colonization of mineral soils by S, and undisturbed native ecosystems with organic soils by U (adapted from Chambers *et al.* 1994).

of the extreme environment and disturbance on alpine ecosystems is increasing, critical information needs still exist. A severe limitation to the successful restoration of these ecosystems is the lack of knowledge concerning the establishment ecology of native species, especially low-nutrient adapted forbs and legumes. Little is known about competitive interactions among native species with varying life histories or adapted introduced cultivars, or the effects of nutrient additions on those interactions. Information on soil nutrient retention or cycling or the development of soil microbial communities is limited. Finally, the long-term effects of various restoration approaches, including the choice of species or soil amendments on ecosystem functioning and successional trajectories, are still poorly understood.

Acknowledgements

Research collaboration with Ray Brown, James MacMahon and James Haefner, technical advice from Jim Richards, Keith Owens, Dave Pyke, Don Sisson and Dave Turner, and research assistance of John Binder, Kate Dwire, Michael Kelrick, Krista Maguire, Nolan Preece, John Mull, Ann Mull, Dave Martin, and Craig Biggart are gratefully acknowledged. The manuscript benefited from review by Ray Brown, Bob Blank, and Krystyna Urbanska, and from editing by Chrystal White. The use of trade or firm names in this chapter is for reader information and does not imply endorsement by the US Department of Agriculture of any product or service.

References

Allen, E. B., Chambers, J. C., Connor, K. F., Allen, M. F., & Brown, R. W. (1987). Natural re-establishment of mycorrhizae in disturbed alpine ecosystems. *Arctic and Alpine Research*, 19, 11–20.

Amen, R. D. (1966). The extent and role of seed dormancy in alpine plants. *Quarterly Review of Biology*, 41, 271–82.

Bell, K. L. & Bliss, L. C. (1973). Alpine disturbance studies: Olympic National Park, U.S.A. *Biological Conservation*, 5, 25–32.

Bell, K. L. & Bliss, L. C. (1979). Autecology of *Kobresia bellardii*: Why winter snow accumulation limits local distribution. *Ecological Monographs*, 49, 377–402.

Bell, K. L. & Bliss, L. C. (1980). Plant reproduction in a high Arctic environment. *Arctic and Alpine Research*, 12, 1–10.

Billings, W. D. (1974). Arctic and alpine vegetation: Plant adaptations to cold summer climates. In *Arctic and Alpine Environments*, eds. J. D. Ives & R. G. Barry, pp. 403–44, London: Methuen.

Billings, W. D. (1988). Alpine vegetation. In *North American Terrestrial Vegetation*, eds. M. G. Barbour & W. D. Billings, pp. 391–420, New York: Cambridge University Press.

Bliss, L. C. (1962). Adaptations of Arctic and alpine plants to environmental conditions. *Arctic*, 15, 117–44.

Bliss, L. C. (1985). Alpine. In *Physiological Ecology of North American Plant Communities*, eds. B. F. Chabot & H. A. Mooney, pp. 41–65. New York: Chapman and Hall.

Bonde, E. K. (1968). Survival of seedlings of an alpine clover (*Trifolium nanum* Torr.). *Ecology*, 49, 1193–5.

Brink, V. C., MacKay, J., Freyman, S., & Pearce, D. G. (1967). Needle ice and seedling establishment in southwestern British Columbia. *Canadian Journal of Plant Science*, 47, 135–9.

Brown, R. W. & Chambers, J. C. (1989). Reclamation of severely disturbed alpine ecosystems: new perspectives. In *Proceedings of the Conference: Reclamation, A Global Perspective*. Compilers, D. G. Walker, C. B. Powter, & M. W. Pole, pp. 59–68. Alberta Land Conservation and Reclamation Council. Report no. RRTAC 89–2.

Brown, R. W. & Johnston, R. S. (1979). Revegetation of disturbed alpine
rangelands. In *Special Management Needs of Alpine Ecosystems*, pp. 76–94.
Denver, CO: Society for Range Management.

Brown, R. W., Johnston, R. S., & Chambers, J. C. (1984). Responses of seeded
native grasses to repeated fertilizer applications on acidic alpine mine
spoils. In *Proceedings: High Altitude Revegetation Workshop No. 6*, eds.
T. A. Colbert & R. L. Cuany, pp. 200–14. Water Resources Research
Institute, Information Series No. 53. Fort Collins: Colorado State
University.

Brown, R. W., Johnston, R. S., & Van Cleve, K. (1978). Rehabilitation
problems of Arctic and alpine regions. In *Reclamation of Drastically
Disturbed Lands*, eds. F. W. Schaller & P. Sutton, pp. 23–44. Madison,
WI: American Society for Agronomy.

Burke, I. C., Lauenroth, W. K., & Coffin, D. P. (1995). Soil organic matter
recovery in semiarid grasslands: implications for the conservation reserve
program. *Ecological Applications*, 5, 793–801.

Cargill, S. M. & Chapin, F. S., III (1987). Application of succession theory to
tundra restoration: a review. *Arctic and Alpine Research*, 19, 366–72.

Chambers, J. C. (1989). Seed viability of alpine species: variability within and
among years. *Journal of Range Management*, 42, 304–8.

Chambers, J. C. (1993). Seed and vegetation dynamics in an alpine herbfield:
effects of disturbance type. *Canadian Journal of Botany*, 71, 471–85.

Chambers, J. C. (1995a). Disturbance, life history strategies, and seed fates in
alpine herbfield communities. *American Journal of Botany*, 82, 421–33.

Chambers, J. C. (1995b). Relationships between seed fates and seedling
establishment in an alpine environment. *Ecology*, 76, 2124–33.

Chambers, J. C., Brown, R. W., & Johnston, R. S. (1984). Examination of
plant successional stages in disturbed alpine ecosystems: a method of
selecting revegetation species. In *Proceedings: High Altitude Revegetation
Workshop No. 6*, eds. T. A. Colbert & R. L. Cuany, pp. 215–24. Water
Resources Institute. Information Series No. 53. Fort Collins: Colorado
State University.

Chambers, J. C., Brown, R. W., & Williams, B. D. (1994). An evaluation of
reclamation success on Idaho's phosphate mines. *Restoration Ecology*,
2:4–16.

Chambers, J. C., MacMahon, J. A., & Wade, G. W. (1992). Differences in
successional processes among biomes: importance for obtaining and
evaluating reclamation success. In *Evaluating Reclamation Success: the
Ecological Considerations – Proceedings of a Symposium*, eds. J. C.
Chambers & G. W. Wade, pp. 59–72. USDA Forest Service, Northeastern
Forest Experiment Station, General Technical Report NE-164.

Chambers, J. C., MacMahon, J. A., & Brown, R. W. (1987a). Germination
characteristics of alpine grasses and forbs: a comparison of early and late
seral dominants with reclamation potential. *Reclamation and Revegetation
Research*, 6, 235–49.

Chambers, J. C., Brown, R. W., & Johnston, R. S. (1987b). A comparison of
soil and vegetation properties of seeded and naturally revegetated pyritic
alpine mine spoil and reference sites. *Landscape and Urban Planning*, 14,
507–19.

Chambers, J. C., MacMahon, J. A., & Brown, R. W. (1990). Alpine seedling
establishment: the influence of disturbance type. *Ecology*, 71, 1323–41.

Chambers, J. C., MacMahon, J. A., & Haefner, J. A. (1991). Seed entrapment in disturbed alpine ecosystems: effects of soil particle size and diaspore morphology. *Ecology*, 72, 1668–77.

Chapin, F. S., III (1983). Patterns of nutrient absorption and use by plants from natural and man-modified environments. In *Disturbance and Ecosystems*, eds. H. A. Mooney & M. Godron, pp. 175–87. Ecological Studies 44. New York: Springer-Verlag.

Chapin, F. S., III. (1987). Environmental control over growth of tundra plants. In Research in arctic life and earth sciences: present knowledge and future perspectives, ed. M. Sonneson. *Ecological Bulletin*, 38, 69–76.

Chapin, F. S., III. & Chapin, M. C. (1980). Revegetation of an arctic disturbed site by native tundra species. *Journal of Applied Ecology*, 17, 449–56.

Chapin, F. S., III., Walker, L. R., Fastie, C. L., & Sharman, L. C. (1995). Mechanisms of primary succession following deglaciation at Glacier Bay, Alaska. *Ecological Monographs*, 64, 149–75.

Cochran, P. H. (1969). Thermal properties and surface temperatures of seedbeds. Corvallis, OR: USDA Forest Service, Pacific Northwest Forest and Range Experiment Station.

Densmore, R. (1994). Succession on regraded placer mine spoil in Alaska, U.S.A., in relation to initial site characteristics. *Arctic and Alpine Research*, 26, 354–63.

Eddleman, L. E. & Ward, R. T. (1984). Phytoedaphic relationships in alpine tundra of North-central Colorado, U.S.A. *Arctic and Alpine Research*, 16, 343–59.

Everett, K. R., Vassiljevskaya, V. D., Brown, J., & Walker, B. D. (1981). Tundra and analagous soils. In *Tundra Ecosystems: A Comparative Analysis*, eds. L. C. Bliss, O. W. Heal, & J. J. Moore, pp. 139–80. New York: Cambridge University Press.

Ferchau, H. A. (1988). Rehabilitating ecosystems at high altitude. In *Rehabilitating Damaged Ecosystems*, ed. J. Cairns, vol. II, pp. 193–209. Boca Raton, FL: CRC Press.

Freedman, B., Hill, H., Svoboda, J., & Henry, G. (1982). Seed banks and seedling occurrence in a high Arctic oasis and Alexandra Fjord, Ellesmere Island, Canada. *Canadian Journal of Botany*, 60, 2112–8.

Fyles, J. W., Fyles, I. H., & Bell, M. A. M. (1985). Vegetation and soil development on coal mine spoil at high elevation in the Canadian Rockies. *Journal of Applied Ecology*, 22, 239–48.

Grabherr, G., Gottfried, M., Gruber, A., & Pauli, H. (1995). Patterns and current changes in alpine plant diversity. In *Arctic and Alpine Biodiversity – Patterns, Causes and Ecosystem Consequences*. Ecological Studies 113, eds. F. S. Chapin III & C. Körner, pp. 167–82. New York: Springer-Verlag.

Haggas, L., Brown, R. W., & Johnston, R. S. (1987). Light requirements for seed germination of Payson sedge and its application to alpine revegetation. *Journal of Range Management*, 40, 180–4.

Hobbie, S. E. (1995). Direct and indirect effects of plant species on biochemical processes in arctic ecosystems. In *Arctic and Alpine Biodiversity – Patterns, Causes and Ecosystem Consequences*. Ecological Studies, 113, eds. F. S. Chapin III & C. Körner, pp. 213–24. New York: Springer-Verlag.

Isard, S. A. (1986). Factors influencing soil moisture and plant community distribution on Niwot Ridge, Front Range, Colorado, U.S.A. *Arctic and Alpine Research*, 18, 83–96.

Jeffries, R. A., Wilson, K., & Bradshaw, A. D. (1981). The potential of legumes as a nitrogen source for the reclamation of derelict land. *Plant and Soil*, 59, 173–7.

Johnson, D. A. & Caldwell, M. M. (1975). Gas exchange of four arctic and alpine tundra species in relation to atmospheric and soil moisture stress. *Oecologia*, 21, 93–108.

Johnson, D. A. & Rumbaugh, M. D. (1986). Field nodulation and acetylene reduction activity of high-altitude legumes in the western United States. *Arctic and Alpine Research*, 18, 171–9.

Körner, C. (1995). Alpine plant diversity: a global survey and functional interpretations. In *Arctic and Alpine Biodiversity – Patterns, Causes and Ecosystem Consequences*. Ecological Studies 113, eds. F. S. Chapin III & C. Körner, pp. 45–62. New York: Springer-Verlag.

Körner, C. & Larcher, W. (1988). Plant life in cold climates. In *Plants and Temperature, Symposium of the Society for Experimental Biology Vol 42*, eds. S. F. Long & F. I. Woodward, pp. 25–57. Cambridge: The Company of Biologists Limited.

Lent, P. C. & Klein, D. R. (1988). Tundra vegetation as a rangeland resource. In *Vegetation Science Applications for Rangeland Analysis and Management*. ed. P. T. Tueller, pp. 307–37. Boston: Kluwer Academic Publishers.

MacMahon, J. A. (1981). Succession of ecosystems: a preliminary comparative analysis. In *Successional Research and Environmental Pollutant Monitoring Associated with Biosphere Reserves. Proceedings – Second U.S. – U.S.S.R. Symposium on Biosphere Reserves*, eds. M. A. Hemstrom & J. A. Franklin, pp. 5–26. Everglades National Park, FL.

MacMahon, J. A. & Jordan, W. R. (1994). Ecological restoration. In *Principles of Conservation Biology*, eds. G. K. Meffe & C. R. Carroll, pp. 409–38. Sunderland, MA: Sinauer Associates, Inc.

Macyk, T. B. Rehabilitation of alpine and subalpine lands. In *Reclamation of Drastically Disturbed Lands*, eds. R. I. Barnhisel, W. L. Daniels, & R. Dormondy, American Society of Agronomy. (in press).

Marschner, H. (1986). *Mineral Nutrition of Higher Plants*. Academic Press, Orlando, FL.

Marr, J. W., Buckner, D. C., & Johnston, D. L. (1974). Ecological modification of alpine tundra by pipeline construction. In *Revegetation of High Altitude Disturbed Lands*. eds. W. A. Berg, J. A. Brown, & R. I. Cuany, pp. 10–23. Fort Collins, CO: Environmental Resources Center.

May, D. E. & Webber, P. J. (1982). Spatial and temporal variation of the vegetation and its productivity, Niwot Ridge, Colorado. In *Ecological Studies in the Colorado Alpine*, University of Colorado, Institute of Arctic and Alpine Research, ed. J. C. Halfpenny. *Occasional Paper* 37, 35–62.

May, D. E., Webber, P. J., & May, T. A. (1982). Success of transplanted alpine tundra plants on Niwot Ridge, Colorado. *Journal of Applied Ecology*, 19, 965–76.

McGraw, J. B., & Vavrek, M. C. (1989). The role of buried viable seeds in arctic and alpine plant communities. In *Ecology of Soil Seed Banks*, eds. M. A. Leck, V. T. Parker, & R. L. Simpson, pp. 91–106. New York: Academic Press.

Nilsson, C. & Grelsson, G. (1995). The fragility of ecosystems: a review. *Journal of Applied Ecology*, 32, 677–92.

Nimlos, T. J. & McConnell, R. C. (1965). Alpine soils in Montana. *Soil Science*, 99, 310–21.

O'Lear, H. A. & Seastedt, T. R. (1994). Landscape patterns of litter decomposition in alpine tundra. *Oecologia*, 99, 95–101.

Pastor, J. (1995). Diversity of biomass and nitrogen distribution among plant species in arctic and alpine tundra ecosystems. In *Arctic and Alpine Biodiversity – Patterns, Causes and Ecosystem Consequences*. Ecological Studies 113, eds. F. S. Chapin III & C. Körner, pp. 255–70. New York: Springer-Verlag.

Ratcliffe, M. J. & Turkington, R. (1987). Vegetation patterns and environment of some alpine plant communities on Lakeview Mountain, southern British Columbia. *Canadian Journal of Botany*, 65, 2507–16.

Retzer, J. L. (1974). Alpine soils. In *Arctic and Alpine Environments*, eds. J. D. Ives & R. G. Barry, pp. 771–802. London: Methuen and Company.

Reynolds, D. A. (1984). Population dynamics of three annual species of alpine plants in the Rocky Mountains. *Oecologia*, 62, 250–5.

Roach, D. A. & Marchand, P. J. (1984). Recovery of alpine disturbances: Early growth and survival in populations *Arenaria groenlandica, Juncus trifudus*, and *Potentilla tridentata. Arctic and Alpine Research*, 16, 37–43.

Stanton, M. L., Rejmanek, M. & Galen, C. (1994). Changes in vegetation and soil fertility along a predictable snowmelt gradient in the Mosquito Range, Colorado, U.S.A. *Arctic and Alpine Research*, 26, 364–74.

Taylor, R. V. & Seastedt, R. T. (1994). Short- and long-term patterns of soil moisture in alpine tundra. *Arctic and Alpine Research*, 26, 14–20.

Urbanska, K. M. (1986). Behaviour of alpine plants and high altitude revegetation research. In *Proceedings of the High Altitude Revegetation Workshop No. 7*, eds. M. A. Schuster & R. H. Zuck, pp. 215–26. Information Series No. 58. Fort Collins, CO: Water Resources Research Institute.

Vitousek, P. M. & Walker, L. R. (1987). Colonization, succession and resource availability: ecosystem-level interactions. In *26th Symposium of The British Ecological Society – Colonization, Succession and Stability*. eds. A. J. Gray, M. J. Crawley, & P. J. Edwards, pp. 207–23. Cambridge, MA: Blackwell Scientific Publications.

Walker, D. G., Sadasivaiah, R. S., & Weijer, J. (1977). The selection and utilization of native grasses for reclamation in the Rocky Mountains of Alberta. In *Proceedings of the Second Annual General Meeting of the Canadian Land Reclamation Association*, pp. 33–48, 17–20 August 1977. Edmonton, Alberta, Paper No. 18.

Walker, L. R. (1989). Soil nitrogen changes during primary succession of a floodplain in Alaska, U.S.A. *Arctic and Alpine Research* 21, 341–9.

Webber, P. J. & Ives, J. D. (1978). Damage and recovery of tundra vegetation. *Environmental Conservation* 5, 171–82.

Willard, B. E. & Marr, J. W. (1970). Effects of human activities on alpine tundra ecosystems in Rocky Mountain National Park, Colorado. *Biological Conservation*, 2, 257–65.

10

Restoration of eroded areas in Iceland

SIGURÐUR H. MAGNÚSSON

Introduction

Iceland lies on the North Atlantic Ridge and is 103 000 km² in size. It is a mountainous country with 75% of the land area above 200 m elevation. The climate is cool temperate, characterized by cool summers and mild winters and frequent and strong winds (Einarsson 1976).

Studies in vegetation history in Iceland show that great changes have occurred during the postglacial time. Before the human settlement, 1100 years ago, the composition of the vegetation varied, controlled by climatic changes and volcanic activity (Hallsdóttir 1987). During most of this period, soil erosion was relatively low and there was an equilibrium between destruction and building up of soil and vegetation (Thórarinsson 1961). The human settlement in the country caused a dramatic change in the vegetation (Einarsson 1963, Hallsdóttir 1987).

It has been estimated that vegetation covered about 65 000 km² (63%) of the country at the time of settlement (Thorsteinsson 1978). At that time, the total area of birch (*Betula pubescens* Ehrh.) woodland was *c.* 30 000 km² (Sigurdsson 1977), but birch is the only native woodland-forming species in Iceland. Due to human influence, such as woodland clearance by burning, charcoal production, and livestock grazing, the woody areas were quickly reduced in size, while grassland increased. In the lowland, the landscape therefore changed from a closed woodland into an open one with grassland and mires (Hallsdóttir 1987). In the highland, considerable changes occurred and, for example, large areas of *Salix* shrubland developed into *Racomitrium* moss heath with *Betula nana* L. as the dominant vascular species (Kristinsson 1979). These vegetation changes led to increased water run-off, solifluction, and cryorturbation. The continuing influence of man and domestic animals, together with deteriorating climate and volcanic activity, further reduced the resistance of the vegetation to the eroding

188

factors, wind and water, which led to accelerated soil erosion. The accelerated soil erosion has had an enormous effect on the Icelandic ecosystems and changed the life conditions of the human population, their domestic animals, as well as Iceland's fauna and flora (Fridriksson 1972). Vegetation and soil have been destroyed in extensive areas, and the ecosystem has turned back to an early successional stage.

As a result of severe soil and vegetation deterioration, controlled revegetation of eroded areas started at the turn of this century and has continued since. The objectives and methods in revegetation have changed considerably with time, which has greatly affected the results. The purpose of this chapter is to give an overview of the development of the erosion in Iceland and the measures which have been carried out to revegetate and restore the eroded land.

Soil erosion in Iceland – ecological catastrophe

The course of the soil erosion

Several studies have been performed which illustrate the course of soil erosion in Iceland. (e.g., Sigbjarnarson 1969; Arnalds 1990). Most likely the erosion started from small scars formed in the vegetation cover, probably as an effect of trampling by grazing animals or through other types of nudation of the vegetation. The most vulnerable sites were hilltops exposed to strong winds and hillsides with heavy run-off of water. Erosion has also been initiated through Aeolian deposition of volcanic tephra over vegetated areas, and through drifting of such material or sand over vegetated sites from marginal zones along glaciers, sandur plains, lake and sea shores, and through flooding from glacier-fed rivers (e.g., Thórarinsson 1961; Arnalds 1990). These factors prevent vegetation recolonization from occurring and the Aeolian–Andic topsoil eroded down to the underlying substrates resulting in deflated surface consisting of, for example, lavas, glacial deposits, or alluvial material (Arnalds 1990). These deposits are normally coarse and therefore much more resistant to erosion than the finer Aeolian–Andic top soil. Commonly, in depressions or other poorly drained sites, only the upper layers of the Aeolian–Andic soil have been removed due to the effect of high groundwater level (Sigbjarnarson 1969; Magnús-son S. H. 1994).

As erosion progresses, sharp borders, known as erosion escarpments, are formed between eroded and uneroded sites (Figure 10.1). At the escarpments, the Aeolian–Andic soil layer continues to erode, undercutting the

Figure 10.1. Erosion escarpments are forming sharp borders between deflated and vegetated land.

root mat of the adjacent vegetation, destroying vegetation and soil. With time, the escarpments therefore move forward. In some cases, the erosion develops into another much faster and more destructive type, a so-called advancing erosion front (Arnalds 1990). The result of these two main erosion types is the same, a total destruction of the existing vegetation and topsoil, leaving behind almost completely barren areas.

As a result of the erosion, several types of surfaces have formed. Arnalds, Aradóttir, & Thorsteinsson (1987) have classified them into five classes, namely glacial deposits, sandy areas, postglacial lavas, alluvial and colluvial materials, and areas covered with pumice.

The continual soil erosion has also had a large influence on the vegetation of uneroded areas, as airborne eroded particles accumulated in the vegetation, increased the soil thickness, and often had a drying effect on the soil. This led to a change in floral composition, and in some cases made vegetated land more susceptible to soil erosion (e.g., Sigbjarnarson 1969; Magnússon S. H. 1994).

Although soil erosion has been active in almost all parts of Iceland, the intensity has been greatest within and near the volcanically active zone which runs through the country from the south-west to the north-east.

The deflation of much of the Icelandic landscape, that has taken place since the early settlement years, culminated in the late nineteenth and early twentieth centuries (Sigurjónsson 1958), when very large areas in the southern and north-eastern part of Iceland became eroded and numerous farms had to be abandoned (Sigurjónsson 1958). Although the rate of erosion has decreased in the twentieth century, it is still very active in many places and is considered to be the most serious environmental problem in Iceland today (Arnalds 1987).

The erosion has had a disastrous effect on Icelandic ecosystems, and can therefore be classified as a major ecological catastrophe (Magnússon S. H. 1994). The rate of plant succession in the eroded areas is, in general, slow, and therefore extensive areas which became eroded several centuries ago still have only a very sparse vegetation cover (Gunnlaugsdóttir 1985; Arnalds *et al.* 1987). Although it is not known in detail, the total area of eroded land is immense, and extends over tens of thousands of km^2. Satellite images show that only 28 000 km^2 (27%) of the country are now covered with continuous vegetation or are fairly well vegetated. More than 37 000 km^2 are barren deserts, and an additional 24 000 km^2 have vegetation of low productivity with moss and sparse vegetation (Iceland vegetation map 1994). The size of the birch woodland is now only 1250 km^2 or 4% of the size it was at the time of settlement (Sigurdsson 1977).

The former pattern of vegetation types across many of the barren areas is disputed. However, evidence from historical documents like the Icelandic Sagas, farm registers, annals, place names, and pollen analytical results can give indications of the former vegetation types (e.g., Arnalds 1987). Also plant and soil remnants found in eroded areas provide us with information concerning the vegetation which existed before the land became eroded (e.g., Arnalds 1987; Magnússon S. H. 1994). Based on these sources, it is probable that very large areas of moss heathland dominated by *Racomitrium* moss, and shrub heath dominated with *Salix* species, *Betula nana*, and other shrub species were destroyed in the highland. In the lowland it is known that large areas of birch woodland, as well as *Salix* shrubland, grassland, and heathland of different types were devastated (Sigurjónsson 1958).

Revegetation and restoration of eroded land

Before the turn of the last century, soil erosion and vegetation destruction were by many considered to be part of nature's forces, and were therefore thought to be impossible to control (Sigurjónsson 1958). In spite of this opinion, a few farmers made some attempts to halt the soil erosion, and revegetate eroded sites on their own land, first by raising barriers of stones, and later by seeding the native sand-dune grass *Leymus arenarius* (L.) Hochst. The first known attempt was as early as *c.* 1700 (Sigurjónsson 1958). Following the very extensive erosion between 1880 and 1890, there was an increased interest in the country to find methods to fight erosion and revegetate eroded areas. During these years, further tests were performed with seeding of *Leymus* and the erection of barriers of stones. Also, irrigation was attempted to stabilize eroded soil and improve plant colonization. The results of these small-scale trials were, in general, positive. At that time, more and more people realized that it was necessary to use radical and co-ordinated methods to cope with the soil erosion and to revegetate land. Therefore, a new law on soil conservation and revegetation was passed in 1907, which led to the foundation of two state institutions, the Soil Conservation Service (scs) and the Forestry Service (fs). These institutions are both concerned with conservation of vegetation and soil. scs is responsible for erosion control and revegetation of eroded land, while the main objectives of fs are protection of the remaining birch forests and reforestation with native and imported tree species.

The aim and methods used for erosion control and revegetation have changed considerably with time, and the following three relatively well-defined periods emerge (Table 10.1): the erosion control period (1907–45), the cultivation period (1946–85), and the ecological revegetation period (1986–).

I The erosion control period (1907–1945)
Purpose and practice
In the first period, the main purpose of the work was to halt the soil erosion (Table 10.1). The principal method was exclusion of grazing animals by setting up fences. At the end of the period, a total of 524 km² had been fenced off by scs alone (Sigurjónsson 1958) (Figure 10.2). In addition, several areas of birch woodland were protected from grazing by fs, some of which were badly affected by erosion (Blöndal S., personal communication). Within the enclosed areas different techniques were used to halt the erosion. Barriers of stones and timber were set up perpendicular to the prevailing wind for trapping sand, and the native grass *Leymus arenarius* seeded and planted for the same purpose. Seeding of native birch and some exotic species was also tried on a small scale. At this time the supply of seed for the revegetation was very limited, and most seeds were collected by hand or by other simple methods in natural communities. A small number

Table 10.1. *Summary of revegetation periods in Iceland from 1907,
showing objectives of the work, who carries it out, methods, use of
species, and research (see also text)*

	1907–45 Erosion control period	1946–85 Cultivation period	1986– Ecological revegetation period
Objectives	Halt destruction of vegetation and soil	Grass cultivation, range improvements	Forming sustainable ecosystems

Performing bodies
  State institutions
  Volunteers
  Farmers
  Private companies

Methods
  Protection from grazing
  Barriers for trapping of sand
  Buiding of dams for irrigation
  Artificial fertilizers
  Use of aeroplanes
  Seed processing

Use of species
Natives
  Leymus arenarius
  Betula pubescens
  Deschampsia caespitosa
  Festuca richardsonii
  Salix species
Exotics
  Various exotic grass species
  Festuca rubra (Leik) – Norway
  Deschampsia beringensis – Alaska
  Lupinus nootkatensis – Alaska
  Larix, Picea, Pinus, Salix

Research
  Testing of exotic grass species
  Testing of native grass species
  Effects of fertilizer on succession
  Ecology of *Leymus*, birch & lupin
  Soil erosion
  Soil biota
  Decomposition of organic matter
  Testing of exotic & native legumes

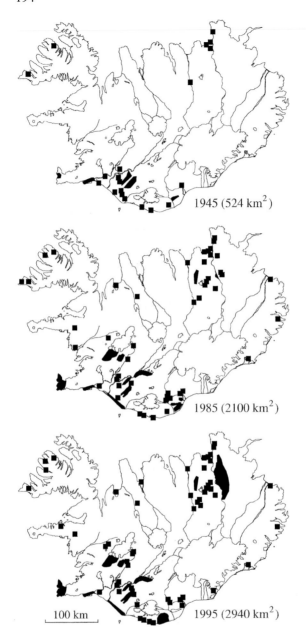

Figure 10.2. Protected revegetation areas of the State Soil Conservation Service in 1945, 1985, and 1995 and their size. The smallest areas are shown as squares.

Figure 10.3. From the early beginning of revegetation of eroded areas in Iceland the native *Leymus arenarius* has been the most important plant species for stabilizing moving sand and other unstable surfaces.

of river dams were built, and water was directed over unstable, sandy, and eroded areas in order to stop sand drift and enhance vegetation regrowth.

During this period the work was carried out exclusively in the lowlands, mostly in areas where erosion threatened hayfields or pasture land. This work was mainly performed by scs (Sigurjónsson 1958). At that time, the technique and choice of species for erosion control was not based on direct scientific research but on 'common sense', and by watching the outcome of applied methods and on observations of the natural plant colonization of eroded land (Sigurjónsson 1958).

Success of erosion control

In most of the protected areas, further vegetation and soil erosion was prevented and the re-establishment of the natural vegetation induced (Sigurjónsson 1958). The seeding and planting of the native grass *Leymus arenarius* proved to be very effective in stabilizing moving sand, and the use of this species is still fundamental in the process of the revegetation of unstable sandy areas in Iceland (Figure 10.3, Table 10.1). Erecting barriers for trapping sand was also important as they formed safe sites for the establishment of *Leymus* grass.

Although the main purpose of the work during this first period was to control erosion, rather than to direct succession into a specific pathway, these methods often led to the restoration of former vegetation types. For example, they increased the colonization of native *Salix* species, and a *Salix*-shrubland was formed at many sites (Sigurjónsson 1958). The seeding of the native birch, which was the first attempt to restore birch woodland on eroded land, was also successful. However, the exotic species tested were not adapted to the harsh conditions found on degraded land, and therefore did not become established (Sigurjónsson 1958).

II The cultivation period (1946–1985)

Purpose and practice

In the mid forties, considerable changes occurred in the aims and methods used in revegetation of eroded areas. These changes were caused partly by the changing attitude to land use by Icelandic farmers, and partly by new revegetation techniques. At that time it was a common belief that it would be profitable to increase agricultural production and therefore necessary to increase fodder production and pasture yield for sheep and cattle (Sigurjónsson 1958). This clearly affected the revegetation work. As before, the aim of the revegetation efforts was to halt erosion, but a greater emphasis was now put on the cultivation of grass on eroded land, with hay production and range improvement as the main goal (Figure 10.4, Table 10.1). This was made possible by the introduction of artificial fertilizer and imported commercial grass seed.

For revegetation practice most of the former methods from the first period were used (Table 10.1). Areas to be revegetated were fenced off. By 1985 a total of 2 100 km² had been protected from livestock grazing under the care of SCS (Iceland Ministry of Agriculture 1986) (Figure 10.2). It was becoming more important to test scientifically the latest planting methods, and to monitor the success of different species and varieties. During this period the approach in the revegetation work was primarily based on common agricultural practices.

In 1946, experiments were initiated to test different exotic grasses and legumes and also to study the effects of fertilizer application on the revegetation of eroded land. Based on the results of these studies, the seeding of grasses and fertilization was started on degraded land on a large

Figure 10.4. During the cultivation period 1946–85 great emphasis was put on revegetation of eroded land by grass seeding and fertilizer application.

scale (Sigurjónsson 1958). A further increase in the use of fertilizer and seeding occurred in the 1950s when aircraft were introduced in the revegetation work. Since then they have been widely used for revegetation practice (Table 10.1), especially in distant and inaccessible areas. The common practice of this revegetation technique included the seeding of grasses and fertilizer application in the first year, and then fertilizer application in the subsequent one or two years.

As most of the seeded grasses did not last long in the vegetation, extensive experiments were carried out to find native and exotic grass species adapted to the conditions at the eroded sites (Helgadóttir 1988a,b). Grasses which were found to be the most hardy for land revegetation were *Deschampsia beringensis* Hult. from Alaska, *Festuca rubra* L. (var. Leik) from Norway, and the native species *Deschampsia caespitosa* (L.) Beauv and *Festuca richardsonii* Hooker. These species are now widely used for revegetation of eroded land.

As the main emphasis in the revegetation work was cultivation of grasses, other species received less attention. The exotic legume the Nootka lupin (*Lupinus nootkatensis* Sims) was, however, seeded and planted within protected areas, mainly by the FS. As in the first period, the native birch was seeded on a small scale. Trials were also established with exotic tree species, mainly *Picea sitchensis* (Bong.) Carr. and *Larix sukaczewi* Dylis (Blöndal S., personal communication).

During the cultivation period, public interest in revegetation increased considerably, and volunteers took an active part in revegetation work (Table 10.1). Co-operation between local communities and the scs was developed, and several areas of eroded land were seeded and fertilized to increase pasture for sheep as well as to reduce grazing pressure in nearby areas which were vulnerable to grazing and in danger of erosion (Arnalds 1988).

Most of the revegetation sites were situated in the lowlands, but some work was also carried out in the highlands. The largest highland revegetation project was in north central Iceland where more than 45 km² have now been seeded with grasses and fertilized (Magnússon & Magnússon 1995). That revegetation project was started in 1981 to compensate for loss of land due to the construction of a hydroelectric power station on the river Blanda (Arnalds *et al.* 1987).

The supply of seed for use in the revegetation projects increased greatly during the cultivation period. Seed from several species and varieties was imported from abroad and also collected in natural communities or cultivated for seed production.

In accordance with the objectives, the results of seeding and fertilization were assessed mainly from the perspective of erosion control and based on the evaluation of cover and production of the seeded grasses (Sigurjónsson 1958; Fridriksson 1960, 1971; Helgadóttir 1988a). In other studies, mainly performed during the latter half of the period, several additional aspects were investigated, such as ecological genetics of the *Leymus* grass (Sigurbjörnsson 1960), vegetation dynamics, soil conditions, and the composition of surface and soil fauna (Fridriksson 1969; Fridriksson & Pálsson 1970; Fridriksson, Magnússon, & Gunnarsson 1977; Gunnlaugsdóttir 1985). Studies were also carried out to investigate the characteristics and development of soil erosion (Sigbjarnarson 1969) which improved the understanding of conditions for plant establishment and succession at eroded sites.

Success of cultivation

Grass seeding and fertilizer application proved to be very effective in increasing vegetation cover and production (Fridriksson & Pálsson 1970; Fridriksson 1971; Gunnlaugsdóttir 1985). However, the stability of the grass-dominated vegetation was limited as it depended on continuous fertilizer application (Gunnlaugsdóttir 1985). Although not studied in detail, the long-term effects of the common method of revegetation (grazing exclusion, seeding of grasses and fertilization for few years) appears to be variable. In some cases these treatments have led to the formation of grassy heathland, in others mossy heath, often with some lichens, has developed (Thórhallsdóttir 1991; Magnússon S. H., personal observations). In still others the effect of fertilization on cover is insignificant, especially at sites with very unstable surfaces (Magnússon S. H., personal observations). In several cases, the method has led to an increase in the colonization of native *Salix* and birch (e.g., Aradóttir 1994).

III The ecological revegetation period (1986–present)

The purpose of revegetation

The next major change in the revegetation work occurred in the mid eighties. As before, the erosion control was still the main objective, but cultivation of grass for range improvement or hay production was no longer the primary goal. Instead, greater emphasis was put on the formation of sustainable ecosystems (Table 10.1). The change has partly been derived from the experience from the fertilization programme used during the cultivation period. It is also evident that increased ecological understanding has accelerated this development. A decrease in sheep numbers in recent years has also promoted these changes. In this third and ongoing period, an ecological approach has become increasingly important both in research and in the practical revegetation work.

Revegetation research

The problems addressed in research have changed considerably, reflecting the new emphasis. Studies were carried out to answer basic questions about the prevailing environmental conditions on eroded sites. Soil erosion processes were investigated (Arnalds 1990) and the different erosion forms classified. Based on this classification, the erosion severity has recently been mapped for the whole country (Arnalds 1996). These maps will be used as a reference when revegetation efforts are planned and designed. Several of the factors affecting the plant colonization and establishment on eroded land have been investigated. They include soil nutrient status, seed bank, emergence of seedlings, growth and survival, seed dispersal (e.g., Arnalds & Pálmason 1986; Aradóttir 1991; Gudmundsson 1991; Magnússon S. H. 1994), and the effects of surface characteristics for seed accumulation (Magnússon S. H. 1994).

Several aspects of the ecology of the native birch (Magnússon & Magnússon 1990; Aradóttir 1991; Magnússon S. H. 1994) and *Leymus* grass (Greipsson 1991; Greipsson & Dawy 1994) were studied in order to improve restoration strategies. Ecological studies on the Nootka lupine have also been carried out to obtain a basic knowledge of the behaviour of the species in the Icelandic environment (Magnússon 1990, 1995). In addition, exotic and native legumes, shrubs, and trees are now being tested for use in revegetation of eroded land.

Studies in the development of ecosystems following grass seeding and fertilization have been continued. In these studies several ecological variables have been addressed, such as composition of plant species and soil biota, soil nutrient conditions (Gudmundsson 1991; Sigurdardóttir 1991; Thorsteinsson 1991; Thórhallsdóttir 1991; Magnússon S. H. 1994), and decomposition of organic matter (Sigurdardóttir, H. unpublished results).

Revegetation practice

Seed production has increased significantly, and revegetation techniques have broadened and improved considerably during this third period. Seeds of the *Leymus* grass are collected by machines in natural communities, and seeds of the grasses *Deschampsia beringensis, D. caespitosa, Festuca richardsonii* and the Nootka lupin are now produced on a large scale in fields for use in revegetation. A seed-processing factory was opened by SCS and the Agricultural Research Institute (RALA) in 1988 where seeds are treated in different ways. Most seeds are cleaned mechanically and coated before seeding. The seeds of the Nootka lupin are infected with *Rhizobium* bacteria, and methods are being developed to inoculate plants with mycorrhiza and to add germination-inducing compounds to seeds.

During the third period, revegetation has both continued at previous sites and expanded to new areas. In 1995, the total size of areas protected by SCS was 2 940 km^2 (SCS, unpublished data) (Figure 10.2), which is 2.8% of the total area of Iceland.

The use of species for revegetation has changed considerably, and now the exotic Nootka lupin and the native birch are much more used. The lupin has been seeded and planted as a pioneer plant at barren sites. In the years 1992–5, more than 15 km^2 have been seeded with lupin annually by SCS alone (SCS, unpublished data). The birch has been planted and seeded particularly in areas with sparse vegetation cover, often at sites which had earlier been seeded and fertilized. During the years 1990–2 about 0.6 million birch plants have, for example, been planted annually for restoration of birch woodland at more than 80 sites in different parts of the country (Aradóttir & Magnússon 1992; Aradóttir & Grétarsdóttir 1995). Several other tree species have been planted at degraded sites like the exotic *Larix sibirica* Ledeb., L. *Larix sukaczewi* Dylis, *Pinus contorta* Dogl. Ex Loud. (Aradóttir & Magnússon 1992; Aradóttir & Grétarsdóttir 1995).

Seeding and fertilizer application has been carried out by aeroplanes, tractors, and by hand. It is quite common to use tractors with specially designed seeding machines, and this has proved to be very effective on unstable soils such as sand-dune areas and erosion escarpments. Planting is generally done by hand.

As in earlier periods, the scs has carried out most of the revegetation work, but revegetation operations have been increased by the fs. Due to increased interest in revegetation work among the local communities, the work has been increasingly practised by farmers, private companies, club members, and volunteers (Table 10.1).

The success of the revegetation work

Within the enclosed areas, erosion has been controlled in most places. For example, in the north-eastern part of the country several actively eroding fronts were stabilized with *Leymus* grass and fertilization and therefore further deterioration of vegetation and soil has been halted. The new ecological approach is, as yet, in its infancy, so it is not possible to ascertain how effective it has been to influence the succession in eroded areas.

Ecological factors affecting restoration

The initial conditions

As pointed out by Bradshaw (1987) it is important to understand the natural processes of succession as they can be used as models for revegetation methodology. Observations and experimental studies into the mechanisms, processes, and results of erosion have led to a number of insights into the conditions necessary for plant colonization at these vulnerable sites.

Seed sources

As most plant species are killed during erosion, plant colonization on newly eroded land is dependent on dispersal of diaspores, either from plants which have already established on eroded land or from nearby vegetation. Studies indicate that the seed bank of eroded soils is small (Arnalds et al. 1987; Magnússon S. H. 1994) as a result of the topsoil having been totally removed during the erosion process. Therefore, the seed bank has a limited effect on the initiation of plant succession (Magnússon S. H. 1994). However, seeds may be transported together with soil material from eroding escarpments in the neighbourhood of degraded areas (Magnússon S. H. 1994).

Physical environment

Initial life conditions on eroded surfaces are relatively harsh for colonizing species. Most of the surface types found on degraded land are characterized by high instability due to wind abrasion, surface erosion, and/or frost heaving (e.g., Arnalds et al. 1987; Aradóttir 1991; Magnússon S. H. 1994). These soils are generally coarse and well drained, and, as with most other severely degraded soils (Bradshaw 1987), the low levels of nitrogen, phosphorus, and organic carbon limit (1%-dw) plant growth (Arnalds et al. 1987; Magnússon S. H. 1994). Eroded sites therefore have an environment of relatively high stress and disturbance (Magnússon S. H. 1994).

Seedling establishment

The frequency of safe sites for most species is low. Due to the high levels of disturbance and thus the continually changing microenvironment, the ability of seeds to germinate and establish at any particular site may vary from year to year (Magnússon S. H. 1994). In unstable eroded soils, seedling mortality is generally high in winter and is caused mainly by intensive frost heaving and/or surface erosion (Magnússon & Magnússon 1990; Aradóttir 1991; Magnússon S. H. 1994). Winter desiccation may also be an important cause of mortality (Magnússon 1994). The signifi-cance of nutrients for seedling establishment has been demonstrated in experiments (Magnússon S. H. 1994) and repeatedly shown by the rapid increase in cover of several species following fertilization of eroded soils (Fridriksson 1969; Fridriksson & Pálsson 1970). In this regard, size of seedlings seems to be of particular importance for establishment (Mag-nússon & Magnússon 1990; Magnússon S. H. 1994). The advantage of increased size may be due to higher levels of nutrient storage (Chapin 1980) and large root systems which make the seedlings more resistant to frost heaving (Péres 1987).

Time of germination affects seedling size and survival, as germination late in the autumn produces small seedlings which in turn leads to high winter mortality (Magnússon S. H. 1994). Seeding is therefore either carried out in late autumn or from spring to early summer in order to ensure the emerged seedlings have a long growing period. For the same purpose, germination-inducing compounds are now commonly added to *Leymus* seeds sown in spring and early summer.

Pioneer species may further increase colonization by stabilizing the surface and trapping diaspores (Magnússon S. H. 1994). It is known that fertilization of eroded soils increases not only the grass cover, but also the cover of low growing *Bryum* and *Ceratodon* mosses (Gunnlaugsdóttir 1985; Magnússon & Magnússon 1995) as well as several lichens which form a thin crust on the surface. The stabilization has been seen to benefit the colonization of *Salix* and birch. However, intense fertilization may increase the growth of grasses to a level which may retard colonization of other species and thus impede restoration (e.g., Magnússon & Magnússon 1995). If fertilization is to be used as a restoration technique, the quantity and duration must be accurately and carefully balanced.

Research into establishment of birch on eroded land also demonstrates important effects of established plants on plant colonization. In an experiment performed on a sparsely covered (20%) eroded gravel flat area, the growth of birch seedlings was enhanced near established *Salix* plants at the site (Figure 10.5) (Magnússon & Magnússon 1992). The seedlings within 70 cm of *Salix* plants were 2–6 times larger after 2 years than the seedlings further away. Several factors could be responsible for this pattern, including shelter, moisture, and nutrient enrichment around the *Salix* plants and mycorrhiza. In the study it was suggested that the growth response was caused mainly by early mycorrhizal infection of the birch seedlings. A similar pattern has been found at several other eroded sites (Magnússon S. H., personal observations).

As pointed out earlier, sheep grazing has had tremendous effect on vegetation in Iceland, and protection from grazing has always been an important part of revegetation practice. Although protection from grazing has in many places led to increased cover of the vegetation, there are other eroded sites that have not recovered despite several decades of protection. Therefore other factors must overrule the positive effects of protection. Studies show that it is possible to revegetate eroded areas by applying grass seed and fertilizer even under considerable grazing pressure (Arnalds *et al.* 1987; Thorsteinsson 1991). This indicates that the limiting factors are related to nutrient conditions and/or seed sources.

Figure 10.5. Experiments show that on unstable and nutrient-poor eroded soils the growth of birch seedlings is enhanced near established *Salix* plants, probably caused by mycorrhizal infection from the *Salix*. Here 'large' birch seedlings and fruitbodies of the fungi *Laccaria laccata* are forming a circle around the low growing *Salix herbacea* in an eroded and fertilized area in south Iceland (see also text).

Ecosystem development

Revegetation in Iceland has, in most cases, been initiated without much information about how different treatments would affect the development of the ecosystems. This is understandable, as the major aim in revegetation has been to halt erosion as a matter of urgency and to prevent further destruction of vegetation and soil.

The communities and soils which have been lost due to erosion are very different regarding their nutrient status. The birch woodland and grassland are the most fertile and the moss heathland is the poorest. Low shrub heaths (*Salix* species, *Betula nana*, and other shrub types) are probably of intermediate level. When restoration is planned for different areas, several factors which effect the site's environmental conditions must be considered, such as height above sea level, soil moisture, and topography. It is thus not possible to create a stable grassland on the top of a mountain or moss heath on a valley floor. In the perspective of ecological restoration, the main emphasis has been put on the creation of grassland, a community with relatively high nutrient requirements. With regard to the low nutrient status of eroded soils, it can be concluded that most of the previous effort has been into attaining a goal which is relatively difficult to reach.

Nitrogen and phosphorus, the most limiting nutrients on eroded soils, are probably the main factors affecting which type of community can be sustained (cf. Bradshaw 1983). The nitrogen deposition (NH_4^+ and NO_3^-) in Iceland is relatively low or about 2 kg ha^{-1} yr^{-1} in the years 1981–90 (Icelandic Meteorological Office, unpublished data). Nitrogen fixing of free-living microbes in eroded soils is not known. It can, however, be concluded that, without fertilizer application or use of legumes or other nitrogen-fixing plants, a long time will be needed before a N-pool of considerable size has accumulated.

Although the ecology of the introduced Nootka lupin has been studied considerably during the last few years (Magnússon B. 1994), the long-term effects of the species on succession are not sufficiently known. However, it is clear that the lupin will have a large influence on the ecosystem (Magnússon B. 1994). The lupin is a perennial, nitrogen-fixing species which spreads by seeding. It has the ability to colonize bare ground and unstable areas and is relatively fast growing. The adult plants are 50–100 cm in height, and where the species colonizes it forms continuous dense patches. Nitrogen fixation has been measured around 80 kg N ha^{-1} yr^{-1} (Pálmason, Gudmundsson, & Helgadóttir 1995) and with the passage of time the carbon content in the soil increases (Magnússon B. 1994). The species appears to have the ability to utilize phosphorus in the soil better than many other species, as an application with phosphorus is not necessary for its growth. The ability of the species to restore the function (productivity, nutrient cycling) of the ecosystem seems clear, and for this reason many consider it to be of considerable value for revegetation in Iceland (Arnalds 1988).

The Nootka lupin can not only colonize eroded soils. It can also invade natural communities such as dwarf shrub heathland and other communities with disturbed and open ground (Magnússon B. 1994). Where the lupin invades, it often displaces native vegetation and totally changes the structure and function of the systems. There is a growing concern about the undesirable effect of the lupin on the native vegetation and landscape.

In conclusion, surface stabilization is an important first step in the restoration of eroded sites. Today the prevailing physical and biological conditions of eroded land are relatively well understood, but much less is known about how different treatments affect the successional pathways, or how it is possible to alter ecosystem properties to reach a specific goal in restoration. This knowledge is very important because initial treatments can have lasting affects on the future pathway of succession and on the function of the ecosystem (Chambers, Brown, & Williams 1994). Directing the development of ecosystems in the eroded areas toward specific goals must be based on an understanding of the most important determinants of succession. Therefore, good knowledge of the ecology of the introduced species and on other important factors is needed. In this regard factors affecting utilization, accumulation, and cycling of nutrients such as mycorrhiza, nitrogen fixers, and soil biota seem to be of special importance.

The scale of land degradation in Iceland is enormous, and thus it is not possible to use intensive and costly methods of restoration in all places (Aradóttir 1994). The need for an ecological and less intensive approach is thus imperative. Based on present knowledge of site conditions suitable for germination and establishment of birch (Magnússon & Magnússon 1990; Aradóttir 1991; Magnússon S. H. 1994), restoration of birch woodland could be, for example, initiated on a large scale by seeding (Magnússon & Magnússon 1990). It could also be achieved by planting birch in small islands from which the birch would gradually colonize the whole area by seeding (Aradóttir 1991, 1994). Similar methods could be used to introduce other species or organisms such mycorrhiza and soil animals by introducing inoculated plants or soil containing the desired organisms. Another approach could be formation of a whole community either by seeding and/or planting several desired species or with transplantation directly from donor populations (cf. Urbanska 1995).

Restoration perspectives

It can be assumed that a great part of the revegetation work carried out at degraded sites in Iceland will lead to restoration of former communities. There are, however, several limitations to ecological restoration projects in Iceland, which include social factors such as the contrasting opinions and objectives of different-interest groups in the community (cf. Jackson, Lopoukhine, & Hillyard 1995). Although most people agree on creating self-sustainable ecosystems with ecological methods, there is no joint view on what kind of systems should be created or which methods used. The opinions range from reclamation to ecological restoration (cf. Jackson *et al.* 1995). In other words, the objectives of the different parties range from those who believe that revegetation should be achieved by using any suitable native or exotic species, to those who wish to restore the ecosystems which existed before the disturbance.

The Society for Ecological Restoration defines restoration as 'the intentional alteration of site to establish a defined indigenous, historic ecosystem. The goal of this process is to emulate the structure, functioning, and dynamics of the specified ecosystem' (see Aronson *et al.* 1993). Referring to this definition, only a part of the revegetation practice carried out in Iceland at present is ecological restoration. This is due to extensive use of exotic species. A large proportion of the work can be classified as rehabilitation or reclamation (Jackson *et al.* 1995).

Referring to the present social influences, it is unrealistic to expect that ecological restoration, in its purest sense, will be a common practice of revegetation in Iceland in the near future. There is, however, a growing interest for ecological restoration, mainly because it will create ecosystems which are similar to the surrounding native vegetation and landscape (cf. Urbanska 1995). The species that comprise the system are adapted to the environmental conditions and to each other, as they have been developing together during long periods of time, and therefore each species is an integrated part of the system.

With the exception of halting erosion, the purpose of revegetation in Iceland has not been well defined, and comprehensive revegetation plans have only been made for a limited number of areas. To achieve a good result in revegetation it is important to set goals for the work, make suitable plans, and have an effective system of evaluation of the work (e.g., Jackson *et al.* 1995). This is particularly important in Iceland, as much of the revegetation is performed no longer by a few professional institutions, but increasingly by volunteers and others who have limited expertise and knowledge in ecology. An important factor in the future will be to ensure that the relevant information and assistance is available to all those who are taking part in the work.

Acknowledgements

I am grateful to J. Foskett, Á. Helgadóttir, B. Magnússon, S. Runólfsson, and two anonymous referees for valuable comments on the manuscript, and to S. Blöndal at the FS and several people at the SCS for information on revegetation of eroded land. I also thank Á. Jónsson for drawing one figure.

References

Aradóttir, Á. L. (1991). Population biology and stand development of birch (*Betula pubescens* Ehrh.) on disturbed sites in Iceland. Dissertation. Texas A&M University.

Aradóttir, Á. L. (1994). [New methods for restoration] Nýjar leidir vid
    endurheimt landgaeda. In *Graedum Ísland*, ed. A. Arnalds, pp. 65–72.
    Reykjavík: Landgraedsla ríkisins (in Icelandic).
Aradóttir, Á. L. & Grétarsdóttir, J. (1995). [*Monitoring of Restoration Planting
    1991 and 1992*] Úttektir á gródursetningum til landgraedsluskóga 1991 og
    1992. Fjölrit Rannsóknastödvar Skógraektar ríkisins Nr. 9. Mosfellsbaer:
    Rannsóknastöd Skógraektar ríkisins (in Icelandic).
Aradóttir, Á. L. & Magnússon, S. H. (1992). [Planting of restoration forests in
    1990 – seedling establishment] Raektun landgraedsluskóga 1990. Árangur
    gródursetninga. *Ársrit Skógraektarfélags Íslands*, 1992, 58–69 (in Icelandic,
    English summary).
Arnalds, A. (1987). Ecosystem disturbance in Iceland. *Arctic and Alpine
    Research*, 19, 508–13.
Arnalds, A., ed. (1988). [*Reclaim Iceland*] Graedum Ísland. Reykjavík:
    Landgraedsla ríkisins (in Icelandic).
Arnalds, Ó. (1990). Characterization and erosion of Andisols in Iceland.
    Dissertation. Texas A&M University.
Arnalds, Ó. (1996). [Mapping of soil erosion – results and usage] Kortlagning á
    jardvegsrofi – nidurstödur og notkunarmöguleikar. *Rádunautafundur*, 1996,
    72–8. (in Icelandic).
Arnalds, Ó., Aradóttir, Á. L., & Thorsteinsson, I. (1987). The nature and
    restoration of denuded areas in Iceland. *Arctic and Alpine Research*, 19,
    518–25.
Arnalds, Ó. & Pálmason, F. (1986). [*Soil at Reclaimed Sites in the Blanda area*]
    Jardvegur í landgraedslutilraunum á virkjunarsvaedi Blöndu. Fjölrit RALA
    118. Reykjavík: Rannsóknastofnun landbúnadarins (in Icelandic).
Aronson, J., Floret, C., Le Floc'h, E., Ovalle, C., & Pontanier, R. (1993).
    Restoration and rehabilitation of degraded ecosystems in arid and
    semi-arid lands. I. A. view from the south. *Restoration Ecology*, 1, 8–17.
Bradshaw, A. D. (1983). The reconstruction of ecosystems. *Journal of Applied
    Ecology*, 20, 1–17.
Bradshaw, A. D. (1987). The reclamation of derelict land and the ecology of
    ecosystems. In *Restoration Ecology: a Synthetic Approach to Ecological
    Research*, eds. W. R. Jordan, M. E. Gilpin, & J. D. Aber, pp. 53–74.
    Cambridge University Press.
Chambers, J., Brown, R. W., & Williams, B. D. (1994). An evaluation of
    success on Idaho's phosphate mines. *Restoration Ecology*, 2, 4–16.
Chapin, F. S. III (1980). The mineral nutrition of wild plants. *Annual Review of
    Ecology and Systematics*, 11, 233–60.
Einarsson, M. Á. (1976). [*The Climate of Iceland*] Vedurfar á Íslandi.
    Reykjavík: Idunn (in Icelandic).
Einarsson, Th. (1963). Pollen-analytical studies on vegetation and climate history
    of Iceland in late and post-glacial times. In *North Atlantic Biota and their
    History*, eds. Á. Löve & D. Löve, pp. 355–65. Oxford: Pergamon Press.
Fridriksson, S. (1960). [Reclamation and cultivation of highland ranges]
    Uppgraedsla og raektun afréttarlanda. *Árbók landbúnadarins*, 11, 201–18
    (in Icelandic).
Fridriksson, S. (1969). [Reclamation investigation on a highland range in the
    east central part of Iceland] Uppgraedslutilraun á Tungnáróraefum.
    Journal of Agricultural Research in Iceland, 1, 38–44 (in Icelandic, English
    summary).

Fridriksson, S. (1971). [Landreclamation studies in the district Kjölur, central Iceland] Raektunartilraunir á Kili. *Journal of Agricultural Research in Iceland*, 3, 12–27 (in Icelandic, English summary).

Fridriksson, S. (1972). Grass and grass utilization in Iceland. *Ecology*, 53, 785–96.

Fridriksson, S., Magnússon, B., & Gunnarsson, T. (1976). [*Studies in Erosion and Reclamation 1976*] *Uppblásturs- og uppgraedslurannsóknir 1976*. Fjölrit RALA 159. Reykjavík: Rannsóknastofnun landbúnadarins (in Icelandic).

Fridriksson, S. & Pálsson, J. (1970). [Landreclamation studies on the desert, Sprengisandur in south central part of Iceland] Landgraedslutilraun á Sprengisandi. *Journal of Agricultural Research in Iceland*, 2, 34–49 (in Icelandic, English summary).

Greipsson, S. (1991). Population studies on the dune-building grass *Leymus arenarius*. Dissertation. Norwich: University of East Anglia.

Greipsson, S. & Davy, A. J. (1994). Germination of *Leymus arenarius* and its significance for land reclamation in Iceland. *Annals of Botany*, 73. 393–401.

Gudmundsson, Th. (1991). [Soil investigations at reclamation sites] Jardvegsrannsóknir á tilraunasvaedunum. In *Uppgraedsla á Audkúluheidi og Eyvindarstadaheidi 1981–1989*, ed. I. Thorsteinsson, pp. 51–70. Reykjavík: Rannsóknastofnun landbúnadarins (in Icelandic).

Gunnlaugsdóttir, E. (1985). Composition and dynamical status of heathland communities in Iceland in relation to recovery measures. *Acta Phytogeographica Suecica*, 75, 1–84.

Hallsdóttir, M. (1987). Pollen analytical studies of human influence on vegetation in relation to the Landnám tephra layer in southwest Iceland. Lundqua thesis 18. Lund: Lund University.

Helgadóttir, Á. (1988a). Testing grass species and varieties for land reclamation in Iceland. *Journal of Agricultural Science in Finland*, 60, 191–200.

Helgadóttir, Á. (1988b). [In search of suitable grass varieties for reclamation purposes in Iceland]. Leit ad hentugum grastegundum til uppgraedslu. *Icelandic Agricultural Sciences*, 1, 11–33. (in Icelandic, English summary).

Iceland Ministry of Agriculture (1986). [*Land Utilization in Iceland*] *Landnýting á Íslandi og forsendur landnýtingaráaetlunar*. Reykjavík: Landbúnadarráduneytid (in Icelandic).

Iceland vegetation map (1994). Iceland vegetation map. Reykjavík: Iceland Geodetic Survey, Soil Conservation Service, Agricultural Research Institute.

Jackson, L. L., Lopoukhine, N., & Hillyard, D. (1995). Ecological restoration: A definition and comments. *Restoration Ecology*, 3, 71–5.

Kristinsson, H. (1979). [The vegetation in islands protected from grazing in the Icelandic Highlands] Gródur í beitarfridudum hólmum á Audkúluheidi og í Svartárbugum. *Týli*, 9, 33–46 (in Icelandic, English summary).

Magnússon, B. (1990). [Studies in the biology and ecology of Nootka lupin] Rannsóknir á líf- og vistfraedi alaskalúpínu. In *Graedum Ísland*, ed. A. Arnalds, pp. 157–9. Reykjavík: Landgraedsla ríkisins (in Icelandic).

Magnússon, B. (1994). Effect of introduced Nootka lupin (*Lupinus nootkatensis*) on vegetation and soil in Iceland. *Nordisk Jordbruksforskning*, 76, 15.

Magnússon, B., ed. (1995). [*Biological Studies of Nootka Lupin* (Lupinus nootkatensis) *in Iceland. Growth, seed set, chemical content and effect of cutting*] Líffraedi alaskalúpinu (Lupinus nootkatensis). *Vöxtur, fraemyndun, efnainnihald og áhrif sláttar.* Fjölrit RALA 178. Reykjavík: Rannsóknastofnun landbúnadarins (in Icelandic, English summary).

Magnússon, S. H. (1994). Plant colonization of eroded areas in Iceland. Dissertation. Lund University.

Magnússon, S. H. & Magnússon, B. (1990). [Seeding of birch for land reclamation and woodland establishment] Birkisáningar til landgraedslu og skógraektar. *Ársrit Skógraektarfélags Íslands*, 1990, 9–18 (in Icelandic, English summary).

Magnússon, S. H. & Magnússon, B. (1992). [Effects of willow (*Salix*) on the establishment of birch (*Betula pubescens*) from seeds] Áhrif vídis á landnám birkis á skóglausu svaedi. *Náttúrufraedingurinn*, 61, 95–108 (in Icelandic, English summary).

Magnússon, S. H. & Magnússon, B. (1995). [*Reclamation in Audkúluheidi and Eyvindarstadaheidi. Estimation of success 1994*] Uppgraedsla á Audkúlu- og Eyvindarstadaheidi. *Mat á ástandi gródurs sumarid 1994.* Fjölrit RALA 180. Reykjavík: Rannsóknastofnun landbúnadarins (in Icelandic).

Pálmason, F., Gudmundsson, J., & Helgadóttir, Á. (1995). Symbiotic nitrogen fixation in lupin and clover in Iceland. *Nordisk Jordbruksforskning*, 77, 77.

Péres, F. L. (1987). Needle-ice activity and the distribution of stem-rosette species in a Venezuelan Páramo. *Artic and Alpine Research, 19*, 135–53.

Sigbjarnarson, G. (1969). [The loessial soil formation and the soil erosion on Haukadalsheidi] Áfok og uppblástur. *Náttúrufraedingurinn*, 39, 49–128 (in Icelandic, English summary.

Sigurbjornsson, B. *Studies on the Icelandic* Elymus. Ph. D Thesis. Cornell University.

Sigurdardóttir, H. (1991). [Studies of *Collembola* at reclamation sites in the Blanda area, Audkúluheidi] Athuganir á stökkmor í uppgraedslusvaedum á virkjunarsvaedi Blöndu á Audkúluheidi. In *Uppgraedsla á Audkúluheidi og Eyvindarstadaheidi 1981–1989*, ed. I. Thorsteinsson, pp. 77–87. Reykjavík: Rannsóknastofnun landbúnadarins (in Icelandic).

Sigurdsson, S. (1977). [Birch in Iceland] Birki á Íslandi. In *Skógarmál*, eds. H. Gudmundsson, I. Thorsteinsson, S. Sigurdsson, H. Ragnarsson, J. Jónsson, & S. Blöndal, pp. 146–72. Reykjavík (in Icelandic).

Sigurjónsson, A., ed. (1958). [*Celebration of 50th anniversary of the Soil Conservation Service of Iceland*] Sandgraedslan. *Minnst 50 ára starfs Sandgraedslu Íslands.* Reykjavík: Agricultural Society of Iceland and Soil Conservation of Iceland (in Icelandic).

Thorsteinsson, I. (1978). [*Vegetation and Land Use*] Gródur og landnýting. Lesarkir Landverndar 3. Reykjavík: Landvernd (in Icelandic).

Thorsteinsson, I., ed. (1991). [*Land Reclamation on Audkúluheidi and Eyvindarstadaheidi 1981–1989*] Uppgraedsla á Audkúluheidi og Eyvindarstadaheidi 1981–1989. Reykjavík: Rannsóknastofnun landbúnadarins (in Icelandic).

Thórarinsson, S. (1961). [Wind erosion in Iceland. A tephrochronological study] Uppblástur á Íslandi í ljósi öskulagarannsókna. *Ársrit Skógraektarfélags Íslands*, 1961, 17–54 (in Icelandic, English summary).

Thórhallsdóttir, Th. E. (1991). [Effects of fertilization and grass seeding on vegetation in experimental plots in Audkúluheidi and Eyvindarstadaheidi and residual effects of fertilization] Áhrif áburdar og sáningar á gródur í tilraunareitum á Audkúlu- og Eyvindarstadaheidi og eftirverkun áburdar. In *Uppgraedfsla á Audkúluheidi og Eyvindarstadaheidi 1981–1989*, ed. I. Thorsteinsson, pp. 89–103. Reykjavík: Rannsóknastofnun landbúnadarins (in Icelandic).

Urbanska, K. M. (1995). Ecological restoration above the timberline and its demographic assessment. In *Restoration Ecology in Europe*, eds. K. M. Urbanska & K. Grodzinska, pp. 15–36. Zürich: Geobotanical Institute STIT.

11

Invertebrates assist the restoration process: an Australian perspective

JONATHAN D. MAJER

Introduction

When disturbed lands are restored, there is a tendency for the agencies concerned to be satisfied with the end-product if the area is stabilized, appears green, supports a variety of 'healthy' plants, and contains at least some types of animals. Judgment is often made within the first few years following restoration.

The attainment of successful, self-sustaining restoration is more complicated. The restoration may initially look successful. Later, however, some of the fast-growing but short-lived plants such as *Acacia* species may die, and trees may cease to increase in size once the effects of the initial fertilizer treatment have worn off. Certain plants may not reproduce successfully if they are not pollinated or their propagules are not dispersed, the area may become dominated by one or a few fast growing species at the expense of some of the herbs and shrubs, and the soil may not develop the texture or structure of the original substrate from the area. Weeds may invade, pests may attack some of the plants, and those animals present may simply be cosmopolitan species which can be found in any disturbed area.

The goal of restoration to native vegetation should be to emulate the structure, diversity, function, and dynamics of a specific ecosystem. Even if a pasture or plantation is the endpoint, some of these features are still desirable. Restoration staff may try to re-create adequate structure and function by propagating a wide range of plant species, representing the full range of structural layers in the ecosystem which is being re-created. However, if the dynamics of the restored area are not in place, the desired end-product may not be reached.

Figure 11.1 shows the various ecosystem functions and processes which need to be re-established in the restored area, and some of the outcomes and typical organisms which are involved. Animals, particularly

ECOSYSTEM FUNCTIONS AND PROCESSES	PEDOGENESIS	DECOMPOSITION	MYCORRHIZAL ACTIVITY	PHOTOSYNTHESIS	HERBIVORY	POLLINATION	PROPAGULE DISPERSAL	PREDATION/ PARASITISM	OTHER SPECIES INTERACTIONS (mutualists, symbionts, competition)
OUTCOME	improves soil structure	cycles nutrients	enhances nutrient uptake, some stimulation by soil fauna	provides cover and diversity, contributes to water cycling	limits excessive growth, enhances plant diversity	enables reproduction of plants	enables dispersal of plants	limits pests, enhances animal diversity	Limits pests, enhances plant and animal diversity
SOME ORGANISMS WHICH ARE INVOLVED	ants, termites, worms	millipedes, springtails, mites, worms	soil microarthropods	lichens, ferns, mosses, higher plants	beetles, caterpillars, kangaroos	wasps, flies, birds	ants, birds, mammals	wasps, flies, beetles, reptiles	ants - nectaries, mites - domatia

Figure 11.1. The various ecosystem functions and processes which should be established in rehabilitation, and some of the outcomes and typical organisms associated with each.

invertebrates, play an important role, so much so that they have been referred to as 'the little things that run the world' (Wilson 1987). This chapter explores some of the issues concerning invertebrates on restored lands.

Most restoration publications concern soil and vegetation, and remarkably few consider the fauna (on average 6.3% of entries make some reference to wildlife, 4.9% to fisheries, and 0.3% to livestock, Majer 1989b). Invertebrates are particularly poorly represented, being considered in only a minority of papers. This lack of information on invertebrates in relation to restored land is further exacerbated by the parochial citation of literature (Figure 11.2). If scientists and practitioners are to share and benefit from the meagre amount of information that is available worldwide, this is not an encouraging observation.

The analysis of publications mentioned above was performed in 1989. How much has changed since then? Perusal of the first five volumes of *Land Degradation and Rehabilitation* revealed no contributions on invertebrates, although the situation was a little better in the first three volumes of *Restoration Ecology*, which contained 8 articles on this topic. A search of the 1994/5 *Biological Reviews* produced 183 references, of which only 12 related specifically to terrestrial invertebrates. A further 20 references pertained to aquatic invertebrates, reflecting the long tradition of considering aquatic invertebrates in relation to disturbance (see Rosenberg & Resh 1993); these are outside the scope of this chapter.

Most of the species of animals alive today are invertebrates; depending on whose estimates are used, the number of extant insect species alone range from 8–100 million (Groombridge 1992). In terms of biomass, invertebrates usually exceed vertebrate animals in the same area (New 1995). Yet there is usually no problem in justifying the outcome of dollars spent on research into vertebrate animals. The low profile of invertebrates in restoration research is totally unjustified in view of their importance in ecosystem functioning.

In this chapter I outline from an Australian perspective some of the current directions which invertebrate work is taking within the area of restoration research. I hope this will emphasize some of the benefits of deriving an understanding of this component of the biota. In describing these studies, I will highlight some of the principles which should be considered and the deficiencies in the current approaches. Finally, I will conclude by revisiting the need to consider invertebrates, placing in context the types of restoration where invertebrate studies could be important, and providing some ideas for changing public opinion in relation to this group of animals.

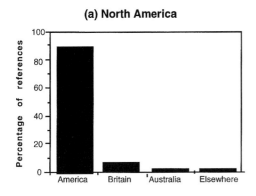

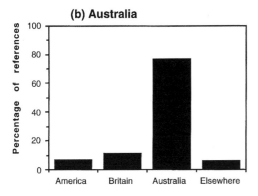

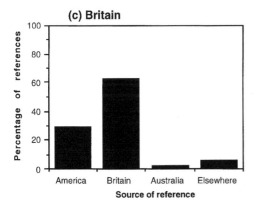

Figure 11.2. References cited by (a) North American, (b) Australian, and (c) British authors who have contributed to recent issues of *Restoration Ecology*, expressed as percentage from broad geographic regions (from Majer & Recher 1994).

Relationship between invertebrates and ecosystem functions and processes – case studies

Most restoration studies which have linked invertebrate abundance or diversity to ecosystem structure and functioning have been inferential (see Noss 1990; Aronson *et al*. 1993) in assuming that animal abundance in a particular feeding guild indicates their contribution to ecosystem structure or function (e.g., Williams 1993, and this volume). It does not prove, however, that a particular function will not operate or will be enhanced if a particular group of animals is absent or abundant and detracts from attempts to convince restoration practitioners that invertebrates are important.

Demonstration projects, which link invertebrate groups with ecosystem structuring or functioning, and which show how the abundance and/or activity of such animals may be encouraged, are required. Researchers, however, tend to avoid this approach because of the difficulties in demonstrating causal links (Lamont 1995), although Handel (this volume), shows how bees and frugivorous birds may be encouraged to facilitate pollination and seed dispersal. In the following three sections I describe Australian studies which relate to the re-establishment of soil structure, nutrient cycling, and plant dispersal systems. They emphasize the importance of invertebrates in the restoration process, and illustrate models of approaches which might be taken.

Soil structure

Abbott (1989) has reviewed the various ways in which invertebrates contribute to the maintenance of soil structure in restored lands. The wheatbelt of Western Australia has been largely cleared for agriculture, resulting in a dramatic shift in soil conditions. In comparison with virgin soils, cultivated soils are less tractable; they often have a compacted zone beneath the surface and are more prone to surface run-off after heavy rains (Abbott, Parker, & Sills 1979). The structure of these soils must be improved if sustainable agriculture is to continue (Parker 1989).

Abbott *et al*. (1979) describe a 'passive' restoration attempt at Kodj-Kodjin in which ploughing and stock were excluded from fields for 7 years. They compared this 'formerly cultivated' soil with cultivated soil and soil under virgin woodland. Physical and chemical variables were measured, and the density of large soil animals estimated by taking soil cores. Although cultivated soil was 'inferior' to virgin soil in terms of pH, organic

Table 11.1. *Winter measurements of soil chemical and physical parameters and also density of larger (>2 mm) soil invertebrates in virgin, formerly cultivated, and cultivated soils at Kodj-Kodjin in the Western Australian wheatbelt (data from Abbott* et al. *1979)*

	Soil type		
Soil parameter	Virgin	Formerly cultivated	Cultivated
pH	5.6	5.2	4.9
Organic matter %			
<2 mm	3.00	1.08	1.00
>45 mm	11.05	8.41	5.62
Mean weight diameter (mm) of			
water stable aggregates	3.28	2.78	1.20
Soil compaction[a]	239.3	207.6	192.2
Area of cavities and holes	+++	++	−
Infiltration[b]	53.1	47.6	150.3
Number of soil invertebrates per			
500 ml core	21	15	0

a Depth of penetration (mm) of a spike after constant force applied.
b Time(secs.) for water in a hollow cylinder to penetrate soil.

matter content, size of water stable aggregates, compactability, and ease of water infiltration, the formerly cultivated soil had substantially recovered towards virgin soil levels (Table 11.1). This was associated with a recovery of the large soil invertebrates, such as ants, termites, and beetles, and the creation of pores and holes within the soil (Table 11.1). Continuing this work at nearby Kellerberrin, Lobry de Bruyn, and Conacher (1994a,b, 1995) quantified the influence of ants and termites on soil structure. They specifically examined the role of ants and termites in soil turnover (bioturbation) and the influence of ant biopores on water infiltration under negative tensions (−5, −10, −40 mm) and positive pressure (+10 mm). Ant biopores were found to conduct water four to six times faster than the control soil, but only under ponded conditions, which would occur under high-energy rainfall events. However ant biopores had no detectable influence on water infiltration at negative tensions, a situation which was analogous to rainfall events which did not result in surface run-off. The density of ant biopores in farmland soils was comparable to the naturally vegetated habitat, and varied according to soil type, which indicates they are capable of maintaining soil structure even in disturbed environments such as a wheat paddock (Lobry de Bruyn 1993).

These studies highlight how the soil invertebrates rejuvenate degraded agricultural soils. The cessation of agriculture is generally not an option for restoring the soil, although modified farming practices such as minimal tillage and direct drilling of seeds (Bauermer & Bakermans 1973), alley farming between rows of revegetated crop trees (Lefroy, Hobbs, & Scheltema 1993), and more appropriate crop/stock rotations can lessen the negative impact of cultivation on invertebrates.

Nutrient turnover

Hutson (1989) has reviewed the role of fauna in decomposition and nutrient turnover in restored lands, examining reclaimed pit heaps in England (e.g., Hutson & Luff 1978), open-cast coal mines in the United States (e.g., Elkins *et al.* 1984), peat extractions in Ireland (Curry, Kelly, & Bolger 1985) and polders in Holland (van Rhee 1963). In addition, Dunger (1989) reviewed the extensive work on the soil and litter fauna of coal-mined areas in the former German Democratic Republic.

A parallel study on restored bauxite mines was conducted in the forested south-west part of Western Australia. It examined the development of the biota on a series of 30 bauxite mines, representing a wide range of restoration prescriptions and ages, and three jarrah (*Eucalyptus marginata*) forest controls. Ward, Majer and O'Connell (1991) quantified the rate of decomposition of eucalypt litter using litter bags. Decomposition was assessed by weight loss of leaves and also by carbon dioxide production from leaves. Greenslade and Majer (1993) also sampled the Collembola fauna by pitfall trapping and by heat extraction of soil and litter samples. A range of environmental variables was measured in each plot (see Majer *et al.* 1984) and their relationships with decomposition and collembolan variables were examined using multivariate statistics.

The collembolan data included total species and numbers of individuals and were further divided into species associated with litter, shrubs, and grasses, as well as introduced species. Many of the collembolan variables were significantly associated with particular environmental parameters (Table 11.2), with a species-rich fauna building up in areas with a rich flora and tree cover. Decomposers built up in areas with a dense litter layer and also high shrub and tree cover. Grass-associated species were most numerous in areas in good shrub cover, while introduced species declined as the restoration matured with age. Decomposition was often higher in areas which were moist and which had a higher litter and shrub cover (Ward *et al.* 1991) (Table 11.2). These data suggest that collembolan populations are mediating decomposition. The need to differentiate con-clusively between correlation and causation still exists, so further studies using microcosms, are required to confirm the association between collembolan build-up and decomposition activity in these restored areas.

Propagule dispersal

The majority of mining companies in Australia use direct seeding to revegetate mine sites. However, the dispersal and survival of many Australian plant seeds is intimately linked with the ant fauna of the region. The removal of seeds or diaspores by ants conforms to three categories: *granivory* – removal of the diaspore and subsequent consumption of the embryo; *nest decoration* – removal and incorporation of the diaspore into the nest structure; and *myrmecochory* – dispersal of the diaspore while leaving the embryo intact. Granivory is detrimental, nest decoration is not widespread, but myrmecochory is particularly prevalent in Australia. In this last category, seeds possess an elaiosome, often an oil- or fat-bearing body, which is attractive to ants. After the diaspore is transported, the ants eat the elaiosome and discard the seed. This may benefit the seed by dispersing it, isolating it from seed predators, isolating it from wildfires while exposing it to germination-inducing temperatures, enhancing longevity, placing it in a nutrient enriched environment, or a combination of these (Andersen 1990a; Majer 1990).

The beneficial effects of myrmecochory to seed survival are probably not all relevant to the initially seeded mine site. Seeds are sown in a dispersed pattern, into fertilized soils, and they have often been pre-treated by heat or smoke to accelerate germination. However, as the restoration matures, it is desirable that myrmecochorous relationships are restored for improved seed survival. This is important because restored areas are often subjected to prescription- or accidentally-lit fires.

Seed removal rates in 3-year-old restored areas in Western Australian bauxite mines (Majer 1980) and 2.5-year-old mineral sand mines in Queensland (Majer 1985) were similar to those in the original vegetation, suggesting that relationships have been restored. The relative rates of seed removal by granivores and elaiosome collectors were similar in the maturing regrowth and in the forest, suggesting that the relationship was recovering. However, in Queensland, although seed was taken in approximately equal proportions by granivores and elaiosome collectors in the forest, only the latter were involved in the regrowth.

The examples given above highlight the difficulties of linking the composition of the biota to ecosystem functioning (see Lamont 1995). Manipulations involving deletion or addition of species, or alterations in

Table 11.2. *Significant positive and negative associations (<0.05) between collembolan variables, and also weight loss and respiration of litter, with environmental variables in a range of restored bauxite mines and jarrah* (Eucalyptus marginata) *forest controls (data from Greenslade & Majer 1993; Ward et al. 1991)*

	Soil moisture	Litter depth	Litter cover (%)	Shrub cover (%)	Tree cover (%)	Plant species-richness	Time since restoration
Collembola variable							
Total species	.	.	.	.	+	+	.
Total individuals	.	-	-	.	.	.	.
Total introduced species	+	.	.	-	-	-	.
Total introduced individuals	.	.	.	.	-	-	-
Total decomposer species	.	+	+	+	+	.	.
Total decomposer individuals	.	+	.	+	+	.	.
Total shrub species	.	.	.	.	.	.	+
Total shrub individuals	.	+	.	.	.	.	+
Total grass species	.	-	.	.	.	.	+
Total grass individuals	.	.	.	+	.	+	.
Decomposition variable							
Loss of weight of litter	.	.	+	+	.	.	.
Carbon dioxide production	+	.	+	+	.	.	.

their abundance's, are necessary to describe their role with complete confidence; Lamont (1995) has outlined test procedures which might be adopted.

Invertebrates as indicators of restoration

By contrast, there have been many studies involving the use of invertebrates as bio-indicators of restoration success (see Williams, this volume), particularly in Australia, where studies have been performed in every state and territory (see Majer 1989a; Beattie 1993 for bibliographies). Environmental consultants now include invertebrates in their monitoring programmes.

Some surveys have sampled the entire invertebrate fauna and used the abundance of various taxa as indicators of ecosystem functioning (e.g. Williams 1993, and this volume). A more common strategy in Australia has been to focus on one or two invertebrate groups (e.g., spiders, collembolans, and ants) and use the data–trends as a surrogate for the whole invertebrate fauna (see Majer 1983; Greenslade & Greenslade 1984; Andersen 1990b, 1996). This idea has attractions, since it is easier to make meaningful interpretations of data when focusing on better-known groups. A further benefit of concentrating on particular taxa is that it may provide a cost-effective means of indicating the biodiversity status of an area, an approach referred to as Rapid Biodiversity Assessment (Beattie 1993). The procedures and rationale for using invertebrates as bio-indicators have been outlined by Majer (1983), Andersen (1990b), New (1995), and Stork (1990). I here add some considerations which should be taken into account if this procedure is adopted.

Selection of indicator taxa

Several indicator taxa have been evaluated in restored areas throughout Australia, although ants are the most commonly utilized taxon (e.g., Majer 1983; Andersen 1990b). Ants are good indicators because they are abundant, exhibit high species-richness, contain many specialists, occupy higher trophic levels, are easily sampled and identified, and are responsive to changing environmental conditions. Collembola (e.g., Greenslade & Majer 1993), termites (e.g., Bunn 1983) spiders (e.g., Simmonds, Majer, & Nichols 1994), and predatory invertebrates (Nichols & Burrows 1985) have also been used as bio-indicators.

Most work in Australia has been carried out on decomposers and predominantly predator groups. The concentration on ants has been largely based on the assumption that ant richness and community composition reflects patterns in other arthropod groups. Indeed, within restored sites this has been shown to be the case (Majer 1983; Anderson, Morrison, & Belbin 1996). However, in studies across a range of native habitats, where differences in habitat composition are more subtle, correlations between the richness of ants and other arthropods may be relatively low (Abensperg-Traun *et al.* 1996; Oliver 1995) or non-existent (Cranston & Trueman, 1996), although differences in community composition undoubtedly exist. Thus a wider range of indicator groups should be used, representing different organisms associated with different ecological processes. Candidates include: termites – soil structure; Collembola – decomposition; Homoptera – herbivory; and flies, beetles, or ants as indicators of several processes.

Ants as indicators of restoration success

The most simplistic approach has been to measure species-richness, diversity, and/or evenness and to relate this to habitat factors and sometimes to the richness of other arthropod groups. Majer *et al.* (1984) have used the first approach in a study of 30 restored bauxite mines and 3 forest controls. Step-wise multiple regression was used to identify the combination of variables which best described variation in ant species-richness and diversity. Plant species-richness and/or diversity, followed by restoration age, plant cover in lower strata, litter cover, and the presence of logs were important variables (Table 11.3). These variables were important in encouraging the return of a rich ant and other invertebrate fauna, so restoration prescriptions were subsequently adopted to encourage the development of these habitat features.

The lumping of species, without considering their biology, masks important information. A second approach classifies species into functional groups. Greenslade (1978) recognized seven functional groups of ants (Table 11.4), with the most important group comprising the dominant species of *Iridomyrmex*, whose members exert a strong competitive influence on other ants because of their high abundance, activity, and aggressive behaviour. The remaining groups comprise species that occur in habitats not favoured by *Iridomyrmex*, or possess specializations reducing their interaction with this genus (Table 11.4). Andersen (1990b) refined this scheme, using ants as indicators of biogeographical affiliation, habitat composition, environmental degradation, and, more recently, habitat restoration (Andersen 1993; Andersen *et al.* 1996).

Table 11.3. *Habitat variables which explain variance in an ant species-richness and diversity in 30 restored bauxite mines and 3 forest controls. Values are percentage of variance explained (adapted from Majer et al. 1984)*

Ant richness and/or diversity positively associated with:	Ant variables	
	Richness (S)	Diversity (H')[a]
Plant species-richness	24%	
Plant species-diversity		27%
Time since rehabilitation	13%	27%
% plant cover (especially 50-125 cm strata)	13%	38%
% litter cover		13%
Presence of large logs	+++[b]	+++

Note: [a]'H' is Shannon's diversity index.
[b]The contribution of large logs to the return of an fauna was assessed by direct observation and found to be important, although the variance which they contribute to the ant parameters is not quantified here.

Table 11.4. *Functional groups of Australian ants, showing the major taxa occurring in each category (taken from Greenslade 1978 and Andersen 1990b)*

Group	Major taxa	Attributes
Dominant Dolichoderinae	*Iridomyrmex*	highly abundant, active and aggressive; exert a strong competitive influence on other ants
Associated subordinate Camponotini	*Camponotus. Polyrhachis*	co-occur with *Iridomyrmex* but competitively subordinate; large body size, often nocturnal foragers, submissive behaviour
Hot climate specialists	*Melophorus, Meranoplus*	co-occur with *Iridomyrmex* but with morphological, physiological, or behavioural specialization
Cryptic species	*Solenopsis, Hypoponera*	occur primarily within soil and litter and therefore do not interact much with other ants
Opportunists	*Rhytidoponera, Tetramorium, Paretrechina*	unspecialized and poorly competitive ants characteristic of disturbed habitats and other sites of low ant diversity
Generalized Myrmicinae	*Monomorium Pheidole, Crematogaster*	unspecialized but highly competitive myrmicines; rapid forager recruitment and ability to defend food resources
Large, solitary foragers	*Leptogenys, Pachycondyla*	large body size, low population density, often specialized diet; unlikely to interact much with other ants

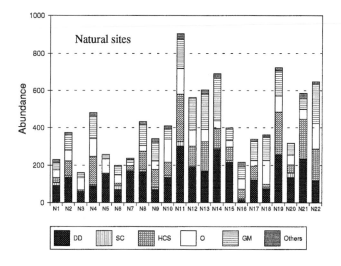

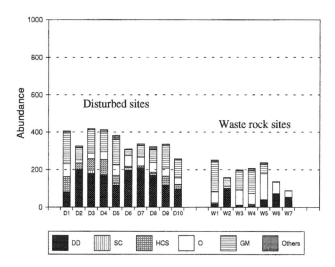

Figure 11.3. Abundances of major ant functional groups recorded in pitfall traps; DD = Dominant Dolichoderinae; SC = Subordinate Camponotini; HCS = Hot climate specialists; O = Opportunists; GM = Generalized Myrmicinae (from Andersen *et al.* 1996).

In a study of 22 natural sites, 10 disturbed areas and 7 sites at varying stages of restoration at the Ranger uranium mine in Australia's Northern Territory, Andersen *et al.* (1996) (Figure 11.3) found clear trends between ant groups. The most abundant ants were Dominant dolichoderines (mostly species of *Iridomyrmex*), Hot climate specialists (mostly species of *Melophorus*), Opportunists (mostly species of *Rhytidoponera, Tetramorium,* and *Paratrechina*), and Generalized myrmicines (mostly species of *Monomorium* and *Pheidole*). These four functional groups were abundant at virtually all natural and disturbed sites, but at waste rock sites Dominant dolichoderines were patchy and Hot climate specialists were mostly absent. Andersen (1996) has now shown that the abundance of ants within certain functional groups can be used as a surrogate for overall ant species-richness in the Australian seasonal tropics.

The third approach is to use an ordination-type of analysis to display hypothetical data on the variation in site descriptors through both space and time. It is seldom possible to follow succession in restored areas over a long period of time. As a result, workers often use a 'chronosequence' approach in which a range of sites which represent known ages after disturbance is selected and sampled at the same time. The resulting differences are then taken to be representative of different stages in the successional process. This technique can be fraught with problems, since the chosen sites may not represent areas which originally possessed identical communities. Thus attempts to detect trends in the chronosequence of sites may be confounded by inherent differences in community composition. This is not such a problem with mine-site restoration studies, since the sites tend to have similar characteristics and the restoration procedures are often standardized between sites or, if they are not, they have probably been documented.

Two overseas studies which I have been involved with illustrate the application of this approach. Bauxite is being mined at Poços de Caldas in the state of Minas Gerais, Brazil. The native vegetation of the area is a patchwork of subtropical rainforest (mata) and grassy woodland (campo). The company is attempting to restore the area to mata by returning the topsoil and revegetating the area with mata plant species. Application of an ordination procedure to ant data from restored plots ranging from 1 to 10 years old and also from a mata and a campo control suggests that the ant fauna in the younger plots is not developing towards that of the mata ant community (Figure 11.4). Furthermore, application of minimum spanning-tree analysis to the points on the ordination indicates that the fauna in the younger plots has more in common with that of the campo than of the mata (Figure 11.4a). Only in the oldest two plots, where the tree canopy has closed up, is the fauna more allied to the mata than to the campo.

The second example comes from Richards Bay, South Africa where a mosaic of cleared and pristine coastal dune forest is being mined for

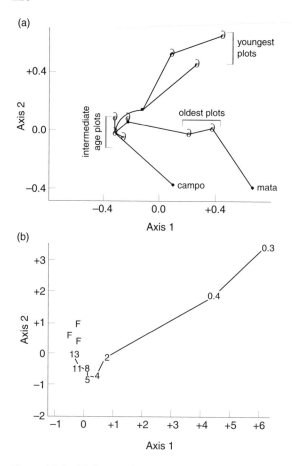

Figure 11.4. (a) Separation of control and rehabilitated plots at Poços de Caldas, Brazil derived by the use of principal co-ordinates analysis of ant species presence/absence data using Sørensen's similarity quotient. The lines were derived by minimum spanning-tree analysis and connect plots which have the most similar ant fauna (adapted from Majer 1992). (b) Separation of control and rehabilitated plots at Richards Bay, South Africa, derived by the use of correspondence analysis on ant species presence/absence data. Numbers represent the age, in years, of the rehabilitation, and 'F' represents the forest controls. The lines have been drawn to indicate the path of the succession (adapted from Majer & de Kock 1992).

mineral sands. The company is attempting to restore much of the area to coastal dune forest by revegetating the area with forest species and also with those plants which characterize the succession which occurs when shifting cultivation-type farms are abandoned. Application of an ordina-tion-type procedure to the ant data from plots ranging from 0.3 to 13 years old and to three forest controls indicates that the first part of the succession is not 'directed' towards the original forest community; only in the older plots does the ant community start to resemble that of the original forest (Figure 114b). Consideration of temporal changes in the physical and biological components of the environment suggests that this dichotomy in the direction of the succession is mediated by the presence of the pan-tropical ant species, *Pheidole megacephala*, which progressively attains massive densities in the youngest restoration and declines to negligible levels from the 6-year-old through to 13-year-old restoration (Majer & de Kock 1992).

I have found the various ordination-type procedures to be very useful in understanding the temporal variation in complex datasets. Provided that users take steps to account for site differences and design their sampling programmes so that the trends are not confounded by seasonal effects, this is a useful method for visualizing successional processes.

Each approach has its benefits, and it is probable that the maximum information would be obtained if all three approaches were used in a complementary manner. Furthermore, although the examples given here are of ants, the three approaches undoubtedly have applicability to other taxa as well.

Adopting a sampling protocol

The most commonly used procedure for sampling invertebrates in restored areas is pitfall trapping; some studies have relied solely upon this method. Pitfall traps have been adopted so enthusiastically because they are relatively simple to use, they operate continuously through day and night over extended periods, and yield high numbers of animals representing a range of species. They are, however, subject to a range of limitations (see Adis 1979; Luff 1975). Majer (1996a) has recently looked at the perform-ance of pitfall traps against a more complete suite of techniques for censusing the entire ant community in habitats of increasing complexity. Three studies of mine site restoration were used for this evaluation as they represent a gradation in habitat complexity from eucalypt forest in North Stradbroke Island, Queensland, to dune forest at Richards Bay, South Africa, through to tropical rain forest at Trombetas, Brazil (data from Majer 1985; Majer & de Kock 1992; Majer 1996b). Within each study, the succession from the newest restoration through to the original vegetation also represents a trend of increasing habitat complexity.

Ants were sampled by pitfall trapping and also by day and night hand

Table 11.5. *Number of ant species caught by pitfall trapping expressed as a percentage of those caught by the 'standard' and 'extended' sampling regimes in restoration and native vegetation controls at North Stradbroke, Richards Bay, and Trombetas (from Majer, 1996a)*

Number of ant species in pitfall traps as a percentage of:	North Stradbroke		Richards Bay		Trombetas	
	Restoration	Control	Restoration	Control	Restoration	Control
Standard samples	59.5	47.3	46.4	35.3	41.9	22.3
Extended samples[a]	56.0	44.0	45.0	32.0	40.0	17.7

Note: [a]Note that the percentages for the 'extended' samples at Richards Bay and Trombetas are not totally comparable with those from the 'standard' samples since they represent a more limited range of plots.

collections, which included sweeping undergrowth and beating trees. The combination of pitfall trapping plus these collecting procedures is referred to as the 'standard' sampling procedure. In certain plots the ants were also sampled by litter extraction (funnels or Winkler sacks) and by baiting. This is referred to as the 'extended' sampling procedure.

Table 11.5 shows the mean number of ant species caught by pitfall trapping expressed as a percentage of those caught by the standard and extended samples in restoration and native vegetation at the three localities. A number of trends are clearly evident. First, pitfall trapping never sampled more than 60% of the ant species obtained from the more complete sample sets. Secondly, looking at the standard sampling dataset first, the percentage of ants trapped by pitfall trapping in the control plots was always considerably lower than in the restored plots. Thus, pitfall trapping does not sample a constant proportion of the fauna if widely divergent habitats such as restoration and native vegetation are considered. Thirdly, the shortfall in pitfall trap catch increased in both restoration and controls with the increasing habitat complexity from North Stradbroke, through Richards Bay to Trombetas. In the forest at Trombetas, the pitfall traps only sampled an average of 22.3% of the species obtained by the standard sampling regime. If the data from the extended sampling regime are used for the calculation of percentage catch by pitfall traps, the trends are further exaggerated (Table 11.5).

In part, the discrepancy between pitfall and standard or extended sample catches is related to the low number of pitfall traps used in the mine site studies; pitfall trapping was never intended to be the main sampling tool.

An adequate number of suitably sized pitfall traps is indeed a good method for sampling the surface-active ant community in open habitats, although authors who use this approach should specify that the study pertains to the epigaeic ant community. However, traps generally undersample the entire ant community in more closed formations. The more structurally complex the habitat, the more serious becomes the problem, with cryptic, hypo-gaeic, arboreal, and rare species being particularly prone to undersampling. Unless the study is specifically of the surface-active ant community, it is not appropriate in structurally complex habitats to rely upon pitfall traps alone. In line with the conclusion of Disney *et al.* (1982), it is recommended that a combination of sampling procedures must be employed if a reasonably complete census of the ant community is to be obtained. A suitable sampling protocol, which involves pitfall trapping, vegetation sweeping, tree beating, and also day and night hand collection has been described in Allen (1989). Although ants have been used to illustrate this point, the conclusions and recommendations may well apply to other invertebrate taxa as well.

In the following section I raise a broader issue which arises from the use of animals, such as ants, as indicators.

Invertebrates in relation to the scope of the restoration problem

The aims and requirements of the restoration process are, to an extent, influenced by the type of disturbance which is involved. Mining, for instance, destroys most or all of the biota of the quarried area, and therefore halts the associated ecosystem functions and processes. At the other end of the disturbance spectrum is rangeland grazing of native vegetation, which may stress the biota and associated ecosystem functions and processes, while not actually eliminating or halting them.

With this in mind, it is useful to quantify the extent of the various types of disturbances so that an indication of the magnitude of the restoration problem can be provided. Majer and Beeston (1996) have developed a biodiversity integrity index (BI) which provides a measure of the degree of intactness of the original species-richness over a particular land use. It is a product of the species-richness of a particular land use unit and the area which that unit occupies.

Consider a landscape which contains four major habitat units (Figure 11.5). The units are first standardized to the same area, since the index attributes equal importance to each habitat, whatever the area it occupies. Unit 1 is in a totally pristine state, unit 2 contains a mine which occupies

230   *J. D. Majer*

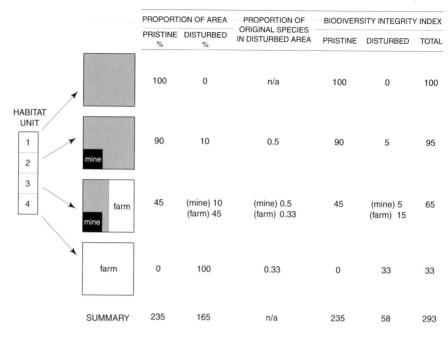

PROPORTION OF AREA		PROPORTION OF ORIGINAL SPECIES IN DISTURBED AREA	BIODIVERSITY INTEGRITY INDEX		
PRISTINE %	DISTURBED %		PRISTINE	DISTURBED	TOTAL
100	0	n/a	100	0	100
90	10	0.5	90	5	95
45	(mine) 10 (farm) 45	(mine) 0.5 (farm) 0.33	45	(mine) 5 (farm) 15	65
0	100	0.33	0	33	33
SUMMARY 235	165	n/a	235	58	293

Figure 11.5. Diagram of hypothetical region that contains four habitat units which have been subjected to differing amounts of mining and farming, showing how the biodiversity integrity index (BI) is affected by these land uses. The BI value is derived by multiplying the percent area under each land use by the proportion of the original diversity that remains in that land use.

10% of the area, while unit 3 contains a mine of similar percentage contribution to the area and also farmland covering 45% of the region. The remaining unit has been totally cleared for agricultural purposes. Richness is set at 1 in the pristine state. No weighting is given to habitat units which support exceptionally low or high richness, as equal importance is assigned to the biological diversity of each unit when it is in its pristine state. The richness of a taxonomic group is then assessed within each habitat unit and in each type of disturbance. In the example given, richness drops to a half its original value in the post-mining situation and to a third in the farmland. The BI index in unit 1 is 100×1.0, or 100, which is the maximum attainable figure. In unit 2 it is 90×1.0 (pristine) plus 10×0.5 (mine), which gives a value of 95. In unit 3 the BI index in the disturbed areas is obtained by summing the indices for the pristine area (i.e. 45×1.0) and the two types of disturbance (10×0.5 (mine) $+45 \times 0.33$ (farm)), which gives value of 65, while in unit 4 there are no pristine habitats so the BI is 100×0.33, or 33.

The resulting BI indices may be used in a number of ways. First, they can provide numerical data which can contribute towards an audit of the state of biological diversity across the entire landscape. Thus, in the hypothetical region mentioned above, the BI index has dropped from a maximum of 400 down to 293. It is also possible to report on the habitat units where biological diversity is most adversely affected. Thus, the BI index is lowest in unit 4 (33), followed by unit 3 (65). The BI index in unit 2 is only slightly lower (95) than that in the pristine unit 1. An additional use of the procedure is to provide summaries of the effect of different land uses on biological diversity across the entire landscape, or subsets thereof. This information is obtained by subtracting the BI value for a particular land use from that value which would have been obtained had species-richness been 1. Thus mining, which occupies 10% of each of two units, has caused a cumulative loss of 10 BI units (10 × 1.0 minus 10 × 0.5 for each unit). Farming, on the other hand, occupies 45 and 100% of two units and has caused a cumulative loss of 30 plus 67, or 97, BI units.

Majer and Beeston (1996) used ants in Western Australia as a demonstration of this index, since their distribution is well known and their response to major land uses has been subject to a range of investigations. The vegetation of Western Australia has been mapped by Beard (1990) and can be reduced to 24 districts or sub districts. The major land uses which have occurred in the state can broadly be described as mining (generally with subsequent restoration), agricultural clearing, rangeland grazing, urbanization, and roadways. The areas of each land use in each phytogeographic district was derived from GIS maps. These were then expressed as percentages of each area and multiplied by the fraction of ant diversity remaining in each land use within that area.

Using this procedure, Majer and Beeston (1996) were able to identify the phytogeographic regions where the BI of ants was most reduced. The resulting rankings closely corresponded with the subjective ordering of areas in the recent State of the Environment (Environmental Protection Authority, 1992) report. Thus, by considering the ant fauna in this way, an objective means of identifying degraded areas is available which may be used for identifying areas for environmental mitigation.

A further spin-off of this procedure is that it provides a statement on the relative impact of different land uses on BI. This may be considered within a particular district or group of districts, or across the whole country or state. The state-wide summary for Western Australia (Figure 11.6) indicates that agricultural clearing has had by far the greatest impact on ant BI, closely followed by rangeland grazing. The lower losses of BI as a result of urbanization, roads, and mining puts into context the lower impact of these

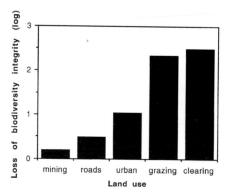

Figure 11.6. Loss of biodiversity integrity (BI) values in the 24 phytogeographic regions (maximum loss is 24×100 BI units $= 2400$) as a result of five broad land uses in Western Australia. Loss is calculated by subtracting the BI values associated with the five land uses in each region from the values that would have been produced if ant diversity values were still 1.00 (i.e. unaffected) in each of the land uses (data from Majer & Beeston 1996).

relatively restricted land uses. The corollary of this is that restoration effort might best be directed at those land uses which have the greatest impact across the entire landscape.

Although the example used ants in Western Australia for deriving the BI, there is no reason why this procedure should not be applied to other regions of the world and to many other plant and animal taxa. However, in order to calculate reliably the fractional changes in richness, it is desirable for the case taxon to be speciose and ubiquitous. It is here that invertebrates are eminently suited to this procedure.

Conclusions

Are invertebrates worth considering?

This review of a range of issues involving invertebrates and the restoration problem clearly shows that these animals can influence the outcome, possibly even the success or failure, of a restoration programme. Additionally, knowledge of the way in which the invertebrate fauna is developing can provide valuable information on the efficacy of restoration attempts. Also evident from this review is that this area of biology is still not receiving adequate attention – a deficiency which partly results from our lack of knowledge about their roles, but none the less one which is detracting from our ability to fully understand our restoration programmes. Granted that our incomplete knowledge creates taxonomic and ecological impediments (Taylor 1983; New 1995) to the uptake of invertebrates into the research and monitoring agenda, we do possess sufficient information on roles and methodologies to incorporate invertebrates into future restoration programmes. In the final section I outline some ideas for gaining a wider acceptance of this viewpoint by restoration practitioners, researchers, and the public at large.

Changing public opinion about invertebrates

When I started talking about invertebrates at mining conferences some 20 years ago, the presentation was treated with some amusement, even derision, by many participants. Nevertheless, two or three companies were sufficiently impressed that they commissioned invertebrate studies in their restored areas. Not only have such studies become commonplace in Australia, invertebrate biologists are frequently asked to speak at restoration conferences. This is not the case in all parts of the world and it is incumbent on scientists to push for their inclusion, and for conference organizers to ensure that they are included.

As mentioned above, restoration practitioners would be more readily convinced if the link between invertebrates and the various ecosystem functions and processes could be firmly demonstrated. This should be a number one priority for research funding. Secondly, land users need to be convinced that a consideration of invertebrates will lead to better restoration. When results are presented at industry conferences, they should be presented with a certain amount of flair, bearing in mind that the audience is comprised of personnel from disciplines who need to be convinced of the importance of these animals.

A further opportunity is to include invertebrates on the list of completion criteria which must be attained before declaring the restoration a success and, where relevant, release of bonds (see discussion in Williams, this volume). As outlined in the section on bio-indicators, invertebrates are ideally suited for conveying information about the environmental status of an area. Although soil and vegetation factors are important parameters to quantify, invertebrates are a valuable adjunct to these and they can integrate information on a variety of factors which are normally difficult to quantify.

A considerable amount of information has now been written about the importance of invertebrates (see textbooks by Gaston, New, & Samways

1994; New 1984, 1995; Samways 1994). Much of the necessary arguments for considering invertebrates has been amply spelt out in the literature. It is now incumbent on restoration practitioners to consider the animals which make up over 95% of terrestrial species which are alive today. If they were to do so we would be more likely to see restored lands developing in a sustainable way!

References

Abbott, I. (1989). The influence of fauna on soil structure. In *Animals in Primary Succession: The Role of Fauna in Reclaimed Lands*, ed. J. D. Majer, pp. 39–50. Cambridge University Press.

Abbott, I., Parker, C. A., & Sills, I. D. (1979). Changes in the abundance of large soil animals and physical properties of soils following cultivation. *Australian Journal of Soil Research*, 17, 343–53.

Abensperg-Traun, M., Arnold, G., Stevens, D., Smith, G., Atkins, L., Viveen, J., & Gutter, M. (1996). Biodiversity indicators in semi-arid agricultural Western Australia. *Pacific Conservation Biology*, 2, 375-89.

Adis, J. (1979). Problems of interpreting arthropod samples with pitfall traps. *Zoologischer Anzeiger*, 202, 177–84.

Allen, N. T. (1989). A methodology for collecting standardised biological data for planning and monitoring reclamation and rehabilitation programmes. In *Animals in Primary Succession: The Role of Fauna in Reclaimed Lands*, ed. J. D. Majer, pp. 179–205. Cambridge University Press.

Andersen, A. N. (1990a). Seed harvesting ant pests in Australia. In *Applied Myrmecology: A World Perspective*, eds. R. K. Vander Meer, K. Jaffe, & A. Cedeno. pp. 34–9. Boulder: Westview Press.

Andersen, A. N. (1990b). The use of ant communities to evaluate change in Australian terrestrial ecosystems: a review and a recipe. *Proceedings of the Ecological Society of Australia*, 16, 347–57.

Andersen, A. N. (1993). Ants as indicators of restoration success at a uranium mine in tropical Australia. *Restoration Ecology*, 1, 156–67.

Andersen, A. N. (1996). Measuring invertebrate biodiversity. Surrogates for ant species richness in the Australian seasonal tropics. *Memoirs of the Museum of Victoria*, 56, 355–60.

Andersen, A. N., Morrisson, S., & Belbin, L. (1996). *The Role of Ants in Minesite Restoration in the Kakadu Region of Australia's Northern Territory, with Particular Reference to their Use as Bio-indicators.* Unpublished report to the Environmental Research Institute of the Supervising Scientist. Darwin: CSIRO.

Aronson, J., Floret, C., LeFloc'h, E., Ovalle, C., & Pontanier, R. (1993). Restoration and rehabilitation of degraded ecosystems in arid and semiarid regions. I. A view from the South. *Restoration Ecology*, 1, 8–17.

Bauermer, K. & Bakermans, W. A. P. (1973). Zero-tillage. *Advances in Agronomy*, 25, 77–123.

Beard, J. S. (1990). *Plant Life of Western Australia*. Perth: Kangaroo Press.

Beattie, A. J., ed. (1993). *Rapid Biodiversity Assessment: Proceedings of the Biodiversity Assessment Workshop, Maquarie University*. Sydney: Research Unit for Biodiversity Assessment, Maquarie University.

Bunn, S. E. (1983). Termite (Isoptera) fauna of jarrah forest in the Wagerup-Willowdale region, Western Australia: relevance to the rehabilitation of bauxite minesites. *Forest Ecology and Management*, 6, 169–77.

Cranston, P. S. & Trueman, J. W. H. (1996). Indicator taxa in invertebrate biodiversity assessment. *Memoirs of the Museum of Victoria*, 56, 267–71.

Curry, J. P., Kelly, M., & Bolger, T. (1985). Role of invertebrates in the decomposition of *Salix* litter in reclaimed cutover peat. In *Ecological Interactions in Soil: Plants, Microbes and Animals*, eds. A. H. Fitter, D. Atkinson, D. J. Read, & M. B. Usher, pp. 355–65. Oxford: Blackwell Scientific Publications.

Disney, R. H. L., Erzinçlioglu, Y. Z., Henshaw, D. J. de C., Howse, D., Unwin, D. M., Withers, P., & Woods, A. (1982). Collecting methods and the adequacy of attempted fauna surveys with reference to the Diptera. *Field Studies*, 5, 607–21.

Dunger, W. (1989). The return of soil fauna to coal mined areas in the German Democratic Republic. In *Animals in Primary Succession: The Role of Fauna in Reclaimed Lands*, ed. J. D. Majer, pp. 307–37. Cambridge University Press.

Elkins, N. Z., Parker, L. W., Aldon, E., & Whitford, W. G. (1984). Responses of soil biota to the organic amendments in strip-mine spoils in northwest New Mexico. *Journal of Environmental Quality*, 13, 215–19.

Environmental Protection Authority (1992). *State of the Environment Report*. Perth, Western Australia: Environmental Protection Authority.

Gaston, K. J., New, T. R., & Samways, M. J. (1994). *Perspectives on Insect Conservation*. Andover: Intercept.

Greenslade, P. J. M. (1978). Ants. In *The Physical and Biological Features of Kunnoth Paddock in Central Australia*, ed. W. A. Low. pp. 109–13. Technical Paper, CSIRO Division of Land Resources Management, Australia.

Greenslade, P. J. M. & Greenslade, P. (1984). Invertebrates and environmental assessment. *Environment and Planning*, 3, 13–15.

Greenslade, P. & Majer, J. D. (1993). Recolonization by Collembola of rehabilitated bauxite mines in Western Australia. *Australian Journal of Ecology*, 18, 385–94.

Groombridge, B., ed. (1992). *Global Biodiversity: Status of the Earth's Living Resources*. Cambridge: World Monitoring Centre/London: Chapman and Hall.

Hutson, B. R. (1989). The role of fauna in nutrient turnover. In *Animals in Primary Succession: The Role of Fauna in Reclaimed Lands*, ed. J. D. Majer, pp. 51–70. Cambridge University Press.

Hutson, B. R. & Luff, M. L. (1978). Invertebrate colonization and succession on industrial reclamation sites. *Scientific Proceedings, Royal Dublin Society, Series A*, 6, 165–74.

Lamont, B. B. (1995). Testing the effect of ecosystem composition/structure on its functioning. *Oikos*, 74, 283–95.

Lefroy, E. C., Hobbs, R. J., & Scheltema, M. (1993). Reconciling agriculture and nature conservation: Toward a restoration strategy for the Western Australian Wheatbelt. In *Nature Conservation 3: Reconstruction of Fragmented Ecosystems*, eds. D. A. Saunders, R. J. Hobbs, & P. R. Ehrlich, pp. 243–57. Sydney: Surrey Beatty and Sons.

Lobry de Bruyn, L. A. (1993). Ant composition and activity in naturally vegetated and farmland environments on contrasting soils at Kellerberrin, Western Australia. *Soil Biology and Biochemistry*, 25, 1043–56.

Lobry de Bruyn, L. A. & Conacher, A. J. (1994a). The effect of ant biopores on water infiltration in soils in undisturbed bushland and in farmland in a semi-arid environment. *Pedobiologia*, 38, 193–207.

Lobry de Bruyn, L. A. & Conacher, A. J. (1994b). The bioturbation activity of ants in agricultural and naturally vegetated habitats in semi-arid environments. *Australian Journal of Soil Research*, 32, 555–70.

Lobry de Bruyn, L. A. & Conacher, A. J. (1995). Soil modification by mound-building termites in the central wheatbelt of Western Australia. *Australian Journal of Soil Research*, 33, 179–93.

Luff, M. L. (1975). Some problems influencing the efficiency of pitfall traps. *Oecologia*, 19, 345–57.

Majer, J. D. (1980). The influence of ants on broadcast and naturally spread seeds in rehabilitated bauxite mines. *Reclamation Review*, 3, 3–9.

Majer, J. D. (1983). Ants: Bio-indicators of minesite rehabilitation, land use and land conservation. *Environmental Management*, 7, 375–83.

Majer, J. D. (1985)., Recolonization by ants of rehabilitated mineral sand mines on North Stradbroke Islands, Queensland, with particular reference to seed removal. *Australian Journal of Ecology*, 10, 31–48.

Majer, J. D., ed. (1989a). *Animals in Primary Succession: The Role of Fauna in Reclaimed Lands*. Cambridge University Press.

Majer, J. D. (1989b). Fauna studies and land reclamation technology – a review of the history and need for such studies. In *Animals in Primary Succession: The Role of Fauna in Reclaimed Lands*, ed. J. D. Majer. pp. 5–33. Cambridge University Press.

Majer, J. D. (1990). The role of ants in Australian land reclamation seeding operations. In *Applied Myrmecology: A World Perspective*, eds. R. K. Vander Meer, K. Jaffe, & A. Cedeno, pp. 544–54. Boulder: Westview Press.

Majer, J. D. (1992). Ant recolonisation of rehabilitated bauxite mines of Poços de Caldos, Brazil. *Journal of Tropical Ecology*, 8, 97–108.

Majer, J. D. (1996a). The use of pitfall traps for sampling ants and other invertebrate fauna – a critique. *Memoirs of the Museum of Victoria*, 56, 323–30.

Majer, J. D. (1996b). Ant recolonisation of rehabilitated bauxite mines at Trombetas, Pará, Brazil. *Journal of Tropical Ecology*, 11, 1–17.

Majer, J. D. & Beeston, G. (1996). The biodiversity integrity index: an illustration using ants in Western Australia. *Conservation Biology*, 10, 65–73.

Majer, J. D., Day, J. E., Kabay, E. D., & Perriman, W. S. (1984). Recolonization by ants in bauxite mines rehabilitated by a number of different methods. *Journal of Applied Ecology*, 21, 355–75.

Majer, J. D. & de Kock, A. E. (1992). Ant recolonization of sand mines near Richards Bay, South Africa: an evaluation of progress with rehabilitation. *South African Journal of Science*, 88, 31–6.

Majer, J. D. & Recher, H. F. (1994). Restoration ecology: An international science? *Restoration Ecology*, 2, 215–17.

New, T. R. (1984). *Insect Conservation: An Australian Perspective*. Dordrecht: W. Junk.

New, T. R. (1995). *Introduction to Invertebrate Conservation Biology.* Oxford University Press.

Nichols, O. G. & Burrows, R. (1985). Recolonisation of revegetated bauxite minesites by predatory invertebrates. *Forest Ecology and Management,* 10, 49–64.

Noss, R. F. (1990). Indicators for monitoring biodiversity: A hierarchical approach. *Conservation Biology,* 4, 355–64.

Oliver, I. (1995). Rapid biodiversity assessment and its application to invertebrate conservation in production forests. Ph.D. thesis, Sydney: Maquarie University.

Parker, C. A. (1989). Soil biota and plants in degraded agricultural soils. In *Animals in Primary Succession: The Role of Fauna in Reclaimed Lands,* ed. J. D. Majer. pp. 423–38. Cambridge University Press.

Rosenberg, D. M. & Resh, V. M., eds. (1993). *Freshwater Biomonitoring and Benthic Invertebrates.* London: Chapman and Hall.

Samways, M. J. (1994). *Insect Conservation Biology.* London: Chapman & Hall.

Simmonds, S. J., Majer, J. D., & Nichols, O. G. (1994). A comparative study of spider (Araneae) communities of rehabilitated bauxite mines and surrounding forest in the southwest of Western Australia. *Restoration Ecology,* 2, 247–60.

Stork, N. E., ed. (1990). *The Role of Ground Beetles in Ecological and Environmental Studies.* Andover: Intercept.

Taylor, R. W. (1983). Descriptive taxonomy: past, present and future. In *Australian Systematic Entomology: A Bicentenary Perspective,* eds. E. Highley & R. W. Taylor, pp. 93–133. Melbourne: CSIRO.

van Rhee, J. A. (1963). Earthworm activities and the breakdown of organic matter in agricultural soils. In *Soil Organisms,* eds. J. Doeksen & J. van der Drift, pp. 54–9. New Holland: Amsterdam.

Ward, S. C., Majer, J. D., & O'Connell, A. M. (1991). Decomposition of eucalypt litter on rehabilitated bauxite mines. *Australian Journal of Ecology,* 6, 251–7.

Williams, K. S. (1993). Use of terrestrial arthropods to evaluate restored riparian woodlands. *Restoration Ecology,* 1, 107–16.

Wilson, E. O. (1987). The little things that run the world (the importance and conservation of invertebrates). *Conservation Biology,* 1, 344–6.

12

Terrestrial arthropods as ecological indicators of habitat restoration in southwestern North America

KATHY S. WILLIAMS

Introduction

While habitat construction and rehabilitation have undergone many modifications since the first 'reclamation' attempts were performed after mining and intense agriculture (reviewed in Jordan, Gilpin, & Aber (1987), devising monitoring programmes that will provide performance evaluations of management plans remains one of the most urgent needs of conservation and restoration ecology (Anderson 1990; PERL 1990; Williams 1993a; Kremen *et al.* 1993; Kremen 1994). Many restoration attempts are based on the assumption that if appropriate vegetation is planted, appropriate native animal and plant species will colonize restored sites (see examples in Jordan *et al.* 1987; Thomas 1994). Often in the United States, habitat restoration is undertaken to create habitat for specific endangered species and applies that assumption (Landres, Werner, & Thomas 1988; Baird 1989, Noss 1990; Kremen *et al.* 1993). Official criteria for evaluating 'success' of restoration projects is typically based on the planting and establishment of specific plants at densities prescribed to mimic natural habitats, and documenting use of constructed habitats by targeted rare and endangered species (e.g., see Baird 1989; Kus in press). Thus, management of restored habitats may focus largely on maintaining plants or just monitoring targeted rare species.

In some systems, forbs and herbaceous early successional plants may respond quickly to disturbance and can be useful indicators of habitat quality (Cottam 1987; Gross, 1987). However, in other systems, such as those dominated by long-lived woody vegetation, plants may not be appropriate indicators of management problems or of progress towards goals of habitat self-maintenance and stability, since such plants may not respond dramatically or rapidly to environmental change, and indirectly reflect ecosystem processes (Landres *et al.* 1988; Majer 1989; Noss 1990;

238

Kremen *et al.* 1993). Several studies have shown how insects and other arthropods can be used to monitor and manage habitats (Hopkins & Webb 1984: Morris & Rispin 1987; Foster *et al.* 1990, Andersen 1990; Erhardt & Thomas 1991; Pearson & Cassola 1992; Rushton & Eyre 1992; Simmonds, Majer, & Nichols 1994; New 1995), and in this chapter I describe how they may be used to evaluate systems and provide management recommendations where restoration goals are to provide self-sustaining habitats for specific endangered species.

Several characteristics contribute to the value of terrestrial arthropods as indicators of habitat quality (Wilson 1987; Andersen 1990; Collins & Thomas 1991; Kremen *et al.* 1993; Williams 1993a; Kremen 1994; Simmonds *et al.* 1994). Insects and their allies represent the greatest morphological and functional diversity in the animal kingdom, playing essential roles as herbivores, pollinators, detritivores, mutualists, predators, parasites, and prey for reptiles, birds, and mammals (Wilson 1987; Samways 1994; Handel this volume). Additionally, the short generation times of many taxa can cause dramatic population fluctuations that signal variations in habitat quality and ecosystem processes (Wolda 1978; Southwood, Brown, & Reader 1979; Brown & Southwood 1983; Andersen 1990; Williams 1993a). Also, because their population densities are usually extremely high relative to vertebrates, terrestrial arthropods usually can be sampled repeatedly without altering population dynamics (Southwood *et al.* 1979; Erwin & Scott 1980; Kremen *et al.* 1993; Williams 1993a).

When urgent decisions with large economic ramifications are being made, it may be difficult to convince decision-makers that arthropods should be monitored, however. Concerns include determining what taxa to monitor and how to do it cost-effectively (Landres *et al.* 1988; Noss 1990; Kremen *et al.* 1993). If monitoring is to be conducted across arthropod taxa (orders), the number of species to identify rapidly and at relatively low cost appears overwhelming. If species from only one or a few taxa are to be monitored, how should the taxa be selected? Since little natural history is known for most species, choice of one taxon for monitoring and decision-making may be problematic; one taxon may not represent responses of other taxa (Prendergast *et al.* 1993; Majer this volume).

In this chapter, I present a method for monitoring a variety of terrestrial arthropod taxa, grouped by functional relationships into assemblages and comparing assemblages among sites to provide management recommendations and help assess success of restoration projects. With arthropods, all or most members of certain higher-level taxonomic groups, like orders or families, belong to the same trophic guild or functional group. Homoptera (the suborder of sucking insects), for example, are all herbivores. There-fore, it may be possible to carefully construct assemblages of orders or families of terrestrial arthropods to provide management information (Moran & Southwood 1982; Stork 1987; Hutcheson 1990; Kremen *et al.* 1993; Chessman 1995).

Riparian and coastal wetland ecosystems are two threatened habitats of southern California and several attempts to mitigate loss by reconstructing and creating wetland habitats are planned or are underway (Zedler 1988; Baird & Rieger 1989; Hendricks & Rieger 1989; PERL 1990). Goals of such projects are two fold: creating habitat for targeted endangered species, and creating self-sustaining, resilient ecosystems (Baird 1989; Rieger 1992). Measuring success of restoration by monitoring establishment of dominant vegetation planted at such restored habitats may not be appropriate, however. Riparian restoration primarily has been aimed at creating habitat, including vegetation for nest sites and food resources, for the endangered least Bell's vireo (*Vireo bellii pusillus*), an insectivore. There, vegetation is dominated by woody species, and criteria for success may be based largely on establishment of trees and shrubs (Baird 1989; Baird & Rieger 1989; Hendricks & Rieger 1989). Coastal restoration has focused on creating cordgrass (*Spartina foliosa*) saltmarsh habitats for threatened light-footed clapper rail (*Rallus longirostris*) and endangered California least tern (*Sterna antillarum*), and success may be based on establishment of *S. foliosa*, a clonal species, and use of the wetland by birds and fish (PERL 1990). Since appropriate indicators of habitat quality in these habitats were not clear, I examined terrestrial arthropod communities at three recon-structed sites and compared them with communities at nearby relatively natural reference sites to evaluate progress towards the goals of creating habitat for endangered species and creating self-sustaining, resilient ecosys-tems. In this chapter, I will provide examples of how terrestrial arthropod communities can be used to answer several questions regarding restoration success, and offer management recommendations based on the results obtained.

Does habitat restoration provide avian food resources that are as abundant as those at reference sites? In attempting to restore suitable habitat for sensitive avian insectivores, it has been assumed that recon-structed habitats will provide avian food resources that are as abundant as those at reference habitats. Results from riparian systems demonstrate how food resources for avian insectivores can be evaluated.

Do potential prey abundances differ among vegetation types at restored and reference sites? Riparian revegetation involved planting dominant woody species found at riparian sites, like trees, *Salix* spp. (willow) and *Populus fremontii* (cottonwood), the shrub *Baccharis*, and herbaceous vegetation, in densities similar to those of woodlands occupied by least Bell's vireo (Baird 1989; Baird & Rieger 1989; Hendricks & Rieger 1989). In the case of habitat restoration for least Bell's vireo, riparian woody vegetation appeared critical for nesting and foraging (Miner 1989; Kus 1994, in press), so I compared potential prey communities among vegetation types at riparian restoration sites and those of reference sites.

Are herbivores more abundant at newly planted, created habitats than at reference areas? Often criteria for 'success' of restoration efforts involves the establishment and maintenance of plant communities of well-defined structure (Baird 1989; Baird & Rieger 1989; Hendricks & Rieger 1989; Kus in press). This presents a potential management paradox when target species are foliage-gleaning insectivores, like least Bell's vireo. Many suitable prey are also herbivores, so when insect prey are abundant, does that reflect increased densities of herbivores in the managed plant community (Louda 1988; Handel, Robinson & Beattie 1994)? To answer this question, insect communities were monitored to quantify dynamics of insect herbivore assemblages at newly planted, created habitats.

What can insects tell use about colonization rates and establishment of populations? Restoration plans generally assume that colonization by native plant and animal species can and will occur. Examples from riparian and coastal systems demonstrate how terrestrial arthropods can indicate limits to immigration and colonization problems.

Study sites

Arthropod population densities vary naturally, both within and among years (Wolda 1978, 1988). Therefore, to evaluate variation in arthropod abundances at restoration sites, restoration site arthropod communities were compared to those occurring at relatively natural reference sites. Reference sites were selected as close as possible to restoration sites to minimize population variations due to climate. Since restoration sites were planted to 'mimic' plant communities typical reference sites, vegetation was intended to be similar. Comparing arthropod communities was used as one method of detecting possible effects of differences in vegetation between sites.

As mitigation for highway construction, the California Department of Transportation restored native vegetation to several sites along rivers in

San Diego County, California, to crate habitat for least Bell's vireo (Baird 1989; Baird & Rieger 1989; Hendricks & Rieger 1989; Rieger1992; Kus 1994, in press). One pair of riparian sites was along the San Luis Rey River, near Oceanside, CA (Williams 1993a). The constructed site was relatively small, with an area of 3 ha, and planting was completed in 1989 (SLR Restoration site). An adjacent site, 3 km away, was studied as a reference site (SLR Reference site). Least Bell's vireo had nested there each year since monitoring began in 1989 (B. Kus, personal communication). A second pair of riparian sites was planted along the San Diego River, near Santee, California, in 1991. That study area was about 7 times larger than the San Luis Rey site, encompassing about 20 ha. On the north side of the river (SD Restoration site), a 13.5 ha section of the drainage was almost entirely replanted. On the south side of the river (SD Reference site), riparian restoration involved revegetation of campsites in a 6.5 ha woodland that had been used as a public campground. Since disturbance and revegetation was relatively limited there, compared to the north site, the south site was considered to be less disturbed and was used as reference for the restoration site north of the river.

As mitigation for a dredging project in south San Diego Bay, the San Diego Unified Port District constructed a 22.25 ha marsh using dredged material at the end of a dike in south San Diego Bay (now known as the Chula Vista Wildlife Reserve, or CVWR). Cordgrass (*Spartina foliosa*) was transplanted from a natural salt marsh 8 km north of CVWR, the Paradise Creek marsh, beginning in 1984, and over the next 3 years the plants flourished and spread naturally in much of the area (Williams 1988, 1989; PERL 1990; Johnson 1991). The aim was to provide habitat for many bird species, including the endangered California least tern, and the threatened light-footed clapper rail. In 1986, however, an outbreak of cordgrass scale insects (Homoptera: *Haliaspis spartina*) was noticed on CVWR cordgrass plants. The cordgrass scale only feeds on *Spartina* (Essig 1958) and is normally present in very low densities at natural marshes (personal observation; D. McIntire, personal communication). Like aphids, cordgrass scales feed on plant vascular fluids, which tends to reduce the vigour of the cordgrass and can limit its growth and reproduction. Since *Spartina* is a dominant and critical member of the marsh community, the uncontrolled scale infestation at the Chula Vista Wildlife Reserve threatened the success of the artificial wetland project. To determine whether predators or parasites of *Haliaspis* might be absent, insect communities were studied at the constructed marsh, CVWR, and at the natural Paradise Creek marsh.

Riparian restoration

Terrestrial arthropods – including insects, spiders, and isopods – were collected at 4 to 6 wk intervals in spring and summer and once each in autumn and winter, 1989–1995. Data presented here compare collections made during spring and summer (April–August) when bird foraging and arthropod activities are greatest. All arthropod collecting methods are somewhat biased (Southwood 1978); some selectively catch flying insects, ground-dwelling insects, insects attracted to light, insects attracted to pheromone traps, etc. Individuals were collected in these studies using two standard techniques: pan trapping and sweep netting. Pan traps were used to collect flying insects that are attracted to yellow colour, ground-dwelling insects that fall into traps, and insects that drop off foliage above pans (Southwood 1978). Pan traps were 22.5 × 32.5 cm by 5 cm deep, filled with 90–100% ethylene glycol (500 ml), put in place between 900 and 1200 hours, and were removed 24 hr later. Traps were placed at ground level, approximately 40 m apart along regularly arranged transects. Along the San Luis Rey River, 26 pans were placed at the Restoration site and 21 at the Reference area. At the San Diego River, 34 pan traps were placed at the Restoration site and 15 at the smaller area used for Reference collections. Nesting birds and standing water prevented access to some trap stations at some times.

Sweep netting or beating of vegetation was used to collect resident external herbivores and other insects associated with plants (Southwood 1978). Many of those insects are also prey for foliage gleaning birds (Ehrlich, Dobkin, & Wheye 1988). To estimate relative densities of arthropods, a standard number of sweeps were made through 4 dominant southern California riparian vegetation types: (1) willow (*Salix goodingii, S. hindsiana, S. laevigata,* and *S. lasiolepis* and hybrids), (2) cottonwood (*Populus fremontii*), (3) baccharis (*Baccharis glutinosa*), and (4) annual and perennial herbaceous vegetation. Herbaceous vegetation included *Escholtzia californica, Lupinus bicolor, Oenothera hookeri, Raphanus sativus, Phacelia parryi, Taraxacum officinale,* and *Trifolium* sp. (Beauchamp 1986; Baird 1989; Baird & Rieger 1989; Hendricks & Rieger 1989). Sweep sampling stations were approximately 50 × 50 m in size. At the San Luis Rey study site, 6 sweep sampling stations were placed randomly at the Restoration site and 11 at the larger Reference area. At the San Diego River, stations were placed in a regular dispersion to provide uniform coverage of the 50 ha area, with 23 sweep sampling stations placed at the Restoration site and 6 at the smaller Reference area. At each sampling station, foliage of each vegetation type was swept using a 39 cm insect sweep net, a total of 25 times, sampling from at least 3 different individual plants or patches of herbaceous vegetation at a height of 0–3 m. Nesting birds and standing water prevented access to some sample stations at times.

Collections were returned to the laboratory, where arthropods were sorted from plant material or ethylene glycol, identified to taxonomic order or family (Essig 1958; Borror & DeLong 1971; Powell & Hogue 1979; Williams 1993a), and preserved in 70% ethanol. Numbers of individuals of each order, per sample, were recorded. Data were analyzed to determine the effects on arthropod abundance of site (Restored vs. Reference habitats) and vegetation type (sweeps samples only).

To identify differences in ecosystem processes or trophic guilds between reference and restoration sites, riparian arthropods were grouped into indictor assemblages containing certain taxa, and relative abundances of those assemblages were compared (Southwood, Moran, & Kennedy 1982; Hendrix, Brown, & Dingle 1988; Noss 1990; Chapin, Schulze, & Mooney 1992; Kremen *et al.* 1993; Williams 1993a; Simmonds *et al.* 1994). Additionally, effects of site and vegetation type on abundances of the subset of large and small arthropods that are considered to be potential prey taken by passerine birds in riparian habitats were quantified (Ehrlich *et al.* 1988). Since least Bell's vireo is a Federally Endangered Species, handling of birds is limited and direct examination of gut contents is not permitted, so observations of vireo researchers (Hamilton 1958; Miner 1989; B. Kus personal communication) were used to construct prey assemblages appropriate for this species. Individuals representing potential avian prey were further identified as 'small' (body length < 0.5 cm) or 'large' (body length > 0.5 cm) to indicate relative biomass. In this chapter I will discuss only 'Herbivore' and 'Prey' assemblages. Taxa chosen to indicate relative abundance of 'Herbivores' were Lepidoptera (moths, butterflies), Orthoptera (grasshoppers, crickets), herbivorous families of Coleoptera (beetles), Homoptera (suborder containing aphids), and small Heteroptera (suborder containing plant bugs Miridae and Pentatomidae). 'Large Prey' was the assemblage including large Araneae (spiders), Coleoptera, Diptera (flies), Homoptera, Heteroptera, Hymenoptera (bees and wasps), Lepidoptera, and Orthoptera. The 'Small Prey' assemblage consisted of small Araneae, Coleoptera, Ephemeroptera (mayflies), Hemiptera, Homoptera, Lepidoptera, Neuroptera (lacewings), and Trichoptera (caddisflies).

Over 280 000 terrestrial arthropods were collected between 1989 and 1992 at San Luis Rey River sites, and over 296 000 were collected between

1991 and 1995 at San Diego River sites. Fourteen orders were collected (Coleoptera, Diptera, Ephemeroptera, Hemiptera, Hymenoptera, Lepidoptera, Neuroptera, Orthoptera, Thysanoptera, Trichoptera, Collembola, Psocoptera, Isopoda, Araneae). Mean numbers of individuals per sample unit were compared between sites and within years using one-way analyses of variance (Abacus Concepts, Statview II, V.1.04, and SuperANOVA, v.1.11). When necessary, data were first transformed to achieve normality. When significant differences among several means were detected, Ficher's Protected Least Squares Difference (FPLSD) multiple comparisons were performed to determine which means were significantly different from others. Data are presented here in the non-transformed form, but statistical differences refer to transformed data. In all figures, significant differences between means (at P < 0.05) are represented by an asterisk*.

Coastal restoration

Scale densities were quantified by sampling 100 *Spartina* stems in each of 3 areas of the CVWR, and in the only area of Paradise Creek marsh where *Haliaspis* was found. Since these armoured scale insects are immobile after selecting a feeding site (McKenzie 1956), counts were made in July and August after juveniles had settled and represented maximum densities for 1988. To quantify differences in arthropod communities, including natural enemies, at each site, nine 4 × 4 m sampling stations were defined at each of the two study sites. Arthropods were censused at each station in spring (April), summer (July), autumn (September), and winter (December), 1989, by sweeping foliage with a standard 39 cm insect net (30 sweeps per station). Arthropods were returned to the laboratory in paper bags and refrigerated until they were identified by taxonomic order, counted, and preserved in 70% ethanol. Potential predators of *Haliaspis*, coccinellid beetles (Coleoptera: Coccinellidae), were quantified by sweeping cordgrass along 10, 10 m transects arbitrarily placed across Paradise Creek marsh and CVWR. Collections were made on 5 occasions during August and September, 1988, when beetles are seasonally active (Johnson 1991; Williams 1988).

Prey assemblages

To quantify potential avian food resources, researchers must first realize that all insects are not appropriate prey for foliage-gleaning passerines, and

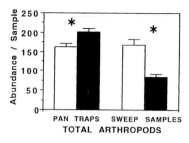 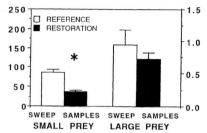

Figure 12.1. Terrestrial arthropods collected in pan traps and sweep samples at SLR sites, 1991. Total individuals collected compared to Small Prey and Large Prey assemblages (mean/sample ± s.e.; Reference site n = 63 pan traps, 50 sweep samples; Restoration site n = 77 pantraps, 132 sweep samples).

sample accordingly to draw accurate conclusions. Examples of this come from comparing pan and sweep collections from SLR sites in spring/summer 1991. Total number of arthropods caught in pan traps at the Restoration site was greater than collections from the Reference site (Figure 12.1). Conversely, the total number of arthropods caught in sweep samples of vegetation at the more natural Reference site was greater than collections from the Restoration site (Figure 12.1). This was because, in part, pan traps caught different arthropods, such as superabundant ground-dwelling scavengers like Collembola (Williams 1993a). However, since not all arthropods are suitable food resources for foliage-gleaning birds, the appropriate comparison to determine relative prey abundance is between potential prey assemblages collected by sweep sampling vegetation (where foraging occurs) at the Restored and Restoration sites. Those results showed that Small Prey were more abundant at the Reference site, while abundance of Large Prey was similar at both sites (Figure 12.1), indicating in the third year after reconstruction that some, but not all, prey resources were more abundant at the more natural Reference site than at the constructed Restoration site. Thus, a management recommendation following from these results is that care must be taken in framing questions and selecting sampling methods.

Prey abundance and plant type

Relative abundances of potential avian prey also differed among vegetation types. For example, at the SD site in 1994, members of the Small Prey assemblage were more numerous in sweep samples from willows and herbaceous vegetation than in sweep samples of *Baccharis* and cottonwood (Figure 12.2). Members of the Large Prey assemblage were significantly

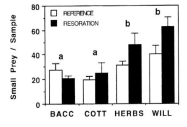 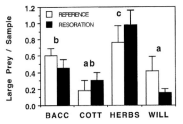

Figure 12.2. Relative abundances (mean/sample ± s.e.) of Small Prey and Large Prey assemblages collected from 4 plant types at SD sites, 1994; BACC = baccharis, COTT = cottonwood, HERBS = herbaceous vegetation, WILL = willows (see text for details). Means of Restoration and Reference sites were not significantly different (P > 0.05), and means by plant type identified by the same letter were not significantly different (P > 0.05; FPLSD). Reference site n = 11 sweep samples/plant type; Restoration site n = 34 sweep samples/plant type (not all plant types were represented at each sample station).

more abundant on herbaceous vegetation than on the three woody-plant types (Figure 12.2). Thus, although riparian habitants are dominated by woody plants, native herbaceous species appear to be critical resources for riparian arthropod populations and should be planted and managed accordingly. Differences between Restoration and Reference collections of both Small and Large Prey were not significantly different (Figure 12.2). However, collections tended to be greater at the Restoration site, indicating that the large constructed riparian site was supporting relatively large Prey assemblages in 1994, the third year after its construction.

Herbivore assemblages

Herbivores rapidly appeared at constructed sites and relative abundances were greater there than at Reference sites. For example, in the year following transplantation at the SD site, the relative abundance of the Herbivore assemblage exceeded that at the Reference site (Figure 12.3), primarily reflecting abundances of Lepidoptera and Homoptera. In 1993 and 1994, the abundances were not significantly different between sites (Figure 12.3), suggesting that conditions in those years either reduced herbivore population growth or enhanced population regulation by natural enemies. However, Herbivore collections from along the San Diego river in 1994, like Prey assemblages, tended to be greater at the Restoration site (Figure 12.3), indicating that when prey for foliage-gleaning birds is

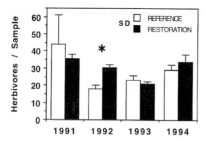

Figure 12.3. Relative abundances of Herbivore assemblages
(mean/sample ± s.e.) collected from vegetation at sᴅ sites, 1994. Significant
differences between means, by date, are designated by * (P < 0.05). Reference
site n = 48 sweep samples in 1991, 96 in 1992, 72 in 1993, 96 in 1994;
Restoration site n = 222 in 1991, 320 in 1992, 260 in 1993, 266 in 1994.

relatively abundant, herbivores are likely to be abundant also. Therefore,
using only vegetation-based criteria for success may be inappropriate,
especially when herbivores can be beneficial for other ecosystem processes.

Colonization and population establishment

Two taxa of insects provided information about colonization rates at
riparian restoration sites, Collembola (springtails) and Hymenoptera:
Formicidae (ants). Collembola are primitive, wingless insects that feed on
decaying plant and animal material. Bark chips and litter were scattered
over the soil surface as planting was completed at the sʟʀ Restoration site
(Baird 1989; Williams 1993a). In 1989 at the sʟʀ site, abundance of
Collembola was significantly greater in the Restoration site collections
than in the Reference collections (Figure 12.4a). In the following 3 years,
Collembola still were significantly more abundant at the Restoration site,
but the differences were substantially smaller (Figure 12.4a), probably
reflecting the decomposition of initially abundant litter. At the sᴅ site,
where less bark was used and was tilled into soil, Collembola were more
abundant in Reference site collections than in Restoration collections in all
years (Figure 12.4b). Apparently, when application of bark chips for soil
moisture retention was modified, the soil arthropods responded as expected. This result also points out the value of inoculating restoration
attempts with soils from natural habits, as a means of transplanting
propagules of native animals.

     Ants have colonized the highly disturbed areas more slowly, however. At
both riparian restoration projects, Formicidae (primarily Argentine ants,
Iridomyrmex humilis) were collected more frequently at Reference sites

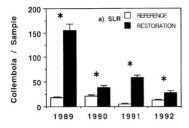
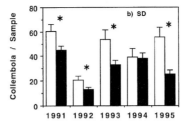

Figure 12.4. Relative abundances of Collembola (mean/pan trap ± s.e.) collected at (a) SLR sites (Reference n = 63 pan traps in 1990–2, 84 in 1989; Restoration n = 78 pan traps in 1990–2, 104 in 1989), and (b) SD sites (Reference n = 60 pan traps in 1992, 45 in other years; Restoration n = 97, 133, 98, 96, 100 in years 1991–5, respectively).

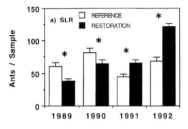
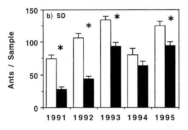

Figure 12.5. Relative abundances of ants (Formicidae) (mean/pan trap ± s.e.) collected at (a) SLR sites and (b) SD sites (sample sizes as in Figure 12.4).

than at Restoration sites in the first two years (Figure 12.5). At the SLR site, ants became more abundant at the Restoration site in the third and fourth years (Figure 12.5a). However, at SD sites, ants continued to be caught more frequently at the Reference site through 1995 (Figure 12.5b), possibly indicating limits to immigration or establishment of colonies at the heavily disturbed SD Restoration site.

At the coastal restoration site, beetles provided another example of limits to dispersal, in this case directly causing problems for habitat restoration. *Haliaspis* scales were significantly more abundant on CVWR *Spartina* than on Paradise Creek *Spartina*. Scale densities at the three sampling stations at CVWR marsh were 151 ± 11 scales/cordgrass stem, 158 ± 11 scales/stem, and 602 ± 21 scales/stem. Conversely, scales were found at very low densities (28 ± 8 scales/stem) in only one small area (< 0.5 ha) of the large natural Paradise Creek marsh. Those scales occurred at the area in which transplanted cordgrass originally grew, supporting the idea that propagules of scales were introduced onto CVWR when cordgrass was

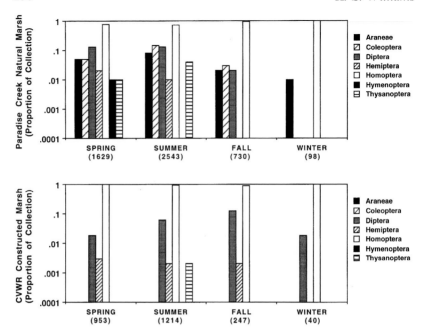

Figure 12.6. Arthropod communities at coastal marshes, 1989. Community composition is represented as proportions of total sweep sample collection, by season. Numbers in parentheses indicate total individuals collected by season.

transplanted (PERL 1990). In 1989, 5 years after planting the marsh, the arthropod community at CVWR remained depauperate. While 7 orders of insects were found at Paradise Creek marsh, only 4 were found at CVWR, and members of 2 of those orders comprised only 2% each of the arthropods collected (Figure 12.6). Sweep samples of CVWR collected no possible insect predators of *Haliaspis*. No Araneae (Spiders), Hymenoptera (bees, wasps, and ants), and no Coleoptera (beetles, including predacious ladybird beetles (Coccinellidae)) were found there. Conversely, the coccinellid beetles *Coccinella californica*, *Chilocorus orbus*, *Hippodamia convergens*, and *Coleomegilla fuscilabris* were regularly collected in high densities at many points at Paradise Creek marsh. *Coleomegilla* was collected from Paradise Creek marsh at a rate of 49 ± 12 per 100 sweeps. In cage trials of coccinellids, only *Coleomegilla fuscilabris* consumed any *Haliaspis*. *Coleomegilla* appeared to be a ravenous predator of *Haliaspis* juveniles and adults, even though they were covered with waxy 'armor'. When 20 beetles/cage were allowed to feed on moderately infested *Spartina* for 4 days, they consumed 45 ± 8 adult (mean ± s.e., n = 4 cages), and

23% ± 6% of juvenile *Haliaspis* that were present. However, no *Coleomegilla fuscilabris* had colonized the marsh over the 5 years after its creation and no parasites of *Haliaspis* were ever observed, either in collections, or emerging from captive *Haliaspis*, supporting the hypothesis that the *Haliaspis* outbreak at CVWR was due, at least in part, to the absence of natural enemies at the constructed marsh. This case points out the need for establishment and maintenance of corridors for dispersal between restored and natural habitats.

Terrestrial arthropods as indicators

I have presented information to demonstrate the value of using terrestrial arthropod assemblages to provide information about the progress towards management goals. However, one of the first problems to address is the careful framing of questions and selection of methods to provide rigorous conclusions (Landres *et al.* 1988; Andersen 1990; Chapin *et al.* 1992; Kremen *et al.* 1993; Kondolf 1995). Because of their diversity, terrestrial arthropods can be sampled in many ways and answers to questions can be contradictory, such as the examples of collections from pan traps vs. sweep sampling vegetation given here. While food abundance is only one aspect of habitat suitability for avian species (others discussed by Kus in press), prey abundance is a requirement. If a primary management question concerns food for target taxa, the sampling must be conducted using spatially and temporally appropriate methods to quantify available resources. These ideas may seem obvious to researchers in the field, but are critical concepts to communicate to decision-makers and managers. The studies of riparian restoration attempts in southern California indicate that, when sites are adjacent to relatively undisturbed habitats, many arthropods emigrate rapidly, as has been shown in other studies (Munguira & Thomas 1992) and that, at least in terms of lower biomass prey (Small Prey), prey resources are apparently sufficient to attract and support foraging activities of least Bell's vireo and other riparian birds (Kus 1994; Kus in press). However, the arthropod community structures at California and other restoration sites remain different even after 5 or more years (Brown & Hyman 1986; Majer 1990; Williams 1993b; Simmonds *et al.* 1994; Williams 1994).

Management strategies may conflict when objectives are aimed at creating habitat for single species rather than preserving or managing ecosystems. Many factors may provoke herbivore outbreaks at restoration sites (Louda 1988; Handel *et al.* 1994). Herbivores like Homoptera (aphids and leafhoppers) can reach outbreak densities when host plant quality is enhanced either by fertilization or damage that mobilises nutrients (Strong, Lawton, & Southwood 1984; White 1984; Williams 1988, 1989). Thus, members of the Herbivore assemblage at riparian restoration sites may have shown rapid population growth in response to enhanced foodplant quality due to transplant stress, poor soil quality, or harsh weather in the year following construction of the Restoration site. Regardless of cause, such responses pose a paradox for species-based management: prey abundance for gleaners also reflected herbivore abundance. If management goals focus on short-term establishment of defined plant communities, the presence of herbivores might reduce the progress towards meeting criteria for 'success' (Baird 1989). If management goals focus on immediate establishment of defined conditions for target animals, such as the insectivorous birds, presence of herbivores represents abundance of potential prey. However, when management goals address establishment of resilient, self-sustaining habitats, herbivores could be expected to increase initially at created sites, and evidence of herbivore regulation should be an indication of plant recovery and/or establishment of natural enemy assemblages.

Herbivore populations seemed to be demonstrating system stability in the riparian system described here, but not at the coastal wetland (Williams 1989; PERL 1990). Apparently *Haliaspis* was introduced onto the island-like marsh when *Spartina* was transplanted from natural marshes, and the absence of predacious insects appeared to be a major factor promoting the explosion of *Haliaspis* at the CVWR. Unfortunately, few terrestrial arthropods (and no cordgrass scale predators or parasites) were introduced or became established, probably because dispersal to the isolated marsh from natural marshes is inhibited by lack of terrestrial corridors or prevailing off-shore breezes blowing against potential colonists (Williams 1988, 1989). Since this study, *Haliaspis* has reached outbreak densities in other reconstructed marshes (Boyer 1994; personal observation), possibly due to the same factors. Unfortunately, early careful arthropod monitoring at coastal restoration sites might have identified the lack of scale predators before scales reached outbreak densities and severely damaged vegetation.

Conclusions

Several general management recommendations derive from the results presented here. First, in the planning stages of restoration efforts, careful assessment of plant community structure is required, since animal communities reflect vegetation composition and architecture (Stinson & Brown 1983; Holmes & Robinson 1984; Stork 1987). While the planted riparian habitats described here appeared to provide resources for foraging passerines (Kus 1994; in press), the architecture of a mature riparian habitat was lacking and the restored habitat was not used as nesting habitat for several years (Kus 1994; Kus in press). Secondly, long-term monitoring is necessary to determine the significance of variations in community structures (Kremen *et al.* 1993; Simmonds *et al.* 1994; Kondolf 1995). Although some aspects of the systems show indications of ecological 'resilience' and successful functioning, other aspects of the sites may not fully mimic natural habitats after several years. Collembola at the riparian restoration sites probably were introduced with root balls on transplanted vegetation (Baird 1989) and their density increased when decaying litter and bark chips were abundant, as would be expected in natural systems when resources are abundant, then subsequently declined. The lack of a similar pattern at the SD river site was probably due to bark chips being tilled into the soil, i.e. not leaving chips in thick layers on the soil surface as was done at the SLR site. Ants were not quick to colonize either restoration site, but seemed to successfully colonize the small SLR site after 2–3 years. Since the SD Restoration site was larger than the SLR Restoration site, the difference in ant abundances might reflect edge effects (larger distance to edges of disturbance at the SD site) (Majer 1990). Additionally, some SD Restoration site soils had relatively high clay contents (personal observation) and those areas had drainage problems (especially after storms), so perhaps soil moisture or temperature regimes inhibited colony establishment (Holldobler & Wilson 1990; Majer 1990).

Although it is virtually impossible to perform replicated experiments at the landscape level of habitat restoration, 8 seasons of study have shown that quantifying riparian insects and related arthropods can provide information about performance and management of restoration projects. By comparing relative abundances of specific assemblages of taxa that represent ecosystem processes, such as herbivores and prey, at constructed and more natural sites used as references, trends can suggest management alternatives. The finding that the reconstructed riparian systems appeared to be functioning better than reconstructed coastal wetlands is probably not due to inherent differences in the ecosystems. Rather, successes appear to be more directly related to management, i.e. early monitoring and diagnosis of problems, and spatial arrangement, i.e. reconstructing habitats adjacent to established habitats to facilitate colonization. Those same factors also appear to have contributed to differences in performances among riparian restoration sites in California (Williams 1993b, 1994; Kus in press).

Widespread development has created the urgent need for programmes intended to 'replace' or 'repair' devastated wetlands. To date, the success of those programmes is in question. The benefits of creating indicator assemblages of taxonomic groups higher than species levels include saving time and money, and the archived collections can be analysed by species as appropriate. However, this method involves assumptions that species that comprise indicator taxa of different sites are the same, or that differences in species diversity do not affect ecosystem functions attributed to assemblages (Chapin et al. 1992). Ultimately, of course, this method assumes that the assemblages do accurately reflect ecosystem processes, and tests of that assumption are valuable. Examples presented in this chapter show how that assumption can be supported by comparing relative abundances of assemblages to performance of other organisms, specifically that bird foraging behaviour reflected prey assemblage abundance, and that insect herbivores at a restored habitat increased when the invertebrate predator assemblage was small. Until we obtain a more thorough, quantitative understanding of both animals and plants interacting in the aquatic/terrestrial interface of wetlands, we will be unable to predict accurately the success, or understand the failure of restoration programmes.

Acknowledgements

Projects were funded by awards from California Department of Transportation, San Diego Unified Port District, and California State University. San Diego Gas and Electric Co., US Fish and Wildlife Service, US Army Corps of Engineers. J. Zedler of SDSU-PERL, and J. Rieger of CalTrans provided assistance and support. A. Brower, B. Cabrera, D. Gibson, K. Johnson, A. Peirce-Calvano, H. Smead, S. Snover, R. Watts, and A. Williams-Anderson assisted with collections and identification of over 500 000 arthropods. Anonymous reviewers of this chapter offered helpful comments.

References

Andersen, A. N. (1990). The use of ant communities to evaluate change in Australian terrestrial ecosystems: a review and a recipe. *Proceedings of the Ecological Society of Australia*, 16, 347–57.
Baird, K. (1989). High quality restoration of riparian ecosystems. *Restoration & Management Notes*, 7, 60–4.

Baird, K. & Rieger, J. P. (1989). A restoration design for Least Bell's Vireo habitat design in San Diego County. In *Proceedings of the California Riparian Systems Conference: Protection, Management, and Restoration for the 1990s; 1988 September 22–24, Davis, CA.* General Technical Report. PSW-110, pp. 462–6. Berkeley: USDA Forest Service.

Beauchamp, R. M. (1986). *A Flora of San Diego County, California.* National City, California: Sweetwater River Press.

Borror, D. J. & DeLong, D. M. (1971). *An Introduction to the Study of Insects.* New York: Holt, Rinehart & Winston.

Boyer, K. E. (1994). Scale insect damage in constructed salt marshes: nitrogen and other factors. M.S. Thesis. San Diego State University.

Brown V. K. & Hyman, P. S. (1986). Successional communities of plants and phytophagous Coleoptera. *Journal of Ecology*, 74, 963–75.

Brown, V. K. & Southwood, T. R. E. (1983). Trophic diversity, niche breadth and generation times of exopterygote insects in a secondary succession. *Oecologia*, 56, 220–5.

Chapin, F. S. III, Schulze, E.-D., & Mooney, H. A. (1992). Biodiversity and ecosystem processes. *Trends in Ecology and Evolution*, 7, 107–8.

Chessman, B. C. (1995). Rapid assessment of rivers using macroinvertebrates: a procedure based on habitat-specific sampling, family level identification and a biotic index. *Australian Journal of Ecology*, 20, 122–9.

Collins, N. M. & Thomas, J. A., eds. (1991). The conservation of insects and their habitats. In *15th Symposium of the Royal Entomological Society of London.* London: Academic Press.

Cottam, G. (1987). Community dynamics on an artificial prairie. In *Restoration Ecology*, eds. W. R. Jordan III, M. E. Gilpin, & J. D. Aber, pp. 257–70. Cambridge University Press.

Ehrlich, P. R., Dobkin, D. S., & Wheye, D. (1988). *The Birder's Handbook: A Field Guide to the Natural History of North American Birds.* New York: Simon & Schuster.

Erhardt, A. & Thomas, J. A. (1991). Lepidoptera as indicators of change in the seminatural grasslands of lowland and upland Europe. In *The Conservation of Insects and Their Habitats*, eds. N. M. Collins & J. A. Thomas, pp. 213–36. London: Academic Press.

Erwin, T. F. & Scott, J. C. (1980). Seasonal and size patterns, trophic structure, and richness of Coleoptera in the tropical arboreal ecosystem: the fauna of the tree *Luehea seemannii* Triana and Planch in the Canal Zone of Panama. *Coleopterists Bulletin*, 34, 305–22.

Essig, E. O. (1958). *Insects and Mites of Western North America.* New York: The Macmillan Company.

Foster, G. N., Foster, A. P., Eyre, M. D., & Bilton, D. T. (1990). Classification of water beetle assemblages in arable fenland and ranking of sites in relation to conservation value. *Freshwater Biology*, 22, 343–54.

Gross, K. (1987). Mechanisms of colonization and species persistence in plant communities. In *Restoration Ecology*, eds. W. R. Jordan III, M. E. Gilpin, & J. D. Aber, pp. 173–88. Cambridge University Press.

Hamilton, T. H. (1958). Adaptive variation in the genus *Vireo. Wilson Bulletin*, 70, 307–46.

Handel, S. N., Robinson, G. R., & Beattie, A. J. (1994). Biodiversity resources for restoration ecology. *Restoration Ecology*, 2, 230–41.

Hendricks, B. J. & Rieger, J. P. (1989). Description of nesting habitat for the least Bell's vireo in San Diego County. In *Proceedings of the California Riparian Systems Conference: Protection, Management, and Restoration for the 1990s, 1988 September 22–24, Davis, CA*. General Technical Report. PSW-110, pp. 285–92. Berkeley: USDA Forest Service.

Hendrix, S. D., Brown, V. K., & Dingle, H. (1988). Arthropod guild structure during early old field succession in a New and Old World site. *Journal of Animal Ecology*, 57, 1053–65.

Holldobler, B. & Wilson, E. O. (1990). *The Ants*. Cambridge, MA: Harvard University Press.

Holmes, R. T. & Robinson, S. K. (1984). Effects of plant species and foliage structure on the foraging behavior of forest birds. *Auk*, 101, 672–84.

Hopkins, P. J. & Webb, N. R. (1984). The composition of the beetle and spider faunas on fragmented heathlands. *Journal of Applied Ecology*, 21, 935–46.

Hutcheson, J. (1990). Characterization of terrestrial insect communities using quantified, Malaise-trapped Coleoptera. *Ecological Entomology*, 15, 143–51.

Johnson, K. M. (1991). The effects of host quality on a phytophagous insect (Homoptera: Delphacidae) and its predators in a California salt marsh system. M.S. thesis. San Diego State University.

Jordan, W. R. III, Gilpin, M. E., & Aber, J. D., eds. (1987). *Restoration Ecology*. Cambridge University Press.

Kondolf, G. M. (1995). Five elements for effective evaluation of stream restoration. *Restoration Ecology*, 3, 133–6.

Kremen, C. (1994). Biological inventory using target taxa: a case study of the butterflies of Madagascar. *Ecological Applications*, 4, 407–22.

Kremen, C., Colwell, R. K., Erwin, T. L., Murphy, D. D., Noss., R. F., & Sanjayan, M. A. (1993). Terrestrial arthropod assemblages: their use in conservation planning. *Conservation Biology*, 7, 796–808.

Kus, B. E. (1994). Use of restored riparian habitat by endangered bird species. In *First Annual Conference of The Wildlife Society, Abstracts*, pp. 56–7. Bethesda: The Wildlife Society.

Kus, B. E. (in press). Use of restored riparian habitat by the endangered least Bell's vireo (*Vireo bellii pusillus*). *Restoration Ecology*.

Landres, P. B., Verner, J., & Thomas, J. W. (1988). Ecological uses of vertebrate indicator species: a critique. *Conservation Biology*, 2, 316–28.

Louda, S. M. (1988). Insect pests and plant stress as consideration for revegetation of disturbed ecosystems. In *Rehabilitating Damaged Ecosystems*, vol. 2, ed. J. Cairns, pp. 51–67. Boca Raton: CRC Press, Inc.

Majer, J. D. ed. (1989). *Animals in Primary Succession: The Role of Fauna in Reclaimed Lands*. Cambridge University Press.

Majer, J. D. (1990). Rehabilitation of disturbed land: long-term prospects for the recolonization of fauna. *Proceedings of the Ecological Society of Australia*, 16, 509–19.

McKenzie, H. L. (1956). The armored sclae insects of California. In *Bulletin of the California Insect Survey*, vol. 5, Berkeley: University of California Press.

Miner, K. L. (1989). Foraging ecology of the least Bell's vireo, *Vireo bellii pusillus*. M.S. thesis, San Diego State University.

Moran, V. C. & Southwood, T. R. E. (1982). The guild composition of arthropod communities in trees. *Journal of Animal Ecology*, 51, 289–306.

Morris, M. G. & Rispin, W. E. (1987). Abundance and diversity of the coleopterous fauna of a calcareous grassland under different cutting regimes. *Journal of Applied Ecology*, 24, 451–65.

Munguira, M. L. & Thomas, J. A. (1992). Use of road verges by butterfly and burnet populations, and the effect of roads on adult dispersal and mortality. *Journal of Applied Ecology*, 29, 316–29.

New, T. R. (1995). *Introduction to Invertebrate Conservation Biology.* Oxford University Press.

Noss, R. F. (1990). Indicators for monitoring biodiversity: A hierarchical approach. *Conservation Biology*, 4, 355–64.

PERL (Pacific Estuarine Research Laboratory). (1990). *A Manual for Assessing Restored and Natural Coastal Wetlands with Examples from Southern California*, Report No. T-CSGCP-021. La Jolla, California: California Sea Grant.

Pearson, D. L. & Cassola, F. (1992). World-wide species richness patterns of tiger beetles (Coleoptera: Cicindelidae): indicator taxon for biodiversity and conservation studies. *Conservation Biology*, 6, 376–91.

Powell, J. A. & Hogue, C. J. (1979). *California Insects.* Berkeley: University of California Press.

Prendergast, J. R., Quinn, R. M., Lawton, J. H., Eversham, B. C., & Gibbons, D. W. (1993). Rare species, the coincidence of diversity hotspots and conservation strategies. *Nature*, 365, 335–7.

Rieger, J. (1992). Western riparian and wetland systems. *Restoration & Management Notes*, 10, 52–5.

Rushton, S. P. & Eyre, M. D. (1992). Grassland spider habitats in north-east England. *Journal of Biogeography*, 19, 99–108.

Samways, M. J. (1994). *Insect Conservation Biology.* New York: Chapman & Hall.

Simmonds, S. J., Majer, J. D., & Nichols, O. G. (1994). A comparative study of spider (Araeae) communities of rehabilitated bauxite mines and surrounding forest in the southwest of western Australia. *Restoration Ecology*, 2, 247–60.

Southwood, T. R. E. (1978). *Ecological Methods.* London: Chapman and Hall.

Southwood, T. R. E., Brown, V. K., & Reader, P. M. (1979). The relationship of plant and insect diversities in succession. *Biological Journal of the Linnean Society*, 12, 327–48.

Southwood, T. R. E., Moran, V. C., & Kennedy, C. E. J. (1982). The richness, abundance and biomass of the arthropod communities on trees. *Journal of Animal Ecology*, 51, 635–49.

Stinson, C. S. A. & Brown, V. K. (1983). Seasonal changes in the architecture of natural plant communities and its relevance to insect herbivores. *Oecologia*, 56, 67–9.

Stork, N. E. (1987). Arthropod faunal similarity of Bornean rain forest trees. *Ecological Entomology*, 12, 219–26.

Strong, D. R., Lawton, J. H., & Southwood, T. R. E. (1984). *Insects on Plants.* Cambridge: Harvard University Press.

Thomas, C. D. (1994). Extinction, colonization, and metapopulations: environmental tracking by rare species. *Conservation Biology*, 8, 373–8.

White, T. C. R. (1984). The abundance of invertebrate herbivores in relation to the availability of nitrogen in stressed food plants. *Oecologia*, 63, 90–105.

Williams, K. S. (1988). *Scale Insect Infestation of Chula Vista Wildlife Reserve.* Project Report No. EM 81-1.30. San Diego Unified Port District.

Williams, K. S. (1989). Insect outbreak on a unique wetland habitat of San Diego Bay. *Supplement to Bulletin of the Ecological Society of America,* 70, 299–300.

Williams, K. S. (1993a). Use of terrestrial arthropods to evaluate restored riparian woodlands. *Restoration Ecology,* 2, 107–16.

Williams, K. S. (1993b). *Riparian Insect Populations in Restored and Natural Habitats Along San Luis Rey and San Diego Rivers, San Diego Co., CA, 1992.* Publication No. 11C113.15A. San Diego: California Department of Transportation.

Williams, K. S. (1994). Terrestrial arthropods as indicators of riparian habitat restoration in southern California. *Supplement to Bulletin of the Ecological Society of America,* 75, 249–50.

Wilson, E. O. (1987). The little things that run the world (The importance of conservation of invertebrates). *Conservation Biology,* 1, 344–6.

Wolda, H. (1978). Seasonal fluctuations in rainfall, food and abundance of tropical insects. *Journal of Animal Ecology,* 47, 369–81.

Wolda, H. (1988). Insect seasonality: why? *Annual Review of Ecology and Systematics,* 9, 1–18.

Zedler, J. B. (1988). Restoring diversity in salt marshes: can we do it? In *Biodiversity,* ed. E. O. Wilson. Washington DC: National Academy Press.

13
Tidal wetlands restoration and creation along the east coast of North America
WILLIAM A. NIERING

Introduction

With increasing development along the eastern coastline of North America, tidal wetlands have been severely affected over the last century. From 1950 to 1970, some 146 000 hectares of estuarine wetlands, primarily salt marshes, were lost in the United States (Tiner 1984). Originally considered wastelands, these resources are now regarded as among the most productive ecosystems in the world (Mitsch & Gosselink 1993). With increasing awareness of their ecological importance in recent years, their development is now regulated in most coastal states. In fact, there is a concerted effort to restore or re-create these coastal wetlands in order to compensate for those lost, and to respond to a Federal no-net-loss-wetland policy (Thayer 1992). Salt marshes in this context are *Spartina*-dominated estuarine emergent wetlands that fringe the land/water interface of temperate regions. They are part of a larger tidal marsh estuarine ecosystem integrally related to finfish and shellfish productivity. These wetlands also play an important role in nutrient cycling, sediment accretion, pollution filtration, and erosion control. In addition, they are known for their distinctive flora and rich spectrum of wildlife, especially waterfowl, which make them attractive to both hunters and naturalists. The economic value of these wetlands has been estimated at $16 000–70 000/ha (Mitsch & Gosselink 1993).

Worldwide, Chapman (1960) recognizes nine different geographical marsh regions. Along the north-east coast of North America, the New England type marshes extending from Maine to New Jersey have developed along resistant rocky shores, and exhibit distinctive peat deposits. To the south they are replaced by the Coastal Plain marshes which extend to Florida and the Gulf Coast. As one moves to the south-east, both tall and intermediate height forms of *Spartina alterniflora* (smooth cordgrass) are encountered on the lower marsh and *Spartina patens* (salt meadow cordgrass), *Distichlis spicata* (spike grass), and *Juncus roemerianus* (black needlerush) are frequent on the upper marsh. These marsh systems have been profiled by Niering & Warren (1980b), Redfield (1972), Nixon (1982), Teal (1986), Wiegert & Freeman (1990), and Bertness (1992).

Along the north-east shoreline, vast areas of these salt marshes have been filled, dredged, tidally restricted, or otherwise modified from their natural condition (*Connecticut's Coastal Marshes: a Vanishing Resource* 1961). Along Long Island Sound, 30% of Connecticut's tidal wetlands have been destroyed by human activities. With the enactment of tidal wetlands legislation in recent decades, this destructive trend has been abated and considerable progress made towards marsh restoration in New England, especially in the south-east, where such activities have been underway since the 1970s (Woodhouse, Seneca, & Broome 1972; Matthews & Minello 1994).

Restoration is here defined as an attempt to restore a degraded system by removing the stressors and restoring those factors which will allow the area to restore itself naturally or by plantings, so that it will tend to mimic a given reference system. Wetland creation may be considered a form of restoration, but it often involves the creation of a wetland on a site where no previous such system existed. It often also involves planting indigenous species to accelerate the restoration process. For example, planting *S. alterniflora* on dredged material is an example of marsh creation, but it is also contributing to the overall restoration of coastal wetlands. Marsh creation is often employed in conjunction with wetland mitigation which is used to compensate for wetland loss (Kusler & Kentula 1989).

The purpose of this chapter is to highlight coastal wetland restoration and creation strategies being employed primarily on the tidal salt marshes of the north-east. This will feature a set of case histories, some of which will involve my research and that of my colleagues, in order to document the diversity of efforts underway in restoring tidal marsh productivity. This work will also consider the importance of functional equivalence in evaluating restoration success.

The tidal saltmarsh community

A brief overview of the saltmarsh plant community as a relatively unaffected system will serve as a point of reference as we look at degraded wetlands with the aim toward restoration. In the north-east, tidal marshes formed within the last 3000–4000 years as sea level rise slowed to about 1 mm/yr, favouring the establishment of the initial colonizer *Spartina alterniflora*, a tall-growing grass 1–2 m in height which formed a distinctive

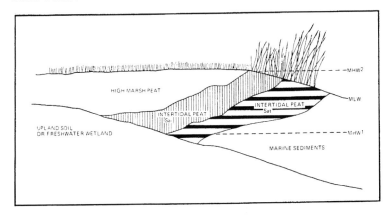

Figure 13.1. Bisect showing marsh development oceanward with intertidal *Spartina alterniflora* tall (Sat) and intermediate (Sai) peat being replaced by high marsh peat. Key: MHW[1] = mean high water when marsh development began; MHW[2] = mean high water at present; MLW = mean low water at present (after Redfield 1965).

low marsh belt along the bay front (Bloom & Stuiver 1963; Redfield 1965; Orson, Warren, & Niering 1987). With continued sediment accretion it was replaced landward by the lower growing *Spartina patens* (Figure 13.1). As the marsh systems continued to develop, they eventually exhibited four distinctive vegetation belts – the *S. alterniflora* zone flooded by every tidal cycle, the high marsh *S. patens* and *Juncus gerardii* (black grass) belts only periodically flooded, and the final belt bordering the upland–marsh interface where *Panicum virgatum* (switch grass) and *Iva frutescens* (marsh elder) are indicator species (Miller & Egler 1950) (Figure 13.2). Another especially salt-tolerant grass frequently found on the high marsh is *Distichlis spicata* (Niering and Warren 1980a,b). In more disturbed sites, *Phragmites australis* (common reed) hereafter referred to as *Phragmites*, may comprise a conspicuous belt along the marsh edge. Due to depressions or pans on the high marsh, site conditions may become unfavourable for *S. patens* and it is replaced by a short or stunted form of *S. alterniflora*, an ecophene of the taller-growing low-marsh species (Shea, Warren, & Niering 1975). This form, growing less than 0.4 m in height, often grows in pure stands that may be contiguous to forb-dominated areas which are also associated with stressful sites. Soil peat in pans or forb areas is often more saline (40–60 ppt) and has lower oxygen levels than the surrounding high marsh. Primary productivity is strikingly reduced in pan or forb areas, compared to the contiguous *S. patens* or *J. gerardii* communities.

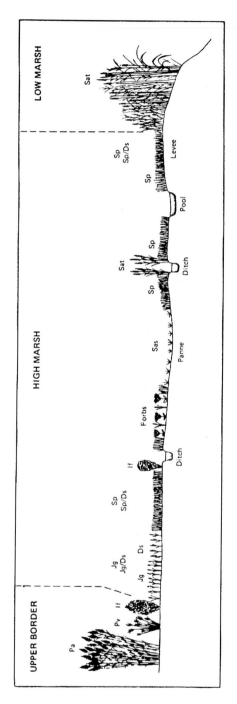

Figure 13.2. Generalized vegetation profile from low marsh to upper border showing major vegetation types that may be encountered on southern New England marshes. Key to symbols: Sat = *Spartina alterniflora*, tall; Sp = *Spartina patens*; Ds = *Distichlis spicata*; Sas = *S. alterniflora*, short; If = *Iva frutescens*; Jg = *Juncus gerardii*; Pv = *Panicum virgatum*; Pa = *Phragmites australis*.

Dominant invertebrate populations associated with these various belts include *Geukensia demissa* (ribbed mussel) and *Uca pugnax* (fiddler crab) which are most frequent in the low marsh, and *Melampus bidentatus* (saltmarsh snail) a distinctive high-marsh species (Olmstead & Fell 1974). As one moves upstream from salt marsh with salinities of 20–30 ppt, the *Spartina*-dominated marshes are replaced by *Typha angustifolia* (narrow-leaved cattail) and/or *Phragmites* in the brackish wetlands. In the upper-most reaches of the riverine system one encounters tidal freshwater marshes where the salinities are < 0.5 ppt. Here a rich diversity of emergent wetland species occurs with *Zizania aquatica* (wild rice) as the indicator species (Metzler & Rosza 1982). This tidal freshwater marsh type is infrequent in New England, but increases in importance southward.

Marsh impacts and need for restoration

During the Colonial period (seventeenth–nineteenth century), salt marshes were mowed, grazed, ditched, and diked in order to make them more suitable for agricultural use. In conjunction with these early activities, some ditching and diking were done to regulate tidal flushing. However, these impacts were minor compared to those that followed the Industrial Revolution (1850s) when, with increased mechanization, marshes were dredged for marinas, filled for development, ditched for mosquito control, and tidal-gated in order to prevent upland flooding. Although marsh ditching started early, it was during the 1930s that extensive mosquito-control ditching occurred along the east coast. Such activity dried out some marshes, changing the vegetation to a more xeric type (Bourn & Cottam 1950), whereas in others it favoured the formation of levees along the ditches. The levees impounded water within the interditch areas and in turn favoured wetter conditions and the less productive panne vegetation previously mentioned. Ditching has had a major impact on many marsh systems of the north-east. However, within the past decade Open Marsh Water Management has been widely practiced using biological control which favours small fish such as *Fundulus heteroclitus* (mummichogs) to control mosquitoes and simultaneously promoted marsh restoration (Capostosto 1994).

A major effect on north-east marshes has been tidal restriction or the exclusion of normal tidal flushing by the installation of tide gates which results in a decrease in salinity and a replacement of the *Spartina*-dominated grasses by *Phragmites* (Tiner 1995). In the 1970s it was estimated that 10% of Connecticut's *Spartina*-dominated marshes had been replaced by *Phragmites*. Although this more aggressive grass is circumpolar in distribution and, based on peat profiles (Niering, Warren, & Weymouth 1977; Orson *et al.* 1987), has presumably been present in north-east marshes for centuries, it has become especially widespread in the last 50–70 years with increased tidal restriction and disturbance. Once established, especially if the salinity is less than 20 ppt, it can form dense monocultures and exclude most typical saltmarsh species. Its woodier stems are also more resistant to decomposition than *Spartina* grasses, thus decreasing the contribution to the detrital food chain. Dense deposits of its flotsam can also cause die-outs on the high marsh. Furthermore, growing in dense stands to a height of four metres or more, it is highly flammable and a fire hazard, especially in urban centers. The aggressiveness of this taxon within the last century may be related to new ecotypes that have either evolved or been introduced. Present populations appear to have no natural predators compared to populations elsewhere in the world, which may further suggest its recent origin. *S. alterniflora* is frequently associated with the *Typha angustifolia* brackish marsh type along the major rivers, like the Connecticut, where salinity levels are especially favourable for its growth (Buck 1995). Here its leaf contribution to the detrital food chain may be equal to that of *Typha*. In contrast to these negative aspects there are situations along the eastern seaboard where it may be playing a positive role. In the Hackensack Meadows (New Jersey), in the shadow of New York City, *Phragmites* forms an extensive monoculture. Here, where restoration of the historic mosaic may not be feasible, this grass may well be the best possible landscape cover in terms of pollution filtration, erosion control, and wildlife cover. Its economic contribution elsewhere in the world has been well documented (Haslam 1973; Cooper & Hobson 1989).

Some representative case histories

Over the past few decades, there has been a diversity of tidal-wetland restoration projects (Rosza & Orson 1993) which illustrate natural marsh restoration by restoring tidal flushing, natural restoration following removal of dredged material from a former *Spartina*-dominated marsh, and *Spartina* marsh restoration by planting following an oil spill. In addition, marsh creation on dredged material by planting is reported from the south-east coastal region, and in the District of Columbia by the creation or restoration of a tidal freshwater marsh in which the destroyed marsh substrate had to be re-created prior to planting.

Restoration of a tidally restricted valley marsh

Tracing the restoration of a restricted *Phragmites* valley marsh over half a century will demonstrate a type of restoration which is being used extensively and which will increase in the future (Rosza 1987; Capotosto & Spencer 1988; Roman, Garvine, & Portnoy 1995). This 100 ha valley marsh on the Hammock River, Connecticut was originally a *Spartina*-dominated salt marsh with a direct connection to the estuarine waters of Long Island Sound. However, installation of a tidal gate early in the century (1913) in conjunction with a causeway crossing the marsh, initiated the restriction. The present tidal gates (four flapper gates) were installed in 1947, and below the gates the 68 ha marsh, which receives full tidal flushing (mean tidal range 1.5 m), is covered by *Spartina*-dominated grasses and other typical saltmarsh species (Figure 13.3). The portion above the gates (32 ha), where tidal flushing had been eliminated for over a half century, was covered by a dense monoculture of *Phragmites* reaching 4 m in height (Figure 13.3). With tidal restriction, sediment accumulation slowed and peat decomposition increased so that the high-marsh elevation is 40 cm lower and the water table was also lower (13.4 vs. 27.8 cm) compared to the unrestricted marsh (Roman, Niering, & Warren 1984). These factors, including the lower salinity (5–18 ppt) compared to the control marsh (20–30 ppt), have favoured the replacement of *Spartina*-dominated species by *Phragmites*. Cutting off this extensive wetland from normal flushing has resulted over many decades in the annual loss of the *Spartina* biomass detrital contribution to the estuarine productivity of Long Island Sound.

In order to reverse this trend, the Connecticut Department of Environmental Protection opened one of the four gates during the summer of 1985. After the first year, height growth of *Phragmites* decreased about 1 m and over the fifth and sixth year *Phragmites* ceased growing in some areas and *Spartina* spp. again became the dominant vegetation. Typical saltmarsh fauna also began to return. Although *Phragmites* declined throughout most of the system, one sector was not affected. Therefore, a second gate was opened. Unfortunately, residents of low-lying properties located too close to the marsh complained of flooding, so by 1994 restoration efforts reverted to a single gate.

The restoration site, at the Pine Creek marshes in Fairfield, Connecticut, is surrounded by urban development and has self-regulating tide gates to minimize residential flooding (Steinke 1986). Here the diked *Phragmites*-dominated marshes have also subsided as much as 0.45 m in 26 years (1968 & 1994) compared to undiked systems that have accreted 6 cm in the same

Figure 13.3. Above – Tidal gates installed across the Hammock River in 1947 restricting tidal flow up the valley marsh. Below – Dramatic vegetation change evident above tidal restriction (foreground) and below (background) causeway where tidal gates are installed. Typical *Spartina* marsh dominates below restriction; *Phragmites australis* (darker vegetation) has replaced *Spartina* spp. over several decades above restriction.

period (Thomas Steinke, personal communication). Under such conditions the self-regulating tidal gate can be adjusted to close automatically during very high water associated with storms, and thus prevent flooding of low-lying properties (Steinke 1995a Figure 13.4). Restoration results to date have been impressive (Steinke 1995b). The height of *Phragmites* has been reduced from 3.3 m to less than 1.2 m in four growing seasons, and, with growth decreasing each year, it is anticipated that within 10–12 years *Phragmites* may be eliminated. In 5 years, stem density was also reduced from several hundred stems per square metre to twenty. Saltmarsh vegetation that has become established includes *S. alterniflora* (dominant) in association with *S. patens, Salicornia europaea*, and *Atriplex patula*. This recovery has taken place under salinities ranging from 6 to 28 ppt. Pre-restoration salinities were < 5 ppt. When the *Phragmites* was burned each year before 4 July, growth was reduced 50% each year. However, by the fourth year there was inadequate fuel to carry the fire. This restoration work is ongoing under the direction of Thomas Steinke, inventor of the self-regulating tidal gate and Conservation Director of the Town of Fairfield. These tide gates will be used in marsh restoration in California, Massachusetts, and Rhode Island.

In the north-east, numerous other such restoration projects are planned or are underway where tidal restriction has degraded the tidal salt marshes (Cook, Lindley Stone, & Ammann 1993; US Department of Agriculture 1994; Golet, Myrshrall, & Tefft 1995; US Army Corps Engineers 1995a,b). In the future, restoration of tidal flushing will aid in restoring *Spartina*-dominated marshes, and contribute to the potential productivity of the contiguous estuarine waters.

Restoration of an impounded valley marsh using GIS to document vegetation change

This restoration effort concerns one of six valley marshes in south-eastern Connecticut within a 0.5 square mile unit known as the Barn Island marshes. Over 50 years ago, the vegetation pattern of these salt marshes was described in a classic paper by Miller and Egler (1950) as the Wequetequock-Pawcatuck tidal marshes. They have also been the site of considerable research by biologists at Connecticut College, since the marsh vegetation has undergone dramatic changes in the last half century.

The state of Connecticut owns 400 acres including 5 of the 6 valley marshes and adjacent upland known as the Barn Island Wildlife Management Area. In the 1940s the state impacted 4 of the valley marshes by the

Figure 13.4. Self-regulating tide gates designed to automatically control water level or degree of flooding. Upper–Both gates open automatically when tide reverses flow. Low-tide view with both gates discharging water from diked marsh. Lower–Floats close gates automatically at predetermined water levels to allow marsh restoration without upland flooding. Rear gate is now closed while the near gate is open with tide water flowing to the diked marsh. Near tide gate will close as tide rises. Turkey/Ash Creeks, Fairfield Connecticut. (Photos: Thomas Steinke, November 1995).

construction of causeways across the marshes, and limited culvert openings for tidal exchange. The objective was to create brackish water impoundments to provide favourable feeding and breeding grounds for waterfowl, primarily ducks. This case history concerns the largest western impoundment, which had only a 0.5 m culvert connection with the adjacent estuarine waters after impoundment in the late 1940s. In its pre-impoundment state, the marsh was dominated by *Spartina* grasses and associated saltmarsh species (Miller 1948). Following impoundment, the area became dominated by *Typha angustifolia* and salinity dropped to <5 ppt. When studied during the 1970s, *T. angustifolia* dominated with *Phragmites* as an associated species (Hebard 1976). The marsh primarily supported muskrats rather than, as intended, waterfowl. Therefore, local citizen pressure resulted in the reintroduction of tidal flushing. The first effort began in 1978 with the installation of a 1.5 m culvert followed in 1987 by a second 2.1 m diameter culvert, which reconnected the impounded marsh with the adjacent estuarine waters (28–32 ppt). This resulted in the rapid decrease of *Typha* from 74% to 16% and the recovery and natural re-establishment of *Spartina alterniflora* from <1 to 45% by the late 1980s (Sinicrope *et al.* 1990). Phragmites did not decrease as expected, but increased from the 6% reported by Hebard (1976) in the early 1970s to 17% total cover in the late 1980s (Sinicrope *et al.* 1990). This overall recovery of *Spartina* and associated saltmarsh species along with the saltmarsh animal populations continues to the present. The unimpounded bay front marshes serve as reference sites; although some areas of the marsh have changed dramatically (Warren & Niering 1993), other portions still exhibit the pattern initially described by Miller & Egler (1950). The mean tidal range is 0.82 m in the marsh system.

Within this restored valley marsh, it has been possible to analyse data collected by Sinicrope *et al.* (1990) using a Geographic Information System (GIS) to document the pattern of vegetation change from the pre-impoundment to the post-impoundment conditions, and to assess the restoration success (Barrett & Niering 1993). In 1988, based on GIS data, 63% of the marsh was restored to *Spartina* species or other saltmarsh species (Figure 13.5). Of this restored area, 28% represents identical vegetation restoration, whereas 28% represents a more hydric saltmarsh vegetation, primarily short or intermediate *S. alterniflora*, and 7% a less hydric saltmarsh cover. It was also possible to indicate newly created wetlands (3%), wetland loss (1%), and marsh area not recovered (33%) still dominated by *Typha angustifolia* and limited primarily to the upper reaches of the valley system. The fact that a considerable area of the restored marsh exhibits a wetter

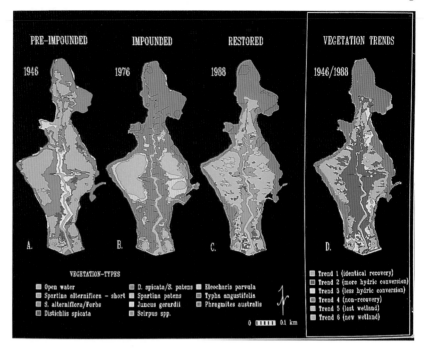

Figure 13.5. Hydrologic conditions and vegetation of Impoundment 1, Barn Island Wildlife Management Area, Stonington, Connecticut. (A) pre-impounded tidal marsh (1946); (B) impounded marsh (1976); (C) restored tidal marsh (1988); (D) trends in vegetation recovery: Trend 1 (identical recovery), Trend 2 (conversion – more hydric), Trend 3 (conversion – less hydric), Trend 4 (nonrecovery), Trend 5 (lost wetland), and Trend 6 (new wetland). (GIS by Nels Barrett).

vegetation is correlated with the lower peat surface elevations due to limited marsh accretion and possibly more rapid decomposition during the impounded period (Roman *et al.* 1984). *Phragmites* still persists, especially along the upper borders of the marsh. Further recovery of this system may require an additional culvert; however, much of the marsh is lower than the reference marsh below the impoundment dike, and excessive flooding might then occur and be detrimental to the already recovering high-marsh communities, especially *Spartina patens*. Completely opening the causeway to the width of the original tidal creek might have created too much flooding for natural recovery, which confirms the extreme caution needed in such restoration efforts. Since post-restoration site conditions have changed over the decades of impoundment, one would not expect identical vegetation recovery. The fact that nearly two-thirds of the system has been restored to a *Spartina*-dominated vegetation is an indication of the restoration potential. The evaluation of restoration success involves such criteria as plant productivity, which is comparable to the reference marsh, and the re-establishment of saltmarsh animal populations or food-chain support which would further document that functional equivalence is being restored. Re-establishment of animal populations will be discussed in a later section. This marsh restoration has been under the supervision of the Connecticut Department of Environmental Protection.

Restoration following dredged spoil removal

Another type of successful restoration has been the removal of dredged material from a salt marsh filled several decades ago. In the early 1950s, the Mumford Cove (Groton, Connecticut) salt marsh was covered with dredged material, and subsequently there developed a vigorous monoculture of *Phragmites* which was dominant when the restoration was initiated. A four-phase restoration was carried out from 1989 to 1992 resulting in the removal of the spoil by forming mounds and peripheral dikes (Capotosto 1993). Elevation and grade of the system were designed to simulate a remnant of adjacent natural salt marsh. Ponds and channels were created to allow diurnal tidal flushing with a mean tidal range of 0.78 m. In 1991–2, 2 to 3 years after the initiation of the project, a vegetation inventory documented the initial stages of restoration (Waters 1995). Except for a small planting of *Spartina alterniflora* (12 plugs) in autumn 1989, all plant colonization was natural on the newly re-exposed marsh peat. After three growing seasons, this *S. alterniflora* locally formed a relatively continuous sward (75% cover). Elsewhere, during the initial growing season, *Salicornia europaea* colonized and dominated the exposed peat with a few scattered clumps of *S. alterniflora*. However, a year later *S. alterniflora* 0.5–1.25 m in height formed the dominant aspect (35% cover), indicating not only rapid establishment, but also vegetative increase of this low-marsh species being flooded by each tidal cycle. Plants vegetatively increased fourfold from 1991 to 1992. Graded to favour low-marsh establishment, high-marsh species such as *Spartina patens, Juncus gerardii*, and *Distichlis spicata* were rare, contributing less than 1%. Persisting *Phragmites* was stunted to 0.8–1 m in height compared to pre-restoration conditions when it was continuous and reached several metres in height. This is a dramatic example of how fast a salt marsh can recover when given the proper hydrological conditions. Some of the typical marsh invertebrates were also observed, but it may be a decade or more until functional equivalence is attained. This work was a joint effort of the US Fish and Wildlife Service and the State of Connecticut Department of Environmental Protection.

Saltmarsh creation and restoration by planting

Saltmarsh creation or restoration by planting saltmarsh graminoids has been carried out along the eastern seaboard for the past few decades (Daiber 1986). The most extensive work has been along the North Carolina coast where Woodhouse *et al.* (1972) and Broome (1990) have pioneered this work using dredged material and *Spartina alterniflora* seedlings (Broome, Seneca, & Woodhouse 1982, 1986; Broome, Craft, & Seneca 1988). Since hydrology is critical, creating a gentle 1–3% slope is essential in order that the planting will occur between mean low and mean high tide. The nature of the substrate is also important; sandy soils are often more easily graded, but may need an organic supplement or even the addition of P or N when planting occurs. Over time, silt and organic material will further enrich the substrate. In some projects, original soils can be stockpiled, since such material often enhanced the rapidity of plant establishment as well as the more rapid re-establishment of trophic structure. Every effort should be made to use locally grown genotypes. The importance of different genotypic forms and the role of their differential functional characteristics in restoration have been reviewed by Seliskar (1995). In general, spacing of plants varies from 0.6 × 0.6 m to 1.0 × 1.0 m. Planting details and care thereafter can be found in Broome (1990). Frequently, newly planted material will need protection from geese or other browsers until well established. Occasionally, plantings of *S. alterniflora* can be invaded by *Phragmites*, especially if there is upland freshwater seepage near the edge of the marsh which reduces salinity levels. Additional saltmarsh species used in restoration include *Spartina patens, S. cynosuroides,* and *Juncus roemarianus,* the latter two species typical of the south-east marshes.

Over the last two decades, the work in Chesapeake Bay, Maryland, in terms of stabilization of shoreline bank erosion, has been most impressive (Garbisch & Garbisch 1994). Over 216 marsh construction projects involving restoration of former site elevations through shoreline filling and gradings and the planting of *S. alterniflora* (low marsh) and *Spartina patens* (high marsh) as bordering belts have provided successful upland bank erosion control. This technique demonstrates the re-creation of a functional attribute that tidal marsh systems normally provide, i.e. shoreline stabilization. Although high-marsh restoration using *S. patens* is not as widely undertaken, about 3 hectares are being planned for a site in the Hackensack Meadows, New Jersey, with plants made available by Environmental Concern Inc., Maryland, one of the nurseries that provides such natural plant material (Mark Krass, personal communication). Another high-marsh species, *Juncus gerardii*, is also available in the trade but planted less frequently than *S. patens*. These high-marsh species are sometimes more difficult to establish, since the factors controlling them are more multi-factorial (Bertness 1992) than those for tall *S. alterniflora* which is primarily controlled by diurnal tidal flushing along the bay or creek fronts.

Saltmarsh restoration – five years after oil spill

In January 1990, an oil spill in Linden, New Jersey, released 567 000 gallons of number 2 heating oil into the New York Harbour area (Arthur Kill Van Kull and Newark Bay) fouling contiguous saltmarsh systems (Bergen *et al.* 1995). Another half million gallons from various sources were also released from mishaps between 1980 and 1990. Most obvious degradation as a result of these spills was to the dominant low marsh *Spartina alterniflora* (Figure 13.6). In addition to significant mortality of *Spartina*, associated animals, especially waterfowl (694 birds confirmed dead) and ribbed mussel, were also affected. Damage claims totalled $75 000 000, a portion of which was used by the New York City Parks Natural Resources Group to undertake tidal marsh restoration. Polluted and restored marshes, non-restored and non-affected salt marshes were monitored for total petroleum hydrocarbon content (TPH) and associated microbial populations in the surface sediments. Also studied was primary productivity of *Spartina*, along with shellfish, fish, mammals, and bird populations. Since 1992, a total of 6 acres of *S. alterniflora* salt marsh has been restored as a result of planting. Plants were spaced 30 to 45 cm on centre and each plant received 30 gms of Osmocote 18-6-12 plus Fe (8–9 months time release). Of the 200 000 seedlings planted, survival has been 75%. Only in the 1995 planting did extensive browsing by geese decrease the restoration success, a problem which has been overcome by proper fencing. After two growing seasons above ground, *Spartina* biomass was about 60% of that of the control (909 vs. 1680 gm²), and below ground biomass (1395 vs. 1360 gm²) was comparable (Figure 13.6). Height and stem density were also comparable after 2 years. The TPH levels were reduced from 17 534 ppm (pre-planting) to 6188 and 4425 ppm. respectively by the end of the first and second growing season, respectively. It is hypothesized that the presence of

Figure 13.6. Above – Mortality of *Spartina alterniflora* following 1990 oil spill in New York harbour. Below – Planted *Spartina alterniflora* after second growing season. (Photos from Department of New York City Parks and Recreation, Natural Resources Group, 13 September 1994).

Spartina may indirectly be accelerating the breakdown of the oil. *Geukensia demissa* showed evidence of returning to restored marsh, 6 m^2 compared to 41 m^2 on the control marsh. Fiddler crabs are also present in small numbers. Avian and fish populations have shown a marked preference for the restored marshes. According to Carl Alderson (personal communication), seven species of wading birds are using restored marsh, and overall bird usage is four-fold greater on restored compared with nearby control marsh. Fish catches, primarily mummichogs and silversides, are double on restored compared with control marshes. Thus, after just 3 years, data suggest that primary production of low-marsh *Spartina* is being rapidly restored by planting, and that the associated biota are also being established. This work documents the ability of the low marsh to rejuvenate following planting and natural re-colonization thereafter.

Tidal freshwater marsh restoration

One of the most recent and challenging restoration efforts involved the 28 ha Kenilworth Marsh (District of Columbia) along the upper reaches of the Anacosta River where the water is essentially fresh (<0.5 ppt), but tidal effects still occur. Before 1948, these freshwater tidal wetlands had been dredged and so highly modified that the former marsh site was mostly open water and exposed mud flat at low tide. Thus it was necessary to bring in 84 000 cubic metres of fill in order to attain suitable surface elevations for plantings. Since maintenance channel dredging was occurring nearby in the river, the dredged material was used as a source of fill. The objective was to restore 11.7 hectares of wetlands, including 8.3 ha of mid marsh, 3 ha of high marsh, and 0.4 ha of low marsh, in a pattern which would mimic the original wetland. To stabilize the fine dredge spoil sediments, brush bundle enclosures ('brush fence' developed in The Netherlands) were placed adjacent to the channel. Since the fine sediments moved through the brush fences, straw and hay bales were added as a further barrier to de-water the dredged spoil. Large geotextile tubes filled with water were used to provide a temporary barrier from tidal inundation. Planting was carried out over a six-week period beginning in May 1993. A total of 340 000 plant specimens was planted in very unconsolidated sediments. Of the 16 species, only 1, *Nuphar advena*, was planted in the low marsh; 11 were planted in mid marsh, primarily *Peltandra virginica, Sagittaria latifolia,* and *Scirpus validus,* and in the high marsh 4 species, primarily *Leersia oryzoides.* Seeds of *Zizania aquatica* were also planted in an attempt to restore this annual wild rice, which was historically one of the dominant species of the upper

Anacosta River. To control geese and waterfowl foraging on the succulent plantings, a string fence 0.3 m above the water, and additional strands strung at the same interval above solved the problem. This work was carried out by Ecological Restoration and Management, Inc. and Biohabitats, Inc., Towson, Maryland. Currently the area is being evaluated in terms of restoration success. This summary was based on an account by Bowers (1995).

Assessing functional equivalence

The ultimate aim in coastal wetland restoration or creation is to produce a self-perpetuating sustainable ecosystem that does not need a continuous input of human energy. This involves attaining functional equivalence in such processes as primary productivity, nutrient cycling, and food-chain support as compared to a given reference or control system. This section will examine some studies which have addressed these issues. Most are from the south-east where coastal wetland creation and restoration have been underway for a longer time.

Standing Crop Biomass

In North Carolina, *Spartina alterniflora* aboveground biomass, stem density, height of plants, number of flowering stalks and belowground biomass were similar on both the created (planted) and reference wetlands after five growing seasons (Broome *et al.* 1986). Some of these parameters, such as standing-crop biomass, stem height, and number of flowering stalks, were achieved in as few as 3 years. In brackish marsh creation, where additional species (*S. patens, S. cynosuroides*, and *J. roemerianus*) were evaluated, aboveground biomass was similar after only 3 years (Broome *et al.* 1982, 1988).

In the north-east, comparable standing crop has been achieved after a decade by natural recolonization following restoration of tidal flushing (Warren & Niering, unpublished data). Graminoids involved include tall and intermediate *S. alterniflora, S. patens, Distichlis spicata*, and *Juncus gerardii*.

Soil development and nutrient cycling

Restoring the soil ecosystem and nutrient cycling are also essential attributes in the restoration process. The nature of the soils can vary greatly depending upon whether one is working with dredged or original soil substrates. Development of nutrient cycles is dependent upon the soil structure; if one starts with sandy soil, the organic components and soil structure will require considerable time to develop. Created soils frequently have less organic matter, and thus porosity and conductivity are lower, and bulk density higher. Such soils may also exhibit more oxidized compounds such as those derived from iron and magnesium. Studies from North Carolina reveal that created marshes on dredged soils have less silt and organic matter than reference wetlands (Sacco *et al.* 1994). Restoration of comparable redox potentials on dredged material has been reported after 2 years, which supports the hypothesis that reducing conditions develop more rapidly on dredged materials where such conditions previously existed (Broome & Craft, unpublished manuscript). In tidally restricted marshes, restoration of tidal flushing to a peat substrate often provides suitable conditions for natural vegetation recovery if a seed source is nearby.

Restored marshes often have less carbon, nitrogen, and phosphorus as well as dead roots and rhizomes, and thus exhibit higher C:N ratios. Developing equivalence for these parameters may take 10–30 years, with considerable variability depending upon the region and nature of the initial substrate. However, over time it is assumed that the planted or re-established vegetation will reconstitute the nutrient pool and soil structure that will begin to mimic the natural wetland systems. Studies by Craft, Broome, & Seneca (1988) have shown that this is occurring for organic matter and nutrients, but rates are variable depending upon redox potential and effects of the N and P fertilizer used when planting. The amount of organic matter being sequestered as belowground biomass in created marshes is lower than on natural marshes. In contrast, denitrification was much lower on restored marshes (Thompson, Paerl, & Go 1995), probably correlated with lack of anaerobic conditions. One study found nitrogen fixation rates several times greater on restored wetlands with a sandy substrate which may have favoured the nitrogen fixing cyanobacteria (Currin, Newell, & Paerl 1995).

Data on the role of marshes as a nutrient pump or sink are limited; however, it appears that created marshes export nitrogen and dissolved organic matter (carbon) and remove inorganic nitrogen (NH_4) and PO_4 from the surrounding waters, compared to natural systems which often export these inorganic compounds (Craft, Broome, & Seneca 1988). The overall trend appears to be that young restored marshes are supported by external nutrient input, whereas reference marshes are often export systems.

Based on these studies it appears that over time many of the functional attributes are restored within the low-marsh *S. alternifora* community. Denitrification may be one of the slower processes to develop fully, since it is dependent upon the development of anaerobic soil conditions.

Food-chain support

Another vital functional attribute is the development of trophic structure or food-chain support involving a complex food web of animal populations linking the marsh and the surrounding estuarine waters. This involves myriad invertebrate populations including shellfish and finfish that not only utilize ditches and tidal creeks, but also feed on the marsh proper when it is flooded. In North Carolina, studies of the invertebrate fauna over 17 years revealed that their densities were lower on restored marshes, but no clear age correlation could be made (Sacco, Seneca, & Wentworth 1994).

In respect to shellfish and finfish, some studies report smaller populations on restored compared with natural marshes, whereas others find relatively comparable populations. In the south-east, restored marshes less than 3 years old showed fewer shrimp and *Fundulus heteroilitus* than reference marshes. In the north-east (Connecticut), Allen, *et al.* (1994) found *Fundulus* populations relatively similar after a decade, and in Texas similar fish densities on restored compared with natural marshes have been reported, although different fish species are involved (Minello & Zimmerman 1992). Feeding differences for *Fundulus* have been documented between restored and natural marshes (Moy & Levin 1991). Lower organic sediment content on the restored marsh had a marked impact on *Fundulus* which were more abundant on the reference system. On created marshes they feed primarily on polychaetes and algae, whereas detritus is a more important food item on natural marshes. In the north-east, algae were also an important food in the natural marshes, especially on the ebbing tide. These data indicate certain regional differences and similarities, as one might predict.

Studies involving $^{13}C^{15}N^{34}S$, to trace the fate of microalgae and dead standing *S. alterniflora* in terms of *Littoraria irrorata* and *Ilyanassa obsoleta, Uca* spp and *Fundulus* spp, indicate that both the natural and restored food chain are very similar (Currin *et al.* 1995).

In the north-east, the work of Fell *et al.* (1991) and his students (Allen *et al.* 1994; Peck *et al.* 1994 Spelke, Fell, & Helvenston, 1995) have contributed significantly to our understanding of the re-establishment of invertebrate, shellfish, and finfish populations on an impounded restored marsh compared to a natural valley marsh in eastern Connecticut. After 12 years, *Melampus bidentatus* biomass was relatively similar on restored compared with natural marsh (4.96 g dry wt/m² vs. 6.96 g dry wt/m²). Although their density was much lower on the restored marsh (332/^{m2} compared with 712/^{m2}), the snails were substantially larger (Peck *et al.* 1994). Furthermore, *Melampus* raised in the laboratory on mixed *S. alterniflora* (intermediate height form)/forb turf from the restored marsh or *S. patens* turf from a natural marsh below the impoundment dike grew more rapidly on the restored marsh turf. The large snails from the restored marsh also deposited larger and twice as many egg masses compared to those from the natural marsh (Spelke *et al.* 1995). Other high-marsh invertebrates, including *Orchestia grillus* (amphipod) and *Philoscia vittata* (isopod), were also present on the restored marsh (Fell *et al.* 1991). *Geukensia demissa* along the tidal creeks and *Uca pugnax* in the banks of mosquito ditches appeared in comparable densities on both restored and natural valley marshes (Peck *et al.* 1994). Fish populations sampled in ditches cut through the marshes (Allen *et al.* 1994) and trapped on the flooded marsh surface were similar on the restored marsh compared with natural reference marshes (Fell, Tarlow, and Shain, unpublished manuscript). *Fundulus heteroclitus* was the dominant fish, but several other species were moderately abundant. Gut content analysis on *Fundulus* from the ditches showed that the major food components were similar on the various marshes, but that fish in the restored marsh consumed more insects and less detritus and algae than did fish in the control marshes. They also tended to consume less food per unit of body weight (Allen *et al.* 1994). *Fundulus* also foraged on both the flooded restored and natural marshes. These data support the author's claim that this 'impounded marsh is in an advanced phase of restoration' in terms of functional equivalence. This is further corroborated by the comparable rate of primary productivity of the aboveground biomass. After more than a decade of more adequate tidal exchange, this system is becoming a part of the larger tidal marsh-estuarine ecosystem of Long Island Sound.

Conclusions

Along the east coast of North America, coastal wetland creation and restoration are viable techniques for compensating for the vast acreage of tidal wetlands lost historically, as well as for creating new wetlands on dredged material and abating shoreline erosion. Both natural plant establishment and planting saltmarsh graminoids are contributing to this restoration. In the north-east, *Phragmites* control is one of the objectives in restoring salt marshes. By restoring tidal flushing it has been possible to arrest *Phragmites* and create saline conditions favourable to the natural establishment of *Spartina* grasses and recreate an ecological link with estuarine productivity. Although *S. alterniflora* low marsh has been most widely created or restored, high marsh *Spartina patens* has been naturally restored or planted to control shoreline erosion. Since frequency and duration of flooding are critical to successful graminoid establishment, creating proper elevations is essential to restoration success. Following oil pollution, it is possible to re-establish successfully *S. alterniflora* marsh by planting within the marsh sediments a few years after the oil spill. Some of the associated animal populations are also returning within a few years. Here the soil biota may be aiding in the degradation of the petroleum residues within the marsh peat. Removal of dredged material from formerly filled marshes will also result in the natural re-establishment of *S. alterniflora* low marsh. Future restoration efforts should not exclude urban sites, since it does not necessarily follow that those wetlands surrounded by intense development have lost their ecological value (Oviatt, Nixon, & Garber 1977).

The basic goal in restoration or creation is to restore functional equivalence when compared to a reference system. Such aspects as productivity, soil development, nutrient cycling, and food-chain support are among the functional roles that should be evaluated. Studies suggest that 5 to 15 years are required, depending upon geographic region and specific aspects of the site, to begin to mimic some of the basic ecological processes occurring in the reference site. As stated by Kusler & Kentula (1989) 'Restoration or creation of a wetland that "totally duplicates" a naturally occurring wetland is impossible, however, some systems may be approximated and individual wetland functions may be restored or created.' This is further reinforced by Moy & Levin (1991) in comparing man-made *Spartina* salt marsh 1 to 3 years old with adjacent natural marshes – 'The extreme spatial and temporal variability inherent to salt marshes make it virtually impossible to exactly replace a marsh by planting one on another site.' It should also be noted that functional equivalence may often be more rapidly ascertained following wetland restoration in contrast to wetland creation. In fact, it may well take decades to restore certain functions. It should also be recognized that, in order to compensate for sea-level rise, upland buffers or undeveloped barriers are indispensable in order to accommodate continued landward migration of coastal wetlands, especially with accelerated sea-level rise which may increase in the future with climatic warming.

Finally, our ability to create or restore tidal wetlands, should not give us licence for the 'trading of natural salt marshes for man-made marshes' (Race & Christie 1982). Any mitigation should be evaluated very carefully and undertaken only as a last resort after all prudent and feasible alternatives have been explored. In the future, creation and restoration efforts along the Atlantic seaboard will contribute to the overall no-net-loss of wetlands, and increase the total acreage of these resources along with all the associated benefits of these liquid assets.

References

Allen, E. A., Fell, P. E., Peck, M. A., Gieg, J. A., Guthke, C. R., & Newkirk, M. D. (1994). Gut contents of common mummichogs, *Fundulus heteroclitus* L., in a restored impounded marsh and in natural reference marshes. *Estuaries*, 17, 462–71.

Barrett, N. E. & Niering, W. A. (1993). Tidal marsh restoration: trends in vegetation change using a Geographical Information System (GIS). *Restoration Ecology*, 1, 18–28.

Bergen, A., Levandowsky, M., Gorrell, T., & Alderson, C. (1995). Restoration of a heavily oiled salt marsh using *Spartina alterniflora* seedlings and transplants: effects on petroleum hydrocarbon levels and soil microflora. Presented to: The 10th Annual Conference on Contaminated Soils; Analysis, Site Assessment, Fate, Environmental and Human Risk Assessment, Remediation, and Regulation. University of Massachusetts, October 1995. Unpublished.

Bertness, M. D. (1992). The ecology of a New England salt marsh. *American Scientist*, 80, 260–8.

Bloom, A. L. & Stuiver, M. (1963). Submergence of the Connecticut coast. *Science*, 139, 332–4.

Bourn, W. S. & Cottam, C. (1950). *Some biological effects of ditching tidewater marshes*. Research Report 19. US Department of the Interior, Fish and Wildlife Service, Washington, DC.

Bowers, J. K. (1995). Innovations in tidal marsh restoration: the Kenilworth marsh account. *Restoration & Management Notes*, 13, 155–61.

Broome, S. W. (1990). Creation and restoration of tidal wetlands of the southeastern United States. In *Wetland Creation and Restoration: the Status of the Science*, eds. J. E. Kusler & M. E. Kentula, pp. 37–72. Washington, DC: Island Press.

Broome, S. W., Craft, C. B., & Seneca, E. D. (1988). Creation and development of brackish-water marsh habitat. In *Increasing Our Wetland Resources. Proceedings of the Corporate Conservation Council of the National Wildlife Federation, Washington, DC. 4–7 October 1987*, eds. J. Zelazny & J. S. Feierabend, pp. 197–205. Washington, DC: National Wildlife Federation.

Broome, S. W., Seneca, E. D., Woodhouse, Jr. W. W. (1982). Establishment of brackish marshes on graded upland sites. *Wetlands*, 2, 152–78.

Broome, S. W., Seneca, E. D., Woodhouse, Jr. W. W. (1986). Long-term growth and development of transplants of the salt-marsh grass *Spartina alterniflora*. *Estuaries*, 9, 63–74.

Buck, E. L. (1995). Selected environmental factors and the spread of *Phragmites australis* (Common Reed) in the tidelands of the lower Connecticut River. Honors Thesis, Connecticut College, New London, Connecticut.

Capotosto, P. M. (1993). Restoration of a dredge disposal site in Mumford Cover, Groton, Connecticut. State of Connecticut. Department of Environmental Protection, Field Services & Boating Division, Unpublished.

Capotosto, P. M. (1994). From mosquito control to wetlands restoration. State of Connecticut, Department of Environmental Protection, Field Services and Boating Division, Wetlands Restoration Unit, Madison, Connecticut, Unpublished.

Capotosto, P. M. & Spencer, E. (1988). Controlling *Phragmites* by tidegate management in the State of Connecticut. State of Connecticut, Department of Health Services, Madison, Connecticut. Unpublished.

Chapman, V. J. (1960) *Salt Marshes and Salt Deserts of the World*. New York: Interscience.

Connecticut's Coastal Marshes: A Vanishing Resource. (1961). The Connecticut Arboretum Bulletin no. 12. Connecticut College, New London, Connecticut.

Cook, R. A., Lindley Stone, A. J., & Ammann, A. P. (1993). *Method for the evaluation and inventory of vegetated tidal marshes in New Hampshire (coastal method)*. Audubon Society of New Hampshire, Concord, New Hampshire.

Cooper, P. F. & Hobson, J. A. (1989). Sewage Treatment by Reed Bed System: the Present Situation in the United Kingdom. In *Constructed Wetlands for Wastewater Treatment*, ed. D. A. Hammer, pp. 153–72. Chelsea, Michigan: Lewis Publishers, Inc.

Craft, C. B., Broome, S. W., & Seneca, E. D. (1988). Nitrogen, phosphorus and organic carbon pools in natural and transplanted marsh soils. *Estuaries*, 11, 272–80.

Currin, C. A., Newell, S. Y., Paerl, H. W. (1995). The role of standing dead *Spartina alterniflora* and benthic microalgae in salt marsh food webs: considerations based on multiple stable Isotope analysis. *Marine Ecology Progress Series*. 121, 99–116.

Daiber, F. C. (1986). *Conservation of tidal marshes*. New York, Van Nostrand Reinhold Company.

Fell, P. E., Murphy, K. A., Peck, M. A., & Recchia, M. L. (1991). Re-establishment of *Melampus bidentatus* (Say) and other macroinvertebrates on a restored impounded tidal marsh: comparison of populations above and below the impoundment dike. *Journal Experimental Marine Biology Ecology*, 152, 33–48.

Garbisch, E. W. & Garbisch, J. L. (1994). Control of upland bank erosion through tidal marsh construction on restored shores: application in the Maryland portion of Chesapeake Bay. *Environmental Management*, 18, 677–91.

Golet, F. C., Myrshrall, D. H. A., & Tefft, B. C. (1995). Salt marsh restoration monitoring at the Galilee Bird Sanctuary, Narragansett, RI. Research proposal. Submitted to Rhode Island Department of Environmental Management, Division of Fish and Wildlife.

Haslam, S. M. (1973). Some aspects of the life history and autecology of *Phragmites communis* Trin.: a review. *Polske Archiwum Hydrobiologii*, 20, 79–100.

Hebard, G. (1976). Vegetation patterns and changes in the impounded salt marshes of the Barn Island Wildlife Management Area. Masters thesis, Connecticut College, New London, Connecticut.

Kusler, J. A. & Kentula, M. E. (1989). *Wetland creation and restoration: the status of the science.* Vol. 1: Regional reviews. EPA/600/3-89/038. US Environmental Protection Agency, Washington, DC.

Matthews, G. A. & Minello, T. J. (1994). Technology and success in restoration, creation, and enhancement of *Spartina alterniflora* marshes in the United States. Vol. 1: Executive summary and annotated bibliography. NOAA Coastal Ocean Program, Decision Analysis series no. 2, National Oceanic and Atmospheric Administration, Coastal Ocean Office, Silver Spring, Maryland.

Metzler, K. & Rosza, R. (1982). Vegetation of fresh and brackish tidal marshes in Connecticut. *Connecticut Botanical Society Newsletter*, 10, 2–4.

Miller, W. (1948). Aspects of waterfowl management for Barn Island public shooting area. Masters thesis, University of Connecticut, Storrs, Connecticut.

Miller, W. R. & Egler, F. E. (1950). Vegetation of the Wequetequock-Pawcatuck tidal-marshes, Connecticut. *Ecological Monographs*, 20, 143–72.

Minello, T. J. & Zimmerman, R. J. (1992). Utilization of natural and transplanted Texas salt marshes by fish and decapod crustaceans. *Marine Ecology Progress Series*, 90, 273–85.

Mitsch, W. J. & Gosselink, J. G. (1993). *Wetlands*, 2nd edn. New York, Van Nostrand Reinhold.

Moy, L. D. & Levin, L. A. (1991). Are *Spartina* marshes a replaceable resource? A functional approach to evaluation of marsh creation efforts. *Estuaries*, 14, 1–16.

Niering, W. A. & Warren, R. S. (1980a). *Salt marsh plants of Connecticut.* Connecticut Arboretum Bulletin no. 25, Connecticut College, New London, Connecticut.

Niering, W. A. & Warren, R. S. (1980b). Vegetation patterns and processes in New England salt marshes. *BioScience*, 30, 301–7.

Niering, W. A., Warren, R. S., & Weymouth, C. G. (1977). *Our dynamic tidal marshes: vegetation changes as revealed by peat analysis.* The Connecticut Arboretum Bulletin no. 22, Connecticut College, New London, Connecticut.

Nixon, S. W. (1982). *The ecology of New England high salt marshes: a community profile.* FWS/OBS-81/55. US Fish & Wildlife Service, Office of Biological Services, Washington, DC.

Olmstead, N. C. & Fell, P. E. (1974). *Tidal marsh invertebrates of Connecticut.* Connecticut Arboretum Bulletin no. 20. Connecticut College, New London, Connecticut.

Orson, R. A., Warren, R. S., & Niering, W. A. (1987). Development of a tidal marsh in a New England river valley. *Estuaries*, 10, 20–7.

Oviatt, C. A., Nixon, S. W., & Garber, J. (1977). Variation and evaluation of coastal salt marshes. *Environmental Management*, 1, 201–11.

Peck, M. A., Fell, P. E., Allen, E. A., Gieg, J. A., Guthke, C. R., & Newkirk, M. D. (1994). Evaluation of tidal marsh restoration: comparison of selected macroinvertebrate populations on a restored impounded valley marsh and an unimpounded valley marsh within the same salt marsh system in Connecticut, USA. *Environmental Management*, 18, 283–93.

Race, M. S. & Christie, D. R. (1982). Coastal zone development: mitigation, marsh creation, and decision-making. *Environmental Management*, 6, 317–28.

Redfield, A. C. (1965). Ontogeny of a salt marsh estuary. *Science*, 147, 50–5.

Redfield, A. C. (1972). Development of a New England salt marsh. *Ecological Monographs*, 42, 201–37.

Roman, C. T., Garvine, R. W. & Portnoy, J. W. (1995). Hydrologic modeling as a predictive basis for ecological restoration of salt marshes. *Environmental Management*, 19, 559–66.

Roman, C. T., Niering, W. A. & Warren, R. S. (1984). Salt marsh vegetation change in response to tidal restriction. *Environmental Management*, 8, 141–50.

Rosza, R. (1987). An overview of wetland restoration projects in Connecticut. In *Proceedings of the IVth Connecticut Institute Water Resources Wetland Conference*, pp. 1–11.

Rosza, R. & Orson, R. A. (1993). Restoration of Degraded Salt Marshes in Connecticut. In *Proceedings of the Twentieth Annual Conference on Wetlands Restoration and Creation*, May 1993, ed. Frederick J. Webb, Jr., pp. 196–205. Plant City, Florida, Institute of Florida Studies, Hillsborough Community College.

Sacco, J. N., Seneca, E. D. & Wentworth, T. R. (1994). Infaunal community development of artificially established salt marshes in North Carolina. *Estuaries*, 17, 489–500.

Seliskar, D. M. (1995). Exploiting plant genetic diversity for coastal salt marsh creation and restoration. In *Biology of Salt-tolerant Plants*, eds. M. A. Khan & I. A. Ungar, pp. 407–416. Pakistan, University of Karachi.

Shea, M. L., Warren, R. S., & Niering, W. A. (1975). Biochemical and transplantation studies of the growth form of *Spartina alterniflora* on Connecticut salt marshes. *Ecology*, 56, 461–6.

Sinicrope, T. L., Hine, P. G., Warren, R. S., & Niering, W. A. (1990). Restoration of an impounded salt marsh in New England. *Estuaries*, 13, 25–30.

Spelke, J. A., Fell, P. E., & Helvenston, L. L. (1995). Population structure, growth and fecundity of *Melampus bidentatus* (Say) from two regions of a tidal marsh complex in Connecticut. *The Nautilus*, 108, 42–7.

Steinke, T. J. (1986). Hydrologic manipulation and restorating wetland values: Pine Creek, Fairfield, Connecticut. In *National Wetland Symposium: Mitigation of Impacts and Losses*. eds. J. A. Kusler, M. L. Quammen, & G. Brooks, pp. 377–83. New Orleans, Lousiana, Association of State Wetland Managers.

Steinke, T. J. (1995a). *The Self-Regulating Tidegate*. Atlantic Waterfowl Council, Delaware Department of Natural Resources and Environmental Control, Division of Fish & Wildlife, Dover, Delaware.

Steinke, T. J. (1995b). *Restoration of Degraded Salt Marshes in Pine Creek, Fairfield, Connecticut*. Atlantic Waterfowl Council, Delaware Department of Natural Resources and Environmental Control, Division of Fish & Wildlife, Dover, Delaware.

Teal, J. M. (1986). *The Ecology of Regularly Flooded Salt Marshes of New England: a Community Profile.* Biological Report 85(7.4), US Fish & Wildlife Service. Washington, DC.

Thayer, G. W., ed. (1992). *Restoring the Nation's Marine Wetlands.* A Maryland Sea Grant Book, College Park, Maryland.

Thompson, S. P., Paerl, H. W., & Go, M. C. (1995). Seasonal patterns of denitrification in a natural and a restored salt marsh. *Estuaries.* 18, 399–408.

Tiner, R. W. (1984). *Wetlands of the United States: Current Status and Recent Trends.* National Wetlands Inventory, US Department of the Interior, Fish and Wildlife Service, Washington, DC.

Tiner, R. (1995). *Phragmites*–controlling the all-too-common Common Reed. Massachusetts Wetlands Restoration Technical Notes. Wetlands Restoration & Banking Program, Technical Note Number 1:1–3.

US Department of Agriculture. Soil Conservation Service (1994). *Evaluation of Restorable Salt Marshes in New Hampshire.* US Department of Agriculture, Washington, DC.

US Army Corps of Engineers. New England Division (1995a). *Massachusetts Wetlands Restoration Study: a Review of Project Monitoring Procedures.* Wetlands Restoration and Banking Program, Massachusetts Executive Office of Environmental Affairs, Boston, Massachusetts.

US Army Corps of Engineers. New England Division (1995b). *Massachusetts Wetlands Restoration Study: Site Identification and Evaluation Report.* Wetlands Restoration and Banking Program, Massachusetts Executive Office of Environmental Affairs, Boston, Massachusetts.

Warren, R. S. & Niering, W. A. (1993). Vegetation change on a northeast tidal marsh: interaction of sea-level rise and marsh accretion. *Ecology,* 74, 96–103.

Waters, R. F. (1995). Tidal wetland restoration on a dredge disposal site: patterns of initial plant species establishment, Mumford Cove, Groton, Connecticut. MA thesis, Connecticut College, New London, Connecticut.

Wiegert, R. G. & Freeman, B. J. (1990). *Tidal Salt Marshes of the Southeast Atlantic Coast: a Community Profile.* Biological Report 85(7.29). US Department of the Interior, Fish & Wildlife Service, Washington, DC.

Woodhouse, Jr., W. W., Seneca, E. D., & Broome, S. W. (1972). *Marsh building with dredge spoil in North Carolina.* Agricultural Experiment Station Bulletin 445. North Carolina State University at Raleigh.

14

Options for restoration and management of coastal salt marshes in Europe

JAN P. BAKKER, PETER ESSELINK, RENÉ VAN
DER WAL, AND KEES S. DIJKEMA

Introduction

Coastal salt marshes are valued as important habitats for their characteristic plant and animal life (Adam 1990; Allen & Pye 1992). The present area of coastal salt marshes in Europe along the Atlantic coast and the Baltic amounts to 175 800 ha (Dijkema 1984, 1990; Allen & Pye 1992). Salt marshes are either of natural origin, or have been created by man as a result of reclamation activities. Most salt marshes have always been exploited agriculturally. Haymaking has gradually decreased, and nowadays the most widespread use is livestock grazing. Seventy per cent of the north western European salt marshes are still exploited, but the area of abandoned salt marshes is increasing rapidly. In particular, the designation of man-made salt marshes as nature reserves and national parks has led to a change of management aims from reclamation of land for intensive agricultural exploitation towards restoration of 'natural' marshland.

From a nature conservation point of view, different opinions exist about what kind of development of the marshes is desirable. The two extremes can be summarized by the concept of 'wilderness' in which all human interference is abandoned, and by the concept of 'biodiversity' in which management plays a role. The objective of this chapter is to outline the possibilities and the constraints for restoration, the management options, the possible outcome of various management practices on the saltmarsh ecosystem, and to sketch some future developments.

In this chapter we will focus on the salt marshes of the Wadden Sea. The conclusions drawn may be applicable to other temperate salt marshes in Europe. The Wadden Sea fringes the northern coasts of The Netherlands and Germany, and the south of Denmark over a distance of nearly 500 km. Its maximum width is 35 km and it is separated from the North Sea by some 20 large and many small sandy barrier islands and sandbanks. The

Wadden Sea developed in the wake of the Holocene transgression (Veenstra 1980; Oost & De Boer 1994). Today, it encompasses Europe's largest intertidal area, as well as major areas of salt marshes, which extend over 33 000 ha. These marshes feature the remainder of an extensive natural landscape of coastal marshes, peatland, and lakes which once existed at the fringe between the Pleistocene deposits and the sea. Despite the changes, the Wadden Sea remains one of the most natural, large-scale, ecosystems of the European Lowlands, often regarded as the last wilderness of the region (Adam 1990).

Two main types of salt marshes may be distinguished in the Wadden Sea, namely the sandy back-barrier marshes which are mainly found on the islands, and the clayey man-made mainland salt marshes, which have developed from accretional works. The back-barrier marshes form about 40% of the marsh area in the Wadden Sea. They developed in the lee of dune ridges (in some cases artificial ridges) and have a high degree of naturalness. Natural geomorphological processes result in the continuous formation of young successional stages which are the most species-rich.

The mainland marshes cover 19 000 ha, and are mostly man-made. They are characterized by an evenly distributed drainage pattern and a flat topography, and hence show less abiotic variation than back-barrier salt marshes. They nevertheless have considerable importance for nature conservation. Their existence largely depends on the continued maintenance of the network of brushwood groynes, which prevents saltmarsh erosion.

To evaluate the options for restoration and management of salt marshes, we will consider what should be understood by the terms 'restoration' and 'management'. We shall further review the historical changes in saltmarsh areas in the Wadden Sea, the natural marsh succession in relation to abiotic conditions, and the outcome of various management options in these marshes. We will first evaluate, however, how the coastal landscape was altered by man, to create a frame of reference.

Historical development: man and the coastal environment

Before dealing with human impact on salt marshes, a short account will be given on the pristine coastal environment. A continuous sea-level rise has occurred since the last glacial period. Natural drainage of fresh water into the sea became blocked, and an extensive accumulation of organic material took place as far as the edges of the Pleistocene sands. Both fen-peat (tall sedges, reedbeds, and alder carr) and bog-peat (communities with

Figure 14.1. Map of mounds (established before AD 1000) and dikes in the northern Netherlands and adjacent Germany. The intrusions of the sea date back to the Middle Ages, therefore no mounds are found in these newly sedimented areas (after Westerink & Wildeman 1996).

Sphagnum spp. and *Erica tetralix*) developed, depending on the regional and local hydrology. Most peat was covered by clay during transgression periods, vast areas from the Middle Ages onwards (Behre 1979). One example of peat which has not been clay covered is located outside the sea-wall in the Jadebusen in Germany. It floats during very high tides, and has therefore been named 'Schwimmendes Moor' (Wierman 1965; Irion 1994). River-bank gallery forests of hard-wood species (amongst others *Fraxinus excelsior* and *Ulmus glabra*) have been recorded on the elevated levees along the lower parts of rivers, for instance the Ems in Germany, from the early sub-Boreal period (*c.* 4500 BC) until the Iron Age (*c.* 500 BC). Mainly swamps with reed-beds, *Salix* scrub, *Bidens cernua* communities, and some tall-sedge communities occurred in the neighbourhood of the levees in the period from 700 BC until AD 300 as examples of natural treeless communities (Behre 1979). Brackish elements of freshwater reed-beds (especially *Scirpus maritimus*) and of salt-water communities with *Armeria maritima* (and especially *Eleocharis palustris* ssp. *uniglumis*), indicating the transition zone between fresh- and salt-tidal water landscapes, have been found (Behre 1979).

The first people assumed to have exploited the salt marshes lived at the fringes of the Pleistocene Plateau in the north-eastern part of The Netherlands, and were herdsmen who moved far away from the villages. The suitability of the salt marshes for grazing might have resulted in 'transhumance' i.e. the movement of herds of livestock to complementary seasonal pastures in the period 700–500 BC (Waterbolk 1988). This system must have changed gradually into year-round occupation of the salt marshes. The forests on elevated levees along the lower part of the rivers in the freshwater landscape were cleared very early and had completely vanished in the Roman period in north-western Germany. The anthropogenic arable field communities and communities in trodden areas which replaced them, were found from 700 BC onwards (Behre 1979).

Between 500 BC and AD 1200 farmsteads were built, initially on the salt marsh, but later also on mounds of saltmarsh sods because of transgression periods (Oost & De Boer 1994). The mound settlements were widespread all along the Dutch and adjacent German coast (Figure 14.1). The mounds gradually grew higher through the accumulation of waste and dung. The macrofossils contain excellent records of former settlement and land use.

It has been possible to reconstruct the saltmarsh plant communities from the time of the mound settlements in the northern part of The Netherlands and adjacent Germany from paleo-ecological samples (van Zeist 1974; Behre 1979, 1985). According to the macrofossils found, it must be assumed that the salt marshes were heavily exploited (Waterbolk, 1976; Bakker *et al.* 1993). Moreover, *Atriplex portulacoides, Artemisia maritima,* and *Elymus athericus*, dominant species on ungrazed salt marshes, were rarely found as macrofossils. Therefore, it seems likely that by the year AD 0 no pristine mainland salt marshes were left.

For centuries, the only defence against inundations was the mounds. The construction of dikes was probably a response to increased risk of flooding and relative sea-level rise (i.e. land subsidence) which was at least partly due to human impact. Much of the flooding of the land along the western Dutch Wadden Sea was enhanced by the exploitation of the peatland behind the coast. Levelling, drainage, and subsequent oxidation after aeration led to subsidence, and the land became vulnerable to flooding (Oost & De Boer 1994). Counter-measures against flooding started around AD 1000 in the northern Netherlands, when dikes were constructed to enclose sheltered areas and to reclaim lost land (Waterbolk 1976). Dike-building started in adjacent Germany in the eleventh century (Behre 1985).

In the eastern Dutch Wadden Sea, peat has been dug for fuel for at least 2000 years, and later on also for salt production. For this purpose and also for agriculture, the area was drained. As in the western Wadden Sea, a large part of the mainland was flooded as a result of mining of peat. In the period 800–1300, the Zuiderzee, Fivel, Middelzee, Lauwerszee, and Dollard were formed in the Netherlands, and the Leybucht, Harlebucht, and Jadebusen in Germany (Oost & De Boer 1994).

The conquest of land from the sea

The Wadden Sea reached its greatest extent during the Middle Ages, when extensive land losses occurred. In the flooded areas, as well as in other areas outside the existing reclamations, sedimentation allowed the growth of new foreland, especially in sheltered bays formed by the aforementioned intrusions of the sea. During the Middle Ages, loss of land exceeded reclamation, but the process was gradually reversed in the Dutch Wadden Sea during the early seventeenth century. Since then, the Wadden Sea has gradually diminished in size through successive reclamation of the newly accreted salt marshes for agricultural purposes. Although continuing accretion has always developed new salt marshes, reclamation rates in the last centuries have been higher than the accretion rate of new salt marshes. Dijkema (1987) compared saltmarsh areas in different periods and regions on the basis of the areas of salt marsh proportional to the area of the tidal basins. He proposed to take the percentage of saltmarsh area of the tidal

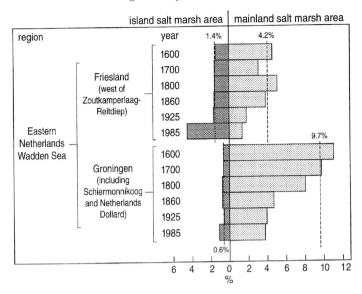

Figure 14.2. Saltmarsh area in the eastern Dutch Wadden Sea after 1600, in percentages of the total tidal area. Figures for 1985 excluding summer polders (1200 ha) and mainland pioneer vegetation (1000 ha). ---- = mean saltmarsh percentage for the period 1600 to 1800 (after Dijkema, 1987).

basin from 1600 to 1800 as a standard for 'naturalness' of the Dutch Wadden Sea, since the rates of saltmarsh increase and of embankment were roughly balanced in that period. The mainland salt marshes of the eastern Dutch Wadden Sea area cover 50 km² below this standard nowadays (Figure 14.2).

Gradually coastal farmers started to promote marsh accretion by digging drainage ditches and building small dams, basically enhancing natural accretion processes. Such techniques were applied by 1740 or even earlier (Stratingh & Venema 1855). In the first decades of the twentieth century, farmers abandoned accretion works. Subsequently, responsibility for accretion measures was taken by government in both Germany and The Netherlands. Such activities included the construction of sedimentation fields surrounded by brushwood groynes in the pioneer zone and at the intertidal flats (Dijkema 1983a) (Figure 14.3). Optimal conditions for the formation of salt marshes are on a gently sloping shoreline with low wave energy and sufficient sediment supply (Dijkema 1987). Surface elevation, tidal amplitude, and drainage must be sufficient to allow periods of soil aeration necessary for plant growth (Armstrong *et al.* 1985). Groynes and sedimentation fields improve both sedimentation and establishment of vegetation as they create more shelter. Hence plant growth by means of

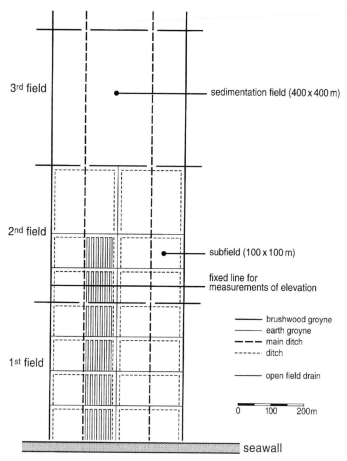

Figure 14.3. Sedimentation fields in the land reclamation works of man-made mainland salt marshes (after Dijkema 1983).

sedimentation fields may start at a lower level (about 20 cm) of the tidal flats then accretion works with drainage only. Pioneer plants (*Salicornia procumbens* and *Spartina anglica*) and continued vertical accretion create an environment which promotes a complete coverage of perennial halophytic plants. Around mean high-tide (MHT)-level, *Puccinellia maritima* reaches sufficient abundance to enhance sedimentation rates. Sedimentation is highest between MHT-level and 20 cm above MHT-level, and decreases again at higher elevation due to less frequent tidal flooding, namely, 0.7–2.0 cm yr^{-1} (at MHT + 0.05 m) to 0.6 cm yr^{-1} (at MHT + 0.80 m) in mainland salt marshes and 0.4 cm yr^{-1} (at MHT + 0.05 m) to

0 cm yr^{-1} (at MHT + 0.80 m) in barrier-island marshes (Dijkema *et al.* 1990).

It seems that the balance between salt marsh expansion and erosion has varied considerably in recent years (Dijkema *et al.* 1990). Until the early 1980s, an average seaward expansion along the mainland coast was found in the Netherlands and in Germany (Dieckmann 1988). The horizontal erosion of salt marshes in the Wadden Sea area in the 1980s might be caused by the increase in MHT-level, namely, 0.37 cm yr^{-1} in the Dutch Wadden Sea (Dijkema *et al.* 1991) and adjacent German Wadden Sea (Schönfeld & Jensen 1991) during the last 30 years. The recent decrease of MHTs in the 1990s (Dijkema 1994) stress the relatively rapidly changing flooding conditions from year to year.

Once sedimentation had yielded a new high salt marsh it was embanked by a high dike and transformed into intensively exploited agricultural land. Often prior to this, a lower summer dike was built, which prevented most of the floodings, and enabled more intensive agricultural exploitation. At present such summer polders are found in Friesland, The Netherlands (1200 ha), and in Niedersachsen, Germany (2100 ha).

The latest development in the conquest of land from the sea are enclosures for coastal protection. Only this century the Dutch Wadden Sea reached its present extent with the large enclosure of the Zuiderzee (1932) and the Lauwerszee estuary (1969). Also several enclosures were established at the west coast of Schleswig-Holstein, like the Hauke-Haienkoog (1959), the Eider estuary (1972), and the Beltringharderkoog (1986), and, at the German–Danish border, the Margarethekoog (1983).

All the aforementioned activities have resulted in a nearly complete loss of the estuarine habitat in the Wadden Sea. Most river mouths have been closed off, sluices being used to discharge the river water into the sea. The Ems, Weser, and Elbe rivers in Germany, and the Varde Å river in Denmark are the only rivers left which still have a free outflow into the sea.

Saltmarsh succession in the Wadden Sea

Since salt marshes have long been exploited for haymaking and grazing, it is hardly possible to study undisturbed vegetational succession from the beginning of saltmarsh formation towards a climax after several centuries. The rare unexploited salt marshes are found on the barrier islands. The largest example is the European nature reserve 'the Boschplaat' at the island of Terschelling, The Netherlands, which developed after the establishment of an artificial sand dike in the 1930s.

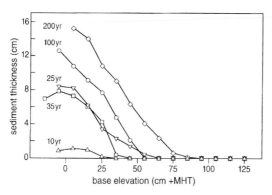

Figure 14.4. Thickness of the clay layer with respect to base elevation (elevation of the sand underground beneath the clay layer) in barrier-island saltmarsh sites on Schiermonnikoog aged 10, 25, 35, 100, and 200 years, respectively (figure from Olff *et al.* 1997).

The island of Schiermonnikoog, The Netherlands, provides the opportunity to study zonation and succession (de Leeuw *et al.* 1993; Olff *et al.* 1997). On bare beach surfaces, small dunes are formed, which later develop into larger dunes. During this second stage, the sand flat behind the dune is no longer inundated frequently by tides from the North Sea; inundation mainly occurs from the Wadden Sea, and the reduced turbulence of the water results in the sedimentation of clay, a process enhanced by the established vegetation. Saltmarsh development can be followed from very young marsh up to about 200-years-old marsh. The oldest parts of the salt marsh have always been grazed, but the island has some unexploited salt marsh parts ranging from a few years to about 100 years of age.

The thickness of the clay layer along the gradient from the feet of the dunes towards the lower salt marsh is determined by two factors: the base elevation, i.e. the elevation of the underlying sand beach, and the soil age, i.e. the duration of sedimentation (Figure 14.4). A thin layer of clay was found at low elevation in the young salt marsh and at higher elevation on the old salt marsh. In each successional stage of the salt marsh, clay sedimentation appeared to be a function of the base elevation and hence inundation frequency (Olff *et al.* 1997). Apparently zonation does not reflect succession in barrier-island systems as it does in mainland salt marshes (de Leeuw *et al.* 1993). It is, however, possible to analyse chronosequences, which represent the succession at the lines of similar elevation for high-, middle-, and low salt marsh. This applies also to other sandy salt marshes at the island of Terschelling, The Netherlands, and

the peninsula of Skallingen, Denmark (van Wijnen & Bakker 1997).
Does continuous sedimentation result in a decreased rate of inundation
and hence a reduced rate of sedimentation eventually? Close to the island of
Schiermonnikoog, annual MHT levels have increased since 1824, at an
average rate of 0.06 mm yr^{-1}. The sedimentation rates at MHT level were
nearly balanced by the sea-level rise, resulting in a very small decrease in
annual inundation frequency of 0.18 (about one inundation every 6 years)
according to Olff *et al.* (1997). Many species revealed some trends with
time, suggesting species replacement during succession over a period of 100
years (Olff *et al.* 1997). The series at the lower salt marsh (base elevation
MHT −0.05 m) featured *Salicornia procumbens*, *Spergularia maritima*,
Suaeda maritima, *Limonium vulgare*, and *Puccinellia maritima*. *Spergularia
maritima* disappeared during the successional series, whereas the other
species maintained themselves. Gradually *Festuca rubra*, *Glaux maritima*,
and *Artemisia maritima* appeared, later on followed by *Juncus gerardii*.
Atriplex portulacoides was dominant between 40 and 60 years. On the
middle salt marsh (base elevation MHT +0.25 m) initially *Limonium vulgare*
and *Fustuca rubra* were dominant. The first species decreased, but *Festuca
rubra* remained dominant in the successional series. *Artemisia maritima*
and *Elymus athericus* increased from the start of the succession onwards.
The first species decreased and *Elymus athericus* and *Festuca rubra* became
co-dominant. On the higher salt marsh (base elevation MHT +0.55 m)
Festuca rubra was initially the dominant species with some *Plantago
maritima* and *Elymus athericus*. *Artemisia maritima* showed an optimum at
60 years, but eventually *Elymus athericus* was the single dominant species
(Olff *et al.* 1997). These successional series show that *Puccinellia maritima*
initially occurred mainly at the lower parts of the salt marsh gradient,
where it nearly disappeared during succession. *Plantago maritima* initially
occurred mainly at the higher part of the gradient, where it maintained
itself for at least 25 years of succession, but had disappeared after 100 years.
Festuca rubra was initially absent only from the lower parts of the gradient,
where it increased. At the highest parts it decreased, however. *Elymus
athericus* occurred initially only at the higher parts of the salt marsh, but
gradually also extended to the lower parts (Figure 14.5).

A significantly positive correlation was found between the total amount
of nitrogen in the top 50 cm of the soil and the thickness of the clay layer at
the barrier island of Schiermonnikoog (Olff *et al.* 1997). In the earliest
stages of succession, the soil nitrogen pool was low. The rate of accumulation of nitrogen on the lower part of the gradient was estimated to be
3.4 g N m^{-2} yr^{-1}, and 0.9 g N m^{-2} yr^{-1} at the higher part (Olff *et al.*

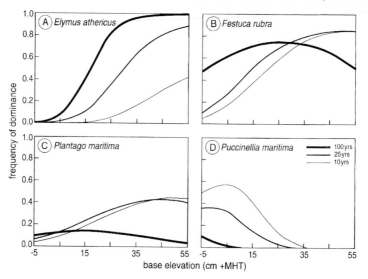

Figure 14.5. Frequency of occurrence as a dominant species with respect to base elevation (elevation of the sand underground beneath the clay layer) for four saltmarsh species in barrier-island saltmarsh sites on Schiermonnikoog aged 10, 25, and 100 years, respectively (figure from Olff *et al.* 1997).

1996). The higher rate of accumulation at the lower part of the gradient might be either attributed to the higher rate of sedimentation or the higher *in situ* production of organic matter by decaying plants.

Measurements of nitrogen mineralization revealed an increase during succession at the Schiermonnikoog salt marsh (van Wijnen, Bakker & de Vries 1997). The nutrient availability was positively related to the standing crop. The standing crop in turn was positively related to the amount of standing dead plant material and height of the canopy (Figure 14.6) (van de Koppel *et al.* 1996). The salt marsh is exploited by rabbit (*Oryctolagus cuniculus*) and hare (*Lepus europaeus*) throughout the year, and by barnacle geese (*Branta leucopsis*) in late autumn and early spring and by brent geese (*Branta bernicla*) in April and May. Use of the marsh by hare, rabbit, and geese, as gauged by the number of droppings, was greatest at intermediate levels of standing crop (Figure 14.7) (van de Koppel *et al.* 1996). Apparently the herbivores were unable to control the standing crop. Van de Koppel *et al.* (1996) suggest that not only the quantity, but also the quality and availability of forage is important for herbivores. During the late 1970s, the prime foraging area for brent geese was about 20 years of age. Grazing pressure determined as the number of goose days spent, as

Table 14.1. *Number of goose hours (and standard error) spent in the same part of the ungrazed salt marsh on the barrier island of Schiermonnikoog in 1979 and 1994*

	Number of goose hours		
1979	1994	*P*	
3343 ± 751 (n = 21)	1197 ± 198 (n = 13)	*	

Note: ($P < 0.05$, Df = 22.8) according to the *t*-test.

recorded from observation towers, had significantly decreased by 1994 (Table 14.1). Apparently saltmarsh ageing leads to less intensive use by brent geese. The geese now occupy young saltmarsh areas a few kilometres to the east (van der Wal, unpublished data). It seems that geese, at least, follow the succession, but are not capable of arresting the process of species replacement. The possible effect of these herbivores on the course of succession, however, needs further study.

Such a system, as described here, seems probably the closest that exists to the pristine saltmarsh ecosystem before man altered the landscape.

Options for saltmarsh restoration and management

Recently we have seen a change in ideas about the function of salt marshes, in particular man-made marshes, as summarized by Kiehl & Stock (1994). This implies that they are subject to discussion on various management options ranging from a lawn to natural succession.

Two options for the future development of salt marshes are possible. The first one is to abandon all human interference and leave the salt marshes to complete natural development: the 'wilderness' concept. In this concept, the management aim and the management practice are identical, namely, the unimpeded outcome of natural development. The outcome of this process with respect to 'target communities' is less important. This is largely the present approach in Germany, where heavy grazing by livestock was practised until recently and resulted in monotonous 'lawns'. The second option is characterized by aiming at 'target communities' including a high species-richness by maintaining or creating a high variation in abiotic conditions: the 'biodiversity' concept. In this concept, which is strived after in Denmark and The Netherlands, the choice for management practices is derived from the precise management aims.

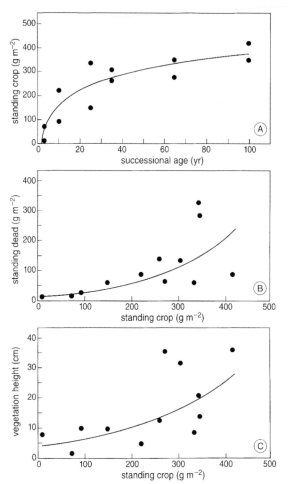

Figure 14.6. (A) Above ground live biomass (standing crop) in relation to successional age of saltmarsh sites on the barrier island of Schiermonnikoog. (b) Standing dead plant material in relation to standing crop. (C) Vegetation height in relation to standing crop. The graphs are based on linear regression after appropriate data transformation (figure from van de Koppel *et al.* 1996).

We define restoration as an attempt to bring back destroyed habitats to the original state. It may be carried out at either the original site, or as a replacement at a different site. The area of mainland marshes is below standard of naturalness (Dijkema 1987). It could be enlarged by further artificial extension of sedimentation fields into the tidal area. This method implies a decrease of the area of tidal flats and may, therefore, conflict with other nature conservation interests like foraging areas for wading birds.

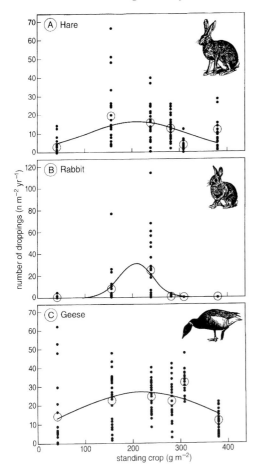

Figure 14.7. Number of droppings of (A) hares, (B) rabbits and (C) geese (barnacle geese and brent geese combined) collected over one year in relation to vegetation standing crop. Open circles indicate mean per site. The graphs are based on Poisson regression over the means only (figure from van de Koppel *et al.* 1996).

Another possibility has been practised in the newly embanked areas of Hauke-Haienkoog and Beltringharderkoog, Germany, where sluices were built to maintain some tidal influence. This alternative cannot be considered as very successful, since extensive salt marsh areas cannot be maintained, due to the decrease in tidal amplitudes. De Leeuw *et al.* (1994) reported a similar outcome for the Easter-Scheldt estuary in the southwestern part of The Netherlands. A minor option for restoration seems the possibility to increase salinity at the landward side of the seawall by the inlet of seawater through sluices. The best option is landward retreat of the marshes by de-embankment of summer polders. In this option the entire tidal amplitude will be maintained enabling saltmarsh development by the interaction of abiotic and biotic components.

We define management as a measure to affect a locally existing community by, for example, grazing, haymaking, or abandonment. A higher degree of naturalness with respect to abiotic conditions in man-made marshes may be achieved by modification or abandonment of the intensive drainage system. It should be taken into account that, in Germany, salt marshes play a more important role in coastal protection than in The Netherlands, because of the different systems of dike construction.

For the biotic conditions the different land use history of island and mainland marshes should be taken into account. Mainland salt marshes have always been intensively exploited. For management scenarios, various possibilities exist, ranging from a *laissez-faire* policy, haymaking and grazing by various livestock and at different stocking rates.

All options should take into account the hierarchical concept of influences. Ecosystems consist of a set of envelopes influencing each other mostly according to a decreasing order of impact: climate – geology – hydrological conditions – soil – plants – (small) animals. This implies that these factors mutually affect each other, but the effects are not equivalent to each other. Animals, such as geese, mostly depend on the vegetation, and can hardly affect the climax vegetation in winter-staging areas. In certain cases, however, the vegetation may be severely effected by a heavy grazing pressure of a herbivore, for instance grubbing geese may destroy the vegetation completely (Smith & Odum 1981; Esselink *et al.* 1997). This applies in particular in breeding areas, and they even may effect soil salinity (Iacobelli & Jefferies 1991).

Before we indicate the possibilities and constraints for restoration and management in the final section, we will deal with studies on the effects of management of abiotic (drainage and sedimentation) and biotic (vegetation, birds, and invertebrates) conditions in more detail. Effects of restoration of salt marshes are not published, and are therefore not discussed in further detail.

Management of abiotic conditions

In the Dollard, part of the Ems Estuary, abandonment of the drainage system in the man-made marshes led to an increase of elevational variation

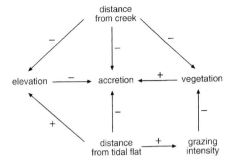

Figure 14.8. Flow diagram describing the accretion pattern and the interrelationships among the independent variables in the man-made mainland salt marsh of the Dollard. '+' and '−' indicate a positive or negative correlation, respectively. See text for further explanation (figure from Esselink *et al.*, in press).

and abiotic diversity. After designation as a nature reserve in 1981, grazing with cattle continued, but in reduced stocking rates (0.5–1 animal ha^{-1}), whereas the maintenance of the drainage system was abandoned by 1984. Many ditches were filled in, which resulted in a rewetting of the marshes and the development of temporarily waterlogged depressions. Vertical accretion rates, derived from levelling programmes carried out in 1984 and 1991/92, were generally correlated negatively with (a) the initial marsh elevation in 1984, (b) the distance from the tidal flats, (c) distance from main creeks, and (d) in many cases, the distance from minor creeks (Figure 14.8). As a consequence of a gradient in grazing intensity, vegetation structure decreased from the outer marsh towards the seawall, and was probably one of the causes for the aforementioned accretion patterns. After the abandonment of drainage, the number of levees along minor creeks (former ditches) increased, as did the elevation differences of many already existing levees (Figure 14.9). The levee development was more pronounced towards the seawall. This could be explained by the greater differences in vegetation structure between the levees and the marsh interiors towards the seawall, and indirectly by the gradient in grazing intensity in the marshes (Esselink, *et al.* in press). The possible effect of grazing on the sedimentation rate was also demonstrated in the mainland marshes of the Leybucht, Germany. After 4 years of measurements, a rate of sedimentation of 2.1 cm yr^{-1} was found in ungrazed sites at 40 cm above MHT, and 1.6–1.7 cm yr^{-1} in grazed sites (Erchinger *et al.* 1994).

A possible consequence of the abandonment of the drainage system in the Dollard was a negative effect on the overall vertical accretion rates.

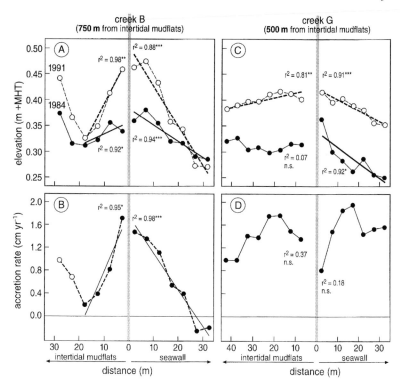

Figure 14.9. Examples of levee development near two minor creeks (former ditches) in the man-made mainland Dollard marshes. (A) The 1984 and 1991 elevation and (B) the vertical accretion rate in relation to the proximity of a creek centre at 750 m from the tidal flats and 420 m from the seawall. (C) The 1984 and 1991 elevation and (D) the vertical accretion rate in relation to the proximity of a creek centre at 500 m from the tidal flats and 670 m from the seawall. In A and B, points at >20 m distance at the tidal flats side of the creek were located at the neighbouring levee of the next creek. In C, the 1984 elevation was not significantly correlated with the distance to the creek. n.s. = not significant, * = $P < 0.05$, ** = $P < 0.01$, *** = $P < 0.001$ (figure from Esselink *et al.*, in press).

These ranged from 0.66 cm yr^{-1} to 1.14 cm yr^{-1} among different study sections. Taking into account the sheltered position of the marshes in the Dollard, these values are rather low in comparison with other man-made marshes in the Wadden Sea, which have mostly vertical accretion rates of well above 1 cm yr^{-1} (Dieckmann 1988; Dijkema *et al.* 1990; Erchinger *et al.* 1994). All these marshes still have a well-maintained drainage system, which will prevent the development of badly drained and sparsely vegetated depressions (Jakobsen 1954; Dijkema 1983a). Though negative accretations could be measured locally in the Dollard (cf. Figure 14.9), on average, vertical accretion rates in these depressions were positive, and ranged from 0.56 cm yr^{-1} to 0.92 cm yr^{-1}. These values exceed the average increase of MHT, which indicates that the development of the waterlogged depressions may not be a threat to the marshes. Maintenance of the artificial drainage system was also suspended in a cattle-grazing trial in the Leybucht marshes, but it was resumed a few years later, since the impact of trampling by cattle on the sward was considered too great (Erchinger *et al.* 1994).

Management of biotic conditions

Management options for biotic conditions includes livestock grazing, haymaking, and a *laissez-faire* policy. As haymaking is not carried out any longer as agricultural exploitation, we only discuss it in comparison with grazing on the basis of experiments.

Vegetation

As we have seen, the comparison between a marsh which has always been grazed and one which has never been grazed is difficult, since the latter is rare. Statements on differences between grazed and ungrazed salt marshes can, therefore, only be made for sites which have been excluded from grazing, or after renewed grazing for relatively short periods of time (in many studies < 10 years, sometimes several decades). Some case studies will elucidate the effects of the exclusion of livestock or the reduction of stocking densities.

The 200-year-old salt marsh at the barrier island of Schiermonnikoog has always been grazed. Parts of it have been protected from cattle grazing since 1973. One enclosure was situated at the gradient from dune to middle salt marsh featuring the zonation from *Ammophila arenaria* via *Festuca rubra* towards a *Juncus maritimus* community (Figure 14.10). Although *Ammophila arenaria* and *Festuca rubra* became more vigorous inside the enclosure, their communities did not spread. Initially the *Festuca rubra* community, including some *Elymus athericus*, spread lower down the gradient and later *Elymus* became so dominant that the *Fustuca rubra* community transformed into the *Elymus athericus* community inside the exclosure. The *Juncus maritimus* community became rapidly overgrown by *Elymus athericus* which also spread higher at the gradient. This process continued, so that after 22 years of cattle exclusion only a narrow zone of

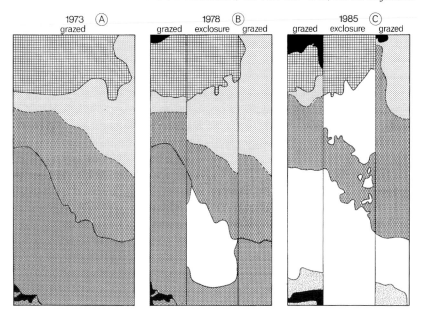

Figures 14.10 and 14.11. (*opposite*) Simplified vegetation maps for (A) 1973; (B) 1978, and (C) 1985 of two enclosures in the salt marsh of the barrier island of Schiermonnikoog established in the autumn of 1973. The upper enclosure (Figure 14.10) was situated at the transition of dune to higher salt marsh, the lower one (Figure 14.11) was at the lower salt marsh (figures from Bakker 1989).

Festuca rubra was left, together with the *Ammophila arenaria* community on the top of the dune. The remainder of the gradient was dominated by *Elymus athericus*. The position of this exclosure with respect to inundation frequency was similar to the sites in the aforementioned chronosequence from young to 100 years old on the ungrazed salt marsh (Figure 14.5). We might therefore conclude that, if a salt marsh becomes older, *Elymus athericus* may spread further downwards along the elevation gradient from the high to the low marsh. This may be explained by the thicker clay layer, which probably enhances nutrient availability to plants.

The second exclosure was established in the mid- and lower salt marsh, with *Festuca rubra-* and *Artemisia maritima* communities alternating with the *Puccinellia maritima* community and *Plantago maritima/Limonium vulgare* community and bare soil due to trampling the soft substrate (Figure 14.11). The area of bare soil completely disappeared inside the exclosure after some years, and transformed into the *Puccinellia maritima* community. This community in its turn, mainly changed into communities with *Plantago maritima* and *Limonium vulgare*, but locally the *Atriplex portulacoides* community established after 12 years. The latter community completely covered the lower parts inside the exclosure after 18 years. After 5 years the initial *Puccinellia maritima* community was replaced locally by

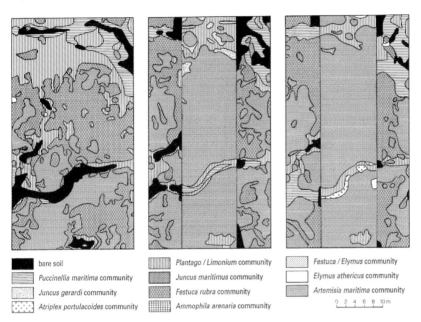

■ bare soil	▥ Plantago / Limonium community	▦ Festuca / Elymus community
▤ Puccinellia maritima community	▦ Juncus maritimus community	□ Elymus athericus community
░ Juncus gerardi community	▧ Festuca rubra community	▦ Artemisia maritima community
░ Atriplex portulacoides community	▦ Ammophila arenaria community	0 2 4 6 8 10 m

the *Juncus gerardii*- and the *Artemisia maritima* communities. After 10 years, the latter overgrew the newly emerged *Juncus gerardii* community and the whole *Festuca rubra* community. It should be noted that the *Elymus athericus* community started to establish after 12 years of exclusion of cattle grazing and has spread (van Wijnen, Bakker & de Vries 1997) since then.

The resumption of cattle grazing 13 years after the abandonment of a barrier-island saltmarsh area on Schiermonnikoog revealed that the proportion of the *Elymus athericus*, *Artemisia maritima*, and *Ammophila arenaria* communities decreased in favour of the *Festuca rubra*, *Armeria maritima*, and *Juncus gerardi* communities (Bakker 1990). Grazing in a previously abandoned salt marsh led to a higher species-richness than haymaking (Bakker 1989, 1990), though it took 5 years before the species number in the grazed sites exceeded that in the mown sites. This may be explained by the immediate removal of the litter, which was accumulated during a long period, by haymaking, whereas it lasted several years before the litter had disappeared in the grazed situation, due to trampling. The extra species are mainly species from the lower salt marsh which spread on the higher salt marsh under grazing. The soil salinity is not higher at the grazed than at the mown sites (Bakker *et al.* 1985). It seems that grazing facilitates the establishment of more species by the creation of gaps, while haymaking causes the formation of a dense turf dominated by *Fustuca rubra*. The experimental sowing of lower-saltmarsh species confirmed that they established better in grazed than in mown sites (Bakker & de Vries 1992). In a low salt marsh, however, cattle grazing may result in a low species number, due to the complete destruction of vegetation and topsoil by trampling (Bakker 1989).

A succession scheme was derived from long-term studies of vegetation changes after abandonment of grazing, and after resumption of grazing (at a stocking rate of 1.6 heifers ha^{-1}) on an abandoned salt marsh on the barrier island of Schiermonnikoog (Figure 14.12). After the resumption of grazing, the return to the initial succession stage generally took 5–10 years. After the cessation of the grazing regime, it takes 10–20 years to reach a new equilibrium (Bakker 1989). During this period, *Elymus athericus* outcompeted most other species on the higher and middle marsh, and the number of plant communities, as well as the number of species in each community, decreased. Only time will tell whether the cessation of grazing in old barrier-island salt marshes will result in zonation other than *Elymus athericus* at the higher and middle salt marsh, and *Atriplex portulacoides* at the lower salt marsh.

A grazing experiment with various stocking rates (0, 0.5, 1, and 2 heifers ha^{-1}) was started in 1980 on the mainland salt marsh in the Leybucht in Niedersachsen, Germany. The marsh, which was previously heavily grazed (2 heifers ha^{-1}), had a homogeneous turf including *Festuca rubra* and *Lolium perenne* in the higher parts, and *Puccinellia maritima* in the lower parts. In the abandoned site, the *Elymus athericus* community largely spread over the higher salt marsh and locally over the lower marsh, too, 8 years after the start of the experiment (Andresen *et al.* 1990). The encroachment of the *Elymus athericus* continued, and after 15 years it also started to spread in the lightly (0.5 heifer ha^{-1}) grazed site (Figure 14.13).

The study described in the Dollard marsh in the Ems estuary is the only one for a man-made marsh to examine the effects of a management of both abiotic and biotic conditions. After 1981, summer grazing was gradually reduced to 0.5–1 animals ha^{-1}, and by 1984 maintenance of the drainage system was abandoned. These changes had a considerable, sometimes interacting, effect on the marsh vegetation. *Elymus repens* decreased substantially from 1984 to 1991, whereas the opposite would have been expected in the light of the effect of the reduced stocking rates in the

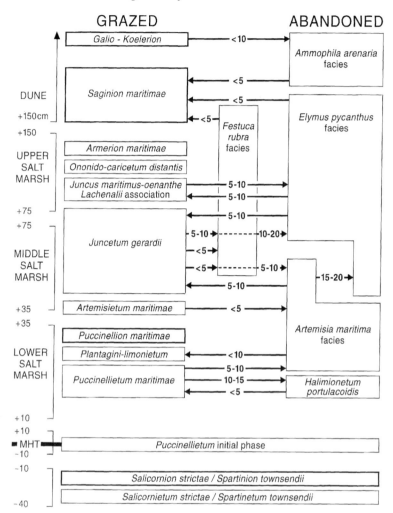

Figure 14.12. The position of plant communities with respect to MHT and the number of years it takes to change after abandoning, or the resumption of, grazing with high stocking rate (1.6 cattle ha^{-1}). As a result of changes in taxonomy of species, which have not taken place in taxonomy of plant communities, *Elymus pycanthus* is synonymous with *Elymus athericus*, and *Halimione portulacoides* with *Atriplex portulacoides* and *Spartina townsendi* with *S. anglica* (figure from Bakker 1989).

Leybucht marshes. *Elymus repens* regained its dominance in an exclosure established in 1991 at a site where the species was dominant in 1983. Apparently, the effect of trampling had become more important, due to the rewetting. *Aster tripolium* showed a considerable increase from 1983 to

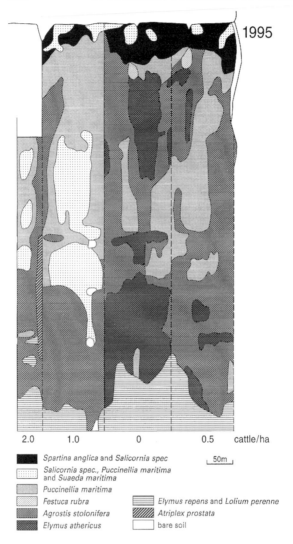

2.0   1.0   0   0.5   cattle/ha

▮ Spartina anglica and Salicornia spec   ⌊ 50m ⌋

▦ Salicornia spec., Puccinellia maritima
    and Suaeda maritima

▦ Puccinellia maritima

▦ Festuca rubra   ▤ Elymus repens and Lolium perenne

▦ Agrostis stolonifera   ▨ Atriplex prostata

▦ Elymus athericus   □ bare soil

Figure 14.13. Simplified vegetation map of part of the man-made mainland salt marsh in the Leybucht after 15 years of cattle-grazing with various stocking rates ranging from 0 to 2 heifers ha^{-1}.

1991. Obviously, the conditions became more favourable for *Aster tripolium* to establish, due to the rewetting and the more open sward. In the 1991 exclosure, the incidence of this short-living species declined rapidly after a peak in the second and third year after grazing had been excluded. The suitability of the Dollard marshes for grazing diminished, because of the rewetting, and this might become a future problem for its management. As a consequence of the reduced stocking rates, *Phragmites australis* increased its dominance in the outer zone of this brackish marsh. As in other brackish marshes and in estuaries of the Wadden Sea, abandonment of grazing will ultimately lead to a climax vegetation of *Phragmites australis* in the entire marsh and the disappearance of the halophytic vegetation (Aerts, Esselink, & Helder 1996).

Apart from the aforementioned examples from barrier-island and mainland salt marshes, we can conclude that cessation of grazing often results eventually in a dominance of one or a few plant species. The species which reach dominance depend on the tidal level and salinity of the sea water, for example, *Festuca rubra* or *Elymus repens* in the southern Baltic (Schmeisky 1977), *Phragmites australis* in brackish conditions in the northern Baltic (Siira 1970; Dijkema 1990), or in the Wadden Sea (Raabe 1981), and *Atriplex portulacoides* and *Elymus repens* in man-made salt marshes in The Netherlands (Dijkema 1983b).

Grazing at a moderate stocking density creates a pattern of closely grazed and lightly grazed patches in the island salt marsh of Schiermonnikoog. These differences emerged soon after the resumption of grazing, and maintained themselves for at least 20 years. The lightly grazed patches range from one ha to small isolated clumps of *Juncus maritimus* (Bakker 1989). Such a pattern does generally not develop in the man-made mainland marshes. In the aforementioned Leybucht marshes, the vegetation height increased from the seawall towards the intertidal flats, which indicated a decrease of the grazing intensity of the cattle in this direction. The gradient in vegetation height was indeed not found in ungrazed sites (Andresen *et al.* 1990). The same pattern in vegetation height was found for sheep grazing in mainland marshes (Kiehl *et al.* 1996).

Kiehl *et al.* (1996) compared the effects of various stocking rates of sheep-grazing on a man-made salt marsh in Schleswig-Holstein, Germany, 5 years after the experiment started. They found great differences in the occurrence of *Atriplex portulacoides* and *Aster tripolium* between the sites with high stocking rate and those with no grazing at all. Sites with intermediate stocking density revealed an increasing occurrence of both species from the dike towards the tidal flats over a gradient of several hundreds of metres (Figure 14.14).

It is obvious that the aforementioned patterns in the structure of the vegetation cannot be established by haymaking. Extensive grazing apparently creates a higher structural diversity as compared to haymaking.

Atriplex portulacoides   **Aster tripolium, flowering plants**

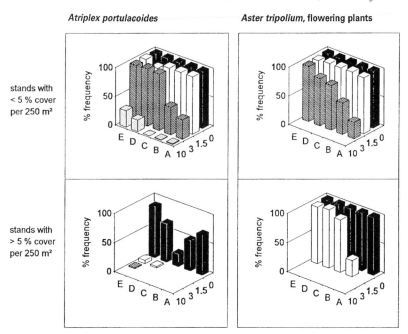

Figure 14.14. Frequency of occurrence of *Atriplex portulacoides* and *Aster tripolium* at various distances from the dike ranging from A to E in the man-made mainland salt marsh of Sönke-Nissen-Koog (Schleswig-Holstein) after 5 years of sheep-grazing with various stocking rates ranging from 0 to 10 sheep ha^{-1} (figure from Kiehl *et al.* 1996).

Avifauna

The effect of grazing on the function of salt marshes as an area for breeding birds was studied in the German Wadden Sea area. An increase in the number of breeding oystercatchers (*Haematopus ostralegus*) was observed, which was positively correlated to the increased grazing of man-made salt marshes in contrast the number of redshanks (*Tringa totanus*) decreased. The avifauna was in this case negatively influenced by the frequency with which the birds were disturbed by flooding, the trampling of nests and young, and the increased stocking rate; the vegetation composition and structure was considered less important (Schultz 1987). In the Dollard marshes, the diversity of the breeding-bird population seemed to be influenced positively by the vegetation development after the reduction in stocking rate (see above), but a well-documented time series is lacking. Bird species of reed-beds, such as marsh-harrier (*Circus aeruginosus*), bluethroat

(*Luscinia svecica*), bearded tit (*Panurus biarmicus*) and sedge warblers (*Acrocephalus schoenobaenus*) nest every year, probably with increasing numbers. In the mean time, the number of breeding avocets (*Recurvirostra avosetta*) have not been effected yet by the increase of stands of tall-growing species. Seven years after the establishment of the reserve, redshanks reached an average density of 4 breeding pairs ha^{-1}, which means that the reserve harboured about 1% of north- and west-European redshank population (de Jong *et al.* 1993). A study on nest-site choice showed that *Phragmites* and *Scirpus* communities, as well as the therophyt communities in the depressions were avoided by the redshanks, whereas communities with *Elymus repens* were preferred (Dallinga, unpublished data). This would indicate that the suitability of the reserve is decreasing for redshanks.

The brent goose (*Branta bernicla*) and barnacle goose (*B. leucopsis*) seem to have become the flagship species for saltmarsh management in the Wadden Sea. Both species breed in the High Arctic, and use the Wadden Sea as a staging area during their autumn and spring migration. In spring, they depend largely on saltmarsh habitats to build the body reserves in order to reach their breeding grounds (van Nugteren 1994). For the brent goose, it has been shown that the breeding success depends on the body mass at departure from the Wadden Sea (Ebbinge 1989). Both goose species have shown an almost exponential population growth during the last two or three decades in western Europe (see Figure 14.15A). which may be related to the extension of protection measures (Ebbinge 1991), and to an increased use of agricultural habitats with high-quality foods, which has led to reduced winter mortalities (van Eerden *et al.* in press).

Brent geese and barnacle geese are mostly found on young salt marshes and grazed marshes. The resumption of cattle grazing 13 years after the abandonment of a barrier-island salt marsh revealed that the proportion of the *Elymus athericus*, *Artemisia maritima*, and *Ammophila arenaria* communities decreased in favour of the *Festuca rubra*, *Armeria maritima*, and *Juncus gerardi* communities (Bakker 1990). Geese, which had been absent in the previously ungrazed conditions, returned after some years.

In man-made mainland marshes, the traditionally intensive livestock grazing mostly resulted in a turf dominated by *Puccinellia maritima* and *Festuca rubra* on the lower and middle marsh, respectively, which formed major feeding sites for geese and other herbivorous waterfowl (Ebbinge & Boudewijn 1984). If such a traditionally managed marsh becomes a protection area with a reduced stocking rate, it may become less important for waterfowl, as has been documented, for instance, by Cadwalladr *et al.*

(1972) for wigeon (*Anas penelope*) on Fenning Island in Bridgwater Bay, England. Aerts *et al.* (1996) analysed the habitat selection of barnacle geese and graylag geese (*Anser anser*) in the Dollard, where traditionally managed marshes, low to moderately grazed marshes (see above), and abandoned marshes are situated closely to each other. Both goose species avoided abandoned areas dominated by *Phragmites australis* and other tall-growing species. The intensively grazed *Puccinellia maritima* community was preferred by barnacle geese. Greylag geese favoured the moderately grazed *Puccinellia maritima* community. Ebbinge (1992) reported higher brent-goose grazing at grazed sites, too.

A very rapid response of geese to management changes was observed at the Hamburger Hallig marshes, Germany. In 1991, a large-scale experiment was started here to study the effects of management on goose visitation. Up to the summer of 1991, the entire marsh area (763 ha) was used for intensive sheep grazing with 10 animals ha^{-1}. Observations on terrain use by barnacle geese showed that the geese did not use all of the marsh (National Park Office, Tönning, unpublished data). Figure 14.15A shows that the Baltic-flyway population of barnacle geese, which winters almost entirely in The Netherlands (Ebbinge, van Biezen, & van der Voet 1991; Netherlands/Belgium Goose Working Group 1992; van Roomen *et al.* 1994, 1995), increased by almost 10% yr^{-1} during the 1980s and early 1990s. The use of the most important autumn and spring staging grounds of the geese in Schleswig-Holstein varied during the last years between 1.9 and 3.1 million goose-days per season. With the start of the experiment in 1991, 25% of the area became moderately grazed with a stocking rate of 3 sheep ha^{-1}, in 40% of the area grazing was abandoned, while the other 35% of the area remained traditionally grazed with 10 sheep ha^{-1}. The rise in barnacle visitation to the Hamburger Hallig marshes came to an abrupt end with the start of this experiment (Figure 14.15B). The geese which continued to use the marsh showed a shift from their traditional area where grazing had been abandoned, to the intensively sheep-grazed area. The figures for the brent geese in the Hamburger Hallig marshes showed similar trends, though with overall smaller numbers. Apparently, livestock grazing conditions facilitate for smaller herbivores like geese.

Invertebrate fauna

The invertebrate species diversity was highest in the *Puccinellia maritima* and the *Armeria maritima* communities of the man-made salt marshes in northern Germany (Rahmann *et al.* 1987). The number of individuals

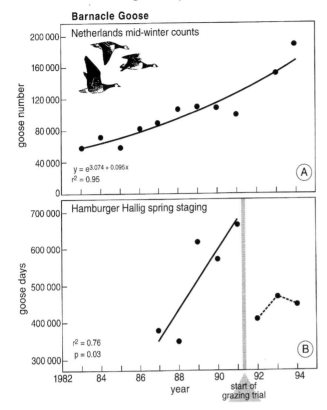

Figure 14.15. (A) The number of barnacle geese wintering in The Netherlands during the 1980s and early 1990s (figure compiled from Netherlands/Belgium Goose Working Group (1984–92), van Roomen *et al.* 1994, 1995 and Spaans, personal communication. (B) Spring staging of barnacle geese in the man-made mainland salt marsh of Hamburger Hallig (Schleswig-Holstein) during the last years of the traditional intensive grazing with sheep, and during the first three years of a grazing trial when only 37% of the marsh remained intensively grazed (figure compiled from unpublished report, National Park Office, Tönning).

decreased in the following sequence: abandoned for 10 years > abandoned for 1 year > cut in July > nearly 2 cattle ha^{-1} > 5 sheep ha^{-1}. The numbers of species and faunal groups were highest in the abandoned area, with a dominance of cicadae (Cicadina), bugs (Heteroptera), and snails (Gastropoda). The grazed areas were very species-poor, with only beetles (Coleoptera) and bugs.

The effects on the macrofaunal invertebrates of cessation of cattle grazing were studied 3 years after the withdrawal of the grazers in the aforementioned Leybucht area in Niedersachsen, Germany (Irmler & Heydemann 1985). The number of species did not change, but the abundances of species sensitive to trampling increased in the abandoned area, either directly or indirectly by damaging tall forage plants. They included springtails (Collembola), spiders (Aranea), butterflies (Lepidoptera), aphids (Aphinidae), bees (Apidae) and hoverflies (Syrphidae). In contrast coprophagous species and those feeding on algae in the bare soil decreased. The cessation of grazing caused litter accumulation and, hence, the food web shifted from predominance of herbivorous animals to a food web dominated by detrivorous animals (Andresen *et al.* 1990). On the most heavily grazed site, the invertebrate community of the lower salt marsh spread to the higher salt marsh. On the ungrazed area, the *Elymus athericus* community started to spread after 8 years. Characteristic saltmarsh invertebrates disappeared within 10 years and were replaced by inland species (Andresen *et al.* 1990).

Effects of sheep grazing on the invertebrate fauna in man-made marshes were reported by Meyer *et al.* (1995). It was concluded that, after 2 and 3 years of excluding sheep, the grazing-induced decrease of food resources brings disadvantages to the larger herbivorous and surface-dwelling species, due to the low abundance of host plants, for example, *Aster tripolium* and *Plantago maritima*. In contrast, small herbivorous and detrivorous species (Collembola) were affected positively. Unfortunately, until now no studies on the invertebrate fauna in relation to grazing management on back-barrier salt marshes have been carried out.

Possibilities and constraints for restoration and management of salt marshes

In this section on possibilities and constraints for restoration and management we start with the question whether salt marshes are able to survive sea-level rise, the only thing man cannot easily affect. The mean relative sea-level rise in the Wadden Sea can be estimated at $0.10–0.16$ cm yr^{-1} over the last decades. The globally expected mean sea-level rise is 0.6 cm yr^{-1} until the year 2030, but the standard deviation equals the expected rise (Warrick & Oerlemans 1990). The present sedimentation rate on mainland salt marshes is high enough to compensate for a future relative sea-level rise of $1–2$ cm yr^{-1}, which is more than the expected global sea-level rise of 0.6 cm yr^{-1}. The barrier-island type of salt marshes in the Wadden Sea will eventually disappear if the relative sea-level rise is more than 0.6 cm yr^{-1} (Dijkema 1994). For the period 1989–1993 sedimentation has been measured in a subsidence area (due to gas extraction) on the barrier island of Ameland, The Netherlands, and amounted to 1.4 cm yr^{-1} in the pioneer zone, 0.8 cm yr^{-1} in the lower saltmarsh, 0.5 cm yr^{-1} in the middle marsh and 0.2 cm yr^{-1} in the high marsh (Dijkema 1997).

The rise of MHT level of 0.37 cm yr^{-1} from 1960 to 1990 is independent of the relative sea-level rise. Moreover, there are no predictions of future MHT levels. The MHT rise has to be considered in relation to both the salt-marsh zone itself and to the tidal flat just in front of it. It seems that the potential loss of saltmarsh area through erosion from the seaward edge is dependent not on the sedimentation processes in the salt marsh itself, but on sedimentation processes in the pioneer zone in front of the marsh (Dijkema *et al.* 1988; Boorman, Goss-Custard, & McGrorty 1989). Sea-edge erosion may result in large-scale cliff formation. In the longer term, if erosion is not prevented by groynes, man-made salt marshes may disappear (Dijkema 1994).

It may be obvious that the aforementioned risk of erosion implies a constraint for the development of natural mainland salt marshes according to the 'wilderness' concept. The second constraint seems the impossibility to reconstruct the extensive prehistoric unprotected mainland landscape including peatland, river-bank gallery forests, and brackish habitats. The third constraint is that we do not have a good idea of natural mainland salt marshes, because they have always been intensively exploited. The few examples of unexploited salt marshes, for a period not longer than decades, are found in back-barrier salt marshes and may represent more sandy marshes.

Possibilities for restoration with respect to the area of salt marshes should consider the mainland salt marshes (Figure 14.2). The present main dikes are expected to be strong enough for protection of the hinterland. This implies that no further embankments are necessary for coastal protection. The need for extension of agricultural areas has diminished, especially in the framework of European Union agricultural policies. This means that the removal of summer dikes has become an option to enlarge the saltmarsh area in the Wadden Sea within a few years. This will be realized for 1200 ha of summer polders in the province of Friesland, The Netherlands. Creation of new marshes by dumping of dredging material from elsewhere is no option, because a salt marsh is the outcome of the interactions of physical and biological processes and not of a dumping site. The area of the island marshes is of no concern with respect to restoration as they cover more than ever before (Figure 14.2). No definite plans exists to create new washover channels through the dunes or artificial sand ridges to start succession anew and establish young marshes at the place of older ones.

Management of abiotic conditions on barrier-island salt marshes is not in discussion, because the meandering creeks and the variation in levees and depressions are regarded as examples for the man-made marshes. The abandonment of the drainage system at man-made salt marshes might enhance the abiotic variation between levees along former ditches and the lower parts in-between ditches. It may contribute to the formation of larger depressions or salt pans (Esselink, unpublished data). In the available study, the variation in structure of the vegetation, as a result of a gradient in grazing intensity, seems to enhance the abiotic variation after less than 10 years. In ungrazed conditions, a dense vegetation may establish all over the salt marsh and perhaps lower again the abiotic variation. A constraint is that it is not known whether the meandering creeks, as present in the barrier-island marshes, can develop in existing mainland salt marshes, or only in the pioneer zone. Nevertheless, experiments will be carried out in man-made Dutch mainland salt marshes with 'self-regulating' drainage systems by diminishing the volume and the length of ditches to values comparable to natural reference sites (Reents and Dijkema, unpublished data).

The effects of cessation of grazing and renewed livestock grazing in barrier-island salt marshes are reversible within 10–20 years. The effects of haymaking are more or less similar to those of grazing at high stocking rate. The constraint is that the plant species-richness is lower than by grazing, because of the dense turf formed by continued haymaking (Bakker 1989). In sandy barrier-island marshes, with a clay layer thicker than 15 cm, cessation of grazing by livestock will result in a dominance of *Elymus athericus* in the higher- and middle-marsh zone. The thicker the layer of clay, and hence the higher nutrient availability, the lower down the salt marsh *Elymus* may spread. At the foot of larger dunes, *Phragmites australis* will become dominant as a result of freshwater seepage. *Atriplex portulaco-ides* and *Salicornia procumbens* will become dominant in the lower salt march and in the pioneer zone respectively. This will be the climax vegetation at the never grazed Boschplaat at Terschelling, The Netherlands (Westhoff & van Oosten 1991). Only in young barrier island marshes with a clay layer thinner than 15 cm will *Elymus athericus* not reach dominance (Dijkema 1990; Bakker 1993). In such relatively low productive conditions, plant species like *Limonium vulgare*, *Plantago maritima*, and *Artemisia maritima*, attractive for their characteristic halobiotic entomofauna, can maintain themselves. These plant species do thrive on older salt marshes after excluding livestock for some years. The vegetation and the entomofauna and the avifauna, including both breeding and migrating birds, will change after cessation of grazing by livestock. The short-term studies on the effects of excluding livestock on man-made salt marshes carried out until now, may not be indicative in relation to long-term effects (Irmler & Heydemann 1985; Meyer *et al.* 1995; Kiehl *et al.* 1996).

Although much knowledge has been gained during the last two decades, many lacunae still exist. More insight is needed on the sedimentation balance and vegetation dynamics in the pioneer zone as a function of year-to-year fluctuations in MHT, wave energy levels, vegetation structure, drainage, and soil fertility. This holds for both existing salt marshes and for salt marshes to be restored after de-embankment. The process of sedimentation, as well as its effects upon succession on sites with low and high sedimentation rates, should be studied. The same holds for the effects of changes in management on vegetation, avifauna, and invertebrate fauna. We need long-term studies and carefully designed experiments to unravel mechanisms involved in changes in salt marshes. These are prerequisites for the development of knowledge on sound and ecologically based plans for restoration and management of salt marshes in the Wadden Sea. The second trilateral working conference on saltmarsh management in the international Wadden Sea, held at Rømø, Denmark, in 1989 (Ovesen 1990; Dijkema 1992) may provide some guidelines. This knowledge should contribute to a coherent management of the entire Wadden Sea – the last wilderness of the European Lowlands.

Acknowledgements

The authors would like to thank K. Wildeman for providing a revised version of the map of Figure 14.1. Dick Visser carefully prepared the figures. Two referees are acknowledged for the improvements they made on the draft of the chapter. The second author was funded by the Prins Bernhard Foundation and the Ministry of Agriculture, Nature Management and Fisheries.

References

Adam, P. (1990). *Saltmarsh ecology*. Cambridge University Press.
Aerts, B. A., Esselink, P., & Helder, G. J. F. (1996). Habitat selection and diet composition of Greylag Geese *Anser anser* and Barnacle Geese *Branta leucopsis* during fall and spring staging in relation to management in the tidal marshes of the Dollard. *Zeitschrift für Okologie und Naturschutz*, 5, 65–75.

318   *J. P. Bakker, P. Esselink, R. van der Wal, K. S. Dijkema*

Allen, J. R. L. & Pye, K. (1992). Coastal salt marshes: their nature and importance. In *Salt Marshes, Morphodynamics, Conservation and Engineering Significance*, eds. J. R. L. Allen, & K Pye, pp. 1–18. Cambridge University Press.

Andresen, H., Bakker, J. P., Brongers, M., Heydemann, B., & Irmler, U. (1990). Long-term changes of salt marsh communities by cattle grazing. *Vegetatio*, 89, 137–48.

Armstrong, W., Wright, E. J., Lythe, S., & Gaynard, T. J. (1985). Plant zonation and the effects of the spring-neap tidal cycle on soil aeration in a Humber salt marsh. *Journal of Ecology*, 73, 323–39.

Bakker, J. P. (1989). *Nature Management by Grazing and Cutting*. Dordrecht: Kluwer Academic Publishers.

Bakker, J. P. (1990). Effects of grazing and hay-making on Wadden Sea salt marshes. In *Salt Marsh Management in the Wadden Sea Region*, ed. C. H. O. Ovesen, pp. 51–65. Copenhagen: Ministry of the Environment, The Natural Forest and Nature Agency.

Bakker, J. P. (1993). Strategies for grazing management on salt marshes. *Wadden Sea News Letter*, 1993/1, 8–10.

Bakker, J. P., Dijkstra, M., & Russchen, P. (1985). Dispersal, germination and early establishment of halophytes and glycophytes on a grazed and abandoned salt marsh gradient. *New Phytologist*, 101, 291–308.

Bakker, J. P. & de Vries, Y. (1992). Germination and early establishment of halophytes on a grazed and mown salt marsh. *Journal of Vegetation Science*, 3, 247–52.

Bakker, J. P., de Leeuw, J., Dijkema, K. S., Leendertse, P. C., Prins, H. H. T., & Rozema, J. (1993). Salt marshes along the coast of The Netherlands. *Hydrobiologia*, 265, 73–95.

Behre, K. E. (1979). Zur Rekonstruktion ehemaliger Pflanzengesellschaften an der Deutschen Nordseeküste. In *Werden und Vergehen von Pflanzengesellschaften*, eds. O. Wilmanns & R. Tüxen, pp. 181–214. Vaduz: Cramer.

Behre, K. E. (1985). Die ursprungliche Vegetation in den deutschen Marschgebieten und deren Veränderung durch prähistorische Besiedlung und Meeresspiegelbewegungen. *Verhandlungen Gesellschaft für Okologie*, 13, 85–96.

Boorman, L. A., Goss-Custard, J. D., & McGrorty, S. (1989). Climatic change, rising sea level and the British coast. HMSO, London. Natural Environment Research Council. *ITE research publication*, 1, 1–24.

Cadwalladr, D. A., Owen, M., Morley, J. V., & Cook, R. S. (1972). Wigeon (*Anas penelope* L.) conservation and salting pasture management at Bridgewater Bay National Nature Reserve, Somerset. *Journal of Applied Ecology*, 9, 417–25.

de Jong, J., Kers, B., Esselink, P., de Bakker, M., & Dijkema, K. S. (1993). Vegetatie-ontwikkeling in de Dollard na het instellen van een extensief beheer. *De Levende Natuur*, 94, 176–82.

de Leeuw, J., de Munck, W., Olff, H., & Bakker, J. P. (1993). Does zonation reflect the succession of salt marsh vegetation? A comparison of an estuarine and a coastal bar island marsh in the Netherlands. *Acta Botanica Neerlandica*, 42, 435–45.

de Leeuw, J., Apon, L. A., Herman, P. J., de Munck, W., & Beeftink, W. G. (1994). The response of salt marsh vegetation to tidal reduction caused by the Oosterschelde storm-surge barrier. *Hydrobiologia*, 282/283, 335–53.

Dieckman, R. (1988). Entwicklung der Vörländer an der nordfriesischen Festlandküste. *Wasser & Boden*, 40, 146–50.

Dijkema, K. S. (1983a). Use and management of mainland marshes and Halligen. In *Flora and Vegetation of the Wadden Sea Islands and Coastal Areas*, eds. K. S. Dijkema & W. J. Wolff, pp. 302–12. Report 9 of the Wadden Sea Working Group. Rotterdam: Balkema.

Dijkema, K. S. (1983b). The salt-marsh vegetation of the mainland cost, estuaries and Halligen. In *Flora and Vegetation of the Wadden Sea Islands and Coastal Areas*, eds. K. S. Dijkema & W. J. Wolff, pp. 185–220. Report 9 of the Wadden Sea Working Group. Rotterdam: Balkema.

Dijkema, K. S. (1984). *Salt Marshes in Europe*. Strasbourg: Council of Europe.

Dijkema, K. S. (1987). Changes in salt-marsh area in the Netherlands Wadden Sea after 1600. In *Vegetation between Land and Sea*, eds. A. H. L. Huiskes, C. W. P M. Blom, & J. Rozema, pp. 42–9. Dordrecht: Junk Publishers.

Dijkema K. S. (1990). Salt and brackish marshes around the Baltic Sea and adjacent parts of the North Sea: their development and management. *Biological Conservation*, 51, 191–209.

Dijkema, K. S. (1992). Sea level rise and management of salt marshes. *Wadden Sea News Letter*, 1992/2, 7–10.

Dijkema, K. S. (1994). Auswirkung des Meeresspiegelanstieges auf die Salzwiesen. In *Warnsignale aus dem Wattenmeer*, eds. J. J. Lozán, E. Rachor, K. Reise, H. von Westernhagen, & W. Lenz, pp. 196–200. Berlin: Blackwell.

Dijkema, K. S. (1996). Impact prognosis for salt marshes from subsidence by gas extraction in the Wadden Sea. *Journal for Coastal Research* (in press).

Dijkema, K. S., van den Bergs, J., Bossinade, J. H., Bouwsema, P., de Glopper, R. J., & van Meegen, J. W. T. M. (1988). Effecten van rijzen dammen op de opslibbing en de omvang van de vegetatiezones in de Friese en Groninger landaanwinningswerken. Rijkswaterstaat Directie Groningen, Nota GRAN 1988-2010, RIN-*report*, 88/66, RIJP-*report* 1988-33 Cbw: 1–119.

Dijkema, K. S., Bossinade, J. H., Bouwsema, P., & de Glopper, R. J. (1990). Salt marshes in the Netherlands Wadden Sea: rising high tide levels and accretion enhancement. In *Expected Effects of Climatic Change on Marine Coastal Ecosystems*, eds. J. J. Beukema, W. J. Wolff, & J. J. W. H. Brouns, pp. 173–88. Dordrecht: Kluwer Academic Publishers.

Dijkema, K. S., Bossinade, J. H., van den Bergs, J., & Kroeze, T. A. G. (1991). Natuurtechnisch beheer van kwelderwerken in de Friese en Groninger Waddenzee: Greppelonderzoek en overig grondwerk. Nota GRAN 1991–2002. RIN-*report*, 91/10, 1–148. Leeuwarden: Rijkswaterstaat Noord-Nederland.

Ebbinge, B. S. (1989). A multifactorial explanation for variation in breeding performance of Brent Geese *Branta bernicla*. *Ibis*, 131, 196–204.

Ebbinge, B. S. (1991). The impact of hunting on mortality and spatial distribution of geese, wintering in the western Palearctic. *Ardea*, 79, 197–209.

Ebbinge, B. S. (1992). Regulation of numbers of Dark-bellied Brent Geese *Branta bernicla bernicla* on spring staging sites. *Ardea*, 80, 203–28.

Ebbinge, B. S., & Boudewijn, T. (1984). Richtlijnen voor het beheer van Rotganzen in het Nederlandse Waddengebied. RIN-*report* 84/4. Wageningen: Institute for Forestry and Nature Research.

Ebbinge, B. S., van Biezen, J. B., & van der Voet, H. (1991). Estimation of annual adult survival rates of Barnacle Geese *Branta leucopsis* using multiple resightings of marked individuals. *Ardea*, 79, 73–112.

Erchinger, H. F., Coldewey, H.-G., Frank, U., Manzenrieder, H., Meyer, C., Schulze, M., & Steinke, W. (1994). *Erosionsfestigkeit von Hellern*. Norden: Staatlisches Amt für Insel- und Küstenschutz.

Esselink, P., Helder, G. J. F., Aerts, B. A., & Gerdes, K. (1996). The impact of grubbing by Greylag Geese *Anser anser* on the vegetation dynamics of a tidal marsh. *Aquatic Botany*, 55, 261–79.

Esselink, P., Dijkema, K. S., Reents, S. & Hageman, G. Vertical accretion rates and profile changes in abandoned man-made tidal marshes in the Dollard Estuary, The Netherlands. *Journal of Coastal Research* (in press).

Iacobelli, A. & Jefferies, R. L. (1991). Inverse salinity gradients in coastal marshes and the death of stands of *Salix*: the effects of grubbing by geese. *Journal of Ecology*, 79, 61–73.

Irion, G. (1994). Morphological, sedimentological and historical evolution of Jade Bay, southern North Sea. *Senckenbergiana Maritima*, 24, 171–86.

Irmler, U. & Heydemann, B. (1985). Der Einfluss der Rinderbeweidung auf die Struktur der Salzwiesen-Biozönose. *Verhandlungen Gesellschaft für Ökologie*, 13, 71–6.

Jakobson, B. (1954). The tidal area in South-Western Jutland and the process of the salt marsh formation. *Geografisk Tidsskrift*, 53, 49–61.

Kiehl, K. & Stock, M. (1994). Natur- oder Kulturlandschaft? Wattenmeersalzwiesen zwischen den Ansprüchen von Naturschutz, Küstenschutz- and Landwirtschaft. In *Warnsignale aus dem Wattenmeer*, eds. J. J. Lozán, E. Rachor, K. Reise, H. von Westernhagen, & W. Lenz, pp. 190–6. Berlin: Blackwell.

Kiehl, K., Eischeid, I., Gettner, S., & Walter, J. (1996). The impact of different sheep grazing intensities on salt marsh vegetation in Northern Germany. *Journal of Vegetation Science*, 7, 99–106.

Meyer, H., Fock, H., Haase, A., Reinke, H.- D., & Tulowitzki, I. (1995). Structure of the invertebrate fauna in salt marshes of the Wadden Sea coast of Schleswig-Holstein influenced by sheep-grazing. *Helgoländer Meeresuntersuchungen*, 49, 563–89.

Netherlands/Belgium Goose Working Group (1984–92). Ganzentellingen in Nederland in het seizoen 1982/1983, 1983/1984, 1984/1985, 1985/1986, 1986/1987, 1987/1988, 1989/1990. *Limosa*, 57, 147–52; 59, 25–31; 60, 31–9; 60, 137–46; 62, 81–90; 64, 7–15; 65, 163–9.

Olff, H., de Leeuw, J., Bakker, J. P., Platerink, R. J., van Wijnen, H. J., & de Munck, W. (1997). Nitrogen accumulation, vegetation succession and geese herbivory during salt marsh formation on the Dutch island of Schiermonnikoog. *Journal of Ecology* (in press).

Oost, A. P. & de Boer, P. L. (1994). Sedimentology and development of barrier islands, ebb-tidal deltas, inlets and backbarrier areas of the Dutch Wadden Sea. *Senckenbergiana Maritima*, 24, 65–115.

Ovesen, C. H. O., ed. (1990). *Salt Marsh Management in the Wadden Sea Region*. Ministery of the Environment, Copenhagen: Ministry of the Environment, The Natural Forest and Nature Agency.

Raabe, E.-W. (1981): Uber das Vorland der östlichen Nordsee-Küste. *Mitteilungen Arbeitsgemeinschaft für Geobotanik in Schleswig-Holstein und Hamburg*, 31, 1–118.

Rahmann, M., Rahmann, H., Kempf, N., Hoffmann, B., & Gloger, H. (1987). Auswirkungen unterschiedlicher landwirtschaftlicher Nutzung auf die Flora und Fauna der Salzwiesen an der ostfriesischen Wattenmeerküste. *Senckenbergiana Maritima*, 19, 163–93.

Schmeisky, H. (1977). Der Einfluss von Weidetieren auf Salzwiesengesellschaften an der Ostsee. In *Vegetation und Fauna*, ed. R. Tüxen, pp. 481–9. Vaduz: Cramer.

Schönfeld, W. & Jensen, J. (1991). Anwendung der Hauptkomponentenanalyse auf Wasserstandzeitreihen von deutschen Nordseepegeln. *Küste*, 53, 191–204.

Schultz, W. (1987). Einfluss der Beweidung von Salzwiesen auf die Vogelfauna. In *Salzwiesen: Geformt von Küstenschutz, Landwirtschaft oder Natur?* eds. N. Kempf, J. Lamp, & P. Prokosch, pp. 255–70. Husum: WWF-Deutschland, Tagungsbericht 1.

Siira, J. (1970). Study on the ecology of the seashore meadows of the Bothnian Bay with special reference to the Liminka area. *Aquilo Series Botanica*, 9, 1–109.

Smith, T. J. & Odum, W. E., (1981). The effects of grazing by Snow Geese on coastal salt marshes. *Ecology*, 62, 98–106.

Stratingh, G. A. & Venema, C. A. (1855). *De Dollard*. Groningen: Oomkens, Zoon & Schierbeek.

van de Koppel, J., Huisman, J., van der Wal, C. F. R., & Olff, H. (1996). Patterns of herbivory along a productivity gradient: an empirical and theoretical investigation. *Ecology*, 77, 736–45.

van Eerden, M. R., Zijlstra, M., Roomen, M. van, & Timmerman, A. The response of *Anatidae* to changes in agricultural practice: long-term shifts in the carrying capacity for wintering waterfowl. *Faune et Gibier Sauvages*. (in press).

van Nugteren, J. (1994). *Brent Geese in the Wadden Sea*. Harlingen: Dutch Society for the Preservation of the Wadden Sea.

van Roomen, M. W. J., Kleman, M. C. M., van Winden, E. A. J., & Netherlands Goose and Swan Working Group. (1994). *Watervogels in Nederland in januari 1993*. SOVON-monitoringrapport 94/01. Beek-Ubbergen: SOVON.

van Roomen, M. W. J., Kleman, M. C. M., van Winden, E. A. J., & Netherlands Goose and Swan Working Group. (1995). *Midwintertelling van watervogels in Nederland, januari 1994*. SOVON-monitoringrapport 95/01. Beek-Ubbergen: SOVON.

van Wijnen, H. J. & Bakker, J. P. (1997). Nitrogen accumulation and plant species replacement in three salt-marsh systems in the Wadden Sea. *Journal of Coastal Conservation*, 3 (in press).

van Wijnen, H. J., Bakker, J. P. & de Vries, Y. (1997). Twenty years of salt-marsh succession on the coastal barrier island of Schiermonnikoog (The Netherlands). *Journal of Coastal Conservation*, 3 (in press).

van Zeist, W. (1974). Palaeobotanical studies of settlement sites in the coastal area of the Netherlands. *Palaeohistoria*, 16, 223–371.

Veenstra, (1980). Introduction to the geomorphology of the Wadden Sea area. In *Geomorphology of the Wadden Sea area*, eds. K. S. Dijkema, H E. Reineck, & W. J. Wolff, pp. 8–19. Report 1 of the Wadden Sea Working Group. Rotterdam: Balkema.

Waterbolk, H. T. (1976). Oude bewoning in het Waddengebied. In *Waddenzee*, eds. J. Abrahamse, W. Joenje, & N. van Leeuwen-Seelt, pp. 210–22. Harlingen: Landelijke Vereniging tot Behoud van de Waddenzee/'s-Graveland: Natuurmonumenten.

Waterbolk, H. T. (1988). Zomerbewoning in het terpengebied? In *Terpen en wierden in het Fries-Groningse Kustgebied*, eds. M. Bierma, A. T. Clason, E. Kramer, & G. J. de Langen, pp. 1–19. Groningen: Wolters-Noordhoff/Forsten.

Warrick, R. & Oerlemans, J. (1990). In *Climate Change, the IPCC Scientific Assessment*, eds. J. T. Houghton, G. J. Jenkins, & J. J. Ephraums, pp. 260–81. Cambridge University Press.

Westerink, B. & Wildeman, K. (1996). Het wierdenlandschap opnieuw in de branding. *Noorderbreedte*, 20, 14–19.

Westhoff, V. & van Oosten, M. F. (1991). *De Plantengroei van de Waddeneilanden*. Utrecht: Uitgeverij Koninklijke Nederlandse Natuurhistorische Vereniging.

Wiermann, R. (1965). Moorkundliche und vegetationsgeschichtliche Betrachtungen zum Aussendeichsmoor bei Schestedt (Jadebusen). *Berichte der Deutsche Botanischen Gesellschaft*, 78, 269–78.

Part IV

Ecological restoration, economics, and sustainability

15

Ecological engineering and sustainable development

PETER J. EDWARDS, AND CYRUS ABIVARDI

Ecology and economics: two views of how the world works

Imagine a group of final year university students who are asked to write an essay on the theme: 'How the world works'. If they were ecology students, they would probably write about the distribution of different kinds of plants and animals, their interactions with each other, and the ecosystem processes, such as nutrient cycling and primary production, which result from their interactions with abiotic factors. They might mention that human beings are an important ecological factor, but they would be unlikely to mention that economic forces have a massive influence upon the ecological processes that they describe. If these students were economists, then their essays would be very different. They would probably describe various types of capital – human capital, manufactured capital, natural resources – and discuss the role of market forces in determining the distribution of these resources. It is unlikely that they would mention the often adverse impacts that economic activity has upon the ecological functioning of the planet.

This imaginary situation serves to illustrate that ecology and economics continue to develop as quite separate disciplines, even though ecological and economic processes are inextricably linked in the real world. Traditionally, for example, natural resources such as air, soil, water, and biodiversity have not been a topic for economics, since they are not traded and there has been no need to assign a value to them. Increasingly, however, we recognize that this limited view of the scope of economics is inadequate (Repetto 1993). Although natural resources such as soil fertility and air may not be tradable, they are essential for human survival, and conventional economic activity is increasingly harming them. Furthermore, as the world population grows and demands on the environment increase, the finite nature of these resources becomes starkly evident. Against this background it is

325

inevitable that ecological issues become part of mainstream economics.

However, it is also essential that ecologists understand better how economic forces affect the systems that they study. This is particularly true for ecologists interested in rehabilitation and restoration since, whether we like it or not, these activities are inextricably embedded within an economic framework. The mere fact that ecological restoration is necessary is usually a product of past economic activity, while the demand for restoration, and the resources which are provided to carry it out, are controlled by current economic circumstances. Yet ecologists remain surprisingly unaware of these economic realities. Our growing ability to apply ecological science to the restoration of damaged ecosystems is a significant achievement, but, as we develop our understanding of the scientific and technical problems, we realize that we are only addressing part of the problem. We must also make a convincing case for the economic need of ecological restoration, especially when this is expensive.

The main theme of this chapter is that ecological rehabilitation and restoration produce a great range of benefits which are often not sufficiently recognized, and yet are important for quality of life and for sustainability. Although these benefits are the product of natural ecological processes such as nutrient cycling and decomposition, they can be treated in the language of economics – as goods and services which have a financial value. Recognition of these benefits can transform the financial case for ecological restoration.

We begin by considering the costs of ecological restoration, which brings us directly to the central economic problem: that all too often the cost of restoration far exceeds the financial value of the restored land. We then examine some of the ways in which ecological restoration produces additional benefits in the form of ecosystem services, before going on to consider how these benefits can be valued in economic terms. Finally, we examine the importance, and also the limitations, of an economic analysis of the case for ecological rehabilitation and restoration. For convenience we shall usually use the word 'restoration', but it should be taken to mean the full spectrum of reclamation, rehabilitation, and restoration *sensu stricto* (Bradshaw this volume).

The costs of restoration

In practical terms, the cost of ecological restoration is usually the first hurdle that has to be overcome before any work can be carried out, and this is therefore the logical point to begin our analysis. However, although cost is so important, it is surprisingly difficult to get accurate information upon how much ecological restoration costs. Perhaps it is a symptom of the separate worlds inhabited by ecologists and economists that the literature on ecological restoration contains almost no information on this subject. In preparing this chapter, we looked at many hundreds of papers about ecological restoration, and from them have assembled a meagre database on costs of various kinds of restoration. These data are summarized in Table 15.1. To simplify the comparisons, all costs in Table 15.1 and elsewhere (unless otherwise stated) are reported in the US dollar, and the dollar value has been adjusted to the 1995 value on the basis of the Hourly Earnings Index (IMF 1996); all values have been rounded to the nearest 100 dollars. Before going on to discuss the conclusions which can be drawn from them, we would put in a plea for more attention to be paid to cost in the literature of ecological restoration. The relative cost-effectiveness of different types of operation is a matter of great practical interest, and it would be a service to all practitioners if the literature on new methods and approaches also considered the cost implications.

Our survey reveals that the cost of ecological restoration varies very widely, and depends on factors such as the size of the site, the degree of damage, the extent of the remedial action, the availability of materials, and the technical difficulties in carrying out the project (Table 15.1). We present here some general conclusions about these factors.

Restoration costs can be very high

The highest costs that we encountered were for the recovery of contaminated wetlands in California, which in two cases exceeded $500\,000\,\text{ha}^{-1}$ (Guinon 1989; NRC 1992). Recovery of other types of contaminated land, especially in urban areas, is often expensive because of the technical problems of removing or isolating toxic materials and the need for high safety standards. For example, Kendle (1992) reports costs of $135\,200\,\text{ha}^{-1}$ in Britain, and Meyer, Williams, & Yount (1995) cite costs of up to $90\,000\,\text{ha}^{-1}$ in the USA for the environmental assessment fees alone. However, more commonly, rehabilitation costs of up to $20\,000\,\text{ha}^{-1}$ are reported, which vary partly according to the degree of damage or contamination of the ecosystem.

One way to put restoration costs into perspective is to compare them with the market value of the restored land. Land prices obviously vary enormously, but the general conclusion is valid that restoration often costs more than the potential value of the restored land. For example,

Table 15.1. *Some examples for cost of land restoration in several countries*

Whenever necessary, all costs have been converted to the US dollar of the appropriate year. The dollar value has been adjusted to the 1995 value using the Hourly Earnings Index in the Manufacturing Sector (IMF 1996). In some cases the end use of the land is to the type mentioned in parenthesis. Costs are per hectare unless otherwise specified.

Region	Type of land (Enduse)	Area (No. of sites)	Cost (US$)	Reference
Japan	Industrial complexes (dense planting)	(285 sites)	63 000	Miyawaki & Golley 1993
United Kingdom	Damaged Peatland	50 ha	5 500–7 800	Wheeler & Shaw 1995
United Kingdom	Abandoned land		<113 300	Bradshaw & Chadwick 1980
United Kingdom	Contaminated land (nature reserve)		9 700	Kendle 1992
United Kingdom	Contaminated land (woodland)		25 100	Kendle 1992
United Kingdom	Contaminated land (agriculture)		38 600	Kendle 1992
United Kingdom	Contaminated land (urban reclamation)		135 200	Kendle 1992
Prairie Potholes (Canada and USA)	Wetland	0.28 and 0.6 ha	<4000	Hey 1992
Colorado, USA	Blanco River Bank	ca. 4 km	110/linear m	Berger 1992
Amite River, USA	Gravel mining	53–57 ha	>850	Vernon et al. 1992
Pennsylvania, USA	Abandoned coal mineland	469 ha (136 sites)	25 300	Bogovich & Member 1992
Los Angeles, USA	Damaged wetland (urban)	120 ha	102 300–511 600	NRC 1992 (p. 270)
San Diego, USA	Riparian (urban)	3 ha	697 900	Guinon 1989
China	Low fertile crop land		40–60	Gu et al. 1989
China	Wasteland		950–1 900	Gu et al. 1989
China	Abandoned strip-mineland		1 900–2 600	Gu et al. 1989
China	Abandoned deep-mineland		ca. 7 800	Gu et al. 1989

Table 15.2. *A summary of restoration costs for different abandoned or destroyed lands according to their future use*

Including current prices for lands in industrial countries of the Europe, and the USA.

	Restoration Costs and Land Values ($1000 ha^{-1})			
Type of land	Natural Reserve/ Woodland	Agriculture	Urban	End use not stated
Contaminated land	9–25	38	135	
Wetland	4	–^{a}	102–>697	
Mine land				5–25
Land values	1–2	2–5	100 ⩾ 2 000	

Note: ^{a}Not applicable

agricultural land in Europe and the USA typically costs in the range of $2000–5000 per hectare, while land for forestry would cost only a fraction as much (Table 15.2).

Costs depend upon objectives

In its strict sense, ecological restoration means putting back what was there before, and the objective of restoration programmes is often to create or recreate a particular habitat with a more or less precisely defined set of species. Very often the work is undertaken in mitigation for the loss of equivalent habitat elsewhere, and the conditions of the planning consent require that the restored area meets strict criteria of species diversity and functional equivalence within a specified time period. Stringent requirements of this kind can make restoration very expensive, since the requirement to achieve a certain result within a specified time limits the opportunities to exploit natural succession for the development of the area. For example, where the restoration involves hand planting of selected species, costs rise rapidly.

Even if the objective is not the creation of a precisely defined community, but merely the restoration of productive land, for example for agriculture, costs may be high. For example, in western Europe the aim of restoration following mining has often been to return the land to agriculture. However, restoration to agriculture has always been an expensive option because of the difficulties of recreating land of high productivity. Since there is now a surplus of agricultural land in western Europe, there is increasing interest in other types of restoration which will make the land suitable for new uses such as recreation or amenity, often at much lower cost.

The data summary in Table 15.2 show how much costs of restoration can vary according to objective. In the case of recovery of contaminated land, costs as high as $135 000 per hectare were incurred when the objective was to restore land to productive use in urban areas. Similarly, costs of ecological restoration of wetland in urban areas can be extremely high. In contrast, the much more modest objectives of establishing some kind of vegetation which would allow the use of land as a nature reserve or for recreation can often be achieved at a fraction of the cost.

Small schemes are relatively more expensive than large ones

The effect of scale on the cost is well illustrated by cost calculations for reclamation on a 39 hectare area in the Swansea Valley ($101 300 per hectare) and on a 4 hectare area of the same site ($350 700 per hectare) (Bradshaw & Chadwick 1980). The reasons for the high costs of restoration on small sites are varied and include problems of access, the need for special protection measures of the developing ecosystems, and the more limited opportunities of exploiting natural ecological processes in developing the new habitats.

Restoration is not always good value for money

The range of costs partly reflects the technical difficulties of dealing with particular kinds of damage. However, costs (and cost effectiveness) also undoubtedly reflect the availability of funding and the political climate for restoration. Since the 1980s, restoration activity in the USA and other industrial countries has boomed, as a result of public pressure and concerns about public health. Special legislation has been passed in the USA to tax mining activity (e.g., Bogovich & Member 1992) and to charge polluters (e.g., Meyer *et al.* 1995). Projects for reclamation of contaminated sites (Table 15.1) and restoration of wetlands have, therefore, enjoyed exceptionally generous funding. For instance, in 1986, SARA (the Superfund Amendment and Reauthorization Act) in the US expanded the 5-year fund for reclamation of a portion of the contaminated sites from the original $1.6 billion to $8.5 billion (Meyer *et al.* 1985). The total reclamation costs, which comprise both transaction costs and actual costs for restoration of contaminated lands, are very high. For instance, the 'Environment Assessment Fees' alone may approach $90 000/ha (Meyer *et al.* 1995).

Since the late 1980s, thanks to ever-increasing water pollution, US federal policies towards management of aquatic systems have undergone a dramatic change: federal incentives to destroy or alter aquatic systems were significantly reduced and funding for restoration work was granted. For example, over $500 million has been considered for the costs of only two restoration projects, i.e., habitat restoration of the Upper Mississippi River and Kissimmee River Restoration Project (NRC 1992, Cairns 1993). As we have seen, restoration of damaged wetlands has often been very expensive (Table 15.1). For instance, restoring of urban wetland in Los Angeles has been estimated for some 120 hectares at $102 300 to $511 600/ha (NRC 1992). Restoring farmlands to wetlands, however, may be relatively inexpensive (as low as $1100/ha) and easier to accomplish.

Although it is to be welcomed that increasingly money has been made available for ecological restoration, it is not always clear whether the results have been value for money. For example, despite the enormous sums of money which have gone into wetland restoration in the USA, the success of many of the projects is limited. An analysis of 75 projects reported in a recent publication of the United States Environmental Protection Agency (see Kusler & Kentula 1990) shows that 31% were deemed to have been successful, while 19% were regarded as unsuccessful. The success of 44% of the projects was unknown, because there were no suitable monitoring data, and for the remaining 6% of projects it was too early to judge the outcome.

Cheaper options are often possible

As we have seen, the costs very often depend on the objectives. Some uses of land, such as forestry and nature conservation, are much cheaper to establish than others (e.g., agriculture) since large-scale landscaping is not required. However cheaper options may take longer, since they rely more upon natural processes for the creation of habitats, such as the development of soil or the immigration of species. For example, Trepagnier, Kogas, & Turner (1995) recommend the removal of levees and subsequent flooding as a cheap way of restoring wetland on former agricultural land in Louisiana. Their conservative estimate of the resulting restoration rate through natural succession is 1% annually, which represents a restoration cost of only $1 per hectare – a tiny fraction of the cost of most wetland restoration, though inevitably also much slower. None the less there is a great deal that restoration ecologists can do to facilitate natural succession, often without incurring high costs. A nice example in this volume is the facilitation of woodland species on reclaimed waste heaps in New York through the establishment of small groves of trees which are used by birds (Handel this volume).

Even in developing countries restoration costs are high

In developing countries, expensive restoration of the kind commonly practiced in the western world is not an option; yet the need for restoration is acute in many parts of the Third World. An example is China, where reclamation is aimed at increasing suitable land for agriculture (Gu, Wu, & Zhu 1989). Two solutions have been suggested: either to increase crop land through reclamation, which is expensive (at least $950–1900 ha^{-1} with an average output of only $150 ha^{-1} year^{-1}), or to improve crop lands with low productivity. The latter alternative, which requires an average investment of about $40–60 ha^{-1} for soil improvement, has increased the yield by 20%. Taking account of the price of staple foods (e.g., pork, 1 kg = $1.44 and rice, 1 kg = $0.48) and the present leasing rate of agricultural lands (an average of $90 ha^{-1} year^{-1}) (Dr Cao Min, personal communication 1996), the first alternative does not appear practical.

However, even these costs are much less than those spent for restoring mined land in China. Total costs, which include site acquisition, earth moving, drainage, fencing, surface treatment and landscaping, fertilizers, seeds, and planting material, have been estimated at $1900–2600 ha^{-1} for restoration following strip-mining, and at about $7800 ha^{-1} following deep mining. The costs quoted are well above what might be regarded as the normal value of the land (Gu *et al.* 1989). In other developing countries, the picture is similar. Restoration costs are generally much lower than in the developed world – for example the costs for rehabilitation and management of upland watersheds in developing countries may range between $70 and $520 ha^{-1} (World Resources Institute 1985) – but these must be set against the extremely low rates of income in these countries.

The problem that restoration very often costs more than the potential value of the land, is a serious one. There are huge areas of the Earth's surface which urgently need some kind of restoration or rehabilitation, but, on purely financial grounds, such work is unjustifiable. In practice this means that restoration projects often depend upon unusual economic circumstances. One of these is the situation where the price of land is high – for example, in prosperous residential areas in affluent countries – and where restoration of part of an area can be linked with planning consents for building on the remainder. Under these circumstances, almost any cost for restoration can be justified financially. Another circumstance is where restoration is required in mitigation for a very expensive project such as the construction of a motorway or an oil pipeline, or the extraction of mineral resources. The fact that the costs of restoration far exceed the market value of the land is unimportant since they are, none the less, relatively minor costs associated with a very profitable activity.

It would be a disaster if ecological restoration could only be undertaken in these special economic circumstances where the relationship between costs and value is unimportant. If we are to achieve a significant improvement to the substantial proportion of the world's terrestrial surface in need of some form of rehabilitation (Daily 1995), then we must become more aware of the costs, and also of the benefits, of restoration. Part of the challenge lies in developing new methods which can be applied on a large scale and cheaply. However, another challenge lies in strengthening the economic argument for ecological restoration. This can be achieved through a better understanding of the full value of restored areas, even if these are not reflected in the market value of the land.

Added value from ecosystem services

The concept of ecosystem services

The formulation of the concept of ecosystem services was a deliberate attempt to draw ecological processes into the domain of economics. We all depend for our survival upon natural processes such as biological productivity, nutrient cycling, and water cycling which provide clean air and water, maintain the fertility of the soil, and help to regulate the climate. As long as these resources were in more than ample supply, there was no need to consider them in economic terms, and economic activity often caused them to be significantly degraded (Repetto 1993; Freedman 1995). An important step in sustaining these conventionally non-valuated resources is to define them as goods and services which can be quantified in economic terms (Ehrlich 1995; Ehrlich & Ehrlich 1992). For example, if ecosystem services can be assigned a value, then damage to them can be seen as an externality of some other economic activity, and appropriate fiscal or legal measures can be devised to prevent or limit the damage. In this section we review briefly some of the more important ecosystem processes and show how they provide benefits which can be described as ecosystem services.

Accumulation and stabilization of soils and sediments

From the point of view of ecological engineering, one of the most important benefits of vegetation is its enormous capacity to stabilize soil and sediments. These processes are the essential precondition for any kind of soil development, and are clearly evident in any primary succession (Figure 15.1a).

Vegetation promotes the accumulation of sediments in various ways (Viles 1990). First, the aerial parts of plants have an important role in creating surface roughness which reduces wind speeds so that airborne sediment is deposited. For example, the succession on outwash gravels of the Muldrow Glacier in Alaska begins with a bare stony surface over which the wind, often loaded with ice particles, blows at high speed (Crocker & Major 1955). As the first plants manage to grow in this hostile environment, they begin to reduce the windspeed so that sand and silt can settle and become trapped amongst the leaves and litter of the developing vegetation. In this way the early successional stages of the vegetation lead to a gradual accumulation of fine material which is important for the development of the soil. In a similar way, plants growing in water also reduce the flow rate and lead to the deposition of sediment. One can see this very clearly on the flood plain of a river, where sediment accumulates in hummocks behind tussocks of grass (Edwards 1985), and also in intertidal regions such as those dominated by species of *Spartina* (Lambert 1964).

A second way in which vegetation stabilizes the soil is through creating a cover of living and dead plant material which protects the mineral soil surface from the energy of wind and rain which would otherwise cause erosion. This process is well understood by ecological engineers, who use organic mulches or geotextiles as a method of protecting developing soil surfaces before vegetation has developed sufficiently to assume this role (Bradshaw & Chadwick 1980; Rickson 1990).

Finally, there is the remarkable capacity of roots and stolons of some species to bind loose sediments together. This is clearly evident in salt marshes stabilized by *Spartina*, which is remarkably effective in binding soft mud, using a combination of stolons which radiate from the bases of the stems, feeding roots which spread out mostly horizontally and ramify through the surface layers of the mud, and stout anchoring roots which extend vertically downwards into the silt (Tansley 1949). Indeed, it is the very tough cord-like vertical roots which give *Spartina* its common name of cordgrass. In sand dunes, major plants capable of binding loose sand together are marram grass (*Ammophila arenaria*) and sand couch (*Agropyron junceum*) in Europe, beach grass (*A. breviligulata*) in America, and sand spinifex (*Spinifex hirsutus*) in warmer climates (Bradshaw & Chadwick 1980). All of these species are deep-rooting and have considerable powers of vegetative spread through tough rhizomes or stolons.

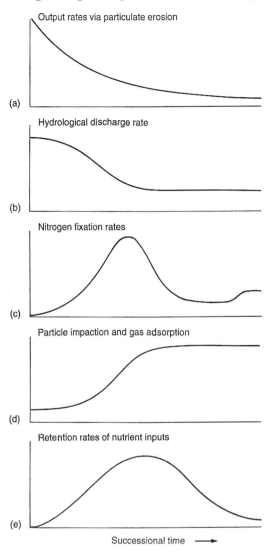

(a) Output rates via particulate erosion

(b) Hydrological discharge rate

(c) Nitrogen fixation rates

(d) Particle impaction and gas adsorption

(e) Retention rates of nutrient inputs

Successional time ⟶

Figure 15.1. Patterns of change in some biogeochemical processes during the course of primary succession. These processes can be thought of as ecosystem services which contribute added value from ecological restoration (adapted from Gorham *et al.* 1979).

The capacity of plants to stabilize and accumulate sediments provides one of the important benefits of ecological restoration. For this reason, plants are widely used in coastal protection, where it is necessary either to accumulate sediments or to stabilize existing sediments. Similarly, the establishment of vegetation in terrestrial areas is one of the most effective methods of reducing the loss of soil, especially in areas such as badlands and mountain regions which are particularly prone to erosion, or where excessive grazing has destroyed the original vegetation cover (Magnússon this volume).

Decomposition and soil microbial processes

An important component of any ecosystem is the community of hetero-trophic organisms which break down organic matter which has been produced, either *in situ* or imported from elsewhere. The processes of decomposition are very complex, and involve a wide diversity of organisms including bacteria, protozoans, fungi, and invertebrates. Organic materials which are easily degraded, such as sugars and amino acids disappear rapidly, but other products, such as lignin and chitin, are degraded much more slowly and accumulate in a chemically altered form as humus in the soil. These partially degraded and chemically altered forms of organic matter are important in the process of soil development, and many important soil properties depend upon this material (Etherington 1982). In particular, the capacity of soils to retain cations is directly related to humus content, and the water-holding and drainage properties of the soil are also determined to a large extent by the nature of the clay–humus complex.

Important ecosystem services depend upon the decomposer subsystem and the soil characteristics which they help to determine. In particular they play an important role in the immobilization and detoxification of pollutants. A good example of ecological engineering which exploits these processes is the increasing use of wetlands as a means of controlling non-point source pollution (Olson 1992). Non-point source pollution contributes a large proportion of the total pollution load of inland surface waters, and derives from sources such as urban storm water and agricul-tural run-off. The important pollutants include nutrients such as phos-phorus and nitrogen, metals such as copper, lead, and zinc, a range of pesticides, sodium chloride, and sediment. Increasingly, engineered wet-lands are being developed to remove pollutants. Their capacity to do so is largely related to the metabolism of micro-organisms (Wetzel 1993). The retentive properties of soils and sediment particles are governed by micro-environmental redox conditions, which are controlled almost exclusively by bacterial metabolism. Microbial biomass is a major sink and repository for organic carbon and many nutrients, and nutrients are strongly retained by wetland communities as a result.

The role of soil organic matter in reducing pollution effects in dryland systems is well illustrated by a study in Czechoslovakia of vegetation development following large-scale forest decline in the Krusne Hory (Moravcik 1994). The area is characterized by a high air pollution level and high proton deposition; under such conditions, organic material plays an important role as a proton buffering layer. The forest floor can buffer most of the incoming H^+ ions. Under these very acid conditions, toxicity of soluble aluminium can potentially influence plant health; however, the presence of humus reduces its influence upon plants due to the binding of aluminium to water-soluble organic matter.

Water balance

Vegetation has major effects on the routing of water, and thus upon the water balance of ecosystems and the hydrological characteristics of catchments (Kittredge 1971; Rutter 1975; Gorham *et al.* 1979) (Figure 15.1b). A forest canopy, for example, has a considerable capacity to intercept water and store it temporarily, before it either evaporates or drips to the forest floor. This process alone means that the flow of water into rivers tends to occur more slowly and with a reduced peak flow in catchments which are forested compared with catchments where the vegetation has been destroyed. Furthermore, total evaporation from forested catchments (the combination of evaporation from the soil and through transpiration) tends to be greater than from equivalent areas of low vegetation or even open water. This effect is due to the increased roughness of tall vegetation which increases air turbulence and therefore promotes evapotranspiration.

From the point of view of ecosystem services, there are several benefits of vegetation in regulating water. The vegetation reduces the erosive force of water falling upon the soil, and the temporary storage of water by vegetation reduces peak flow and hence erosive effects. All too often, we become aware of the powerful influence of vegetation in controlling water only when the vegetation is destroyed: then we understand all too clearly its importance in reducing flooding and preventing soil loss. For example, in India the costs of flood damage and destruction of reservoirs and irrigation systems by sediments from misused slopes averaged $1 billion a year between 1978 and 1985, and the annual expenditure on compensation and damage-prevention measures was $250 million (World Resources Institute 1985). In the upper Mississippi River Basin mean annual flood damage has increased by 140% in the past 90 years (averaging $3.4 billion over the last 30 years), largely as a result of the destruction of wetlands, and despite a massive effort to construct levees. Hey & Philippi (1995) argue, however, that the basin's flooding problems can be solved in an ecologically sound manner by restoration of wetland vegetation in an area of some 13 million hectares.

Nutrient cycling

As vegetation develops, the essential chemical components which make up plants and animals are incorporated into biomass and then returned to the environment. Mature vegetation typically has a closed nutrient cycle in which the nutrients used by plants are regenerated almost entirely *in situ*. In contrast, early successional stages often have an open nutrient cycle which depends upon the input of nutrients from outside the system. The process of succession can be viewed as the gradual accumulation of stocks of nutrients within the ecosystem thus reducing the dependence upon nutrient inputs. The mere presence of a plant canopy increases inputs of elements owing to impaction of particles of various kinds and absorption of gases by plant surfaces (Gorham *et al.* 1979) (Figure 15.1d). Catchment experiments have shown that forested ecosystems, especially during the early stages of succession, are often net retainers of nutrients from such sources (Binkley & Richter 1987) (Figure 15.1e). Of particular importance in many successions is the accumulation of nitrogen (Figure 15.1c), since this element is usually absent from the soil parent material and its accumulation depends mainly upon biological fixation by micro-organisms. Nitrogen is clearly a factor controlling the rate of primary succession on substrates such as sand dunes (Olson 1958), glacial moraines and outwash gravels (Crocker & Major 1955), volcanic ash (del Moral & Bliss 1993), and also in many successions on industrial waste materials such as China clay and mine waste (Roberts *et al.* 1981; Bradshaw 1983).

The benefits which arise from nutrient cycling in ecological restoration include the restoration of soil fertility (Hutnik & Davis 1973; Bradshaw this volume). Where nutrients are in short supply, this can be a slow process, and much research has gone into finding cheap ways of increasing the rate of nutrient accumulation. Marrs *et al.* (1981) found that a total of 1000 kg per hectare of nitrogen was needed in an ecosystem developing on China clay waste before forest vegetation could develop. They showed that this succession could be speeded up by the planting of various fast growing leguminous species, most notably *Lupinus arboreus.*

Another benefit which comes through nutrient cycling is that pollutant nutrients may be immobilized within the ecosystem. This point was referred to in the previous section when considering the development of the decomposer system, but also deserves mention here. Ultimately any ecosystem is likely to become saturated, but the restoration of forest vegetation can, nevertheless, have important benefits over a significant period in reducing unwanted nutrient input into watercourses. Similarly, in wetlands, the macrophyte vegetation can serve as a major storage for nutrients (Wetzel 1993). Enhanced growth of these plants in response to nutrient addition leads to increased production of organic matter which can accumulate in the substrate and thus prevent the contamination of water.

Biodiversity

All of the ecosystem processes so far reviewed depend upon biological diversity. These processes begin to operate whenever we create or restore an ecosystem. However, additional benefits may also come as the ecosystem is colonized by other organisms. The original restoration may introduce only a few species of plants and no animals, but the developing ecosystem provides the opportunity for many other organisms to colonize.

Examples of how species-poor degraded areas can become rich in species are numerous. For example, Bradshaw & Chadwick (1980) present a list of sites of wildlife interest which have developed on derelict land in England, and which have now either been made into nature reserves or at least recognized officially as sites of conservation importance. Attempts to reintroduce floristic diversity into intensive agriculture have also had considerable beneficial effects for biodiversity more generally. For example, in Switzerland there have been programmes to plant narrow strips of wild flower mixtures in cereal fields. These strips provide the habitat for an increased diversity of insect species (Lys and Nentwig 1992). In areas where a large number of such strips have been established, there have been significant increases in populations of larger animals such as the skylark *Alauda arvensis*, quail *Coturnix coturnix*, and hare *Lepus lepus.*

The benefits from increased diversity are not simply for those who are interested in wildlife for its own sake. They can also contribute to ecosystem services. For example, the increase in numbers of beneficial

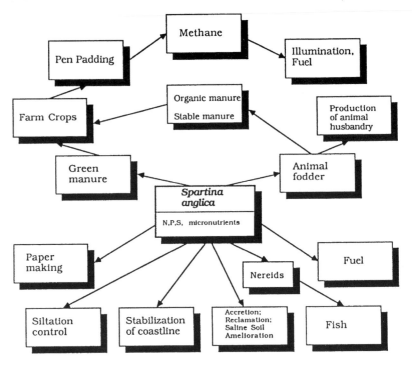

Figure 15.2. The diversity of benefits obtained by the planting of *Spartina anglica* for coastal protection in China (from Chung 1989).

insects such as Carabids and Coccinellids provides the opportunity for reducing pesticide inputs through more effective biological control of insect pests. There is also good reason to suppose that increased diversity will be beneficial for long-term stability of ecosystems, since there is more potential for diverse systems to adjust to changing environmental conditions (Schulze & Mooney 1992).

In addition, the new species may have direct commercial value. For example, in China *Spartina anglica* has been widely planted for coastal defence and land reclamation. Chung (1989) presented a long list of additional benefits, including the role of *Spartina* in improving soil fertility, as a source of food for livestock, as a source of methane for fuel, and as a green manure (Figure 15.2). *Spartina* also provided a habitat for other organisms, some of which were of economic significance. For example, the *Spartina* marshes were a valuable source of nereids and crabs. A curious and unexpected benefit was the effect of the plantings upon Chinese wild geese. Prior to the creation of *Spartina* marshes, these geese had used wheat fields as their feeding ground, but they began to shift to the newly planted vegetation for both nesting and feeding grounds, and ceased to present such a problem.

Benefits and how to assess them

Filion and Adamowicz (1994) present a classification of five major categories of uses of biodiversity, and this also provides a useful framework for considering the benefits of ecological restoration. One type of benefit is *direct extractive uses*, such as the production of timber or the use of an area for hunting or fishing. There may also be *direct non-extractive uses* such as the use of restored land for recreation or tourism. The *indirect uses* of natural resources include their role in providing ecosystem services such as flood control, erosion protection, pest control, and the detoxification of pollutants. *Optional uses* are those related to the possible use of the resource at some point in the future, while *passive uses* (i.e. existence values) are those motivated by sympathy for the natural environment, altruism towards future generations or a feeling of responsibility and stewardship towards nature. The importance of passive values should not be underestimated; a sense of community pride and a corresponding dissatisfaction that derelict areas should be allowed to exist are powerful social pressures for ecological restoration (Lodwick 1994; Bradshaw, personal communication).

To assess the value of the various types of benefit which arise from environmental improvement, several methods are used. Detailed discussion of the methodology is outside the scope of this chapter, but reviews are given by Van Ierland (1993), Filion and Adamowicz (1994), and Perrings (1995). We describe briefly the kinds of considerations which go into producing such a valuation (Table 15.3). Direct extractive uses present the least difficulty, since it is often possible to achieve an evaluation based on actual market prices. Thus, in the example of *Spartina* in China, it was possible to evaluate the production of trees on land reclaimed by the planting of *Spartina*. This method is relatively straightforward if a market exists for the goods produced, and is applicable to a wide variety of goods including agricultural products, forestry output, fisheries etc. In cases in which the goods are not traded, then it is possible to use the replacement-cost method, in which the products are evaluated by comparison with the market value of a traded substitute. For example, the value of wildfowl which are shot could be estimated by considering the market price of poultry.

There are a variety of methods in which non-extractive uses of restored environments could be valued. One is to assess the actual expenditure

Table 15.3. *Examples of methods that could be used for assessing the value of ecological restoration (based on Filion & Adamowicz 1994)*

Methods based on actual market prices	
Market price output method	Uses actual value of goods, e.g., fish, timber products
Actual expenditure method	Measures actual expenditure on goods and services related to use of an area e.g., ecotourism
Methods based on surrogate market prices	
Replacement cost method	Evaluates economic benefit for a given good or service using a tradable substitute, e.g., construction of a dike as replacement value for the benefit of flood control from wetland
Travel cost method	Estimates the value that visitors place on a site, or changes in environmental quality of site, from their travel behaviour, including time and money spent to visit the area
Hedonic methods	Value of an area is assessed by comparing the prices of surrogate goods, such as property, e.g., increased house prices close to an improved area
Methods based on simulated market prices	
Contingent valuation methods (CVM)	Based on sophisticated questionnaires in which people are asked the value they place upon a resource in terms of their willingness to pay, e.g., through taxation
Contingent ranking method	Rather than ask questions about willingness to pay as in CVM, individuals are asked to rank alternatives, e.g., several restoration scenarios differing in environmental quality, employment effects, other facilities etc.

associated with the use of the area for tourism or recreation. Filion *et al.* (1990) estimated the non-extractive value of biodiversity in Canada by surveying how much tourists spend on such things as transportation, accommodation, and equipment. This information represents part of the value that people attach to such areas, and could equally be applied to areas of restored land. A related approach is the travel-cost method, which was developed to estimate the recreational value of public sites. It estimates the value visitors place upon a site, or upon changes in environmental quality of the site, from their travel behaviour. Travel costs consist of the monetary costs, the time spent to get to an area, and any entry fees to use the area. Yet another method that can be considered, though its validity has been hotly disputed, is the contingent valuation method. This method is based upon careful questionnaires in which people are asked what monetary value they placed upon a resource such as a restored ecosystem. The questions thus address people's willingness to pay for the improvement, either through charges to use the new goods and services provided, or through other charges such as increased taxation. The aim is to establish people's perception of the value of these resources, and express it in a monetary value as if a real market existed. Such a methodology can also be applied to passive uses, in which the willingness to pay reflects a desire to see the improvement in the environment, even if the person interviewed does not expect to derive direct benefit from it.

Methods for estimating the value of ecological restoration for ecological ecosystem services often rely upon estimating the replacement costs of those services. For example, the alternative to coastal defence through sand dunes or salt marshes might be the construction of a seawall. The estimated costs of such a structure provides surrogate value for the creation of the ecosystem. Similarly, the value of beneficial insects associated with wild-flower strips sown in farmland could, at least in theory, be estimated in terms of the savings to be achieved from reduction in the use of pesticides. However, in this as in many other cases, we lack the precise ecological knowledge to make an assessment of the benefit.

When an attempt is made to calculate the full value of a natural ecosystem, taking into account the different components of value outlined above, the results can be quite surprising, especially in wetlands. For example, the gross annual income per hectare of wetlands in the Great Lakes region of Canada was estimated as $1600 ha^{-1} (Jaworski and Raphael 1978), based on user-day values and the wholesale value of wetland products. For the same wetlands, Tilton (1978) used an 'ecosystem-replacement' methodology to estimate their value for such functions as runoff-nutrient control and wastewater renovation. The two studies yield a combined value (at 1980 prices) of $4700 ha^{-1} yr^{-1} (Jaworski 1981). Other wetland studies also yield very high values for wetlands. A review of wetland utilization in Canada (National Wetlands Working Group 1988) assigned a value of $51 300 ha^{-1} to their functions in water purification and as pollution sinks, and $139 500 ha^{-1} in regulating flood peaks. Thibodeau and Ostro (1981) calculated the benefits of a hectare of wetland in the Charles River Watershed in Massachusetts as $632 000 to $785 900 ha^{-1}. The economic value of salt marshes dominated by *Spartina* on the eastern coastline of North America have been estimated at $16 800 to $73 500 ha^{-1} (Mitsch & Gosselink 1993; Niering this volume). However, despite these impressive examples of the value of wetlands, there is a serious lack of

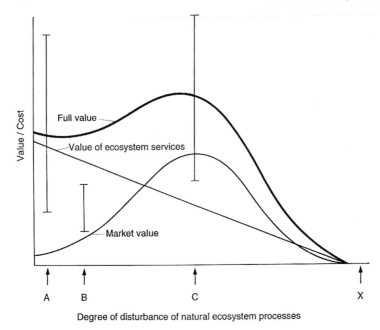

Figure 15.3. A simple model to illustrate how the inclusion of benefits from ecosystem services affects the relative costs and benefits of ecological restoration. Three options (A, B, and C) are shown for restoring an area from the heavily degraded condition X. Option A is restoration aimed at achieving functional equivalence to a defined, natural ecosystem; option B is a cheap rehabilitation aimed at establishing some kind of vegetation; option C is reclamation of the land for productive purposes. The vertical bars represent the range of costs likely for each type of restoration relative to the benefits.

knowledge about the benefits of natural ecosystems. The failure to quantify value for comparison with competing or alternative land uses is certainly one factor responsible for the progressive decline of such areas.

The economics of ecological restoration

Figure 15.3 presents a simple model designed to illustrate some of the issues which arise in developing the economic case for ecological restoration. This model considers how the value of land varies according to the degree of disturbance of ecosystem processes, and relates this to the costs of restoration. The x axis represents the degree of disturbance of the natural ecosystem, and ranges from a completely natural ecosystem to environments which are so degraded that they are of no economic value. The direct economic value of a completely natural ecosystem is assumed to be low, and limited to its value for the harvesting of native plants and animals (direct value – extraction) and uses such as tourism (direct value – no extraction). The greatest value is derived from land systems of intermediate disturbance, which are those used for productive processes such as agriculture and forestry. However, the benefits from ecosystem services are assumed to be greatest in undisturbed, natural ecosystems, and decline linearly with increasing disturbance, with the most degraded areas having no value. In practice such an assumption is probably an understatement of the real situation, since highly degraded areas may represent an actual cost in terms of damage to health and the need for measures to protect the public against effects such as pollution.

The figure also shows three options for restoration or rehabilitation, and a likely range of costs for carrying out the work. Option A is restoration in its strict sense, and is intended to establish an ecosystem with a defined species composition and functional equivalence to a reference ecosystem. As we have seen, such specifications often make restoration expensive, though, if the value of ecosystem services is also considered, the costs may not be excessive. Option C is aimed at rehabilitating the land to its maximum productive capacity; for example for agriculture. Such rehabilitation is also often expensive, and there may be no economic benefit in the restoration of the land, even if the contribution from ecosystem services is included. Option B is a cheap rehabilitation aimed at establishing some kind of vegetation; it is the option often adopted for heavily degraded sites, when the funding available is very limited (e.g., reclaiming wasteland; Handel this volume) and the potential for productive use of the land is small. This financial picture may, however, be transformed if the benefits of ecosystem services are also considered.

The simple model suggests that an assessment of the full benefits can significantly strengthen the argument for restoration. However, although a full valuation may present a realistic assessment of the social benefits of ecological restoration, it does not necessarily represent the benefit to those who must pay for the work. Indeed there are several economic and social factors which may act against restoration, even though a full analysis of costs and benefits is positive.

Social and private benefits

The full benefits of a scheme include direct economic benefits to the person carrying out the project, as well as other benefits which are for society as a

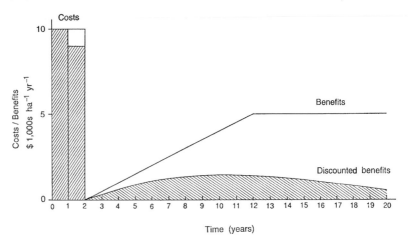

Figure 15.4. An illustration of how discounting of future benefits affects the financial case for restoration. In this example the costs are $10 000 ha^{-1} in each of the first two years. The annual value of benefits from the restored area is $5 000 ha^{-1}, but it takes 10 years after restoration for these to be obtained. When costs and benefits are discounted at 10% yr^{-1} (shaded areas), the total costs are $19 000 ha^{-1} and value of benefits in the first 20 years is $18 400 ha^{-1}.

whole, but may not be reflected in financial advantage to the developer. The developer may see the benefits of restoration simply in terms of the enhanced value of the land, for example for productive use in forestry or for building. Benefits in terms of ecosystem services, for example a general reduction in the risk of flooding or an increase in biological diversity, may not represent any tangible advantage to the land owner, though they are clearly of value to society generally.

Discounting

The environmental benefits from ecological restoration usually accrue slowly with time. Processes such as soil development and colonization by plants and animals are slow, and, even though the initial restoration may be a significant improvement on what was there before, it may take decades or even centuries for the full benefits to be seen. The economic frame for most projects is strongly constrained by the immediate financial benefits of the restoration, since benefits in the future are discounted in value. In practical terms, the discounting rate for a developer will be the prevailing rate of interest (Figure 15.4). However, there may be strong social reasons for choosing a lower rate of discount in assessing the value of the project, in order to consider the interests of future generations (Page 1988, Luckert & Adamowicz 1993).

Spatial scale

The benefits we obtain from recreating ecosystems depend to some degree upon the spatial scale of the restoration. Some benefits arise however small the area restored. For example, soil erosion is reduced locally wherever plants become established; even small areas of wetland may contribute to trapping sediment and reducing input of nutrients into waterways. However, to have a significant effect at a regional scale, a certain minimum area of a particular ecosystem may be needed. For example, Baker (1992) estimated that to achieve a reduction of suspended solids in rivers a ratio of wetlands to total drainage area of approximately 1:20 was desirable. Furthermore, some effects are only produced if restoration is carried out at a larger scale. As we have seen, total biodiversity in intensive agricultural land increases significantly as we increase the numbers of species-rich strips of vegetation (Arnold 1995). Larger organisms, such as many birds and mammals, use more than one habitat and small areas are quite inadequate to support them. Benefits in terms of increasing biodiversity therefore increase as we increase the scale of restoration.

The unknown and the unknowable

Economics helps us to understand the importance of a natural resource by identifying the various benefits it produces and placing a value upon each of them. This is a considerable challenge for ecologists, but one which is generally beneficial. However, there are limits to how far we can go in such an analysis. One of these is the limit of our present knowledge: for example, we still have a very imperfect understanding of the importance of particular species in ecosystem functioning, and it is therefore difficult to assign a precise value to biodiversity. More importantly, there are things we can never know. How important will the existence of certain species be for ecosystem stability under certain unknown conditions in the future? In valuing natural resources, the precautionary principle would suggest that the full value is certainly greater than that which we can estimate simply by summing the known benefits.

All of these factors mean that restoration is usually not something which can be left to a free market. Since much of the benefit from restoration is diffused amongst society as a whole, some form of government intervention is often necessary (for example, direct financing of projects, subsidies, tax incentives, planning incentives, etc.) to ensure that society obtains the full benefits (Tisdell 1991).

Concluding remarks

The environmental resource base, upon which all economic activity ultimately depends, includes ecological processes which produce a wide range of services (Arrow *et al.* 1995). This resource base is finite, and we have already damaged it greatly. Daily (1995) estimates that approximately 43% of the Earth's terrestrial vegetated surface has diminished capacity to supply benefits to humanity as a result of recent, direct impacts of land use. Rehabilitation of the world's degraded land is of the highest importance for the future of our species.

Fortunately, there is an enormous potential for recovery in most land types, and, as the chapters in this book demonstrate, great progress has been made in developing techniques to restore or rehabilitate ecosystems. However, to make the case for ecological restoration, we must analyse in economic terms the ecological benefits that will obtain, and also the full costs if we fail to intervene. Economics can help us to quantify the full value of restoration, and thus bridge the gap between restoration costs and restored value. The recognition of ecosystem services is a valuable step in bringing ecological understanding into the economic analysis. However, economics challenges ecologists to quantify much more precisely than we can at present our dependence upon ecosystem processes.

The economic analysis is also important because it demonstrates the forces which tend to work against ecological restoration. The task of restoration cannot be left to the free market alone. Many of the benefits take the form of ecosystem services which are of value to society as a whole, and are accrued, either slowly, or as part of a more general strategy for environmental improvement. Such benefits, although real, will never appear in the balance sheet of a developer concerned with the immediate financial viability of a project. These are strong reasons for subsidizing restoration programmes for the social good of the present and future generations. If we can achieve an effective fusion of ecological and economic understanding, our efforts at ecological restoration will be seen less as an expensive luxury which can be applied by the affluent developed world, and more as an essential part of reversing global environmental degradation and achieving sustainability.

References

Arnold, G. W. (1995). Incorporating landscape pattern into conservation programs. In *Mosaic Landscapes and Ecological Processes*, eds. L. Hansson, L. Fahrig, & G. Merrian, pp. 309–37. London: Chapman & Hall.

Arrow, K., Bolin, B., Costanza, R., Dasgupta, P., Folke, C., Holling, C. S., Jansson, B.-O., Levin, S., Mäler, K.-G., Perrings, C., & Pimentel, D. (1995). Economic growth, carrying capacity, and the environment. *Science*, 268, 520–1.

Baker, L. A. (1992). Introduction to nonpoint source pollution in the United States and prospects for wetland use. *Ecological Engineering*, 1, 1–26.

Berger, J. J. (1992). The Blanco River. In *Restoration of Aquatic Ecosystems*, ed. National Research Council (NRC), pp. 470–7. Washington, DC: National Academy of Sciences.

Binkley, D. & Richter, D. (1987). Nutrient cycles and H^+ budgets of forest ecosystems. *Advances in Ecological Research*, 16, 1–51.

Bogovich, W. M. & Member, P. E. (1992). Twelve years of abandoned mineland reclamation activities by the United States Department of Agriculture – Soil Conservation Service in Southwest Pennsylvania. In *Land Reclamation: Advances in Research & Technology*, Proceedings of the International Symposium, 14–15 December 1992, Nashville, Tennesse, eds. Y. Younos, P. Diplas, & S. Mostaghimi, pp. 230–9. St. Joseph (Michigan): American Society of Agricultural Engineers.

Bradshaw, A. D. (1983). The reconstruction of ecosystems. *Journal of Applied Ecology*, 20, 1–18.

Bradshaw, A. D. & Chadwick, M. J. (1980). *The Land Restoration: The Ecology and Reclamation of Derelict and Degraded Land*. London: Blackwell Scientific Publications.

Cairns, J. Jr. (1993). Is restoration ecology practical? *Restoration Ecology*, 1, 3–7.

Chung, C.-H. (1989). Ecological engineering of coastlines with salt-marsh plantations. In *Ecological Engineering: An Introduction to Ecotechnology*, eds. W. J. Mitsch, & S. E. Jorgensen, pp. 255–89. New York: John Wiley & Sons.

Crocker, R. L. & Major, J. (1955). Soil development in relation to vegetation and surface age at Glacier Bay, Alaska. *Journal of Ecology*, 43, 427–48.

Daily, G. C. (1995). Restoring value to the world's degraded lands. *Science*, 269, 350–4.

Del Moral, R. & Bliss, L. C. (1993). Mechanisms of primary succession: insights resulting from the eruption of Mount St. Helens. *Advances in Ecological Research*, 24, 1–66.

Edwards, P. J. (1985). Some effects of grazing on the vegetation of streamside lawns in the New Forest. *Proceedings of the Hampshire Field Club Archaeological Society*, 41, 45–50.

Ehrlich, P. R. (1995). Context: biodiversity and ecosystem services. In *Global Biodiversity Assessment*, eds. V. H. Heywood, & R. T. Watson, pp. 282–5. Cambridge University Press.

Ehrlich, P. R. & Ehrlich, A. H. (1992). The value of biodiversity. *Ambio*, 22, 64–8.

Etherington, J. R. (1982). *Environment and Plant Ecology*, 2nd edn. New York: John Wiley & Sons.

Filion, F. L. & Adamowicz, W. L. (1994). Socioeconomic evaluation of biodiversity. In *Biodiversity in Canada: A Science Assessment for Environment Canada*, ed. Biodiversity Science Assessment Team, pp. 221–42. Ottawa: Minister of Supply and Services Canada.

Filion, F. L., Jacquemot, Boxall, A. P., Reid, R., Bouchard, Du Wors, P. E., & Gray, P. A. (1990). *The Importance of Wildlife to Canadians in 1987: The Economic Significance of Wildlife-related Recreational Activities*. Ottawa: Canadian Wildlife Service, Ottawa.

Freedman, B. (1995). *Environmental Ecology: The Ecological Effects of Pollution, Disturbance, and other Stresses*, 2nd edn. London: Academic Press.

Gorham, E., Vitousek, P. M., & Reiners, W. A. (1979). The regulation of chemical budgets over the course of terrestrial ecosystem succession. *Annual Review of Ecology & Systematics*, 10, 53–84.

Gu, H., Wu, D., & Zhu, H. (1989). Land restoration in China. *Journal of Applied Ecology*, 26, 787–92.

Guinon, M. (1989). Project elements determining comprehensive restoration costs and repercussions of hidden and inaccurate costs. In *Restoration '89: the New Management Challenge*, Proceedings of the First Annual Conference of the Society for Ecological Restoration, January 16–20, 1989, Oakland, California. eds. H. G. Hughes, & T. M. Bonnicksen, pp. 162–71. Madison: Society for Ecological Restoration.

Hey, D. L. (1992). Prairie Potholes. In *Restoration of Aquatic Ecosystems*, ed. National Research Council (NRC), pp. 505–9. Washington, DC: National Academy of Sciences.

Hey, D. L. & Philippi, N. S. (1995). Flood reduction through wetland restorations: The Upper Mississippi River Basin as a Case History. *Restoration Ecology*, 3, 4–17.

Hutnik, R. J. & Davis, J., eds. (1973). *Ecology and Reclamation of Devastated Land* (2 vols.). New York: Gordon & Breach.

IMF (International Monetary Fund) (1996). *International Financial Statistics*, 49/4, April, 1996. Washington DC: International Monetary Fund.

Jaworski, E. (1981). The economics of wetland protection. In *Proceedings, Ontario Wetland Conference, September 18–19, 1981*. ed. Federation of Ontario Naturalists, pp. 58–62. Toronto: Federation of Ontario Naturalists.

Jaworski, E. & Raphael, C. N. (1978). *Fish, Wildlife and Recreational Values of Michigan's Coastal Wetlands*. Lansing: Land Resource Programs Division, Department of Natural Resources.

Kendle, A. D. (1992). Reclaiming land to maximize conservation benefits. In *Land Reclamation: Advances in Research & Technology*, Proceedings of the International Symposium. 14–15 December 1992, Nashville, Tennesse. eds. Y. Younos, P. Diplas, & S. Mostaghimi, pp. 346–55. St. Joseph (Michigan): American Society of Agricultural Engineers.

Kittredge, J. (1971). *Forest Influences*. New York: Dover Publications.

Kusler, J. A. & Kentula, M. E., eds. (1990). *Wetland Creation and Restoration: The Status of the Science*. Washington, DC: Island Press.

Lambert, J. M. (1964). The *Spartina* story. *Nature*, 204, 1136–8.

Lodwick, D. G. (1994). Changing worldviews and landscape restoration. In *Beyond Preservation: Restoring and Inventing Landscapes*, eds. A. D. Baldwin, J. de Luce, & C. Pletsch, pp. 97–110. Minneapolis: University of Minnesota Press.

Luckert, M. K. & Adamowicz, W. L. (1993). Empirical measures of factors affecting social rates of discount. In *Forestry and the Environment: Economic Perspectives*, eds. W. L. Adamowicz, W. White, & W. E. Phillips, pp. 262–81. Wallingford: CAB International.

Lys, J.-A. & Nentwig, W. (1992). Augmentation of beneficial arthropods by strip-management: 4. Surface activity, movement and activity density of abundant carabid beetles in a cereal field. *Oecologia*, 92, 373–82.

Marrs, R. H., Roberts, R. D., Skeffington, R. A., & Bradshaw, A. D. (1981). Ecosystem development on naturally-colonized China clay wastes. II. Nutrient compartmentation. *Journal of Ecology*, 69, 163–9.

Meyers, P. B., Williams, R. H., & Yount, K. R. (1995). *Contaminated Land: Reclamation, Redevelopment and Reuse in the United States and the European Union*. Aldershot (UK): Edward Elgar.

Mitsch, W. J. & Gosselink, J. G. (1993). *Wetlands*. 2nd edn. New York: Van Nostrand Reinhold.

Miyawaki, A. & Golley, F. B. (1993). Forest reconstruction as ecological engineering. *Ecological Engineering*, 2, 333–45.

Moravcik, P. (1994). Development of new forest stands after a large scale forest decline in the Krusné hory Mountains. *Ecological Engineering*, 3, 57–69.

National Wetlands Working Group (1988). *Wetlands of Canada*. Ecological Land Classification Series, No. 24. Ottawa: Canadian Government Publishing Service.

NRC (National Research Council). (1992). *Restoration of Aquatic Ecosystems: Science, Technology and Public policy*. Washington DC: National Academy Press.

Olson, R. K. (1992). Evaluating the role of created and natural wetlands in controlling nonpoint source pollution (Editorial). *Ecological Engineering*, 1, xi-xvii.

Page, T. (1988). Intergenerational equity and the social value of discount. In *Environmental Resources and Applied Welfare Economics: Essays in Honor of J. V. Krutilla*, ed. K. V. Smith. Washington DC: Resources For the Future Inc.

Perrings, C. (1995). The economic values of biodiversity. In *Global Biodiversity Assessment*, eds. V. H. Heywood, & R. T. Watson, pp. 827–914. Cambridge University Press.

Repetto, R. (1993). How to account for environmental degradation. In *Forestry and the Environment: Economic Perspectives*, eds. W. L. Adamowicz, W. White, & W. E. Phillips, pp. 3–18. Wallingford: CAB International.

Rickson, R. J. (1990). The role of simulated vegetation in soil erosion control. In *Vegetation and Erosion*, ed. J. B. Thornes, pp. 99–111. New York: John Wiley & Sons.

Roberts, R. D., Marrs, R. H., Skeffington, R. A., & Bradshaw, A. D. (1981). Ecosystem development on naturally-colonized China clay wastes. I. Vegetation changes and overall accumulation of organic matter and nutrients. *Journal of Ecology*, 69, 153–61.

Rutter, A. J. (1975). The hydrological cycle in vegetation. In *Vegetation and the Atmosphere*, ed. J. L. Monteith, pp. 111–54. London: Academic Press.

Schulze, E. D. & Mooney, H. A. (1993). Ecosystem function of biodiversity: a summary. In *Biodiversity and Ecosystem Function*, eds. E. D. Schulze, & H. A. Mooney, pp. 497–510. Berlin: Springer-Verlag.

Tansley, A. G. (1949). *The British Islands and their Vegetation.* Cambridge University Press.

Thibodeau, F. R. & Ostro, B. D. (1981). An economic analysis of wetland protection. *Journal of Environmental Management*, 212, 19–30.

Tilton, D. L. (1978). *The Ecology and Values of Michigan's Coastal Wetlands, Phase II.* St. Paul-Minneapolis: United States Fish and Wildlife Service.

Tisdell, C. A. (1991). *Economics of Environmental Conservation: Economics for Environmental and Ecological Management.* Amsterdam: Elsevier.

Trepagnier, C. M., Kogas, M. A., & Turner, R. E. (1995). Evaluation of wetland gain and loss of abandoned agricultural impoundments in South Louisiana 1978–1988. *Restoration Ecology*, 3, 299–303.

Van Ierland, E. C. (1993). *Developments in Environmental Economics, Volume 2: Macroeconomic Analysis of Environmental Policy.* Amsterdam: Elsevier.

Vernon, R. D., Autin, W. J., & Mossa, J. (1992). Developing a floodplain sand and gravel mine reclamation program in the Amite River Basin of Louisiana. In *Land Reclamation: Advances in Research & Technology*, Proceedings of the International Symposium, 14–15 December 1992, Nashville, Tennesse, eds. Y, Younos, P. Diplas, & S. Mostaghimi, pp. 240–5. St. Joseph (Michigan): American Society of Agricultural Engineers.

Viles, H. A. (1990). The Agency of Organic Beings: A selective review of recent work in biogeomorphology. In *Vegetation and Erosion*, ed. J. B. Thornes, pp. 5–24. New York: John Wiley & Sons.

Wetzel, R. G. (1993). Constructed wetlands: Scientific foundations are critical. In *Constructed Wetlands for Water Quality Improvement*, ed. G. A. Moshiri, pp. 3–7. London: Lewis Publishers.

Wheeler, B. D. & Shaw, S. C. (1995). *Restoration of Damaged Peatlands: with Particular Reference to Lowland Raised Bogs Affected by Peat Extraction.* London: HMSO.

World Resources Institute (1985). *Tropical Forests: A Call for Action. Part I: The Plan.* Report of an International Task Force convened by the World Resources Institute, The World Bank and the United Nations Development Programme. Washington DC: World Resource Institute.

16

Ecological restoration – the magnitude of the challenge: an outsider's view

MICHAEL J. CLARK

It is interesting to contemplate a tangled bank, clothed with many plants of many kinds, with birds singing on the bushes, with various insects flitting about, and with worms crawling through the damp earth, and to reflect that these elaborately constructed forms, so different from each other, and dependent upon each other in so complex a manner, have all been produced by laws acting around us ... There is grandeur in this view of life, with its several powers ... [and] from so simple a beginning endless forms most beautiful and most wonderful have been, and are being evolved.

So begins and ends the final paragraph in Charles Darwin's *Origin of Species* (Darwin 1859) – posing simultaneously the ultimate conceptual challenge to scientists and philosophers of his day, and the ultimate practical challenge to restoration ecologists today, For, if restoration ecology is to justify its place in both the definitive academic texts and the practical manuals of land management, it has to be able to yield something approaching the totality of that 'tangled bank' with all of its complexity and creative dynamism. Despite detailed subsequent critique of the mechanisms proposed by Darwin, there is no denying the overwhelming grandeur of his viewpoint on life, and no escaping the difficulty of rebuilding a self-sustaining ecosystem such as that described in his final paragraph. Above all, Darwin provides us with a challenging perspective, which starts with *interest* and *contemplation* (worthy icons of the scientific process), and ends with the *most beautiful and most wonderful* (which serve to underline the subjective social and aesthetic values which our efforts at restoration also have to satisfy). Do we really have a sufficient mastery of the 'laws acting around us' to claim such an awesome capability?

It seems that the challenge of restoration ecology can be found both in intellectual debate and in field practice: in the virtual world and the real world. As an intellectual construct, it calls into question many fundamental

353

concepts of ecology, and generates such strong contention that at times it appears that the notion lacks all practical validity (Baldwin, de Luce, & Pletsch 1993a). Nevertheless, as a practical device, it serves as a popular sustainability strategy, as a powerful element in the armoury of soft engineering, and sometimes as a token of planning gain or mitigation which is increasingly often traded in the counting-house of environmental impact assessment and the granting of planning permission. Though initially a vision of the conservation idealist, ecological restoration has thus become both a big issue and big business. Not surprisingly, ecologists have found themselves at the centre of this debate and, though sometimes divided on the purity of the claim that a functioning ecosystem can be restored, have been able to demonstrate the massive scale of the world-wide need for such restoration. They have also faced the greater challenge of seeking to identify where priority investment should be made, and have demonstrated that the greatest need may not equate with the highest feasibility or most attractive investment priority. The evaluation of restoration potential and the setting of realistic restoration targets have become tantalizing aims for ecologists, as has the competition between prevention and restoration as investment goals.

An abundant literature, within this volume and beyond, testifies convincingly to the breadth and depth of technical experience of restoration ecology demonstrated by its many professional exponents. A significantly smaller literature acknowledges that behind this practical experience there lie several fundamental issues of mission and priority which colour past achievements and query future directions, validity (e.g., Baldwin, de Luce, & Pletsch 1993b). This apparent separation between philosophy and action is the norm rather than the exception, and it is exacerbated in the case of restoration ecology by the fact that many of the projects through which such restoration is attempted are directed by related but distinct professions, notably landscape architecture and environmental engineering. There is, therefore, a double challenge in ensuring that restoration ecologists are aware of the value system of the society which they serve, and that society (together with its component professions) is well informed on the expert product of ecological restoration research. This task is one of liaison between groups rather than one of the internal ordering of an enclosed profession.

The aim of this chapter is thus to explore those issues which lie most prominently at the intersection between, first, the expert profession of restoration ecology; second, the more constrained world of the many restoration practitioners who may or may not acknowledge affiliation to this profession; and, third, the innate or articulated environmental interests of the society (and the political structures) within which restoration is needed, undertaken and evaluated. Do professional ecologists share the environmental priorities of that wider society? (Often a question of scale.) Is society clear on exactly what is being sought, promised, and achieved in its name through the implementation of ecological restoration? How do the limited targets of restoration ecology relate to the broader political commitments of Agenda 21, with its apparent blanket embrace of sustainable environmental management?

The ecological crisis has been typified as an intellectual crisis (Baldwin *et al.* 1993b), and issues such as those raised above are unashamedly philosophical. They cannot be answered through technical analysis of particular cases, though they can be illuminated by specific case studies – in the present context drawn from the field of river channel restoration. The argument is derived neither from previous discussion within the profession of restoration ecology, nor from a technical analysis of specific projects, but from a consideration of the broader debate within environmental management. Against such a background it is possible to provide an external review of progress within restoration ecology, and to consider both its ultimate mission and its more pragmatic targets. This externality of viewpoint, arguing from the perspective of a broader environmental management position rather than from the specific stance of restoration ecology *sensu stricto*, inevitably introduces a risk of duplication or even of uninformed confusion. It is offered, none the less, in the hope that it opens the possibility of providing valuable reinforcement when the conclusions run parallel, and the potential to provide illumination when the outcomes diverge.

Issues of priority and comparative evaluation surface not only in academic debate, but also in the cost-effectiveness analysis which, formally or intuitively, is likely to figure in the business case for any restoration project, but they are rooted more deeply in the underlying science. They figure in the consideration of mutual understanding and communication between the various sectors of society involved in restoration ecology, so that the distinctions between clean-up, rehabilitation, enhancement, restoration and creation are of much more than semantic interest. Each poses its own technical problems and makes its own demands on ecological concepts. These are the debates which must be resolved if we are to claim some feel for the magnitude of the restoration challenge, but first it is necessary to consider briefly the magnitude of the need for restoration before exploring the way in which the aims and evaluation of restoration-type projects are bound up with a terminology which is far from consistent in its usage and application.

Global and local perspectives on restoration need

While it may well be satisfactory to view the long-term mission of restoration ecology as being to shift the planet significantly back towards the higher environmental status that often prevailed before the 'developments' of the last one or more centuries. However, to design operational short- and medium-term ecological restoration goals requires more careful definition. There is, moreover, merit in confronting the extent to which the goals inherent in practical applications of ecological restoration reflect the overarching mission. That they should represent but a partial step in its direction is both understandable and acceptable, but it remains professionally healthy to keep the link between mission and goals under periodic review.

There is no doubting either the overall scale or ubiquity of environmental degradation. Pollution and pesticides; acidification and eutrophication; deforestation and soil erosion; hunting, fishing, decline in populations and loss of biodiversity; decline in water quality and quantity – the list is long and disturbing. The magnitude of the restoration challenge is in part a reflection of the scale of need, but there are other dimensions of challenge. It is difficult enough to estimate (even to guess) how big the problem is, but substantially more difficult to suggest where the priorities for action lie or how we can ensure that action is directed where it is most needed. Still more worrying is the fact that most current restoration projects are regarded as site-scale prototypes or experiments, and, even at this microscale, both the costs and the professional difficulties can seem insurmountable. As the scale of approach is increased, there is no guarantee that the controlling variables remain the same, or that the optimum remedial responses will be constant; quite the opposite! The most rudimentary review of habitats and ecosystems suggests that they are, in many respects, scale-dependent, so that the chance of site-scale prototypes being successfully extrapolated to higher scales is limited. Moreover, as target habitats become more varied, so too will the restoration performance achieved.

There is a real danger that a mismatch is developing between the scale of the problem and the scale of response. Are we concentrating effort at the scale of the urban river reach or of a grassland or heathland disturbed by a pipeline trench, when the real challenge is the massive loss of temperate forest and the continuing loss of tropical rainforest? Huge sums are spent cleaning and releasing (to an extremely low life expectancy) individual birds and animals involved in accidental oil spills, while at the same time industrial systems produce pollution or acidification at near-continental scale. Should we be satisfied to respond at the particular ecological community scale (a kind of landscape gardening), or insist on action at the functioning ecosystem scale? Momentarily, the answer seems obvious – most present efforts are inadequate, and both attention and investment should shift to national and international scale. It is, perhaps, misleading to assume that the two focuses of response (local and regional) are alternatives which are in competition, rather than interwoven strands to be handled in partnership – but it is important that the very different approaches at these two scales should be clearly acknowledged, so that restoration priorities and goals can be more confidently defined.

Clearly, restoration response is often at a minute scale compared with the overwhelming magnitude of the global problems – yet each response has value in its own right, and there is potential in principle (though not necessarily in practice) for individual responses to be positively compatible so that they combine to produce a regional rather than local amelioration. The scale distinction is nicely posed by two North American projects:

Dedicated environmentalists in St John's, Newfoundland are working to restore the natural environment of the Virginia River. Established in 1992, the Virginia River Conservation Society has worked with a single goal: to return the river to its original condition and to encourage its stewardship. 'The river had a couple of badly eroded banks', says Ken Hannaford, president of the society. 'We made a lattice-work of logs, covered them with soil and peat, and then planted native plants to stabilize the ground.'   (FEF, 1996)

This kind of exercise in local and essentially 'amateur' restoration can be compared with the regional-scale effort of a government programme:

The Clinch River Remedial Investigation is designed to address the transport, fate and distribution of waterborne contaminants from the U.S. Department of Energy's Oak Ridge Reservation and to assess the potential risks to human health and the environment associated with these contaminants ... A phased remedial investigation ... is underway to (1) define the nature and extent of the off-site contamination, (2) evaluate associated environmental and human health risks, and (3) preliminarily identify and evaluate potential remediation alternatives.
                                                            (ORNL, 1995)

Not only is there a significant difference in scale here (though still nothing approaching a macro-regional coverage), but also a not-uncommon distinction between an action-centred local approach and an information-centred regional approach. In essence it seems that the local problems can effectively be tackled by intervening in the outcomes, but we might tentatively suggest that the broader regional system failures require remediation through intervention in the causative processes. Both are valid goals for restoration ecology, but the latter may be expected to make a more substantive contribution towards the underlying mission. The Clinch River Project would not even meet a strict definition of ecological restoration, yet ironically it may be better positioned to achieve a sustainable return to previous conditions than is the local and more limited Virgina River initiative.

This is related to, but not quite the same as, the perennial conflict between a focus on cure and a focus of prevention, which presents both planners and ecologists with a classic dilemma – is prevention better than cure? The precautionary principle enshrined at the heart of sustainability theory would argue in the affirmative, but, faced with present deforestation, actual loss of wetland, or the *fait accompli* of the Gulf War releases of oil, then no real choice is available. Cure appears to be the only reasonable response to continued degradation, and the choice is not whether to prevent or to cure, but at what scale and through what approach attempts at curing might be most feasible. A starting-point is then the challenge presented by the multiplicity of overlapping strategies and related conflicting terminologies on offer to the planner and to those who read the literature.

Once again, we find that there may be at least a temporary contention between the mission of substantive planetary restoration and the reality that, in practice, a multitude of more modest local goals may have more immediate impact. It has to be acknowledged that the issue is both fundamental and complex. If net social benefit is either the primary aim, or at least a significant part of the aim, then the local ownership represented by individual commitment to 'amateur' or small-scale projects has enormous values in its own right. Indeed, Higgs (1994) has commended the 'brilliance' that has emanated from the fusion of amateur and professional traditions in ecological restoration. There is huge merit in maintaining active responsibility with individuals, rather than delegating it to remote and questionably representative and accountable organizations. Yet no matter how the argument is pursued, it tends to reduce ultimately to a recognition of the value of prevention, and to a realization that prevention is a social rather than individual responsibility. In this, as in so many contexts, science is a part of society rather than apart from it, and the scientific role of restoration ecology may be to inform and guide the worthy efforts of non-scientific practitioners (Bradshaw 1994).

Mean what you say and say what you mean

Clarity of definition

It may be suggested that ecological restoration is at heart a social process (perhaps even an art: Turner 1987), but that its component practices of design, implementation, and communication are through the language and convention of science (Bradshaw 1993; Higgs 1994). If mission and goal are to converge, and society at large is to be more centrally involved in discussing priorities, it is important that a consistency of meaning and intent should be agreed and applied. It is clear, from the catalogue of global and regional disasters, that very many different forms of ecological response are feasible and helpful. Intervention into disturbed or degraded ecosystems with a view to their improvement thus yields a spectrum of activities. Selecting between these options, and ensuring that the target is one of reason rather than rhetoric, demands both clarity of thinking and robustness of evaluation. It is in this context that the subtle variants of language and intention become highly significant. Only through a substantial consistency of language is it possible to define the intent of the protagonist or antagonist sufficiently clearly to set targets, devise frameworks for post-project appraisal, and undertake justified assessment of performance. This confrontation of the language is not universally welcome, since it signifies a challenge to the message – does restoration have to be interpreted with absolute purity, or are there compromises that can be accepted?

In practice, confusion often reigns. At a professional level, great strides have been made towards identifying the nuance of terminology that requires resolution (Jackson, Lopoukhine, & Hollyard 1995; Bradshaw this volume). But there remain many practitioners who are largely untouched by the academic debate. Thus, much of the published literature precedes such convergence of terminology, and many practitioners working at a non-specialist level are acting in essential isolation from such professional norms as have been achieved, and their use of terminology rarely approaches consistency. It is thus pertinent to consider the extent to which the pattern of terminological usage throws light on the pattern of aspirations for, and expectations of, ecological restoration and associated activities. The interplay of words and deeds is close, but often unclear, and there is value in considering the implications of particular meanings, as well as merely establishing their optimum definition.

Restoration

Bradshaw (this volume) is unambiguous in insisting that restoration implies both a return to an original state, and a desire that this state should ideally be perfect and healthy. In whatever formulation, these notions underpin a worthy formal definition of ecological restoration, while at the same time permitting sufficient flexibility to incorporate some peripheral but helpful subsidiary meanings. At the heart of the matter is the feeling that the outcome of a restoration project aims to be an ecosystem resembling the original (pre-disturbance) state, or resembling similar undisturbed ecosystems in the vicinity (Gore 1985). This alternative definition is important, since it is quite possible that no information survives on the pre-disturbance state of an impacted environment. Restoration also implies that the habitat concerned previously supported the target ecosystem, and that, with attention to the driving habitat variables could be induced to support it again: the implication is that something is being returned to a previous state at the same location so that between-site variation is likely to be high. In order to achieve the aim of being 'healthy', a fully restored system is likely to be in dynamic equilibrium (which certainly does not imply a static state) and also be self-sustaining. There appears to be a significant similarity of meaning between restoration and habitat re-creation, but a significant difference between habitat restoration (largely physical, chemical, and morphological) and ecosystem restoration (largely biological). These issues are of critical importance in targeting and monitoring restoration projects, and they should not be oversimplified. While restoration rightly poses the ideal of returning an ecosystem to an original state, there is great variation in the way in which 'original' can be interpreted. It certainly does not inevitably mean 'pre-disturbance', but perhaps does mean 'pre-detrimental disturbance'. As will be seen later, the examples of prairie restoration and coppice restoration pose interesting dilemmas of definition, since both return an ecosystem to a previous state of acceptable human intervention, but not to the state before any human disturbance.

Mitigation

Strictly speaking, mitigation is not an ecological practice at all, but a planning-related term that usually signifies a set of actions which are seen as helping to make good a loss (environmental deterioration and conse-quent social disbenefit) that has been or will be suffered. In this regard we may view mitigation as a core component of ecological restoration even if it remains somewhat marginal to the concepts of restoration ecology (Higgs 1994). These actions may conceivably take the form of restoration, but this is not usually the case. More commonly, mitigation implies working towards a different (but acceptably alternative) ecosystem at the same site or, more usually, towards an equivalent ecosystem at a different site. The target is likely to be rehabilitation or enhancement rather than restoration *sensu stricto*. Mitigation sites should nevertheless meet a no-net-loss criterion (to achieve sustainability requirements of net natural capital transfer) even if they cannot achieve the full functional equivalency required of a successful restoration, but this simple criterion is itself difficult to operationalize, despite its crucial importance to the concept of sustainability. Since acceptable mitigation performance is, from the outset, a firm expectation rather than just an aspiration, it requires monitoring as a procedural necessity (because it is an action traded to permit a development elsewhere), whereas, with restoration, monitoring is a useful scientific process but not to such an extent a social obligation. This is an example of the way in which robust definition of terms can carry implications which permit the users of the terminology to agree the consequences of a set of proposed actions.

Why should mitigation warrant discussion in the present context, given that it in no way equates with restoration? The justification lies in the fact that planners may make the assumption that the ecosystem manipulation being targeted by the action offered as a mitigation does indeed represent an equivalency for what is to be, or has been, lost or disturbed. If it does not, then the planners need to know that it does not in advance. Such awareness can only be achieved if the sometimes subtle shades of meaning of different terms are indeed rehearsed openly within the planning domain in which mitigation is offered or demanded. In the absence of such discussion, there is a fear that the availability of supposed mitigation will render actions leading to further detrimental environmental impact easier to justify in planning terms (Baldwin *et al.* 1993b).

For example, 'enhancement' is acknowledged by Bradshaw (this volume) to be a pale shadow of true restoration, yet the term is often used in planning circles where it generally signifies improving the existing conditions at a site, without necessarily attempting to return them to some former or equivalent state. More particularly, enhancement has been applied to any acceleration of the recovery process – and, if that recovery returned the ecosystem to the pre-disturbance state, then the term restoration would be appropriate.

Rehabilitation is also sometimes offered in mitigation under circumstances under which restoration would appear to be a more suitable goal. Rehabilitation implies returning a habitat to a state in which it is more biologically acceptable to plants and animals. This is not dissimilar to habitat creation, which often aims at producing a short-term amenity habitat without any pretence that it is either fully functional or that it will duplicate a previous state. Rehabilitation may be used to imply assistance to a system to equilibriate to a new set of driving variables: if the habitat has changed irreversibly, then a system may be rehabilitated, but certainly not restored.

What is interesting about definitions such as these is not their semantic purity or distinctiveness, but the fact that they tacitly acknowledge that ecosystem improvement strategies take very many different forms, and are motivated by highly contrasting purposes (Newbold 1989). The difference of form represents a spectrum of complexity, with rehabilitation clearly involving a significantly less demanding target than restoration. The difference of purpose is frequently stereotyped as a simple distinction between conservation projects (science-driven) and amenity projects (planning-driven). In practice, however, considerably greater diversity emerges. For example, Sear (1994) notes that river restoration has been used to enhance in-stream habitats, to reduce nutrient and sediment loads from intensive farming, to improve landscape quality, and to stabilize eroding streams. Different purposes inevitably suggest different remedial strategies, so it is not surprising that careful attention needs to be paid to setting appropriate targets for a restoration project.

Criteria for restoration targets and performance monitoring

It is clearly inadequate to view a restoration project as being satisfactory simply because a degree of 'greening' of a previously denuded site has been achieved, though in political and planning circles this unacceptably crude definition does seem to be in use at times (partly because, as we have seen, restoration is often confused with rehabilitation and enhancement). There is, therefore, a danger that transplant or introduction survival could be regarded as a viable measure of restoration success, when in fact the full target has been achieved only when a system carries out the many biological (e.g., food chain) and other (e.g., hydrological) functions pertinent to its undisturbed counterpart. Pragmatically, it may justifiably be claimed that the purpose of restoration is to *initiate* migration of an impacted system in this direction, but this merely exacerbates the difficulty of establishing definitive success for the project. Yet no matter how problematic the task of defining goals, it remains an essential underpinning of the review and accountability of ecological restoration (Jackson *et al.* 1995).

If simple measures of 'greening' are insufficient, then it is surprisingly difficult to propose a sophisticated alternative set of criteria that could be claimed to win general professional approval and usage. Bradshaw (this volume) offers a structured review of the differences of intention and outcome between such targets as ecosystems, habitat, community, and species restoration. In addition, it is helpful to build from a range of case studies a synthesis of the inferred targets and standards, taking care to highlight habitat attributes as well as introduced flora and fauna. Indeed, in many cases it appears to be failure to create habitats in dynamic equilibrium (physical and chemical) that undermines the attempt to introduce viable populations. 'Site preparation' is a term much used in the restoration literature, but it frequently fails to indicate a full understanding of the complexity of the non-biological site attributes. A holistic approach is thus a necessity, not a luxury, in this context, and leads us to criteria which generally include some of the following (arranged in order of decreasing complexity and sophistication):

- *Functional equivalency* of habitats and of organism components (plants, animals, microbes) – demanding both an ability to define the functional status that is the target, and an understanding of what it is that causes functional inequivalency.
- *Structural equivalency* of habitats and of organism components – supposing an equivalence of density; a full representation of trophic groupings (bottom feeders; mid feeders etc.); a proper balance between native and exotic species; and an appropriate distribution of, and connectivity between, habitat elements.
- *Elemental equivalency* of habitats and of organism components – reflected in such indices as biodiversity or a self-sustaining convergence of species composition between the restored system and the target system (it is generally accepted that self-sustenance is an ultimate aim, but that some maintenance may be required in the early years).

Such targets may assist in planning the restoration project, and are certainly useful in devising appropriate performance monitoring strategies, but they presuppose a significant understanding of the ecosystem concerned. It is the realization that, in many respects, existing knowledge is inadequate to this task that motivates the research and development activity that lies behind restoration science.

Research and development targets

While there is clearly enormous scope for continued research on innumerable detailed technical aspects of restoration technique (Thayer 1992), there are also higher-level needs for rigorous evaluation of the objectives and principles. Perhaps the fundamental aim of restoration research should be to achieve predictability of outcome (Zedler 1992), thereby more fully justifying the use of the term restoration science, but this will be possible only through undertaking protracted post-project appraisal (monitoring) over timescales sufficiently long to permit robust evaluation of the extent to which the restored system is self-sustaining as well as target-satisfying. Many facets of performance could be regarded as significant, but some of the priorities would seem to be:

• Development of ecotechnological methods to accelerate the achievement of functional equivalency (e.g., habitat preparation; application of nutrients; control of grazers; control of competitors).
• Understanding of the potential of restored systems to withstand the application of new stresses or interventions (e.g., ability to withstand natural hazard events such as floods or anthropogenic events such as pollution incidents; resilience to introduction of exotic species).
• Demonstration of the performance of restored systems in terms of biodiversity and genetic diversity, both of which attributes may constrain sustainability if they are not satisfied.
• Extrapolation of techniques and understanding from the plot scale to the regional scale, thereby introducing an additional dimension of complexity through those many attributes which may well be scale-dependent, at least in part.
• Development and testing of modes of communication suitable for informing planners and other decision-makers of the issues underlying restoration recommendations. The communication of complex science to executive non-specialists and to interested lay people poses a particular challenge to which ecologists have not always sought to respond positively. Without the transmission of understanding to accompany implementation guidance, it is unlikely that projects will receive the support and long-term maintenance that they deserve.

So great is the intellectual and practical challenge of even this short list of priorities that it might be supposed that a resolution of such issues is likely to remain elusive in the short-term. It is in this context that a new impetus has been given by the emergence of a powerful new mission which virtually demands a rapid increase in restoration skills – a mission encapsulated in the concept of sustainable development which, against all the odds, has achieved high political prominence.

Ecological restoration and sustainability

The exploration of ecological restoration as a supporting device for strategies of sustainable development demands more than passing mention (Edwards & Abivardi, this volume), but no consideration of the scope of the challenge is possible without reviewing in outline the implications of sustainability. It immediately becomes apparent that, while many authors and orators have extolled the virtues of sustainability in principle, relatively few have taken the next step and tied the vision down to its practical implications. An exception is Gardiner (1995), who addresses the principles of sustainable development of water resources in a way which offers an effective foundation for considering the practice of river restoration (Sear, 1994; Brookes, 1995a). It rapidly becomes clear that while sustainability is an invaluable incentive for introducing restoration projects, the cost in terms of complexity and investment can be high.

The precautionary principle is of the utmost importance, given the present limited success rate of major restoration programmes: systems should not be perturbed unless the outcome can be predicted. This is not only a plea to avoid environmental degradation in the first place (the preference of prevention over cure has already been discussed), but also a warning against initiating overambitious restoration plans. It seems reasonable to suggest that, in the present state of the restoration art, only those systems with relatively modest degradation or disturbance can be confidently expected to be restored to the point at which they are undetectably different from non-degraded and undisturbed sites. Even this degree of intervention is likely to be a slow process, and it is therefore imperative to avoid detrimental intervention rather than have to face the unequal challenge of having to repair the subsequent damage. Restoration is indeed a potentially important component in a sustainable strategy, but the ideal situation is that circumstances should not be permitted to deteriorate to the point at which restoration is deemed necessary.

While it must be acknowledged that restoration ecology has little to contribute to several other aspects of sustainable development, there are certainly at least three further contexts in which its role is so significant that we can easily justify the suggestion that restoration is a key component of sustainability:

- The overall stock of natural capital should be kept constant or increased. This is a critically important premise underlying most restoration processes, and is inherent in the mitigation principle in planning. It is the need to maintain natural capital that drives the requirement for restoration to attempt full functional equivalence, since the lesser ecosystem status achieved by alternatives such as enhancement and rehabilitation cannot really be said to maintain capital. Nevertheless, despite this difficulty of non-equivalence, the principle of mitigation in general must be seen as a key sustainability element.
- Thresholds of environmental carrying capacity should be identified and implemented as management constraints. Some restored ecosystems can be developed in a setting protected from external stress, but this ideal cannot always be achieved. Indeed, if the system is to be regarded as self-sustaining, then it must be capable of withstanding extreme natural and anthropogenic events. The design and implementation of a restoration programme with this degree of resilience is a major contribution to sustainability, but is heavily demanding on current levels of skill and understanding.
- System criteria must be satisfied as well as local criteria. The point has already been made, and will be further reinforced below, that ecosystems rarely function as closed systems, which implies that they and the associated habitats are subject to formative influence from external factors. The clear implication is that, unless the current and likely future status of these factors is built into the restoration design, a self-sustaining system in dynamic equilibrium with its environment is most unlikely to emerge. By relating ecosystem to habitat, and habitat to the driving variables such as hydrology and geomorphology, restoration ecology makes a further major contribution to establishing sustainable outcomes.

While, at the operational level, the task of supporting sustainable development through ecological restoration may seem very practical, its justification and its long-term contribution to sustainable development rely upon an interplay between scientific assertion and social values. Nowhere is this interplay more important than in the challenge of setting priorities for restoration action based on some ranking of needs and feasibility.

Restoration need and response priority

It is tempting, but somewhat naive, to assume that a ranking of restoration need based on seriousness of environmental impact or ecological deterioration will relate easily or directly with a planning-based prioritization of restoration response. In many cases it will not. More likely is a situation in which restoration potential and restoration cost (and opportunity cost) will take precedence in influencing the response decision. It will often be the case that the decision-maker will primarily be concerned with achieving optimum return on investment (i.e. maximum net social benefit from the project) and minimum payback period (reflecting society's time preference for benefits in the near future and costs in the distant future). Against these criteria, the poorest ecosystems may offer restricted potential for rapid high returns, while an ecosystem of only moderate deficiency may be amenable to substantial improvement for a limited investment. Such decisions are always multi-component and value-laden. It is not possible to construct an objective scale to determine priority, though it is certainly feasible to identify the rule-base of many of the judgements involved. We are thus likely to see expert systems for the designation of habitat quality being linked with indices of improvement potential to identify restoration investment priority. When we talk of the magnitude of the challenge of ecological restoration, the complexity of the evaluative systems required is as significant as the scale of the ecological deterioration to be overcome. Nevertheless, it begins to emerge that restoration potential reflects a series of attributes including:

- the scale of the ecosystem or habitat quality deficiency to be made good – which provides a first-order estimation of the distance through which the system has to be shifted.
- the extent of understanding of the links within and between ecological and other elements of the system, including energy, nutrient and sediment flows (the 'laws acting around us' in Darwin's (1859) formulation), which indicates whether or not the shift could be designed.
- the clarity with which an equilibrium target ('natural' or pre-impacted) state of the ecosystem or habitat can be defined by the restoration manager – often a major challenge in the absence of close reference comparisons between one site and another (Aronson, Dhillion, & Le Floc'h 1995).
- the time that would be required to achieve a self-sustaining state, or the ongoing maintenance cost required to achieve the required equilibrium. Equilibrium in this context may well be highly dynamic, and certainly does not imply an expectation that the target ecosystem should be static. Moreover, it is entirely possible that the ecosystem in question incorporated an element of acceptable or beneficial human intervention before

the imposition of the detrimental disruption from which restoration is to be attempted – examples as diverse as prairies (Jordan 1993) and coppiced woodlands may be pertinent here. With a traditionally coppiced woodland, it could be suggested that restoration may indeed imply the reimposition of intervention in a system which has more recently fallen into 'neglect'.

The combined scale and complexity of the shift which the system will require in order to move it to a socially acceptable status and self-sustaining (stable or dynamic equilibrium) state will determine the feasibility of achieving restoration, and the costs to be incurred (tangible and intangible; present and future; local and distant). A small required shift will appear attractive, since it suggests a relatively feasible restoration challenge. However, it is interesting to note that, in some systems at least, the net increase in environmental quality necessary to yield a given increase in biomass may be least in the most impoverished (highest environmental stress) conditions (Ewel 1983). Against this kind of background, it becomes clear why the simple notion that restoration investment should be directed towards the 'worst' environments is highly misleading.

Moreover, in actually selecting priorities for restoration activity, it is inevitable that consideration will be given to the extent to which remedial action would require some associated change in social or economic activity. 'Engineering' a new habitat may seem inherently more attractive to many people than making social or economic sacrifices to reduce the disturbing intervention that is causing environmental deterioration. Indeed, in some cases, removal of the disturbing stress may trigger 'natural' restoration without further intervention. Prioritizing decisions will thus reflect a combination of bio-physical and socio-economic criteria (Willeke 1993). For example, Maragos (1989) suggests that preferential attention should be paid to elements which are subjectively viewed as socio-economically important, are highly important to the ecosystem as a whole, and are difficult or slow to re-establish. In the case of a coral reef restoration, for example, reef coral would rank highest, since it has moderate socio-economic value, is essential to the reef, and is slow to recover. Non-edible invertebrates, on the other hand, might score low, since they are of low socio-economic value, are non-essential to the reef, and recover moderately well. Evaluation matrices can be compiled on this basis, though they have low acceptability unless based on broad consultation and 'ownership'. Many ecologists will recoil from the suggestion that ecosystems should be 'valued' so that an assessment of the cost-benefit ratio of a restoration proposal can be assessed, but distaste for the technique will not banish the issue.

Restoration ecology in context

In many contexts, ecological restoration is at best an *ad hoc* product of a series of largely uncontrolled experiments, yet it attracts disproportionately strong support from managers and planners, particularly those who wish to be convinced that the likely outcome of a restoration exercise would indeed serve as a viable mitigation for a proposed project. Restoration undertaken in non-mitigation contexts is significantly easier to evaluate, but, even so, it is important to question unrealistic claims of the degree or pace of success that can be achieved with a given investment. Uncritical faith in the power of restoration can lead to a management underestimation of the seriousness of actual and expected environmental deterioration (Colby 1989), and also can lead to unrealistically high expectations of the restorative powers that can be called upon. Some of the potential and the pitfalls can be illustrated through a single brief example, that of river restoration.

Some implications from river restoration

River channel systems have been abused for very many years, and formal attempts at restoration have been undertaken for well over half a century (Koski 1992). Initially, the focus was strongly on engineering problems and engineering solutions, but, during the 1980s and 1990s, there has been an increasingly important role for conservation values, targets, and techniques. The task of prescribing and reaching a functional freshwater habitat, let alone a full ecosystem, is daunting, but substantial progress has been made (Bickmore & Larard 1989). No attempt is made here to provide a definitive account of river restoration, since the aim is simply to use this context to derive a few general principles of ecological restoration. These will colour our conclusions on ecological restoration in general, but also give substance to the social metagoals – particularly the need for sustainability, adaptability, resilience, and consensus – which have been suggested as motivating and shaping most successful environmental management strategies, particularly those which take place within a context of on-going uncertainty (Clark & Gardiner 1994).

In particular, river restoration challenges the ecologist to design a system capable of surviving effectively in a highly dynamic and spatially/temporally variable environment. Moreover, massive changes of land cover and land use in many river basins over the last two centuries have produced substantial and often irreversible change in the process system. Specifically, both the hydrology (water quality and quantity) and the fluvial geomorphology will have changed, and there has been a growing realization that design and implementation strategies which prioritize geomorphology are equally essential whether the ultimate aim is ecological restoration or the effective conductance of flood flows. Above all, geomorphology stresses the spatial and temporal links (energy, sediment, nutrients, pollutants) which tie together the basin and its entire channel network into a single interdependent systems in which local perturbations or interventions have far-reaching effects. Additionally, channel geomorphology (form, gradient, sediment supply, substrate, etc.) is an essential component of habitat. It is hardly surprising that the twin drives of a 'softer' engineering and a more environmentally accountable society have brought geomorphologically based river management and restoration to the forefront.

Sear (1994) has argued for the acceptance of site geomorphological management as the basis for sustainable river restoration, and has stressed the highly variable function and spatial/temporal scale of geomorphic elements in the system. River restoration schemes which overlook the scale at which these components function cannot expect to yield either equilibrium or self-sustaining systems. Indeed, one of the primary applications of channel geomorphology may be to identify when the river is close to a functional threshold which, if crossed, would induce associated shifts in form, substrate, operation, and habitat. In the particular case of restoration ecology, this would affect both the physical stability of the ecosystem and its carrying capacity – both important elements in achieving a sustainable situation. It can be concluded that scheme designs should shift from regarding geomorphology as an in-stream feature to be manipulated, to seeing it as modulating between the site characteristics and the temporally and spatially broader functioning of the system as a whole. Without this dimension, the aquatic environment may be usefully rehabilitated, but the self-sustaining functional equivalence required for sustainable restoration will not be achieved.

A further implication of this holistic viewpoint is that the restoration itself will have potential implications at much wider spatial and temporal scales than are directly involved in the project, and, for this reason, restoration projects should, in many cases, be subject to an Environmental Impact Assessment (Brookes 1995a). This will not only help to avoid detrimental impacts, but, through a thorough scoping exercise, can materially assist in ensuring that the scheme design is fully system-wide. Again, this would not be essential for enhancement and rehabilitation, but is basic to the concept of restoration. Not least, it will help to identify potential conflicts between restoration (which may be a planning mitigation exercise) and continued riparian or floodplain development (with which the mitigation might be associated). For example, Brookes (1995b) notes that channel restoration may well increase hydraulic roughness and lead to a reduced ability to transmit flood peak flows, thereby lowering the achieved standard of flood protection. These critically important issues of the interplay between system function and local site specification are fully developed by Newson (1995), who provides a timely reminder of the need for caution as well as enthusiasm:

Perhaps the most important current role for fluvial geomorphology is in informing (and in some cases restraining!) headlong moves for river restoration. Once again a reach scale is emerging as a popular management unit, but Sear (1994) has cautioned that reach restoration which ignores the catchment sediment system is bound to be unsustainable.

One of the most important prerequisites of effective river restoration is a clear definition of the pre-disturbance (or appropriate alternative) state to which the system is to be returned. It should be noted that no viable concept of 'original state' exists in this context, since hydrology is systematically variable in response to long-term climatic and vegetative change. The restoration target has to be sufficiently recent in state to be compatible with current river basin climate and land cover. This equilibrium with driving variables subject to secular trends is a challenge both to restoration and to the sometimes-competing philosophy of preservation (Baldwin *et al.* 1993b). It equates well with Pickett & Parker's (1994) view that ecological systems subject to restoration project definition are bounded by local contexts and contingencies which render generalization difficult – but this realization is fundamental to the environmental sciences, and must be regarded as a challenge rather than an insurmountable hurdle. Since systematic manipulation of river channels has been undertaken over very long periods of time, detailed historical evidence of the semi-natural state of the channel may be impossible to define. In such circumstances, it can be invaluable to specify in a representative fashion the 'normal' state of a channel with the prevailing conditions that are associated with the channel to be restored (i.e. similar size, substrate, geology, gradient etc.). While apparently easy in principle, this task can be difficult to achieve at operational scale and cost – but Brookes (1995b) notes that many attempts to restore functionally dynamic river channels have been a success despite the lack of rigorous information on the semi-natural state of the site.

In England and Wales, a highly significant step towards being able to define achievable restoration targets has been taken by the National Rivers Authority in instituting national assessments of channel habitats within the River Habitat Survey (RHS), which is building a major archive of field derived data on a meso-scale sampling framework (initially one site per 10 km^2 grid square). Some 3000 site surveys have been undertaken, and this total has risen to 6000 in 1997. The result is a national database of unprecedented power as a means of generalizing inferences about the likely semi-natural equivalents of an impacted channel. This is by no means the only intended function of the RHS database, but it is certainly a major contribution to sustainable river ecological restoration. At a more macro-regional scale, the SERCON expert-system approach adopted by Scottish Natural Heritage is a further aid to identifying restoration capabilities and targets. While such national-level initiatives may not be necessary for local restoration prototypes, it is difficult to imagine designing and prioritizing a regional restoration strategy without such a substantive information base.

Complexity of habitat context

One of the clear messages that can be derived from the example of river restoration is that ecosystem improvement relies upon a successful restoration of the habitat as a quasi self-sustaining physico-chemical system. In part, this restoration may be 'pure' in the sense that there is a return to a pre-disturbance state. In other cases, however, restoration needs to create a habitat in equilibrium with driving processes which may have altered significantly since the pre-disturbance phase – a river channel, for example, must be in equilibrium with the current hydrological regime (relating to current land cover in the river basin) not with some pre-disturbance historical artefact which can never return. There are, however, vulnerabilities in this notion of the complexity of context, including assumptions about extent to which the underlying drivers of the ecosystem (energy, mass, sediments, nutrients, geomorphology) can effectively be managed.

Interestingly, it may well be that a restoration attempt to return an ecosystem to its predisturbance state is actually inappropriate, since the habitat variables themselves may have changed irreversibly (Cairns 1987). The nature-in-flux model poses much greater challenge to the restoration ecologist than the balance-of-nature model (Jackson *et al.* 1995). In such cases, restoration to a system of similar functional level, but more appropriate to the prevailing habitat status, is fully justified. It is in cases like this that the strict sustainability requirement to consider system-wide parameters, not just local conditions, becomes paramount.

It appears at first sight reasonable to assume that if a site (habitat) with substrate, hydrology, and vegetation virtually indistinguishable from those of a non-degraded site is prepared or available, then a faunal and floral community appropriate to this habitat will colonize the site with or without the assistance of introductions. On such a basis, it would be assumed that if major components of the dominant communities are established, then other components will follow without further intervention provided that suitable conditions exist (Broome 1989). Reflection soon suggests that in many cases this approach is pragmatic, but somewhat simplistic. The timescale for colonization to create a functioning community equivalent to that of the undisturbed site, may well be unacceptably long, and the system may be non self-sustaining in the meantime (since the habitat is in a fully mature state while the communities may be highly immature). Nevertheless, if it is difficult to create functionally equivalent communities on functionally equivalent habitats (broadly defined), we may rest assured that it will be effectively impossible to achieve self-sustaining restoration on a site or habitat that itself does not offer non-biological functional equivalence. The short message is that the site/habitat must come first.

Restoration ecology: faith and future

To play Devil's Advocate, it is tempting to question whether ecosystem restoration might, in some cases, be little more than a sop to the conscience, rather than a serious practical possibility: at the very least, such a critique can yield spirited defence which helps to rationalize the possible roles of restoration. At anything other than the local scale, there may be some justification for having the strength of purpose to regard the creation of a worthwhile enhanced or rehabilitated ecosystem as a better target for society as a whole, than to cling to the ideal that one can alter the habitat drivers (climate, hydrology, geomorphology – Pickett & Parker's (1994) 'flux of nature') and yet still turn the clock back to a something akin to a pristine pre-intervention ecosystem.

We have built an argument on the assumption that the restoration of a complex ecosystem is essentially a management process which builds upon scientific insights: unless we have mastered a functional specification of the target ecosystem, we will fail to restore it except with a significant input of luck. But, in moving towards a concluding perspective, it is enlightening to remind ourselves that the reverse of this argument can also be promulgated. It could be that the very process of restoration has the capability to yield greatly improved scientific understanding. By manipulating the system under at least partially controlled conditions, we have the opportunity to learn from the better specification of the link between input and outcome, and from an understanding of why certain restoration activities work, while others do not. The implication is that there is a more equal two-way partnership between ecological science and ecological restoration than is usually recognized (Jordan, Gilpin, & Aber 1987).

Nevertheless, given both the enormous scale of global environmental degradation, and the almost incredible complexity of even the smallest functioning ecosystem, it may be that pure restoration of large areas is currently largely impracticable, and that the scope for significant saving of threatened species and ecosystems is correspondingly more limited than would be deemed desirable. Alternatively, the opportunity for stabilizing fragile ecosystem functions and controlling exacerbation of major degra-dations such as soil loss (or, in some cases, flooding) may present a better return on social investment. So we end, as we began, querying the complementary relative roles and merits of preventing damage and curing damage. From the outside, it appears that in this respect ecological restoration is the figurehead of the biological sciences, and a fine role model for the environmental sciences as a whole, but in its growing professional and scientific maturity it can also benefit from assimilating some of the perhaps equivalent values of lesser targets such as enhancement and rehabilitation.

As serious scientists, restoration ecologists can gain from having the strength and the courage to question the theoretical robustness and practical feasibility of some of the demands made by politicians drunk on the heady rhetoric of sustainability. The challenge of just one example, river restoration, has provided an effective demonstration of the enormous success that can be achieved, and also of the very practical limitations that can intervene and make restoration impracticable in some cases. The blend of good science and good practice leads in principle to good sense – but this will only be achieved if we insist on the whole exercise being both informed and realist.

At the beginning of this chapter, Charles Darwin challenged us with the complexity of the functioning ecosystem, but embellished his scientific *interest* with a recognition of the *grandeur and beauty* of nature and of the sense of *wonder* that its contemplation yields. A century of material progress left the world impoverished and damaged against the standards of

Darwin's criteria. More recently, however, a growing revulsion at these trends has manifested itself in a number of partially serendipitous icons of renewal – the mission of sustainable development and the, at-least nominal, support for the Earth Summit amongst them. The distinction between what Higgs (1993) has labelled 'technical' and 'engaged' professionals has narrowed or, at least, the two have come to work more closely together. Faced with the opportunities that these trends represent, it would be churlish indeed to denigrate ecological restoration because its focus was too local-scale, or because its time-frame was too short. Through efforts at restoration, society is able to demonstrate a commitment to improvement. Its gross impact on world-scale environment may be limited in the immediate term, but there is every reason to expect that its contribution to a more sustainable attitude may be both tangible and substantial in the long term. We may conclude by sharing with Kane (1993) the view that restoration attempts are an inescapable human obligation even if their success cannot be guaranteed. Ultimately, however, we must tackle the causes and reverse the downward trends: realistically, no amount of blood transfusion can restore the planet to health until the haemorrhage is stemmed. But then it will be the ever-strengthening skills of restoration ecology which must heal the wound and restore the vitality. Not for the first time, we see that the real magnitude of the challenge is to look beyond the technical tasks of today and recognize the broader mission of tomorrow.

Acknowledgement

As a non-ecologist, the author acknowledges with gratitude the editorial and scientific guidance of Peter Edwards, and the patient and highly creative chiding of an anonymous referee whose breadth of experience and viewpoint was both invaluable and much appreciated. The resulting 'external' perspective on restoration ecology has matured greatly through their intervention, but remains a set of observations from an outsider looking in.

References

Aronson, J., Dhillion, S., & Le Foc'h, E. (1995). On the need to select an ecosystem of reference, however imperfect: a reply to Pickett & Parker. *Restoration Ecology*, 3(1), 1–3.
Baldwin, A. D., de Luce, J., & Pletsch, C. eds. (1993a). *Beyond Preservation: Restoring and Inventing Landscapes*. Minneapolis: University of Minnesota Press.

Baldwin, A. D., de Luce, J., & Pletsch, C. (1993b). Introduction: ecological preservation versus restoration and invention. In *Beyond Preservation: Restoring and Inventing Landscapes*, eds. A. D. Baldwin, J. de Luce, & C. Pletsch, pp. 3–16. Minneapolis: University of Minnesota Press.

Bickmore, C. J. & Larard, P. J. (1989). Reconstructing freshwater habitats in development schemes. In *Biological Habitat Reconstruction*, ed. G. P. Buckley, pp. 189–200. London: Belhaven Press.

Bradshaw, A. D. (1993). Restoration ecology as a science. *Restoration Ecology*, 1(2), 71–3.

Bradshaw, A. D. (1994). The need for good science – beware of straw men: some answers to comments by Eric Higgs. *Restoration Ecology*, 2(3), 147–8.

Brookes, A. (1995a). River channel restoration: theory and practice. In *Changing River Channels*, eds. A. M. Gurnell and G. E. Petts, pp. 369–88. Chichester: John Wiley & Sons.

Brookes, A. (1995b). The importance of high flows. In *Ecological Basis for River Management*, eds. D. Harper & A. Ferguson, pp. 33–49. Chichester: John Wiley & Sons.

Broome, S. W. (1989). Creation and restoration of tidal wetlands of the Southeastern United States. In *Wetland Creation and Restoration: the Status of the Science*, eds. J. A. Kusler & M. E. Kentula, pp. 37–66. U.S. Environmental Protection Agency, EPA600/3-89-038a.

Cairns, J. (1987). Disturbed ecosystems as opportunities for research in restoration ecology. In *Restoration Ecology*, eds. W. R. Jordan, M. E. Gilpin, & J. D. Aber, pp. 307–20. Cambridge University Press.

Clark, M. J. & Gardiner, J. L. (1994). Handling uncertainty in integrated river basin planning. In *Integrated River Basin Development*, eds. C. Kirby & W. R. White, pp. 437–45. Chichester: John Wiley & Sons.

Colby, M. E. (1989). The evolution of paradigms of environmental management in development. *World Bank Policy, Planning and Research Working Paper*. WPS313.

Darwin, C. (1859). *The Origin of Species*, 6th edn, 1872. London: John Murray.

Ewel, J. (1983). Succession. In *Tropical Rain Forest Ecosystems, A. Structure and Function*, ed. F. B. Golley, pp. 217–23. Amsterdam: Elsevier.

FEF (Friends of the Environment Foundation) (1996). *River gets New Lease of Life*. Internet publication URL http://www.fef.ca/fef/fefnews/river.html

Gardiner, J. L. (1995). Towards a sustainable water environment. In *Changing River Channels*, eds. A. M. Gurnell and G. E. Petts, pp. 389–411. Chichester: John Wiley & Sons.

Gore, J. A. (1985). *The Restoration of Rivers and Streams*. Boston: Butterworth.

Higgs, E. S. (1993). The ethics of mitigation: SER '92 conference report. *Restoration and Management Notes*, 9, 97–104.

Higgs, E. S. (1994). Expanding the scope of restoration ecology. *Restoration Ecology*, 2(3), 137–46.

Jackson, LL., Lopoukhine, N., & Hillyard, D. (1995). Ecological restoration: a definition and comments. *Restoration Ecology*, 3(2), 71–5.

Jordan, W. R. III (1993). 'Sunflower Forest': ecological restoration as the basis for a new environmental paradigm. In *Beyond Preservation: Restoring and Inventing Landscapes*, eds. A. D. Baldwin, J. de Luce, & C. Pletsch, pp. 17–34. Minneapolis: University of Minnesota Press.

Jordan, W. R. III, Gilpin, M. E., & Aber, J. D. (1987). *Restoration Ecology: a Synthetic Approach to Ecological Research*. Cambridge University Press.

Kane, G. S. (1993). Restoration or preservation? Reflections on a clash of environmental philosophies. In *Beyond Preservation: Restoring and Inventing Landscapes*, eds. A. D. Baldwin, J. de Luce, & C. Pletsch, pp. 69–84. Minneapolis: University of Minnesota Press.

Koski, K. V. (1992). Restoring stream habitats affected by logging activities. In *Restoring the Nation's Marine Environment*, ed. G. W. Thayer, pp. 343–403. College Park, Maryland: A Maryland Sea Grant Book.

Maragos, J. E. (1989). Restoring coral reefs with emphasis on Pacific reefs. In *Restoring The Nation's Marine Environment*, ed. G. W. Thayer, pp. 141–221. College Park, Maryland: A Maryland Sea Grant Book.

Newbold, C. (1989). Semi-natural habitats or habitat re-creation: conflict or partnership? In *Biological Habitat Reconstruction*, ed. G. P. Buckley, pp. 9–17. London: Belhaven Press.

Newson, M. D. (1995). Fluvial geomorphology and environment design. In *Changing River Channels*, eds. A. M. Gurnell and G. E. Petts, pp. 413–32. Chichester: John Wiley & Sons.

ORNL (Oak Ridge National Laboratory, US Department of Energy) (1995). *Phase I data summary report for the Clinch River Remedial Investigation: health risk and ecological risk screening assessment*. Environmental Sciences Division ORNL Publication 4021, Energy Systems Environmental Restoration Program. Internet publication URL http://www.esd.ornl.gov/programs/CRERP/DOCS/ER—155.HTM

Pickett, S. T. A. & Parker, V. T. (1994). Avoiding the old pitfalls: opportunities in a new discipline. *Restoration Ecology*, 2, 75–9.

Sear, D. A. (1994). River restoration and geomorphology. *Aquatic Conservation: Marine and Freshwater Ecosystems*, 4, 169–77.

Thayer, G. W., ed. (1992). *Restoring the Nation's Marine Environment*. College Park, Maryland: A Maryland Sea Grant Book.

Turner, F. (1987). The self-effacing art: restoration as imitation of nature. In *Restoration Ecology*, eds. W. R. Jordan, M. E. Gilpin, & J. D. Aber, pp. 47–50. Cambridge University Press.

Turner, K. (1993). Sustainability: principles and practice. In *Sustainable Environmental Economics and Management*, ed. K. Turner. London: Belhaven Press.

Willeke, G. E. (1993). Landscape restoration: more than ritual and gardening. In *Beyond Preservation: Restoring and Inventing Landscapes*, eds. A. D. Baldwin, J. de Luce, & C. Pletsch, pp. 90–6. Minneapolis: University of Minnesota Press.

Zedler, J. B. (1992). Restoring cordgrass marshes in Southern California. In *Restoring the Nation's Marine Environment*, ed. G. W. Thayer, pp. 7–51. College Park, Maryland: A Maryland Sea Grant Book.

Part V
Conclusions

17

Restoration ecology: science, technology and society

PETER J. EDWARDS, NIGEL R. WEBB,
KRYSTYNA M. URBANSKA,
REINHARD BORNKAMM

Introduction

Restoration is rapidly developing into a profession in its own right. As the contributions in this book demonstrate so well, great progress has already been made in developing techniques to restore a wide range of ecological communities. However, until now the application of these techniques has been relatively limited and largely confined to the developed world. In many areas, especially in the underdeveloped countries, the present rates of destruction of natural ecosystems are manifestly not sustainable. Increasingly, we recognize that these ecosystems, and the resources and services they provide, are a form of natural capital, capable of yielding sustained economic benefits if well managed.

While no one would wish to deny the significant successes that have already been achieved, for example in landmark schemes such as the recovery from industrial devastation of the Lower Swansea Valley in Wales in the 1960s, or the current programmes for restoration of wetland habitats, prairies, and sand-dunes in the USA, it is evident that the scale of present restoration activity is quite inadequate to meet the growing problems of environmental degradation (Daily 1995).

Against this background it is clear that the potential role for restoration ecology is enormous, and that the greatest needs lie in the developing world. Although great progress has been made in understanding the scientific issues associated with successful restoration, restoration ecology is not merely a scientific problem. To carry out restoration requires the approval and support (not least the financial support) of society, and the technology to carry out the work to large enough scale and at a reasonable price. In this concluding chapter, we should like to examine the interrelationship of these complex issues of the interrelationships of society, science, and technology which characterize the practice of restoration science.

381

Science

Restoration ecology must be based on science. While this statement seems perhaps obvious, there has been a flurry of debate in recent years about the exact role of science in restoration. Bradshaw (1993, 1994) was sufficiently concerned about what he saw as a tendency to regard ecological restoration as an art, that he penned two articles in the *Journal of Restoration Ecology* to restate his view of the centrality of science.

There is probably no aspect of ecological science which is irrelevant to the restoration of ecosystems. Our knowledge of the ecological characteristics of species, and their response to environmental conditions, form an essential basis for selecting species for restoration. Ecological genetics teaches us that a knowledge of species characteristics may not be enough. Plants and animals are genetically variable, as the classic case of heavy metal resistent ecotypes of many plant species so clearly illustrates (Antonovics, Bradshaw, & Turner 1971). Similarly, restoration ecologists recognize that plant seed brought in from remote areas will probably not be as effective for restoration as genotypes of the same species collected locally. Population ecology teaches us that effective restoration depends upon understanding ecological processes at all stages in the life cycle of a plant (Urbanska 1997). Community ecology reveals the importance of interactions between species in a functioning community. Examples with direct relevance to restoration ecology are the role of birds for the dispersal of plants (e.g., Robinson & Handel 1993), the role of decomposer organisms in nutrient mineralization, and the role of nitrogen fixing organisms in facilitating the growth of other species. Indeed, ecological restoration may be regarded as an imitation of the process of ecosystem development as revealed in a primary succession (Bradshaw 1983). In particular, the same processes of organisms modifying their environment and thus facilitating the entry of other species are fundamental to the recovery of damaged ecosystems, and the task of the restoration ecologist is, whenever possible, to accelerate these natural processes.

Although the role of ecological science in restoration is probably generally accepted, there remain many outstanding questions where further ecological research is urgently needed. Here are some of the more important of them:

What kind of ecosystem should we aim for?

Even the apparently simple issue of what we are trying to restore is very complex. As the chapter by Pickett and Parker shows, our ideas about what kind of ecosystem and what kind of species composition we should be aiming for are far less clear than previously thought. The apparently clear goal of imitating a well-defined reference system proves to be a shifting target, as we recognize the dynamic nature of natural communities. In defining goals for restoration, Pickett & Parker (1994) urge the need to accept a new paradigm – 'the flux of nature' – in place of the 'balance of nature' which has dominated ecological thinking for most of this century.

How do we get there?

Pimm has argued that it may be more difficult to restore a particular assemblage of species than to restore ecosystem processes. According to this view, species cannot simply be brought together and be expected to form a persistent community with a particular composition. The complexity of species interactions means that there may be many alternative outcomes and many stable states associated with a certain set of available species, depending upon the sequence in which they are introduced. 'In models, persistent communities may not be created from just their constituent species: other species, which may become extinct in the process, may be needed. If this is true in nature, then, when we destroy communities, we may not be able to reassemble them, even if we have kept all the species alive in botanical gardens and zoos' (Pimm 1991). Furthermore, existing communities may be a result of processes which are no longer operating – for example peat formation or podzolization – and for this reason they may be impossible to re-create because they arose through unrepeatable historical circumstances. The lesson for restoration ecologists is that we must accept many different endpoints and not strive too doggedly to achieve a particular, precisely defined community.

Does species diversity matter?

If the objective of a particular restoration is to achieve an ecosystem with certain functional characteristics, does it even matter which species or how many species are present? There is a great debate at present about how important species are within an ecosystem, and the general importance of keystone species remains unresolved. Is it true that most species are functionally unnecessary, as some have argued, or are all species potentially keystone species as others would maintain? And if most species are potentially keystones, under what circumstances do they become essential?

Does genetic diversity matter?

This is perhaps the most neglected question. While most restoration ecologists are sensitive to the need to use genotypes which are of local origin, the question of the importance of genetic diversity is rarely raised. Yet we know that in natural communities a very high degree of genetic diversity exists within species such as *Trifolium repens* and *Quercus robur*, and closer investigation often reveals the most precise partitioning of this variation amongst different microhabitats (Turkington & Harper 1979). There is also evidence that, during the course of succession, the genetic structure of plant populations changes. How important such variation may be for the successful development of an ecosystem and for its long-term stability, however, remains an open question.

Not only are all these questions important for ecological restoration, they are also of fundamental interest to ecological science. Indeed, numerous authors (Harper 1987; Ewel 1987; Bradshaw 1993) have argued that the ultimate test of our understanding of an ecological system is whether we can reconstruct it. Thus, attempts of restorationists to design and create communities for practical or environmental purposes can also be regarded as attempts to test ideas or answer crucial questions in ecology.

This brings us to the last point that we would make about science: that restoration ecologists must be scientists. Bradshaw (1993) has argued the issue well: 'One must have the appropriate background and a logical mind. One must have the ability to appreciate the principles involved, to see the questions that must be asked, and to know how to answer them. One must be prepared not just to say 'I did it this way' but be able to spell out the problems and the logic that led to the solutions, divide if necessary from experimental work.' He goes on to express the cardinal points which are essential for the restoration ecologist to be an effective scientist:

1. to be aware of the work of others;
2. to be prepared to carry out proper experiments and test ideas;
3. to be prepared to monitor fundamental parameters in a restoration scheme;
4. to carry out further tests and experiments suggested by these monitoring observations;
5. to publish the results of the work; unless others can read and benefit from individual experience, then restoration ecology will remain just an art of individuals.

Technology

It is not enough to know, in theory, how an ecosystem can be restored. We must also be able to do it at a scale which is appropriate to the problem, within an acceptable period of time, at a price which is affordable, and in a way which meets any other constraints imposed by society. For all but the smallest of schemes, this means a dependence upon technology.

We see at present an uneasy relationship between ecology and technology, with uncertainty about the proper role for each. At one extreme there is 'restoration' which is virtually a branch of engineering. Adherents to this approach reflect the engineer's concern to build structures according to fixed plans and to a high precision, but not necessarily in sympathy with natural environmental processes. Indeed, the discipline of environmental engineering has developed in parallel to restoration ecology, and the practical objectives are often similar. For example, environmental engineers have made great progress in construction of wetlands for the purpose of water treatment. The difference from ecological restoration is that these are essentially engineered structures, perhaps requiring the building of new levees or excavating of the land in areas which could not otherwise support wetland communities; such structures often require virtually constant aftercare. At the other extreme are the wildlife conservation organizations which attempt to restore ecosystems with only hand tools and willing volunteers. The problems with this approach is that it can be very slow, can only be performed at a small scale, and the results obtained are unpredictable.

One of the reasons for this uncomfortable relationship is certainly a distaste amongst some ecologists for the tools that technology provides. Bulldozers, herbicides, pesticides, chainsaws, and high explosives are, for many conservation-minded ecologists, the instruments of the Devil. It is using precisely these means that the damage that they wish to put right was created. This is an attitude, which, while perhaps understandable, is none the less a barrier to progress. No tool in itself is bad or good; what matters is how it is used.

Restoration ecology must improve its use of technology, and find a middle course between these two extremes. In particular, it must develop techniques which are cheap enough to be applied over a large scale so that projects are financially viable even in developing countries. We need better techniques for harvesting seed, for introducing organic matter into the soil, for providing protection for the developing seedlings, for isolating or removing toxic metals, and so on. Much of this technology does exist – for example, geotextiles for stabilizing soil surfaces, and turf lifters for removing contaminated soil – but there is much scope for further development and for applying it more widely.

Society

Restoration ecology has a social and economic context. This is perhaps in contrast to much ecological research, which can be pursued without the need for consultation with, and acceptance by, the public. As Clark (chapter 16 in this volume) puts it: 'There is, therefore, a double challenge in ensuring that restoration ecologists are aware of the value system of the society which they serve, and that society (together with its component professions) is well informed on the expert product of ecological restoration research.' The relationship between society and restoration ecology is considered in detail by Clark, and we summarize here where interaction between the profession and society is essential:

The ethical basis for restoration

Why restore, and what is our value system for assessing the quality of restoration? These are fundamental questions which concern how nature is valued by society, though clearly the restoration ecologist has a role in stimulating debate about them (Jackson, Lopoukhine, & Hillyard 1995).

Definition of the appropriate response

Society has expectations, but also prejudices, about what to expect from restoration. Very often 'restoration' means the re-creation of conditions which existed at some time in the past which is perceived as having been good. For example, in Britain the re-creation of rolling downland, or heathland, or woodland managed as coppice with standards seems a desirable objective to many people, even though none of these ecosystems could be regarded as natural. Indeed, society may respond negatively to a genuine attempt to restore a natural ecosystem. Nature may be perceived as dangerous (e.g., wild animals), dark (e.g. forests), impenetrable (e.g., wetlands), or in some other way hostile. The objectives for restoration, even though they may be matched against a well-defined reference ecosystem, therefore have to be developed in a democratic and open dialogue (Wiegleb 1995).

Identification of practical consequences

No one enjoys the kind of disruption that is caused, for example, by roadworks or the construction of a building. The same irritation may also be associated with restoration projects, with the added problem that the time course for restoration is often much longer. Restoration ecologists need to explain the consequences of their work. There may be restrictions in access, and the initial appearance may be unsightly, giving rise to a perception that money is being wasted.

Identification of the costs and benefits

The last 10 years have seen a transformation of our view of the importance of natural and semi-natural areas. No longer are they seen simply as scientifically interesting or attractive places for recreation. Increasingly we are recognizing the importance of such ecosystems in providing ecosystem services upon which we all depend for such things as flood control, clear water, and control of pollution (Edwards & Abivardi, this volume). A challenge for restoration ecologists and society is to understand much more fully the full benefits of ecological restoration, including those benefits not valued in financial terms, and also the costs in terms of environmental damage or remedial measures if we do nothing.

Setting professional standards

The responsibility of the restoration ecologist to be responsive to the needs and aspirations of society means that professional standards are important. As the profession develops, it is inevitable that the issues associated with professional standards – ethical responsibilities, quality definition and control, acceptable and unacceptable practices, and the like – will become the topics for vigorous debate.

Meeting the challenge

A full acceptance of restoration ecology requires not only education of the public to make them aware of the state of the environment and opportunities for improvement, but also a much more systematic training of the future restorationists (Figure 17.1). Probably most of those who become restoration ecologists have a training in ecology or environmental science, where they obtain, it is to be hoped, a good grounding in the underlying

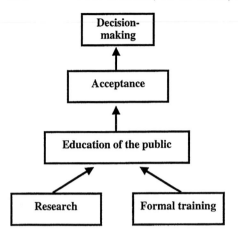

Figure 17.1. Interactions called for in the establishment of restoration ecology as a component of environmental management: gaining of ecological knowledge via research and formal training, and its utilization via communication with the public and decision-makers.

scientific principles. In most cases however, they are unlikely to have the same background in the social and economic issues associated with ecological restoration, nor in the technical opportunities. A quite different route into ecological restoration is through landscape architecture, in which the training in technological and professional aspects may be emphasized rather more than the underlying scientific background. Given this diversity of backgrounds from which restoration ecologists are recruited, it is increasingly important that a well-defined professional curriculum is defined and that opportunities for graduate training exist.

Already a tendency in American universities towards providing training in related disciplines can be detected. Conservation biology represents a well-established element of the academic training in the United States, and restoration ecology increasingly is gaining in importance as a discrete subject. In a recent survey (Jacobson, Vaughan, & Webb Miller 1995), restoration ecology was formally listed in graduate programmes offered by 11 of the 51 schools. Training in issues concerned with environmental engineering and sustainable development were more or less explicitly defined in programmes of a further 12 universities, but only one, Southern Connecticut State University at Newhaven, proposed a fully fledged master's degree in environmental education. Progress in Europe appears to be slower. While environmental sciences is taught as a discipline at many universities, and there may be undergraduate units in restoration ecology, there appear to be no post-graduate training opportunities such as a master's degree in restoration ecology.

Since restoration ecology is a professional activity rather than a purely academic discipline, it seems desirable that the content of training courses should, to some extent, be defined by the profession itself. However, the institutional structure of restoration ecology is almost non-existent, and a considerable effort of co-ordination would be required to provide the necessary collation of views from practitioners and academics. In Europe this co-ordinating role could be undertaken by the European Ecological Federation, which represents the ecological societies of Europe, in collaboration with the European Federation of Environmental Professionals, representing ecologists and environmentalists in professional practice. Whatever the route by which it is achieved, the development of more formal professional training at the post-graduate level is urgently needed, and would be one of the most effective ways to ensure that restoration ecology achieves its full potential.

References

Antonovics, J., Bradshaw, A. D., & Turner, R. G. (1971). Heavy metal tolerance in plants. *Advances in Ecological Research*, 7, 2–85.

Bradshaw, A. D. (1983). The reconstruction of ecosystems. *Journal of Applied Ecology*, 20, 1–18.

Bradshaw, A. D. (1993). Restoration ecology as a science. *Restoration Ecology*, 1, 71–3.

Bradshaw, A. D. (1994). The need for good science – beware of straw men: some answers to comments by Eric Higgs. *Restoration Ecology*, 2, 147–8.

Daily, G. C. (1995). Restoring value to the world's degraded lands. *Science*, 269, 350–4.

Ewel, J. J. (1987). Restoration is the ultimate test of ecological theory. In *Restoration Ecology – A Synthetic Approach to Ecological Research*, eds. W. R. Jordan, M. E. Gilpin, & J. D. Aber, pp. 31–3. Cambridge University Press.

Harper, J. L. (1987). The heuristic value of ecological restoration. In *Restoration Ecology – A Synthetic Approach to Ecological Research*, eds. W. R. Jordan, M. E. Gilpin, & J. D. Aber, pp. 35–45. Cambridge University Press.

Jackson, L. L., Lopoukhine, N., & Hillyard, D. (1994). Ecological restoration: a definition and comments. *Restoration Ecology*, 3, 71–5.

Jacobson, S. K., Vaughan, E., & Webb Miller, S. (1995). New directions in conservation biology: graduate progams. *Conservation Biology*, 9, 5–17.

Pickett, S. T. A. & Parker, V. T. (1994). Avoiding the old pitfalls: opportunities in a new discipline. *Restoration Ecology*, 2, 75–9.

Pimm, S. L. (1991). *The Balance of Nature?* University of Chicago Press, 434pp.

Robinson, G. R. & Handel, S. N. (1993). Forest restoration on a closed landfill: rapid addition of new species by wind dispersal. *Conservation Biology*, 7, 271–8.

Turkington, R. & Harper, J. L. (1982). The growth, distribution and neighbour relationships of *Trifolium repens* in a permanent pasture. *Journal of Ecology*, 67, 245–54.

Urbanska, K. M. (1997). Reproductive behaviour of arctic/alpine plants and terrestrial restoration. In *Disturbance and Recovery of Arctic Terrestrial Ecosystems – An Ecological Perspective*, ed. Crawford, R. M. N., pp. 481–501. Amsterdam: Kluwer Academic Publishers.

Wiegleb, G. (1995). Naturschutzziele in der Bergbaufolgelandschaft. Fakultät Umweltwissisenschaften der Technischen Universität Cottbus, Aktuelle Reihe 7/95, 118pp.

Index

Note: page numbers in **bold** indicate illustrations; those in *italics*, tables